Optical Processing and Computing

Optical Processing and Computing

Edited by

Henri H. Arsenault

Département de Physique
Université Laval
Cité Universitaire, Québec
Canada

Tomasz Szoplik

Institute of Geophysics
University of Warsaw
Warsaw
Poland

Bohdan Macukow

Warsaw Technical University
Warsaw
Poland

ACADEMIC PRESS, INC.
Harcourt Brace Jovanovich, Publishers
Boston San Diego New York
Berkeley London Sydney
Tokyo Toronto

ACADEMIC PRESS, INC.
1250 Sixth Avenue, San Diego, CA 92101

United Kingdom Edition published by
ACADEMIC PRESS INC. (LONDON) LTD.
24-28 Oval Road, London NW1 7DX

Library of Congress Cataloging-in-Publication Data
Optical processing and computing.

Bibliography: p.
Includes index.
1. Optical data processing. I. Arsenault, Henri H.
II. Szoplik, Tomasz. III. Macukow, Bohdan.
TA1630.O643 1989 621.36'7 88-35140
ISBN 0-12-064470-3

Printed in the United States of America
89 90 91 92 9 8 7 6 5 4 3 2 1

Contents

Contributors   xi

Preface   xiii

1   **Optics as an Interconnect Technology** **1**
     Joseph W. Goodman

     1. Introduction   1
     2. Why Use Optics for Interconnections?   3
     3. Types of Optical Interconnections   5
     4. Some Specific Properties of Optical Interconnections . .   9
     5. Power Requirements for Optical Interconnections   12
     6. Fan-In and Fan-Out Properties of Optical Interconnections   15
     7. Power Comparison for Example Electrical and Optical
        Interconnects   18
     8. Optical Clock Distribution to a VLSI Chip   23
        Acknowledgements   31
        References   31

2   **Nonlinear Phenomena in Optical Fibers and
the Feasibility of Their Application in
Optical Computers.** **33**
     Mikhail P. Petrov and Yevgeny A. Kuzin

     1. Foreword   33
     2. Stimulated Raman Scattering (SRS) and Stimulated
        Mandelstam-Brillouin Scattering (SMBS) in Optical
        Fibers   34

3. Basic Principles of Operation of Nonlinear Fiber Optical
   Elements   40
4. SRS Inverter   46
5. Switching of Optical Signals by SMBS in Optical Fibers   52
6. Conclusion.   56
   References   57

3 Fundamental Physical Limitations of the Photorefractive Grating Recording Sensitivity   59
R.V. Johnson and A.R. Tanguay, Jr.

1. Introduction   60
2. Factors Contributing to the Photorefractive Sensitivity   63
3. The Grating Recording Efficiency.   68
4. Representative Grating Recording Efficiency Calculations   95
5. Conclusions   98
   Acknowledgements   99
   References   99

4 Biopolymers for Real-Time Optical Processing   103
Vladimir Yu. Bazhenov, Marat S. Soskin, Victor B. Taranenko, and Mikhail V. Vasnetsov

1. Introduction   103
2. Sensitized Gelatin.   105
3. Materials Based on Bacteriorhodopsin   118
4. Conclusion.   139
   Acknowledgements   140
   References   141

5 Diode Lasers in Optical Computing   145
Valentin N. Morozov

1. Introduction   145
2. Basic Characteristics of Diode Lasers   146
3. Generation of Short Pulses by Diode Lasers   150

4. Recording and Reconstruction of Fourier Holograms with Diode-Laser Radiation 154
5. Diode Lasers in Correlation Systems 161
6. Integration of Holograms with Optical Waveguides . . . 169
7. Optical Logic Gates on Diode Lasers 174
8. Integration of Diode Lasers with Electronic Circuits . . . 179
9. Conclusion 185
   References 186

6 Array Optoelectronic Computers 189
Pyotr E. Tverdokhleb

1. Introduction 189
2. Optoelectronic Computer Structure 191
3. Optical Preprocessor 193
4. Microoperations of the Optical Preprocessor 201
5. Photoelectronic Parallel Processor 210
6. Logic Data Processing 213
7. Data Search in an Array Computer 219
8. Summary 220
   References 220

7 Optical Matrix Computations 223
Mustafa A.G. Abushagur and H.J. Caulfield

1. Introduction 224
2. Linear Algebra 225
3. Optical Computations 231
4. Summary 247
   References 247

8 Optical Implementation of Neural Computers 251
Demetri Psaltis, David Brady, Xiang-guang Gu, and Ken Hsu

1. Introduction 251
2. The Basic Architecture 252
3. Three-Dimensional Storage of the Interconnection Weights 257

4. Adaptive Weights and Real-Time Holography   269
Acknowledgements   274
References   275

9   Computer Synthesis of Diffraction Optical
    Elements   277
    Voldemar P. Koronkevich

1. Introduction   278
2. Production of Diffraction Optical Elements   280
3. Practical Results: Elements of Diffraction Optical Systems   286
4. Optical Systems with Diffraction Elements   301
5. Conclusion   311
References   312

10 Distortion-Invariant Pattern Recognition
    Using Circular Harmonic Matched Filters . . .   315
    Henri H. Arsenault

1. Introduction   316
2. Rotation-Invariant Matched Filters   320
3. Multiple CHC Methods   329
4. Sidelobe Reduction   336
5. Principal Component Filters   338
6. Conclusion   338
References   339

11 Pattern Recognition Using Photon-Limited
    Images   343
    G. Michael Morris

1. Introduction   344
2. Photon Statistics and Detection Systems   346
3. Correlation with a Deterministic Reference Function . . .   350
4. Summary   385
Acknowledgements   386
References   386

12 Line Detection and Directional Analysis of Images 391
Tomasz Szoplik

1. Introduction 391
2. Anamorphic Fourier Transform 392
3. Mesooptical Fourier Transform Microscope 402
4. The Hough Transform 410
5. Conclusion 415
   References 416

13 Incoherent Optical Processing and Holography 421
E.N. Leith

1. Introduction 421
2. The Achromatization of Katyl 422
3. White Light Coherent Correlator 427
4. Further Development of White Light Filtering 428
5. Construction of Diffractive Optical Elements 436
   References 438

14 Generalized Matched Spatial Filters with Optimum Light Efficiency 441
Katarzyna Chalasinska-Macukow

1. Introduction 442
2. Light Utilization Problems in Optical Correlators 443
3. Phase-Only Matched Filtering 446
4. Matched Filtering Using Tandem Component Filters . . . 455
5. Conclusion 463
   References 464

15 Optoelectronic Analog Processors 469
Evgeny S. Nezhevenko

1. Introduction 469
2. Optoelectronic Analog Feedback Processors 472

3. Optoelectronic Pipeline Processors   477
4. Optoelectronic Pipeline Correlator   484
5. Conclusion   486
   Acknowledgements   487
   References   487

Index   489

Contributors

Numbers in parentheses refer to the pages on which the authors' contributions begin.

Mustafa A.G. Abushagur (223), *Department of Electrical and Computer Engineering, University of Alabama in Huntsville, Huntsville, Alabama 35899*

Henri H. Arsenault, (315) *Department de Physique Universite Laval, Cite Universitaire, Quebec, Canada*

Vladimir Yu. Bazhenov (103), *Institute of Physics, Academy of Sciences of the Ukrainian SSR, Kiev 28, 252, 650, USSR*

David Brady (251), *California Institute of Technology, Department of Electrical Engineering, Pasadena, California 91125*

H.J. Caulfield (223), *Center for Applied Optics, University of Alabama in Huntsville, Huntsville, Alabama 35899*

Katarzyna Chalasinska-Macukow (441), *Institute of Geophysics, University of Warsaw, ul. Pasteura 7, 02-093 Warsaw, Poland*

Joseph W. Goodman (1), *Department of Electrical Engineering, Stanford University, Stanford, California 94305*

Xiang-guang Gu (251), *California Institute of Technology, Department of Electrical Engineering, Pasadena, California 91125*

Ken Hsu (251), *California Institute of Technology, Department of Electrical Engineering, Pasadena, California 91125*

R.V. Johnson (59), *Optical Materials and Devices Laboratory, Departments of Electrical Engineering and Materials Science, and Cen-*

xi

ter for Photonic Technology, University of Southern California, University Park, MC-0483, Los Angeles, California 90089-0483

Voldemar P. Koronkevich (277), Institute of Automation and Electrometry, Siberian Branch of the USSR Academy of Science, Novosibirsk, 630 090, USSR

Yevgeny A. Kuzin (33), A. F. Ioffe Physical Technical Institute, Academy of Sciences of the USSR, Leningrad, 194 021, USSR

Valentin N. Morozov (145), P. N. Lebedev Physical Institute, USSR Academy of Sciences, Moscow, 117 924, USSR

G. Michael Morris (343), The Institute of Optics, University of Rochester, Rochester, New York

Evgeny S. Nezhevenko (469), Institute of Automation and Electrometry, Siberian Branch of the USSR Academy of Sciences, Novosibirsk, 630 090, USSR

Mikhail P. Petrov (33), A. F. Ioffe Physical Technical Institute, Academy of Sciences of the USSR, Leningrad, 194 021, USSR

Demetri Psaltis (251), California Institute of Technology, Department of Electrical Engineering, Pasadena, California 91125

Marat S. Soskin (103), Institute of Physics, Academy of Sciences of the Ukrainian SSR, Kiev 28, 252 650, USSR

Tomasz Szoplik (391), Institute of Geophysics, University of Warsaw, ul. Pasteura 7, 02-093 Warsaw, Poland

A.R. Tanguay, Jr. (59), Optical Materials and Devices Laboratory, Departments of Electrical Engineering and Materials Science, and Center for Photonic Technology, University of Southern California, University Park, MC-0483, Los Angeles, California 90089-0483

Victor B. Taranenko (103), Institute of Physics, Academy of Sciences of the Ukrainian SSR, Kiev 28, 252, 650, USSR

Pyotr E. Tverdokhleb (189), Institute of Automation and Electrometry, Siberian Branch of the USSR Academy of Sciences, Novosibirsk, 630 090, USSR

Mikhail V. Vasnetsov (103), Institute of Physics, Academy of Sciences of the Ukrainian SSR, Kiev 28, 252 650, USSR

Preface

Digital optical computing and analog optical processing are rapidly expanding areas of optics. This book includes contributions from researchers from the USA, Canada, the Soviet Union, and Poland. A collection of articles from the principals in the field in Europe and Japan would be a useful complement to this book, and we hope that someone will compile such a collection.

This book will give western readers an exposure to Soviet work in optical computing, some of which has never been published in the West. The collaboration in this book between American and Soviet researchers will also give readers an opportunity to compare the different types of research in the two countries.

Some chapters deal with the fundamental limitations and capabilities of optics in relation to interconnections, switching, computing, materials, and devices; others deal with architectures, technology, and applications. The topics range from new and promising areas in the early stages of development, such as nonlinear effects in fibers, which could bring about the optical transistor, to new developments in areas ripe for technology, such as the production of optical kinoforms, an important type of computer-generated optical component. The flavor of the book is somewhat more fundamental than applied, so the book is of interest not only to specialists, who will find in the book reviews of optical computing by some of the best-known scientists in the field, but also to students and researchers who need a broad coverage of the principles of optical computing and of the underlying physics.

The preparation of this book was an exercise in international cooperation that we hope will be a useful addition to the scientific literature. This book also shows that science is a truly international activity, and we hope that in the near future such cooperation will be considered a normal and everyday activity.

Henri H. Arsenault, Bohdan Macukow, and Tomasz Szoplik

1.

Optics as an Interconnect Technology

Joseph W. Goodman

Department of Electrical Engineering
Stanford University
Stanford, California

Contents

1. Introduction. 1
2. Why Use Optics for Interconnections? 3
3. Types of Optical Interconnections 5
4. Some Specific Properties of Optical Interconnections 9
5. Power Requirements for Optical Interconnections 12
6. Fan-In and Fan-Out Properties of Optical Interconnections 15
7. Power Comparison for Example Electrical and Optical Interconnects . . . 18
8. Optical Clock Distribution to a VLSI Chip. 23
   Acknowledgments 31
   References 31

1.

Introduction

The hardware portion of a digital computing system can be regarded in most general terms as a collection of many nonlinear elements within which signals must interact (the gates), together with interconnections between those elements, or between groups of such elements. The groups of elements can be of various sizes and complexities, depending on the level of architecture

1   Copyright © 1989 by Academic Press, Inc.
All rights of reproduction in any form reserved.
ISBN 0-12-064470-3

of concern. The function of the interconnections may be to communicate information to or from processing subunits, memories subunits, or users, or to transfer control signals or program segments to hardware subunits of various kinds.

The variety of different kinds of interconnect problems can be appreciated in the context of a listing of several levels of computer architecture within which interconnections play a fundamental role. Starting at the highest levels of architecture and working downward to lower levels, we have:

Machine-to-machine interconnections. The interconnections are required to transfer messages of various kinds, including electronic mail, files, and information from shared databases. The distances involved typically vary from several meters to many kilometers.

Processor-to-processor interconnections. In a multiprocessor environment within a single machine, interconnections are required between different processors, and between processors and certain shared resources, such as memory. In many cases it is necessary to change the interconnect pattern dynamically in time. The distances involved may vary from as little as a few centimeters to a few meters.

Board-to-board interconnections. Within a single processing unit, there usually exist several electronic boards. These boards must interchange information and usually do so by means of some form of data bus. The distances involved can vary from a very few centimeters to perhaps as much as one meter.

Chip-to-chip interconnections. On a single board there typically exists a multitude of integrated circuit chips, many of which must communicate with one another. The communication distances involved range from of the order of 0.1 centimeter to as much as a few tens of centimeters. A special case is that of wafer-level interconnection, in which various chips on a single wafer must communicate.

Intrachip interconnections. A single integrated circuit chip typically contains thousands of interconnections between gates and between different functional subunits of the chip. In addition, a substantial system of interconnections exists between the chip itself and the pins that connect it to the outside world. This intrachip level we regard as the lowest level of the interconnection hierarchy. The distances involved range from a few micrometers to at most a very few centimeters.

An examination of the above hierarchy of interconnect problems reveals that optics is now penetrating the highest levels. Machine-to-machine communication via optical fibers is now a commercial reality, and serious attempts are in progress to bring optics to the next lower level of architecture, processor-to-processor interconnection within a single machine. Research is also under way at the chip-to-chip level. How far down this hierarchy of interconnection problems optics will eventually penetrate is a subject for speculation.

It is the goal of this chapter to examine the properties of optical signals that make them attractive as an interconnect technology. Some speculation as to possible future developments will also be included. Several other discussions on this subject are available in the literature (Special issue, 1986; Goodman et al., 1984; Husain, 1984; Hutcheson et al., 1987).

2.
Why Use Optics for Interconnections?

The physical properties desired of an interconnect technology are markedly different (and indeed in many respects quite the opposite of) the physical properties required of a gate technology. An interconnect technology should ideally have the property that interactions between different interconnections are minimum or nonexistent. Thus signals flowing through one interconnection should not couple to or otherwise influence signals flowing in another interconnection. There are fundamental differences between electrons and photons that are pertinent in this regard. Several points of view are possible in explaining these differences. From the most basic perspective, electrons are members of the class of particles known as fermions, while photons belong to the class known as bosons.

According to the Pauli exclusion principal, no two fermions can occupy the same cell of phase space, whereas any number of bosons can share a common cell. This fact can be viewed as implying that electrons must fundamentally suffer mutual interactions that prevent violation of the exclusion principal, while no such interactions need exist for photons.

A somewhat more straightforward point of view rests on the fact that electrons are charged particles while photons carry no charge. Moving electrons thus generate stray electric and magnetic fields, which in turn couple signals into proximate conducting lines. No such fundamental coupling mechanism exists for streams of photons, although from the practical point of view, some level of coupling can arise through optical scattering if care is not taken.

Regardless of the point of view, there is a fundamental conclusion that emerges from the discussion: *Optical interconnections potentially offer a freedom from mutual coupling effects not afforded by conventional electronic interconnects.* This potential advantage of optics becomes more and more important as the bandwidth of the desired interconnections increases, for the strength of mutual coupling associated with electrical interconnects is proportional to the frequency of the signals propagating on the interconnect lines.

A second potential advantage of optical interconnections is an extra flexibility of routing. Electrical interconnect paths can not cross and therefore must be routed over or under one another through multiple interconnect layers. Optical interconnections can indeed be routed through one another without any deleterious effects. Unlike electrical interconnect paths, which must reside near a ground plane to assure that stray electric fields are properly terminated, optical interconnects need not remain near a ground plane and indeed can be routed in a flexible manner through three-dimensional space.

A third advantage of optical interconnects rests on a partial freedom from certain capacitive loading effects. For an electrical interconnection, the delivery of signals to a number of different devices or subunits of a system requires that the interconnect line drive a total capacitance consisting of the capacitance of the interconnect line plus the capacitances of all the devices or subsystems attached to that line. The capacitance of the line itself is proportional to the length of the interconnection. For both optical and electrical interconnects, the basic signal-carrying streams (comprised of photons and electrons, respectively) must be divided between the various termination points where information is to be delivered. However, in the electrical case, if the connection is long enough, a significant number of electrons are diverted to charging the capacitance of the interconnect line and are therefore not available for charging the capacitances of the devices at the termination points. No such line-charging phenomenon is present for an optical interconnection, although the equivalent of a resistive loss is present if the optical interconnect line has significant absorption or scattering, or if the electrical-to-optical or optical-to-electrical converters (sources and detectors, respectively) have low quantum efficiency.

A fourth possible advantage of optics rests on its potential for supplying dynamically changeable interconnect devices. Since photon-based interconnects require no mechanical contacts, interconnect rerouting can be accomplished simply by changing directions of optical beams. While much work remains to realize dynamic routing elements with interestingly large numbers of connections and speeds of reconfiguration, nonetheless the potential for optics in this role is intriguing (Herriau et al., 1984; Wilde et al., 1987).

3.
Types of Optical Interconnections

An optical interconnection performs the task of delivering modulated light generated at a source to a detector where the modulation is recovered. The interconnection should be efficient in that as many as possible of the available photons should be delivered to the desired destination. In addition, the interconnection should be as free as possible from dispersion that might limit the bandwidth of the modulation recoverable at the receiver. There are in fact many optical methods that could be used as the basis for realization of optical interconnections. In this section we briefly describe the various possibilities.

The first method for realizing optical interconnections that comes to mind is by means of *optical fibers,* as indicated conceptually in Fig. 1.1. Fiber-optic technology is having enormous impact on telephone and data communications, particularly over distances of several to many kilometers. Commercial availability of fiber-optic networks is also beginning to be used for connecting a number of digital computers with one another and with

Fig. 1.1.

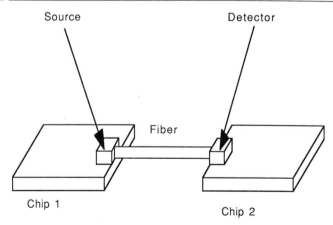

Chip-to-chip interconnect with optical fibers.

shared peripherals. It seems natural, therefore, to consider the possible use of fibers at other high levels of computer architecture. Optical fibers have many of the properties we might desire of an interconnect technology. They efficiently deliver photons coupled into the input to detectors at the output. Their losses are so low at lengths of a kilometer and less (the distances of main interest here) that attenuation by the fibers themselves can often be neglected. In addition, dispersion over such short distances is usually negligible at bandwidths of current interest. The above comments apply for both single-mode and multi-mode fibers, so there seems to be little motivation to utilize the more complicated and expensive single-mode technology in these applications when multimode solutions should be perfectly adequate. However, optical fibers are not necessarily the ideal solution for interconnect problems at all levels. In particular, at the lowest levels, i.e., intrachip and very nearby chip-to-chip interconnections, the problems of bending and looping fibers become severe, due to radiation losses induced by bending. For such problems, it might be argued that fibers are too much like wires, requiring a material path for the interconnection between every two points, and rather inflexible paths at that.

An alternative approach that may be applicable to intrachip communications is the use of *integrated optic* technology, illustrated in Fig. 1.2. This approach rests on the use of waveguides that are integrated in a planar substrate. Most common is the creation of waveguides in lithium niobate by indiffusion of titanium channels, but similar guides can be made by sputtering glass on SiO_2. While the losses associated with such waveguides are orders of magnitude higher than those associated with optical fibers, nonetheless the distances for intrachip communication are so short that these losses

Fig. 1.2. _____

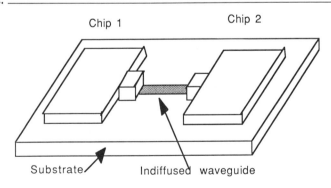

Chip-to-chip interconnect using integrated optic waveguides.

may not be of great importance. However, losses, together with the problems associated with realizing large integrated-optic substrates, appear to rule out the use of integrated optics for levels of interconnection higher than intrachip or very nearby interchip.

An important practical problem with the integrated-optic approach is the coupling of light into and out of the waveguides. Butt coupling of light into such waveguides is common and is applicable when the source is a discrete device. Likewise, end-to-end juxtaposition of a discrete detector and the waveguide output can serve to deliver the optical signals to the photosensitive surface of the detector.

In some applications, it may be desirable to place a passive waveguide substrate over an active integrated circuit in which detectors and/or sources have been integrated. The problem of efficient coupling into and out of the waveguides is more difficult in this case, requiring the use of prism or grating couplers.

Of the various imaginable ways for using optics for interconnects, perhaps the simplest method from the conceptual point of view is that of *free-space unfocused broadcast* shown in Fig. 1.3. For this method, a modulated optical signal, generated, for example, by a laser diode, is transmitted in a broad and unfocused beam, portions of which fall upon one or more detectors. If the interconnection is from one source to a single receiver, then the connection is one-to-one. On the other hand, if the same signal must be delivered simultaneously to several receiving points, then the interconnection is said to have *fan-out* and to be one-to-many. The chief drawback of

Fig. 1.3. _____

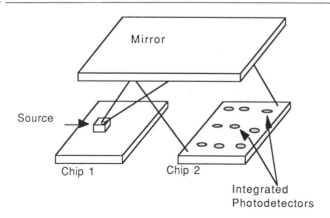

Free-space unfocused broadcast.

this approach to interconnection is the very low degree of efficiency with which photons are utilized. The fact that the light has been spread over a large area implies that only a small fraction of the optical power will be intercepted by any one detector. Since in most applications the electrons generated by photons at the detector must charge a capacitance on a gate, loss of photons implies that longer integration times will be required for the gate threshold voltage to be reached. Thus the speed capability of the circuit will be less than it could be with more efficient delivery of photons. A further disadvantage of this approach in many applications is the lack of parallelism in communication capability. Since all detectors receive all the signals transmitted by any one source, the communication channel realized by this approach must be time shared. Only one source can be active at one time, thus eliminating all potential for parallelism. In spite of the drawbacks of this type of interconnection, it has been used in at least one experimental computer system as the basis for a common bus (Tajima et al., 1984).

The final approach to be discussed can be called *free-space focused interconnection,* or more simply, *imaging interconnections,* as illustrated in Fig. 1.4. This method differs from that discussed above in that rather general optical focusing elements are used to place nearly all the available light onto the detector sites where it is required. The focusing elements generally must be realized by means of holography and are referred to as holographic optical elements. Using such elements, a single source can be imaged onto one or more photodetectors with high efficiency, eliminating much of the waste of

Fig. 1.4. _____

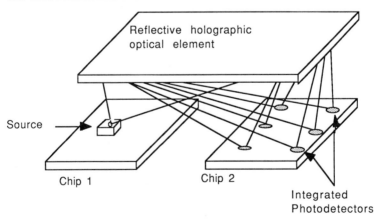

Imaging interconnections.

photons present in the unfocused case. The practical limits to efficiency depend on the amount of fan-out required, the material from which the hologram is made, and the geometry required. With the use of dichromated gelatin as a recording material, simple reflection holograms capable of imaging one source onto one detector using visible light can be made with efficiencies in excess of 99%. Less is known about making good holographic optical elements that work in the near infrared, where high-speed optical communication technology is prevalent (a recent reference is available on this subject (Herzig, 1986). Note that the use of imaging interconnections reserves the possibility of parallelism in the interconnect network. One source can be imaged onto one photodetector, while another independent source is imaged onto another different photodetector. Each such channel can then operate independently. If holographic optical elements are to be used, it should be noted that the Bragg selectivity of a thick *transmission* grating is far superior to that of a thick *reflection* grating. Therefore, when several parallel interconnects are to be made independently, a transmission geometry is preferable to a reflection geometry.

4.
Some Specific Properties of Optical Interconnections

In a previous section, we have discussed in a general way the differences that exist between optical and electronic interconnections, as well as the properties of optics that make it attractive as the basis for an interconnect technology. In this section we will discuss some more specific properties of optical interconnections, particularly properties that strongly influence the practicality of such techniques in real applications.

If optical interconnects are to be used to interconnect two electronic subunits at some level of architecture, then signals that are originally in electronic form must be converted to optical form, and, following reception at the destination, they must be converted back into electronic form. Each conversion step has a finite efficiency, and it is important to quantify the impacts of the associated losses. It should be kept in mind that in most applications the termination of the interconnect link will be a capacitive load that must be charged to the threshold voltage of the logic devices that follow. To reach the threshold voltage, a certain minimum amount of charge must be deposited at the terminating device.

A flow of electrons over an electronic connection must be mimicked by a flow of photons over an optical connection. Thus a flow of current in the electronic case is analogously replaced by a flow of power in the optical case. It is, of course, necessary to take into account the finite efficiency of the optical source and the finite quantum efficiency of the optical detector in making any comparison.

4.1. Detector Efficiency

In the case of a communication link at 800-nm wavelength, we can assume an 80% quantum efficiency for a silicon p-i-n photodiode, corresponding to a responsivity of approximately 0.5 amps/watt. Avalanche photodiodes have inherent gain, and as a consequence they are better converters of optical power into electrical current. Typical values of responsivity for such detectors are 50 to 100 amps/watt. However, we intentionally exclude avalanche photodiodes from consideration here for two reasons. First and foremost, we wish to compare optical and electronic interconnections without any gain mechanism present. Obviously both types of interconnections can be followed by devices or circuits with gain. Comparison of the two technologies then becomes a strong function of the detailed character of the gain mechanism, opening a Pandora's box of details that are beyond our central purpose here. Secondly, once gain is allowed at the end of the interconnection, the total power requirements no longer arise only at the transmitting end of the link. Rather, power is supplied at the receiving end as well, further complicating the comparison. It should also be mentioned that avalanche photodiodes require higher voltages than p-i-n diodes and have greater temperature sensitivities, making their use in practice more complex than p-i-n diodes.

4.2. Source Efficiency

The efficiency considerations discussed above apply only to photon-to-electron conversion at the receiving end of the interconnection. Equally important are the efficiency considerations for the initial electron-to-photon conversion at the transmitting end of the link.

Efficiencies in the range of 1% to 2% are typical of LEDs operating in the near infrared. Such low efficiencies make it difficult for an optical interconnect to compete on a power basis with an electrical link. Therefore higher efficiency laser sources are of greater interest.

High efficiencies are realized in laser diodes only well above lasing threshold. Below threshold, a semiconductor laser source behaves essentially as an LED and as such exhibits a relatively poor overall power efficiency. When using a laser diode, there exists a certain minimum amount of electrical power required to bring the source to threshold, and that electrical power is essentially wasted, since it generates very few photons. Any comparison of electrical and optical interconnects must ultimately take account of this minimum required threshold current. When an electrical interconnect requires less power than that needed to bring a laser diode to threshold, optics can not compete with the electronic solution. On the other hand, when the interconnect is characterized by a high degree of fan-out, the inefficiency associated with the finite laser threshold can be amortized over a large number of connections, making the optical interconnect more attractive as a solution.

As a typical state-of-the-art laser diode attractive for interconnect applications, we consider the GaAs single quantum well laser recently described in the literature (Lau et al., 1987). The threshold current for this laser is just under 1 mA, and the required applied voltage is 1.4 V. Thus to reach threshold a commitment of 1.4 mW of electrical power is required. In the middle of the lasing range, 5 mA of current are required to produce approximately 1.5 mW of output optical power. Thus the efficiency of the device in converting electrical to optical power is 21%. Efficiencies in the range of 20% to 25% are typical of good semiconductor lasers with outputs in the range of a few milliwatts. Higher power semiconductor lasers can achieve higher efficiencies, even in excess of 50%. In our considerations, we will use a 25% efficiency number.

4.3. Interconnect Efficiency

Finally, considerations of efficiency can not ignore the losses associated with the optical path from transmitter to receiver. These losses vary dramatically, depending on which of the various schemes discussed in the previous section are chosen for the optical interconnect. Most efficient would be a fiber-optic link, which for the geometries to which such technology can be applied and for the short distances of interest here, will suffer primarily from coupling losses at the input and output of the fiber. Losses of only a decibel or two should be possible. Least efficient will be the free-space broadcast schemes, for which the losses could easily reach 60 db in some applications (broadcast to a 10 μm × 10 μm detector on a 1 cm × 1 cm chip). Holographic distribution systems exhibit losses of 3 db to 10 db for bleached silver-halide-based reflection holograms and considerably less for dichromated-gelatin-based reflection elements. Larger losses can be expected if the light from the optical source overfills the holographic optical element. Such would be the case for an LED source, but not necessarily for a semiconductor laser source.

5.
Power Requirements for Optical Interconnections (Kostuk and Goodman, 1985; Kostuk, 1986)

An important consideration for any interconnect line is the power required to drive that line, and the devices attached to it, at a given bit rate. It is instructive to compare conventional electronic interconnections with optical interconnections from this point of view, for some fundamental conclusions result. In the electrical case, the power requirements depend on whether the interconnect line is terminated or unterminated. Termination of a line is required if reflections from the end of the line pose a problem; it results in a substantially greater amount of power dissipation than if no termination is used. For an unterminated line a major portion of the power requirement arises from the need to charge the capacitance of the line and the capacitance of the device or devices attached to the line. Such power is entirely reactive in nature. This conclusion changes when the bit rates become high enough, due to skin-effect losses in the conductors.

In the optical case, it is assumed that the same devices that were driven by the electrical interconnect line are now driven by the output of the detector at the end of the line. The capacitance of those devices is unchanged, but the major power requirement now stems from the inefficiencies of the electron-to-photon and photon-to-electron conversion processes. These inefficiencies constitute real power loss, and therefore the drive power requirements are no longer reactive.

A rather simple example is revealing. Consider first the case of an electrical interconnection. Suppose that the electrical interconnect line is unterminated and skin-effect losses are negligible. The drive power requirements in the electrical case then consist primarily of the reactive power needed to charge to the threshold logic voltage the capacitance of the interconnect line itself and the device capacitances attached to the line. The reactive power P required to charge a capacitance C to a voltage threshold level V in a fixed time τ is

$$P = CV^2/2\tau. \tag{1.1}$$

Hence for a fixed voltage threshold level and a fixed charging time, the required power is directly proportional to the capacitance that must be charged. Let the capacitance of the device attached to both of the lines be represented by C_d and the capacitance of the electrical interconnect line itself by C_1. The reactive power P_e required for the electrical interconnect line is then

$$P_e = \frac{(C_1 + C_d)V^2}{2\tau}. \tag{1.2}$$

Consider next the case of an equivalent optical interconnection. A real electrical power P_{eo} must be supplied to the optical source in order to ultimately charge the same device capacitance, as well as the dectector capacitance C_D. We calculate the required P_{eo} in the following manner. First, since by definition capacitance is the amount of charge stored for a given applied voltage, the charge required at the end of the interconnection in order to bring the detector capacitance and device capacitance to voltage V is

$$Q = V(C_D + C_d). \tag{1.3}$$

To deposit that charge in time τ requires a current

$$i = \frac{V(C_D + C_d)}{\tau}. \tag{1.4}$$

Let the responsivity of the detector be R, in which case the optical power required to generate the current above is

$$P_o = \frac{V(C_D + C_d)}{R\tau}. \tag{1.5}$$

Finally, taking account of the finite power efficiency η_s of the source, the total electrical power required to drive the optical link is

$$P_{eo} = \frac{V(C_D + C_d)}{\eta_s R\tau}. \tag{1.6}$$

Note that different methods were required to calculate P_e and P_{eo} due to the fact that in the former case we were dealing with a constant voltage source applied to the line, whereas in the optical case the capacitances are charged by a constant current source.

It is now possible to compare the powers required of the two technologies. The power required of the optical link will be less than the power required of the electrical link when $P_{eo} < P_e$, i.e., when

$$\frac{C_D + C_d}{\eta_s R} < \frac{(C_l + C_d) V}{2}, \qquad (1.7)$$

or, equivalently, when the electrical line capacitance satisfies

$$C_l > 2\frac{C_D + C_d}{V\eta_s R} - C_d. \qquad (1.8)$$

If we take the detector responsivity to be 0.5 watts/amp, and the laser efficiency to be 25%, the optical link will be superior to the electrical link whenever the electrical line capacitance satisfies

$$C_l > \frac{16}{V}(C_D + C_d) - C_d. \qquad (1.9)$$

Note that the higher the threshold voltage required by the devices, the more favorable the optical link becomes. Finally it should be noted that in the chip-to-chip communication problem, the electrical interconnection is usually accomplished via bonding pads at each end of the line. The capacitances of the bonding pads are very large compared with the capacitances of a gate, and hence in this case the bonding pad capacitances should replace the gate capacitance when calculating the required electrical power.

The power requirement comparison above is, in a rather hidden way, intrinsically connected with the issue of the relative isolation of two adjacent interconnections. For the case of an electrical interconnection, a high degree of isolation can be achieved if the conducting lines are kept very close to a ground plane. Thus if the conducting line is separated from a ground plane by a thin dielectric layer, or if it is sandwiched between two ground planes with thin dielectric layers providing separation, the isolation of the line dramatically improves. However, accompanying this increased isolation there comes fundamentally an increase in the line capacitance and therefore a greater power requirement for the electrical interconnection. Improved isolation comes from the more effective termination of electric field lines on the conducting ground plane or planes, resulting in less stray capacitance between lines. In turn, the increased number of field lines terminating on the ground plane implies that the line itself has a greater ability to store charge when a fixed voltage is applied and therefore a greater inherent capacitance. Thus there is a direct trade-off between isolation between lines and the electrical power required to drive those lines. No such tradeoff exists in the case of optical interconnections. High isolation between lines is inherently provided, with no direct cost (other than the fixed factor arising from the imperfect laser and detector quantum efficiencies) in terms of increased driving power.

Much of the above discussion has assumed that the electrical interconnect line is not long enough, and the bandwidth not wide enough, to require termination for suppression of reflections. In the event that electrical termination is required, the electrical drive power requirement increases appreciably. If the termination is perfectly matched to the characteristic impedance R_0 of the line, then the power dissipation is

$$P_e = \frac{V^2}{R_0}.$$

(1.10)

It can now be seen that an optical interconnection will require less power than an electrical interconnection when

$$\frac{C_D + C_d}{R\tau} < \frac{V}{R_0}.$$

(1.11)

Note that this result is independent of length for the case of lossless optical and electrical interconnects.

We defer until Section 7 a more specific comparison of the power requirements for electrical and optical interconnects.

6.

Fan-In and Fan-Out Properties of Optical Interconnections (Goodman, 1985)

An interconnection is said to have an *N-fold fan-out* if it provides a path from a single source of information to N different destinations. Whether the interconnections are electronic or optical, at each of the N destinations there will usually be a device capacitance that must be charged by the electrons delivered or generated by the interconnection. If N-fold fan-out is present, then the electrons or photons must be divided at least N ways (more than N ways if capacitive charging of the electronic lines or losses associated with the optical lines are considered). This fact implies that the time required to charge one device capacitance will be approximately N times as long in the presence of N-fold fan out as in the absence of fan-out. This same conclusion holds whether the interconnect paths are provided by electrons or by photons. The difference between optical and electronic interconnects with regard to fan-out resides only in the capacitances and losses associated with the interconnect lines themselves. Low-loss optical interconnect lines do not provide the equivalent of capacitive or resistive effects associated with electronic lines.

An interconnection is said to have *N-fold fan-in* if it provides simultaneous paths from N different sources of information to a single destination. In this case, a single destination device capacitance must be charged by the N streams of electrons delivered or generated by the interconnections. If the interconnections are electronic, one source will appear to another source as a resistive path to ground, and if the resistance of such paths is sufficiently low, then a portion of the electrons delivered from any one source to the destination device may be diverted to ground through those source resistances. In fact, if the sources all have internal series resistance R_s, and if the load to which power is to be delivered has resistance R_s, then it can be shown that the fraction of power delivered by one source to the load, in the presence of N-1 other sources, is $1/N$ of the power delivered by that source. The fraction $(N - 1)/N$ of the delivered power is dissipated in the internal resistances of the $N - 1$ other sources.

In the optical case, a similar effect is observed as a consequence of fan-in. A basic optical fact, derivable from the laws of thermodynamics and often referrred to as the *constant brightness theorem* (Welford and Winston, 1978—Appendix A), states that no passive linear optical system can increase the brightness (watts per steradian per unit area per unit bandwidth) of an optical beam. This theorem implies that any attempt to superimpose mutually incoherent beams of light in such a way that the resultant brightness would be increased must inevitably fail. More specifically, the optical system devised to accomplish this goal must have associated with it some form of loss mechanism that will prevent the brightness from being increased. A good example is afforded by a holographic optical element designed to merge two mutually incoherent beams of light of the same wavelength into a single beam having the same cross-sectional area and angular divergence as the original beams. Figure 1.5a shows the recording geometry that might be devised to make such an element. A thick hologram is recorded using two object beams and a single reference beam. Figure 1.5b shows the geometry in which such an element would be used for fan-in. Two incident beams, each coinciding in direction with one of the original object beams, are merged into a single beam traveling in the direction of the original reference beam. It can be shown that such an element must have associated with it at least

Fig. 1.5.

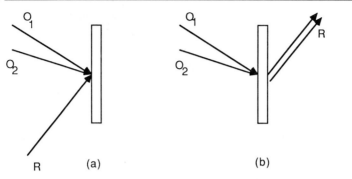

Holographic beam combiner: (a) recording, (b) utilization.

a 50% loss, arising from the fact that at least 50% of the light in each of the incident beams remains in the undeflected transmitted beams. In this way the constant brightness theorem is satisfied. More generally, if an element is made to merge N different optical beams of the same wavelength into a single beam having the same cross-sectional area and angular divergence as its component beams, then at most $1/N^{th}$ of the light in each beam can be placed into the desired output beam. However, lossless fan-in can in principle be accomplished if

$$A_2\Omega_2 > NA_1\Omega_1, \qquad (1.12)$$

where A_1 and A_2 are the cross-sectional areas of a single input beam and the output beam, respectively, while Ω_1 and Ω_2 are the solid angles subtended by one of the N input beams and the output beam, respectively.

If the two beams to be merged are mutually coherent, then the predictions of the constant brightness theorem must be used with care. It has been shown by Rediker and Leonberger (1982) that the merging of two single-mode mutually coherent beams in a waveguide Y junction into a single output waveguide can yield an efficiency anywhere between 0% (input waveguides driven out of phase) and 100% (input waveguides driven in phase). If the phase difference between the two coherent beams is entirely random, then each input beam is coupled into the output waveguide with an efficiency of 50%, consistent with the constant brightness theorem, the rest of the light being lost through radiation modes. Thus average power per output mode obeys the constant brightness theorem.

It should be re-emphasized that in the incoherent case the losses mentioned previously can be avoided if the resultant beam is allowed to have a sufficiently larger cross-sectional area or angular divergence than the component beams. Such is usually the case if the fan-in takes place on a detector that is capable of accepting radiation from a larger solid angle than that occupied by any one of the beams. In such a case, no attempt is made to force the beams to coincide in their directions of propagation.

7.
Power Comparisons for Example Electrical and Optical Interconnects

The power required to drive an interconnect line is one of several characteristics that is important in deciding the superiority of one interconnect technology over another. Note that drive power alone is not a complete characterization of an interconnect problem, for it ignores other important characteristics, such as mutual coupling between adjacent interconnect lines. To understand the power requirements is to understand but one of the dimensions in a multidimensional comparison space, albeit a very important dimension.

In this section we compare the power required for interconnects at two levels of architecture, focusing on the gate-to-gate interconnect problem and the chip-to-chip interconnect problem. In the latter case, both unterminated and terminated electrical interconnect lines are considered.

7.1. Power Requirements in Gate-to-Gate Interconnects

We first consider the simplest of interconnection problems, illustrated in Fig. 1.6. Gates on a single silicon chip are to be interconnected by a single in-

Fig. 1.6.

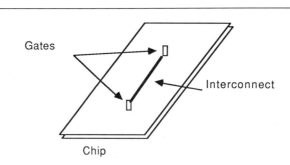

Gate-to-gate interconnect.

terconnection line. In one case the interconnection will be accomplished by conventional electronic means, while in the other the interconnection will be accomplished by optical means.

In both the electronic and the optical interconnect cases, the interconnect must supply sufficient electrical charge in a clock period to charge the capacitance C_g of a destination gate to its threshold voltage V. In the process, an electrical interconnect must supply sufficient reactive power to charge to that same voltage not only the capacitance of the destination gate, but also the capacitance C_l of the interconnect line itself, as well as the capacitance C_g of the source gate. Thus the total capacitance to be charged is

$$C_{TOT} = 2C_g + C_l. \qquad (1.13)$$

The capacitance of a metal plate of area A separated from an infinite ground plane by a dielectric of relative dielectric constant ϵ_r and thickness d is

$$C = \frac{\epsilon_r \epsilon_0 A}{d} \qquad (1.14)$$

where $\epsilon_0 = 8.854 \times 10^{-14}$ F/cm is the dielectric constant of free space. Considering first the gates, projected VLSI device lengths and oxide layer thicknesses are taken to be 0.5 and 0.02 μm, respectively. An SiO_2 oxide is assumed ($\epsilon_r = 3.9$). The resulting gate capacitance is $C_g = 0.4$ fF. Considering the interconnection line itself, C_l is given by

$$C_l = \frac{\epsilon_r \epsilon_0 wl}{h}, \qquad (1.15)$$

where l is the line length, w the line width, and h the height of the line above the ground plane. The width/height ratio is restricted by fringing field effects to a minimum value of about 2. Considering a typical length of the interconnect to be about 1 mm, the line capacitance is 69 fF. Thus the total capacitance of the gate-to-gate link is approximately $C_{TOT} = 70$ fF. Looking to the future, we assume for the purpose of illustration that the gate capacitance must be charged in 1 nsec (implying a data rate of 1 Gb/s). Assuming a 1-volt gate threshold, eq. (1.1) implies that the reactive power to charge the gate in 1 nsec is

$$P_e = 35 \ \mu W. \qquad (1.16)$$

Calculation of the power required to solve this same interconnect problem using optics proceeds as follows. In this case we assume that a laser is driven by a current source, the optical power generated by that laser is coupled into a waveguide with perfect efficiency, and the optical signal is delivered without loss to a detector having a responsivity of 0.5 amps/watt. The detector is taken to be 2 μm thick and to be 25 μm on a side, yielding a detector capacitance of 33 fF. Thus the combined capacity C_t of the parallel detector and gate capacitances is dominated by the detector capacitance, and is therefore about 33 fF. The laser is assumed to have an overall power efficiency of 25%. To reach a 1-volt threshold on a capacitance of 33 fF in 1 nsec requires a charging current ($i = VC_t/\tau$) of 33 μA.

The responsivity of 0.5 amps/watt leads to a required optical power of 66 μW at the detector. The 25% source efficiency in turn requires an electrical drive power of approximately 260 μW at the beginning of the link. Thus power required of the electro-optic link is $P_{eo} = 260$ μW.

The power calculated above is actually an underestimate of what would be required in practice, even for a lossless optical interconnect line. The reason lies in our neglect of the fact that to achieve lasing action in the optical source, which is required for high overall efficiency, a certain minimum threshold current is required. As discussed previously, the smallest threshold currents for sources currently available commercially are of the order of 1 mA. Following the example presented earlier in connection with Lau et al., 1987, the electrical power required to drive the optical link is modestly larger than the threshold power of 1.4 mW. Future improvements of laser devices could drive this number lower, but probably not be more than a factor of 2. Since we are looking to the future here, we assume a minimum electrical drive power of 1 mW. Hence, we use in all future comparisons a drive power required of the electro-optic link given by

$$P_{eo} = 1 \text{ mW}. \qquad (1.17)$$

We see from the above considerations that, for the parameters assumed in this example, *the optical link is not competitive with the electrical link at the gate-to-gate level,* assuming that drive power is the determining factor. This conclusion is likely to be true in general at this lowest level of architecture. Such is not necessarily so at the chip-to-chip level and higher, as we shall now see.

7.2. Power Requirements in Chip-to-Chip Interconnects

As illustrated in Fig. 1.7, in the electrical case the interconnection line must be attached to bonding pads on each of the two chips. We initially consider the case of an *unterminated* electrical interconnect line. To minimize propagation delays, the bonding pad is driven by a series of gates, with gate

Fig. 1.7.

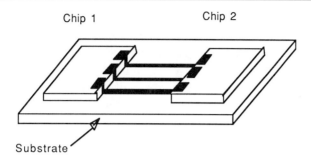

Chip 1   Chip 2

Substrate

Chip-to-chip electrical interconnect.

capacitances gradually increased until the device capacitance is comparable to that of a bonding pad. A current pulse from the driving logic element must be capable of charging capacitances of these larger gates, the bonding pads at both ends of the line, the line itself, and the destination gate. The total capacitance to be charged is thus

$$C_t = 2C_g + 2C_b + C_l, \qquad (1.18)$$

where C_b is the capacitance of a bonding pad, C_g is the capacitance of a gate, and C_l is the capacitance of the metallic interconnect line. The gate capacitances have been discussed in the previous section and again are taken to be 0.4 fF.

Considering the bonding pads, for a pad area of 100 μm^2 and the same SiO$_2$ dielectric layer assumed previously, the bonding pad capacitance is about 173 fF. The line connecting the bonding pads on the two chips is assumed to be 25 μm wide, 500 μm above the ground plane, and about 1 cm in length. The resulting line capacitance is only 4 fF. It is assumed for the present that the line is unterminated.

Examining the capacitances discussed above, we see that the dominant capacitance is that of the bonding pads, which are by far the largest structures on the chips themselves. The total capacitance C_t is 0.35 pF, essentially equal to the combined capacitances of the two bonding pads. Again looking to the future of silicon technology, we assume that the data link between chips will be required to operate at a rate of 1 Gb/s ($\tau = 10^{-9}$ sec). Assuming that the final gate has a threshold voltage of 1 volt, the reactive power required to drive the electrical interconnection is then given approximately by

$$P_\mathrm{e} = 175\ \mu\mathrm{W}. \qquad (1.19)$$

Turning attention to the optical solution to this interconnection problem, we replace the bonding pads and electrical line with an essentially lossless optical path (e.g., a fiber). Again the capacitance of the destination gate must be charged to the threshold voltage, taken to be 1 volt, in a time period of 1 nsec. The electro-optical parameters are all taken to be identical to those used in the gate-to-gate illustration, yielding the same electrical power required to drive the optical interconnection,

$$P_\mathrm{eo} = 1\ \mathrm{mW}. \qquad (1.20)$$

We see that in this case the amount of power required for the electrical interconnection is about one order of magnitude less than that needed to drive the optical interconnection. If the interconnect has some degree of fan-out associated with it, the optical link becomes more attractive in the comparison (to double the optical power emitted by the laser requires only an increase by 1.8 in electrical drive power for the particular laser considered here). We can conclude that in this example the use of an optical interconnection probably can not be clearly rejected based on drive power considerations, but it also can not be justified on this basis. Rather, it is the immunity from mutual interference that is the main attraction of the optical link.

We turn now to the case of a terminated electrical line. The electrical interconnect line must be terminated in its characteristic impedance if the line and the bandwidth of the interconnect exceed a certain limit. In simplest terms, if a reflection from the end of the line travels back to the source, and arrives there with as much as a half a bit period of delay, then potentially the signal transmitted to the gate will have sufficient reflection noise to cause unreliable triggering of the gate. On a lossless line with inductance L per unit length and capacitance C per unit length, the velocity of propagation is

$$v = \frac{1}{\sqrt{LC}}. \qquad (1.21)$$

If the line length is l, then potential problems arise with an unterminated line when

$$l > v\tau. \qquad (1.22)$$

The velocity of progagation on a standard 50-ohm coax line is typically about 0.5 times the free-space velocity of light. For a 1 Gb/s data rate, the maximum allowable line length for an unterminated line would then be of the order of 15 cm.

To avoid reflections, it simply necessary to terminate the electrical line in its characteristic impedance. For the lossless LC line, that impedance is given by

$$R_o = \sqrt{\frac{L}{C}}. \tag{1.23}$$

The power required to drive a terminated electrical line can now be calculated with the help of eq. (1.11). For a 50-ohm transmission line, a 1-volt threshold voltage, the required power for an electrical interconnect becomes

$$P_e = 20 \text{ mW}. \tag{1.24}$$

Note that the presence of the terminating resistor has dramatically increased the drive power necessary for the electrical connection to the point where the optical interconnection now has a distinct advantage in terms of required drive power. Thus we can conclude that in problems where the electrical interconnect solution requires a terminated transmission line, the optical interconnect solution can have a distinct advantage in requiring a smaller drive power.

8.
Optical Clock Distribution to a VLSI Chip

As VLSI chip capabilities increase through the scaling down of feature sizes and the scaling up of chip areas, interconnection delays at the chip level are known to be rapidly becoming the dominant limitation to chip speed. Important among these chip-level interconnect problems is clock distribution, i.e., the transmission of a reference timing signal to all parts of the chip, free from differential delays that could lead to a loss of synchronism. The only previous work on the problem of clock distribution at the chip level is that of Fried (1986). Much of what follows is based on the work of Clymer (1987) and Clymer and Goodman (1986).

There are major problems associated with the distribution of signals within integrated circuit chips via conductors. These problems arise from the finite resistivity, capacitance, and length of the conductors used as the signal paths, and from the limited number of layers available for routing. Chip designers can route signals over different types of conductors, each characterized by a different resistivity, and all having about the same capacitance per unit length. Aluminum conductors have the lowest resistivity, while polysilicon conductors have the highest, the two resistivities differing by two orders of magnitude. Low resistivity implies a small RC time constant for charging the line, and hence implies the smallest amount of delay per unit length. While aluminum is very desirable as an interconnect medium, many VLSI fabrication technologies support only one or two levels of metal interconnection. Aluminum is needed for the distribution of ground, supply voltages, and other special communication lines, and its use for other functions may be restricted by the need to avoid crossing conductors and the limited number of layers for wiring. Even in designs having several layers of wiring paths, the majority of the chip surface area is occupied by interconnections rather than active devices.

The clock signal is used to synchronize the operations of a very large number of devices on a VLSI chip. The large number of devices that the clock distribution system must accommodate, and the wide range of distances that exist between devices, create special limitations in this signal distribution problem. The finite capacitances and resistivity of the rather long wires, as well as the capacitances of the multitude of devices attached to the clock line (i.e., the very large fan-out), result in a very large loading of the clock driver. All capacitances are present in parallel and therefore add to produce a large overall capacitance that must be driven. The large capacitive load causes a broadening of the clock pulses and slows the overall operation of the chip.

There are two design approaches that can be used to reduce the effect of capacitive loading of the clock drivers. The first is characterized by a chain of increasingly larger inverter stages. Such a strategy minimizes the overall delay through the chain of inverters. The second approach is illustrated in Fig. 1.8. This figure shows a hierarchical distribution system in which the fan-out at each node is limited to reduce the transition time for the driver stages at the nodes.

The circuit lines can be modeled as distributed RC paths, and as such the waveform propagation is governed by the diffusion equation. Each length of conductor has an associated delay that is a function of the capacitance per unit length, resistance per unit length, and length of the wire. Furthermore, as feature sizes are made smaller and smaller, the interconnection delay increases quadratically with the reciprocal of feature size for a fixed length of interconnection. The large range of different delays corresponding

Fig. 1.8.

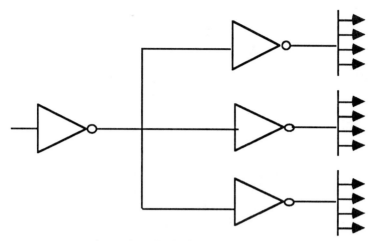

Hierarchical distribution with inverters.

to the conductors connecting the clock driver to many different clocked devices leads to differences of clock pulse arrival times at those devices. Such a phenomenon is commonly referred to as *clock skew,* and it has a large influence in determining the rate at which the chip can run.

Several approaches have been suggested and implemented to reduce or eliminate the clock skew problem. One approach, suggested by Anceau (1982), involves distributing a low-frequency clock chipwide to several functional blocks and internally synthesizing a high-frequency clock to synchronize operations within each block. A second approach, shown in Fig. 1.9, is characterized by the use of metal (heaviest lines) to distribute the clock to a multitude of smaller functional blocks and the use of polysilicon to locally distribute the signal within each block. A third approach forces all lines to be of exactly the same length; one method for realizing this goal is the so-called H-tree distribution system shown in Fig. 1.10 (Dhar et al., 1984). A fourth approach eliminates a chipwide synchronization signal by designing each functional block to be self-timed. This approach allows fast execution of operations within each functional block, but at the expense of handshaking delays for communication and added control lines between functional blocks (Mead and Conway, 1980). All of the above approaches have the unfortunate attribute of requiring massive use of metal wiring due to the large lengths necessary for coverage of the entire chip.

26 Joseph W. Goodman

Fig. 1.9.

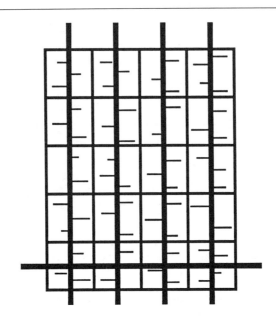

Hierarchical distribution system with metal and polysilicon wiring.

Fig. 1.10.

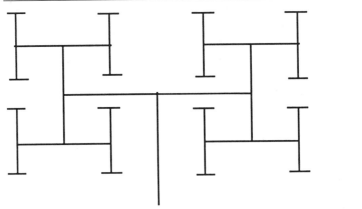

H-tree distribution system.

One possible approach to the design of an optical clock distribution system is shown in Fig. 1.11. An optical clock signal is generated by an off-chip laser diode, shown at the top of the figure. The optical beam is then mapped through a holographic optical element to various photodetector sites on the chip surface. The detected signal is converted to a digital voltage on the chip and is then distributed to nearby clocked devices. Optical clock distribution takes place to small functional cells on the chip, from which the clock signal is sent via polysilicon interconnections to the clocked devices within each functional cell. The communication delay differences from the laser source to the various detector sites are entirely negligible, and the prime source of clock skew is variations of the response time of the photodiodes and amplifiers distributed over the surface of the chip. Of course other optical methods of distributing the clock could also be envisioned, perhaps using optical waveguides on the chip itself.

Two technological problems that arise in the optical clock distribution approach should be mentioned. First, it is highly desirable to use near IR radiation for the optical clock, since the technology of high-speed semiconductor sources is well developed in this wavelength region. However, the penetration depth of such IR radiation in silicon is greater than might be desired, leading to the generation of deep charge carriers that may be able to diffuse to nearby portions of the chip, causing unwanted interference. Design rules may have to take account of this effect, or, alternatively, means for confining the charge carriers may have to be developed. Secondly, small variations in linewidth across the chip, due to nonuniformities of the fabrication process, result in significant variations of time delay through the

Fig. 1.11.

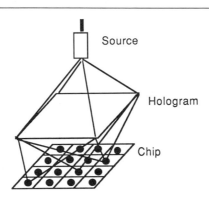

Optical distribution of a clock via a holographic optical element.

detector/amplifier circuits on the chip. A ± 1-μm variation of linewidth in the 4-μm design has been found to result in a ± 5-nsec variation of transition time of the clock waveform. This variation can be reduced if more area is devoted to the clock detector/amplifier circuitry. In addition, the assumption of a ± 1-μm variation is probably far too pessimistic.

An example of a detection and clock driver circuit is shown in Fig. 1.12. In this figure, devices to the left of point A represent a standard transimpedance amplifier chain commonly used in optical communication receivers (Abibi, 1984). The photodiode is shown on the far left. The devices to the right of point A represent a textbook example of a VLSI clock driver (Mead and Conway, 1980, Chapter 7). The outputs correspond to the two-phase clock signals commonly used in VLSI designs.

Figure 1.13 shows a photograph of the layout of a chip that has been fabricated for the purpose of testing the approach outlined above. The function of this chip is simply to conduct a series of tests on its own performance. The nine vertical strips in the upper portion of the chip are the individual optical receivers, with two contained in each strip. The leftmost string of devices in the upper half of the layout comprises a test circuit for measuring the maximum allowable clock rate. The four similar vertical strips to the right of this circuit contain eight receivers used in a clock-skew measurement test. The receivers in the lower half are included to help align the optical input beams to the photodiode windows for the leakage current tests. This chip was fabricated with the MOSIS 3-μm CMOS process. The individual detectors are 20 μm by 20 μm in size. The performance of the receivers has been tested only in the visible portion of the spectrum (632.8 nm wavelength), not yet in the near IR, where the interest is greater.

The yield obtained on this chip was very poor, due primarily to the simultaneous presence on the chip of both analog and digital circuitry. How-

Fig. 1.12.

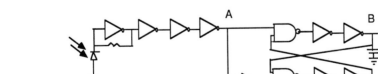

Detection and clock driver circuit.

Fig. 1.13. _____

Optical clock test chip.

ever, it was possible to find chips on which individual tests were operable, and measurements were accordingly taken. The maximum clock frequency, averaged over 10 chips, was found to be 15.1 MHz, with a standard deviation of about 1.4 MHz. A 2-μm design could be expected to have a maximum allowable clock frequency of no more than 40 MHz.

A measurement of the skew introduced by variations of the delay time experienced through different receivers was also made. The results showed an average receiver-to-receiver skew of 13.25 nsec, with a standard deviation of 1.5 nsec.

Finally, leakage current tests were performed to determine the maximum

storage time achievable with dynamic latch cells that are at various distances
from a photodetector. The results are a function of the optical power incident
on a photodiode, but with the maximum available 632.8-nm optical power
(2.2 mW) incident on a single photodetector, spacings of several tens of
microns were found to be required if the storage time of the latch was to
be undegraded. This constraint can be expected to be more stringent if the
clocking wavelength is at 800 nm. Considerations such as these can lead to
new design rules that account for the leakage currents and prevent them from
degrading latch performance at the cost of significant geometrical constraints.

  The test results described above demonstrate that the transimpedance amplifier approach to clock detection and distribution suffers many limitations
and is in general not very competitive with present day nonoptical approaches. For this reason, a second approach was devised that overcomes
many of the above limitations. This alternative approach is now briefly described. Rather than trying to electrically amplify a received optical clock
waveform for direct use in generating an electrical clock on chip, the alternate approach uses a series of free-running digital ring oscillators wherever
the transimpedance amplifiers were located in the previous approach, and
uses a photodetector within a phase-locked loop circuit to force locking of
each ring oscillator to the common frequency of the optically distributed
clock. A circuit diagram showing the phase-locked loop is found in Fig.
1.14.

  SPICE simulations of this approach have yielded very encouraging results,

Fig. 1.14. _____

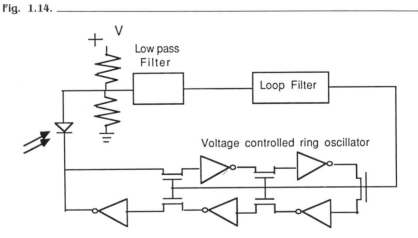

Phase-locked loop containing an optical detector.

indicating that with a 2-μm CMOS process, clock frequencies up to 150 MHz should be possible. Furthermore the skew between individual frequency-locked ring oscillators is predicted to be of the order of 50 psec. Finally, far less chip area is required of a ring oscillator with a phase-locked loop than is required of a transimpedance amplifier. A CMOS chip is currently being designed to check these predictions experimentally. Much work remains to be done on the subject of optical clock distribution at the chip level.

The understanding of the capabilities and limitations of optical clock distribution systems is still at an early stage, and it is not possible to be definitive about exactly what circumstances will justify the use of the optical approach. Undoubtedly there will be much future work in this area, not only on the problem of clock distribution at the chip level, but on the use of optics for distributing timing signals at the board and wafer levels as well.

Acknowledgments

I am indebted to several people for parts of the material presented here. Much of Section 8 is based on an analysis first performed by Raymond Kostuk. Section 9 contains work that is primarily due to Bradley Clymer. I am also grateful to Prof. E.G.S. Paige for many stimulating discussions of these and related subjects.

References

Abibi, A.A. (1984). "Gigahertz transresistance amplifiers in fine line NMOS," *IEEE J. Solid-State Circuits,* **SC-19,** 6, 986–994.

Anceau, F. (1982). "A synchronous approach for clocking VLSI systems," *IEEE J. Solid-State Circuits,* **SC-17,** 1, 51–56.

Clymer, B.D. (1987). "Optical Clock Distribution for VLSI," Doctoral Dissertation, Dept. of Electrical Eng., Stanford University.

Clymer, B.D., and Goodman, J.W. (1986). "Optical clock distribution to silicon chips," *Opt. Eng.* **25**(10), 1103–1108.

Dhar, S., Franklin, M.A., and Wann, D.F. (1984). "Reduction of clock delays in VLSI structures," *Proc. IEEE Conf. on Computer Design: VLSI in Computers,* pp. 778–783.

Fried, J.A. (1986). "Optical I/O for high-speed CMOS systems," *Opt. Eng.* **25**(10), 1132–1141.

Goodman, J.W., Leonberger, F.J., Kung, S.Y., and Athale, R.A. (1984). "Optical interconnections for VLSI systems," *Proc. IEEE* **72**(7), 850–866.

Goodman, J.W. (1985). "Fan-in and fan-out with optical interconnections," *Optica Acta,* **32**(12), 1489–1496.

Herriau, J.P., Deloulbe, A., Loiseaux, B., and Huignard, J.P. (1984). "Optical switching using photoinduced gratings," *J. Optics,* **15**(5), 314–318.

Herzig, H.P. (1986). "Holographic optical elements (HOE) for semiconductor lasers," *Optics Comm.* **58**(3), 144–148.

Husain, A. (1984). "Optical interconnect of digital integrated circuits and systems," *Proc. SPIE* **466** 10–20.

Hutcheson, L.D., Haugan, P., and Husein, A. (1987). "Optical interconnects replace hardwire," *IEEE Spectrum* **24**(3), 30–35.

Kostuk, R.K. (1986). "Multiple grating reflection holograms with application to optical interconnects," Ph.D. Dissertation, Dept. of Electrical Eng., Stanford University.

Kostuk, R.K., and Goodman, J.W. (1985). "Optical imaging applied to microelectronic chip-to-chip interconnects," *Appl. Opt.* **24**(17), 2851–2858.

Lau, K.Y., Bar-Chaim, N., Derry, P.L., and Yariv, A. (1987). "High-speed digital modulation of ultralow threshold (<1 mA) GaAs single quantum well lasers without bias," *Appl. Phys. Lett.* **51**(2), 69–71.

Mead, C., and Conway L. (1980). "Introduction to VLSI Systems," Addison-Wesley.

Rediker, R.H., and Leonberger, F.J. (1982). *IEEE J. Quantum Electronics* **18** 1813–1816.

Special Issue on Optical Interconnections, (1986). *Optical Eng.* **25**.

Tajima, H., Okada, Y., and Tamura, K. (1984). "A high-speed optical common bus for a multiprocessor system," *Trans. Inst. Electron. and Commun. Eng. Jpn.* **24**(17), 850–866.

Welford, W.T., and Winston, R. (1978). "The Optics of Nonimaging Concentrators," Academic Press, New York.

Wilde, J., McRuer, R., Hesselink, L., and Goodman, J.W. (1987). "Dynamic holographic interconnections using photorefractive crystals," *Proc. SPIE* **752** 200–208.

2.

Nonlinear Phenomena in Optical Fibers and the Feasibility of Their Application in Optical Computers

Mikhail P. Petrov and Yevgeny A. Kuzin

A.F. Ioffe Physical Technical Institute
Academy of Sciences of the USSR
Leningrad, USSR

Contents

1. Foreword 33
2. Stimulated Raman Scattering (SRS) and Stimulated Mandelstam-Brillouin Scattering (SMBS) in Optical Fibers 34
3. Basic Principles of Operation of Nonlinear Fiber Optical Elements 40
4. SRS Inverter 46
5. Switching of Optical Signals by SMBS in Optical Fibers 52
6. Conclusion 56
   References 57

1.
Foreword

The initial proposal to use nonlinear optical phenomena for the development of computers appeared just after the invention of the laser. Since then considerable efforts have been focused on the search for media and nonlinear phenomena appropriate for the design of optical computer elements. The complexity of this problem is due to a number of specific requirements relating to optical elements in optical computers. These requirements can change depending on specific conditions, but, as a rule, a nonlinear element should always work at the lowest light power possible without noticeable degradation or deviation from its operational regime during a long period of time.

Optical fibers are a very promising medium for nonlinear optical elements. It is known that one can observe in a fiber a large variety of different nonlinear phenomena at rather small laser radiation powers of less than 1 W. These effects are caused by specific features of light propagation along a fiber, which allow the radiation to be concentrated within the small core diameter and which provide a very long region of interaction between the radiation and the medium.

Further on, we will draw attention to the physical aspects and to the features of nonlinear phenomena in optical fibers. We will discuss how operations such as amplification and switching of optical signals could be done, and then we will finally consider the design principles of fiber-optic logic elements whose parameters can exceed those of most semiconductor optical bistable elements intensively studied today.

2.
Stimulated Raman Scattering (SRS) and Stimulated Mandelstam-Brillouin Scattering (SMBS) in Optical Fibers

The phenomena of SRS and SMBS in fibers were originally reported by Stolen et al. (1972) and Ippen and Stolen (1972). The basic properties of these processes for non-waveguide media were described in a number of review papers and books (Bloembergen, 1967; Pantell and Puthoff, 1969; Shen, 1984); nonlinear properties of fibers were discussed by Stolen (1979). Both SRS and SMBS result from the scattering of photons on molecular oscillations of the medium. However, SRS is known to involve the optical oscillation branch, whereas SMBS is attributed to the acoustic branch, which causes significant differences between them.

Let us consider SRS and then discuss the main difference between SRS and SMBS. The simplest example of observation of SRS in a fiber is shown in Fig. 2.1. A pumping laser pulse with power ranging from tens of watts

Fig. 2.1. _____

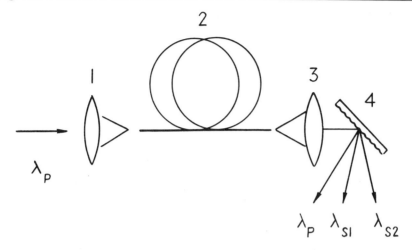

Schematic of a setup for the investigation of stimulated Raman scattering. 1 and 3, focusing lenses; 2, an optical fiber; and 4, a grating.

up to a few kilowatts is introduced into the fiber. The spectral distribution is studied at the fiber output. At a laser pulse power higher than some threshold value there appear one or a few components with longer wavelengths shifted at 450–500 cm^{-1} on the fiber output along with the pumping wavelength. SRS can be represented as the interaction of three particles where a laser photon $\hbar\omega_p$ is scattered into a Stokes photon $\hbar\omega_s$ and a phonon with the energy $\hbar\omega_v = \hbar\omega_p - \hbar\omega_s$. The probability of such a three-particle process is proportional to the rate of alteration of the Stokes photon numbers determined by the following expression (Pantell and Puthoff, 1969):

$$\frac{\partial\langle n_s\rangle}{\partial z} = K_s\,\langle n_p\rangle\,(\langle n_s\rangle + 1)(\langle n_v\rangle + 1) - K_s\,(\langle n_p\rangle + 1)\langle n_s\rangle\langle n_v\rangle, \quad (2.1)$$

where $\langle n_s\rangle$, $\langle n_p\rangle$, and $\langle n_v\rangle$ are the average numbers of particles per mode for the Stokes wave, the laser wave, and the molecular oscillations, respectively, and K_s is a constant that defines the efficiency of the nonlinear interaction. The meaning of this expression is quite evident. The probability of a three-particle interaction producing particles is proportional to the average per mode number of annihilated particles and proportional to the average per mode number plus 1. The first sum in the right part of Eq. (2.1) describes the production of a Stokes photon and phonon from a laser photon. The second sum describes the reversed process of producing a laser photon from a Stokes photon and phonon. Since $\langle n_v \rangle$ is usually $\ll 1$, the process develops with an increasing number of Stokes photons. Expression (2.1) may be used to show the difference between the processes of spontaneous and of stimulated scattering. Spontaneous scattering occurs when $\langle n_s \rangle \ll 1$. In this case Eq. (2.1) can be reduced to

$$\frac{d\langle n_s \rangle}{dz} = K_s \langle n_p \rangle, \tag{2.2}$$

and the production rate of new Stokes photons is proportional to the number of laser photons. This rate is quite low, and the process of spontaneous scattering cannot result in the production of intense Stokes wave. A different situation arises when $\langle n_s \rangle \gg 1$, when Eq. (2.1) can be rewritten in the form

$$\frac{d\langle n_s \rangle}{dz} = K_s \langle n_p \rangle \langle n_s \rangle. \tag{2.3}$$

The increase of Stokes photons becomes exponential and can lead to the generation of a Stokes wave with an intensity comparable to the intensity of the laser wave. The process described by Eq. (2.3) is called *stimulated*, since previously produced Stokes photons stimulate the reproduction of new ones. The generation of Stokes photons leads to a reduction in the number of laser photons, and the intensity of laser radiation can decrease to almost zero during the stimulated scattering process. For further consideration it is important to include one more feature of SRS. During the interaction between a laser photon, a Stokes photon, and a phonon, the following conservation laws of energy and momenta are maintained:

$$\hbar\omega_p = \hbar\omega_s + \hbar\omega_v \tag{2.4}$$

$$\hbar\mathbf{K}_p = \hbar\mathbf{K}_s + \hbar\mathbf{K}_v,$$

where $\hbar\mathbf{K}_p$, $\hbar\mathbf{K}_s$, and $\hbar\mathbf{K}_v$ are the momenta of the laser and of the Stokes photons and of the phonon, respectively. The process of stimulated scattering with a large number of photons in a mode can be considered as an interaction of the pumping wave, the Stokes wave, and the molecular vibration wave. This approach also requires the application of a condition similar to Eq. (2.4) that represents, in this case, the condition of phase matching.

The phase matching condition is determined by the wave frequencies, their wave vectors, and dispersion relations characterizing the dependence of the wave vector on frequency. Dispersion characteristics for light and molecular vibrations are given in Fig. 2.2. The SRS process is connected

Fig. 2.2. _____

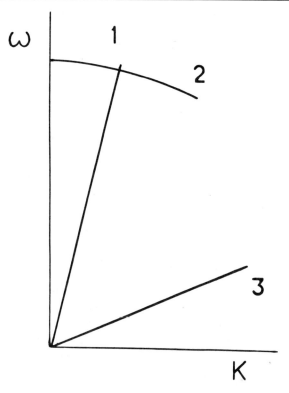

Dispersion characteristics of photons (1), optical phonons (2), and acoustic phonons (3).

to the optical branch of molecular vibrations for which the frequency does not depend on the wave vector in the region of wave vectors small compared to the wave vectors of optical radiation. This provides the possibility of fulfilling the condition of phase matching for both collinear and counter propagation of laser and Stokes waves. In both cases the frequency of molecular vibrations is the same, and the wave vector of molecular vibrations excited by SRS automatically satisfies the phase matching conditions (2.4). Therefore, the SRS process doesn't require any special conditions providing for phase matching. However, the forward SRS process is usually more efficient that the backward one because of longer interaction length.

The process of SMBS is determined by the acoustic branch of molecular vibrations. In this case, a special choice of experimental setup geometry is required to fulfill the condition of phase matching. For single-mode fibers, the phase matching could be fulfilled only for counter propagation of laser and Stokes waves.

The equations describing SRS can be put in a more convenient form in terms of the pumping intensity I_p and of the Stokes intensity I_s. It is possible if there is a great number of photons per mode. For forward SRS these equations take the form

$$\frac{d\,I_2}{dz} = g\,I_s\,I_p \tag{2.5}$$

$$I_p + \frac{\omega_p}{\omega_s}\,I_s = \text{constant.} \tag{2.6}$$

The factor g is the Raman gain coefficient that characterizes the property of a medium, and the Z axis is directed along the direction of propagation of the light waves. If we neglect the decrease of I_p, then from Eq. (2.5) there follows a simple solution for the Stokes wave intensity

$$I_s = I_s(0)\,\exp\{g\,I_p z\}. \tag{2.7}$$

The mechanism leading to high efficiency of SRS in optical fibers is based upon the possibility of providing high values of I_p due to a small crossection of the fiber core and to an extended interaction length z. Table 2.1 presents the data on the gain coefficient g and on the frequency shift of Stokes wave Δv for fused silica and for some liquids often used in SRS experiments.

Equation (2.7) is the intensity of a Stokes wave input on a nonlinear medium $I_s(0)$. In a number of cases this Stokes wave is really introduced and we deal with the amplification of an incoming Stokes wave. However, more often, the SRS is observed only at the introduction into the nonlinear medium of the laser pumping radiation. In this case the Stokes wave primarily arises due to spontaneous scattering, and then this spontaneous Stokes wave is increased by SRS. To take into account spontaneous scattering it is necessary to use a quantum description of the scattering process rather than the

TABLE 2.1

	SRS Gain Coefficient cm/W	Stokes Frequency Shift cm^{-1}
CS_2	$24 \cdot 10^{-9}$	655
Benzene	$2.8 \cdot 10^{-9}$	992
Fused quartz	$2 \cdot 10^{-11}$	490

classical one based on Eqs. (2.5) and (2.6). However, in some cases we can take into account spontaneous scattering, if we assume that one photon is introduced into every longitudinal and transverse mode of an optical fiber (Auyeung and Yariv, 1978). It yields an effective input power for the Stokes wave of the order of 10^{-9} W for each transverse mode of the fiber. Thus to obtain a Stokes wave with a power of the order of a few watts (comparable to the power of the pumping radiation) at the output of the nonlinear element, it is necessary to provide an exponential amplification e^{20}. A pumping power providing for exponential growth in Eq. (2.7) of the order of e^{20} will be referred to as a *threshold power*. For example, for a 1 km long fused silica fiber with a 5 μm core diameter, the threshold power is equal to 2.5 W. For a fabricated 100 m long capillary fiber filled with CS_2, with a core diameter of 5 μm, the threshold power is equal to 2×10^{-2} W.

The SMBS process is similar to SRS in many respects and also represents the formation of a Stokes photon and a phonon from the pumping photon. However, unlike the case for SRS, the participating phonon in SMBS is acoustic. The frequency of the acoustic phonon is a few orders lower than the optical phonon frequency, and hence for SMBS the frequency shift is a few orders smaller than with SRS. In addition, the frequency of the acoustic phonon is no more independent of its wave vector. They are connected by the ratio

$$|\mathbf{k}| = \frac{\omega_v}{v_v}, \tag{2.8}$$

where v_v is the sound velocity in the medium.

It is easy to see now that for the case when the wave vector of the pumping wave is parallel to the wave vector of the Stokes wave and oriented in the same direction, the phase matching conditions could be met only for $|\mathbf{k}_v| = 0$ and $\omega_v = 0$. That means that the SMBS process does not take place for parallel propagation of the laser and of the Stokes wave. Taking into account the phase-matching condition (2.4) and the dispersion relation (2.8) for acoustic waves, one may conclude for the case of counter propagation of the Stokes and the pump waves that the frequency of the acoustic wave obeys the relation

$$\omega_v = \omega_p - \omega_s \approx \frac{2v_v}{c} n \, \omega_p, \tag{2.9}$$

where n is refraction index of the medium, and c is the velocity of light. In typical experiments the frequency of the acoustic wave is of the order of

TABLE 2.2

	SMBS Gain Coefficient cm/W	Hypersonic Wave Velocity m/s
CS_2	$68 \cdot 10^{-9}$	1251
Benzene	$7.6 \cdot 10^{-9}$	1475
Fused Quartz	$5 \cdot 10^{-9}$	5995

10^{10} Hz. Amplification of the Stokes wave for SMBS is described by an expression similar to Eq. (2.7)

$$I_s(z) = I_s(0) \exp\{g I_p z\}. \qquad (2.10)$$

Numerical values of SMBS gains g are obviously different from the SRS values. Table 2.2 shows data featuring SMBS in fused quartz and in some liquids. The SMBS gain is higher than the SRS gain in the same materials. Consequently, the threshold powers in the former case will be lower. For a fused silica fiber 1 km long with a 5 μm core diameter, the threshold power of SMBS can be as low as 10^{-2} W. However, because for SMBS the Stokes wave propagates in the direction opposite to the pumping wave, one should use longer pumping pulses to satisfy the necessary interaction length. Thus, for the particular case of a 1 km long fiber, a 10 μs laser pulse is required to exploit all the opportunities provided by the fiber itself.

3.
Basic Principles of Operation of Nonlinear Fiber Optical Elements

According to Petrov and Kuzin (1985) and Kuzin and Petrov (1986), an amplifier based upon the principle of stimulated light scattering may be considered as an element with two inputs and two outputs, as shown in Fig. 2.3. Input 1 is fed by the Stokes wave λ_s and input 2 by the pumping wave λ_p. Outputs 1 and 2 correspond to the Stokes and pumping waves, respectively. Due to the interaction of the Stokes and pumping waves, the signal intensities of both outputs depend on both input signals. Incoming information can be coded either on one of the radiation fluxes or on both of them. Similarly, either output can be used as the information signal, or both of them can be used simultaneously. Let us consider the situation when one

Fig. 2.3.

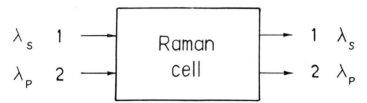

A SRS amplifier as a two-input, two-output nonlinear element.

input flux and one output flux are used as information signals. In such a way four combinations of input and output signals can be used to construct four different active elements. The characteristic curves of two of them derived from Eqs. (2.5) and (2.6) are shown in Fig. 2.4. For example, if the information is coded in the Stokes radiation both at the input and at the output, the element will operate as an amplifier. Its characteristic curve is shown in Fig. 2.4a. The pump power defines the coefficient of amplification.

Fig. 2.4.

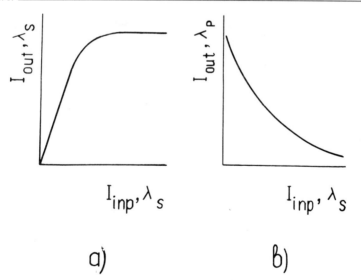

Output intensity of an SRS element versus the input intensity. (a) Both the output signal and the input signal beams at the Stokes frequency. (b) The input signal is a beam at the Stokes frequency, and the output signal is a beam at the pump frequency.

Interesting practical applications can be found for elements in which the Stokes wavelength radiation is used as the input and the pumping wavelength radiation as the output signal. The characteristic curve of this element is shown in Fig. 2.4b. It has a negative slope, so inverters of optical logic signals may be built on the basis of this element. There are 16 logic operations, and in order to synthesize all of them it is sufficient to have a logic gate producing the operations NOT and OR. The OR operation is quite simple to produce in optics. Therefore, by being able to perform the inversion operation we are able, in principle, to realize any arbitrary complex scheme. In practice some obstacles could be very difficult to overcome.

Let us evaluate the attainable pulse repetition rate and the energy consumption of a SRS-inverter shown in Fig. 2.5 and the SMBS-inverter shown in Fig. 2.6. Two laser pulses are introduced simultaneously into the fiber. One of them is a Stokes signal pulse having a wavelength λ_s, and the other is a pump pulse having a wavelength λ_p. The pumping pulse transmitted through the fiber is used as an output signal pulse. In the case of SMBS, the pumping wave and the information signal propagate counter to each other, and in the case of SRS their propagation is parallel. We have already pointed out that for SRS, counter propagation of the pumping wave and of the Stokes wave is also possible, but, as will become apparent from further analysis, this regime is unfavorable for logic elements and we will disregard it. The operation of a "no" element is based upon depletion of the pump in the

Fig. 2.5. _____

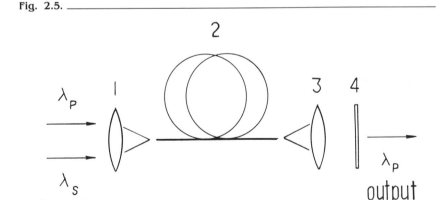

A SRS inverter. 1 and 3, focusing lenses; 2, an optical fiber; and 4, a filter passing the pump beam.

Fig. 2.6.

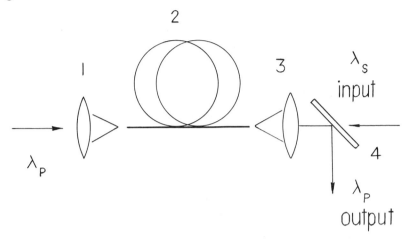

A SMBS inverter. 1 and 3, focusing lenses; 2, an optical fiber; and 4, a beam splitter.

process of Stokes wave amplification. The pumping power introduced into the fiber is chosen to be smaller than the threshold power, so in the absence of input information signals on the Stokes wavelength the pumping radiation passes without depletion along the fiber and reaches the output. This means that in the absence of an input information signal an output signal exists. If a signal at the Stokes wavelength is introduced into the fiber, then the energy transfers from the pumping wave to the Stokes wave, which results in the depletion of the pumping pulse, and the output signal disappears. Thus in the presence of an input information signal, the output signal is absent. The power of the pump radiation should be less than a threshold value, but, as should be clear from Section 2, it should be close enough to the threshold value to allow an efficient interaction between the pump and signal waves. We assume, therefore, for simplicity that for the operation of a logic element, the power of the pump radiation should be equal to the threshold value

$$P_{\mathrm{p}} = 20\,\frac{S}{gl}, \tag{2.11}$$

where P_{p} is the pump pulse power, S is the core area of fiber, and l is the length of the fiber. Let us evaluate the interaction length l. It will be restricted by different mechanisms for parallel propagation and counter propagation of the pump and Stokes pulses. Figure 2.7 illustrates the case of

Fig. 2.7. _____

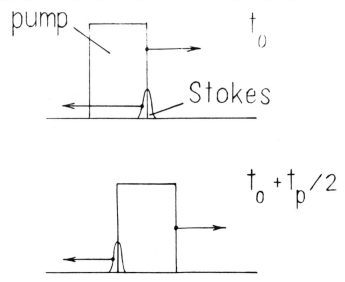

Interaction length estimations for counter-propagating pump and Stokes pulses.

counter propagation. The leading edge of the Stokes pulse meets the pumping wave and begins to interact with it at instant t_o; after $t_p/2$, where t_p is the duration of the pumping pulse, the leading edge of the Stokes pulse reaches the rear edge of the pumping pulse, and its interaction with the pumping pulse ceases. The leading edge of the Stokes pulse thus interacts with the pumping pulse during a time $t_p/2$. The same will be valid for any fraction of the Stokes pulse. The interaction length l for the counter propagation is given by the expression

$$ l = \frac{t_p}{2} \frac{c}{n}, \tag{2.12} $$

where n is the refraction index of the fiber core. The energy of the pumping pulse W_p is equal to the product of the pulse power by its duration, so from Eqs. (2.11) and (2.12)

$$ W_p = \frac{40\, S\, n}{g\, c}. \tag{2.13} $$

Consider now the case of parallel propagation of the pumping and Stokes pulses. SMBS is impossible in this case, as has been shown above. Here the relationship between the interaction length and the pulse duration is governed by the group velocity dispersion in the fiber. Because of dispersion, the propagation velocity of the pumping pulse will differ from the velocity of the signal Stokes pulse, and in long fibers the pulses can spatially separate and cease to interact. The difference in the travel times of the Stokes pulse and of the pumping pulse propagating along the fiber is

$$\Delta t = Dl\ \Delta\lambda, \tag{2.14}$$

where l is the fiber length, $\Delta\lambda$ is the wavelength shift between the Stokes and the pumping pulses, and D is a numerical value characterizing the group velocity dispersion. Let us consider the element as workable until Δt is less that the pulse duration. This leads to the following constraint on the fiber length for a given pulse length

$$l = \frac{t_{\mathrm{p}}}{D\ \Delta\lambda}. \tag{2.15}$$

The expression (2.11) for the pump power and (2.15) for the interaction length allow the determination of the pump pulse energy required for the functioning of a fiber element for parallel propagation of the pump and the information Stokes pulses

$$W_{\mathrm{p}} = \frac{20\ S\ D\ \Delta\lambda}{g}. \tag{2.16}$$

It follows from Eqs. (2.13) and (2.16) that the pumping pulse energy does not depend on the pulse length. This is because extending the pulse length yields the possibility of extending the interaction length while reducing the pulse power. This remains true until the threshold power of Eq. (2.11) is reached. When the pumping pulse duration is reduced to values comparable with the relaxation times of molecular vibrations participating in the scattering Eq. (2.11) becomes invalid. The threshold power begins to increase, and, in addition, a number of peculiarities appear in the process of stimulated scattering. These phenomena have been discussed elsewhere (Shen, 1984).

As a rough estimate we assume that the minimum allowed duration of the light pulse is equal to the relaxation time of the molecular vibration responsible for the scattering. For SMBS these intervals lie in the range 1–10 nsec, and for SRS typical values are in the picosecond range. Hence, the maximum attainable pulse repetition rate for fiber elements can be estimated as 10^2–10^9 pulse/sec for the SMBS process and 10^{11}–10^{12} pulse/sec for SRS.

Let us now estimate the energy of a pumping pulse. According to Kogelnik (1981) the lower value for a beam crossection is restricted by λ^2. Suppose, therefore, that S in Eqs. (2.13) and (2.16) is equal to 10^{-8} cm^2. For SMBS in fused quartz fibers $g = 5 \times 10^{-9}$ cm/W. From Eq. (2.13) an energy of the pumping pulse equal to 4×10^{-9} J is obtained. For parallel SRS the energy depends on the wavelength, since three parameters of Eq. (2.16), g, D, and $\Delta\lambda$, depend on the wavelength. For the particular case of a 1 μm wavelength, the value D for fused quartz is equal to 3.1×10^{-16} sec/nm.cm (Lin et al., 1977), $g = 10^{-11}$ cm/W, and $\Delta\lambda = 28$ nm. The pumping energy for those parameters turns out to be equal to 10^{-11} J. As another example, consider a capillary fiber filled with CS_2. Its SRS-gain g is one of the highest known and is equal to 24×10^{-9} cm/W. From refraction index data one can evaluate the parameter D, which for $\Delta\lambda = 0.50$ μm is equal to $D = 0.1 \times 10^{-14}$ sec/nm.cm, which yields pumping energy value of the order of 10^{-13} J.

These examples show that the pumping powers required to drive fiber-optic logic elements could be sufficiently small, especially for parallel propagation of the pump and of the Stokes pulses.

4.
SRS Inverter

General principles regarding the development of fiber-optic logic elements were discussed above. Here we consider how this general idea has been used to construct an inverter more appropriate for computing (Kuzin et al., 1986). Its layout is shown in Fig. 2.8. The main feature of this inverter is the use of two successive pieces of the fiber. The first is used as an SRS amplifier and produces the inversion previously discussed. It is fed by an input signal on the Stokes wavelength and by an accompanying pumping radiation, which is not picked up as output signal but is introduced into the second fiber used as an SRS generator. The Stokes wave arising in the SRS generator is used as the output signal. The operational conditions of this tandem are chosen in such a way that generation in the SRS generator appears in the absence of an input signal pulse and disappears when it is switched on. That is possible because in the absence of an input signal pulse the pumping light travels through the SRS amplifier without attenuation, and its intensity at the output of the SRS amplifier becomes higher than the threshold power of the SRS generator. When the input signal is switched on, the pumping intensity

Fig. 2.8.

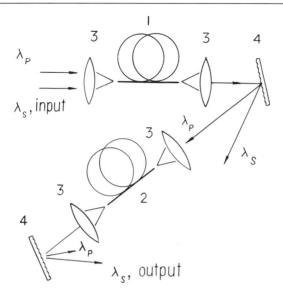

A SRS inverter consisting of two optical fibers. 1, an optical fiber used as a SRS amplifier; 2, an optical fiber used as a SRS generator; 3, focusing lenses; and 4, a grating.

in the SRS amplifier decreases below the level of the threshold power required for the SRS generator. The arrangement shown has a number of advantages compared to the simplest scheme consisting of a single section of fiber. One of the obvious advantages is that using the second fragment gives the possibility of generating the output signal on various desirable wavelengths, including the input wavelength. The latter is very important when elements are stacked in cascade. In addition, a two-piece arrangement has a higher differential amplification coefficient k

$$k = \frac{d\,P_{\text{out}}}{d\,P_{\text{in}}}, \tag{2.17}$$

which is also very important for the construction of computing systems (Smith, 1986). A detailed analysis of the two-piece element requires a solution of Eqs. (2.5) and (2.6), which are represented in the form (Auyeung and Yariv, 1978) for the condition $\lambda_p = \lambda_s$

$$P_{s,\text{out}} = \frac{P_{s,\text{in}} + P_{p,\text{in}} \times \exp\{g(P_{s,\text{in}} + P_{p,\text{in}})\,l/s\}}{P_{p,\text{in}} + P_{s,\text{in}} \times \exp\{g(P_{s,\text{in}} + P_{p,\text{in}})\,l/s\}} P_{s,\text{in}} \tag{2.18}$$

$$P_{p,out} = \frac{(P_{s,in} + P_{p,in})\, P_{p,in}}{P_{p,in} + P_{s,in} \times \exp\{g(P_{s,in} + P_{p,in})\, l/s\}}, \qquad (2.19)$$

where $P_{s,in}$; $P_{s,out}$; $P_{p,in}$; and $P_{p,out}$ are the input and output light pulse powers for the given fiber section at the Stokes wavelength λ_s and the pumping wavelength λ_p, respectively. An alternate procedure is as follows: a pumping power $P_{p,in}$ and a signal Stokes pulse power $P_{s,in}$ are introduced into the first fiber, which acts as an SRS amplifier. Now, Eq. (2.19) can be used to determine the power at the SRS amplifier output. This pumping power is introduced into the second fiber, which acts as a SRS generator. Equation (2.18) can then be used to find the power of the Stokes pulse on the SRS generator output. Since no special Stokes signal is introduced into the SRS generator, the spontaneous Raman signal denoted by P_{so} plays the role of the input signal. We assume that $P_{s,in} < P_p$ and the ratio P_{so}/P_p is independent of P_p. Under these conditions the output signal is related to the input signal by

$$P_{out} = \frac{P_{so}\, \exp\{G^{(2)}\}}{1 + \dfrac{P_{so}}{P_p}\, \exp\{G^{(2)}\}} \qquad (2.20)$$

$$G^{(2)} = \frac{\tau G^{(1)}}{1 + \dfrac{P_{in}}{P_p}\, \exp\{G^{(1)}\}}, \qquad (2.21)$$

where

$$G_{(1)} = \frac{g^{(1)} l^{(1)}}{S^{(1)}}\, P_{p,in}^{(1)}, \qquad G^{(2)} = \frac{g^{(2)} l^{(2)}}{S^{(2)}}\, P_{p,in}^{(2)}, \qquad (2.22)$$

and P_{in} and P_{out} are the powers of the Stokes signals at the input and at the output of the inverter. Superscripts (1) and (2) denote to which fiber the respective value refers. Factors $G^{(1)}$ and $G^{(2)}$ define the amplification of fibers (1) and (2), respectively. For $P_{in} = 0$, $P_{p,in}^{(1)} = P_{p,in}^{(2)}$ because there is no pump depletion in the fiber (1); it follows from Eq. (2.21) that $G^{(2)} = \tau\, G^{(1)}$. The factor τ shows by how much the amplification in the SRS generator differs from the amplification in the SRS amplifier for the same pump power.

Now we turn to a very important question. How will binary pulses with amplitudes equal to 0 and 1 be modified when passing through a long chain of inverters? Two cases are possible. In the first case both amplitudes corresponding to 0 and 1 converge to the same stationary level. In this case after passage through some number of inverters, loss of information occurs, so this inverter is hardly appropriate for computer operation. In the second case, the zero amplitudes converge to one stationary value, whereas unit amplitudes converge to another one. This will not lead to loss of information, and the logic element will possess the necessary functional stability. Analysis of Eqs. (2.20), (2.21), and (2.22) confirms that the SRS inverter under consideration is stable. Figures 2.9 and 2.10 show the results of numerical calculations for stationary amplitudes of logic ones (1) and zeroes (2), and powers P_{in} at which $P_{in} = P_{out}$ (3). The line (3) separates amplitudes of zeroes and ones. If the pulse amplitude lies above the line corresponding to $P_{in} = P_{out}$, this pulse corresponds to unity; otherwise it corresponds to zero. In the calculations the ratio P_{so}/P_p was supposed to be equal to 10^{-6}. Figure 2.9 shows the dependence of the stationary amplitudes of zeroes and ones on $G^{(1)}$, that is, on the amplification coefficient in the SRS amplifier for constant amplification of the SRS oscillator. We see that a different stationary signal power for 0 and 1 exists for a wide range of $G^{(1)}$ values from 0 to 14. It is worth noting that the level of 1 is practically equal everywhere

Fig. 2.9. _____

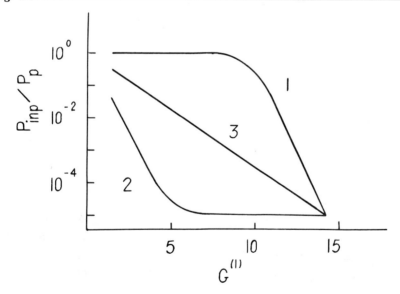

The relative input powers of logic one and logic zeroes versus the amplification coefficient of fiber (1)—$G^{(1)}$. Curve 1 shows the stationary power of a logic one. Curve 2 shows the stationary power of a logic zero. Pulses with power below curve 3 are logic zeroes; those above are logic ones.

Fig. 2.10.

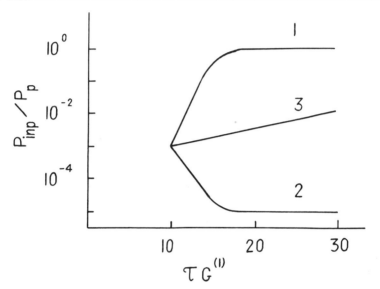

The relative input power of logic ones and logic zeroes versus amplification coefficient $G^{(2)}$ of fiber (2) calculated at a pump intensity equal to that introduced into fiber (1). Curves 1, 2, and 3 are similar to those in Fig. 2.9.

to the pumping power, whereas the level of 0 is close to the efficient input Stokes power in the SRS generator, that is, to the power of the spontaneous Raman scattering. When $G^{(1)}$ exceeds 14, the stationary values of zeroes and ones coincide and the inverter becomes unstable. A value of $G^{(1)} = 14$ corresponds approximately to the threshold of SRS in a SRS amplifier.

Figure 2.10 shows the dependence of the stationary signal power of zeroes and ones on the amplifying properties of the fiber section operating as a SRS generator. We see that the properties of the second fiber section can also vary between significant limits.

In the preceding paragraphs we calculated the energies of the pump pulses required for the logic elements under consideration to operate. Figures 2.9 and 2.10 imply that the minimum energy of input signals that should be recognized as logic ones could be lower by 3–4 orders of magnitude. Hence, the levels of input signals required by a SRS inverter could be as low as 10^{-15} J.

Let us calculate the differential gain coefficient determined by Eq. (2.17). It is easy to derive the expression for the SRS inverter considered for a value of input power corresponding to the condition $P_{in} = P_{out}$. From numerical calculations it follows that $P_{out} \ll P_p$ and the depletion of the pump and of the SRS oscillator can be neglected. Relations (2.20) to (2.22) then reduce to the form

$$P_{out} = P_{so} \exp\left\{\dfrac{\tau G^{(1)}}{1 + \exp\{G^{(1)}\}\dfrac{P_{in}}{P_{out}}}\right\}. \tag{2.23}$$

Differentiating P_{out} with respect to P_{in} one can obtain for the condition $P_{in} = P_{out}$

$$\dfrac{dP_{out}}{dP_{in}} = -\dfrac{P_{in}}{P_p} \cdot \dfrac{\tau G^{(1)} \exp\{G^{(1)}\}}{\left(1 + \exp\{G^{(1)}\}\dfrac{P_{in}}{P_p}\right)^2}. \tag{2.24}$$

This gives the value of the differential gain, as P_{in}/P_p is known from numerical calculations. Figure 2.11 displays the dependance of the differential gain on the value $G^{(1)}$ for a constant $\tau G^{(1)}$ when the input power corresponds to the condition $P_{in} = P_{out}$.

Fig. 2.11.

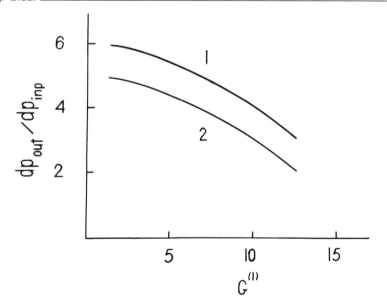

The differential gain coefficient dP_{out}/dP_{in} versus the amplification coefficient $G^{(1)}$ of fiber (1).

To verify the main idea, we investigated a laboratory experimental inverter. It consisted of a capillary filled with toluene functioning as a SRS amplifier (fiber 1 in Fig. 2.8) and a fused silica fiber used as a SRS generator (fiber 2 in Fig. 2.8). The capillary length was chosen to be 7 cm and the core diameter was 30 μm. A 60 m long fused silica fiber had a core of diameter 50 μm.

The use of media with different Stokes shifts in the SRS amplifier and in the SRS oscillator allowed us to get rid of the selecting elements for separating the pump radiation between the SRS amplifier and the SRS generator, and allowed the introduction of all the radiation from the input of the SRS amplifier into the SRS generator. This significantly simplified the alignment of the setup, while changing nothing in the principle of its operation. The pump was produced by the second harmonic of a YAG:Nd laser ($\lambda = 532$ nm, $t_p = 20$ nsec). The input signal was formed from a SRS process in a separate capillary fiber filled with toluene. (This part is not shown in Fig. 2.8). The threshold power for the SRS oscillator measured in the experiment reached ~ 100 W and for the SRS amplifier ~ 400 W. The pump power introduced to the SRS amplifier was ~ 300 W. In the absence of an input Stokes signal, the SRS oscillator generated a Stokes frequency with an output power ~ 100 W. When a 0.1 W input signal was introduced into the SRS amplifier the output Stokes power in the SRS oscillator dropped by a factor of more than 300. A quantitative comparison of the experimental data with theoretical published values is difficult because the laser radiation was multimode, which caused a complex shape of the laser pulse consisting of many spikes. Only the most powerful spikes participated in the SRS process, while photodetectors recorded the mean value of the laser pulse. Nevertheless, the experimentally observed sharp decrease of the input signal intensity is in favor of the validity of our numerical estimates in general.

5.
Switching of Optical Signals by SMBS in Optical Fibers

Nonlinear optical techniques allow the switching of optical beams (Kuzin and Petrov, 1985; Petrov and Kuzin, 1985). The simplest version of this switching device is shown in Fig. 2.12. A similar arrangement has already been considered for the evaluation of the required pump pulse energy to operate a fiber logic element. Here we draw attention to the potential of this

Fig. 2.12. _____

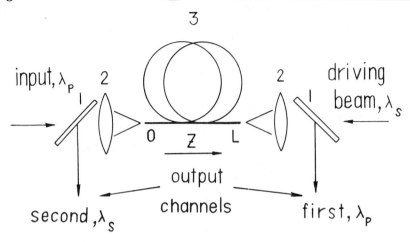

A SMBS switch. 1, beamsplitters; 2, focusing lenses; and 3, an optical fiber.

device as a switching element. The element operates as follows. A comparatively powerful signal with a wavelength λ_p (the signal radiation plays the role of the pump beam) is introduced through the beamsplitter (1) and lens (2) into the fiber (3). In the absence of a driving beam, the signal passes through the fiber without attenuation in the direction $+z$ and feeds the first channel. If simultaneously the other end of the fiber is fed by a counter-propagating driving beam with a wavelength λ_s (the driving beam is a Stokes beam), the nonlinear interaction of the signal with the driving beam will result in the excitation of a hypersonic wave in the fiber and a complete energy transfer from the signal wave to the counter-streaming driving beam can occur. Thus the process of SMBS results in the "reflection" of the signal from the fiber, and the signal will reach the second channel.

Let us evaluate the power of the driving beam required for efficient signal switching. To this end we exploit the theory of stationary SMBS (Tang, 1966), according to which the process of energy transfer from a pump to a Stokes wave is described by the following equations

$$\frac{d\,I_s(z)}{dz} = -g\,I_s(z)\,I_p(z) \tag{2.25}$$

$$\frac{d\,I_p(z)}{dz} = -g\,I_p(z)\,I_s(z), \tag{2.26}$$

where I_p and I_s are the intensities of the pump and of the Stokes waves, respectively, and g is the SMBS gain coefficient.

According to Tang (1966) the solution of this equation has the form

$$I_s(z) = \frac{I_s(0)\{1 - I_s(0)/I_p(0)\}}{\exp\{[1 - I_s(0)/I_p(0)]\, g\, I_p(0)\, z\} - I_s(0)/I_p(0)} \tag{2.27}$$

$$I_p(z) = I_s(z) + I_p(0) - I_s(0). \tag{2.28}$$

The value of interest is the ratio of pumping intensity on the fiber output $z = l$ to that on the input $z = 0$. It can be found more easily by rewriting Eqs. (2.27) and (2.28) in the more convenient form

$$\frac{I_p(l)}{I_p(0)} = \frac{I_s(l)}{I_p(0)} + 1 - k \tag{2.29}$$

$$\frac{I_s(l)}{I_p(0)} = \frac{k(1 - k)}{\exp[(1 - k)\, G] - k}, \tag{2.30}$$

where

$$k = I_s(0)/I_p(0) \text{ and } G = I_p(0) \cdot gl.$$

Substituting in Eqs. (2.29) and (2.30) the optional sequence of k numbers, one can construct the family of the dependence of $I_p(l)/I_p(0)$ on $I_s(l)/I_s(0)$ for various values of G. This family of dependence is shown in Fig. 2.13. It can be used to calculate the properties of a SMBS switch. To reduce the power of the driving beam, the value of G should be as high as possible. However, if G exceeds the threshold value, the SMBS process arises from spontaneous scattering on the thermal hypersonic vibrations, and the total pumping energy will stream to the second channel even in the absence of a driving beam. According to Tang (1966), the power spectral density of a spontaneous Stokes wave for each transverse fiber mode is equal to

$$P_{so} = k_B T \frac{c}{4\pi n^3 v_v}, \tag{2.31}$$

where k_B is the Boltzman constant and T is the temperature.

For silica glass, $v_v = 6 \times 10^5$ cm/sec and the Stokes bandwidth is 100 MHz (Ippen and Stolen, 1972). For those parameters, the power of the spontaneous Stokes wave per single mode of a fiber is of the order of 10^{-9} W. For $G = 20$, the power of the amplified Stokes wave and the corresponding signal power in the second channel will be ~0.5 W, even in the absence of

Fig. 2.13.

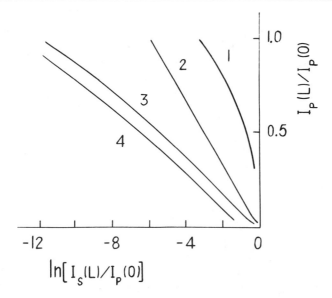

Dependence of signal intensity switched to the first channel on the driving beam intensity: $I_p(l)/I_p(0)$—the ratio of the intensity switched to the first channel with respect to the input signal intensity; and $\ln[I_s(l)/I_p(0)]$—logarithmic ratio of the driving beam intensity to the input signal intensity.

a driving beam. Thus the amplification increment G should be lower than 20.

From Fig. 2.13, for $G = 15$, in order to switch 80% of the signal energy into the second channel, i.e., $I_p(l)/I_p(0) = 0.2$, the power of the driving beam should be equal to 10^{-2} of the input signal power. To obtain an amplification $G = 15$ in a 10 m long single mode fiber with a core diameter of 5 μm, the required pumping power is 2.5 W (for fused silica $g = 5 \times 10^{-9}$ cm/W), and an evaluation of the corresponding driving power gives approximately 25 mW. The switching time of the switch is limited by the relaxation time of the hypersonic wave and is equal to ~10 nsec.

An experimentally studied SMBS switching element consisted of a 7 m long multimode fiber with a 30 μm core diameter. On one end the fiber was fed by 200 to 300 nsec pulses from a ruby laser. This pulse with a power of 30 W was used as a signal pulse. On the other end the driving pulse on the Stokes frequency was introduced with a power level of 3 W. In the absence of a driving pulse, the signal radiation propagated without losses along the fiber and went to the first channel. When the driving pulse was applied, about 70% of the signal energy switched to the second channel. A comparison of the experimental data with theoretical predictions is hindered due to the polarization scrambling in multimode fibers. This deteriorates the interaction of the pump and driving beams. For the case of complete depolarization of both waves the factor G for the experimental conditions was equal to 7, and, according to the diagram in Fig. 2.13, the pump should decrease approximately by a factor of 3, which agrees well with the experimental observations.

6.
Conclusion

Examples of the logic operations of inversion and switching of optical signals show that nonlinear phenomena in optical fibers are promising for the active processing of optical signals. The required energy range of signals and pump pulses for successful operation of fiber elements is of the same order as for corresponding parameters for semiconductor bistable elements that are presently considered as the most advanced. The pulse repetition rate can even attain higher values, especially if one uses SRS in glass fibers. A number of advantages of dealing with fiber-optic elements is also evident. They operate in a convenient range of wavelengths that coincides with the range used in fiber optics communications. In some cases the communication line itself can be utilized as an active element used for signal amplification in optical fiber communication lines. Another important feature of fiber elements is that they are very little affected by external conditions. In the considered SRS and SMBS systems, there is, on the one hand, a weak influence of external conditions on those nonlinear properties of the medium responsible for SRS and SMBS. On the other hand, the nature of SRS and SMBS processes is such that they do not require any special phase matching of the signal wave and of the pump. Phase matching or locking occurs automatically as a result of sound-wave generation with the required phase. With the alteration of external conditions such as temperature, pressure, etc., there occurs automatic tuning of the acoustic wave providing the required phase matching. It should be noted, however, that phase locking is a factor of vulnerability for devices based on the phenomenon of interference, since even moderate variations of external conditions leads to variations of phase relations and improper device behavior. It is worth noting that difficulties with phase mismatch increase with the length of the propagation medium.

Therefore, there is a need to balance the contradictions between the evident trend to increase the length of the medium, in order to raise the sensitivity on the one hand, and the requirement to provide stability with respect to external perturbations, on the other hand.

In our opinion the examples considered are quite typical, but they by no means exhaust all the existing opportunities offered by nonlinear phenomena in optical fibers. Partly because of the novelty and of the related insufficient state of the development of the question at this time, and partly because of limited space, many interesting phenomena remain outside the framework of this review. Among them are phase conjugation (Petrov and Kuzin, 1982, 1983; Kuzin et al., 1984, 1985) and other phenomena, the consideration of which could significantly extend the number of applications based upon the functional abilities of nonlinear phenomena in glass fibers.

References

Auyeung, G., and Yariv, A. (1978). *IEEE J. Quantum Electron.* **QE–14.**, 347–352.

Bloembergen, N. (1967), *Am. J. of Phys.* **35**, 989–1023.

Ippen, E.P., and Stolen, R.H. (1972). *Appl. Phys. Lett.* **21**, 539–540.

Kogelnik, H. (1981). *Proc. IEEE* **69**, 232–238.

Kroll, N.M. (1965) *J. of Appl. Phys.* **36**, 34–43.

Kuzin, E.A. and Petrov, M.P. (1985). *Pisma v Zh. Tekh. Fiz.* **11**, 389–393 (in Russian). English transl. in *Sov. Tech. Phys. Lett.*

Kuzin, E.A., and Petrov, M.P. (1986). *Avtometriya,* **2**, 87–92 (in Russian). English transl. in *Automatic Monitoring and Measuring.*

Kuzin, E.A., Petrov, M.P., and Davydenko, B.E. (1984). *Pisma v Zh. Tekh. Fiz.* **10**, 833–837 (in Russian). English transl. in *Sov. Tech. Phys. Lett.*

Kuzin, E.A., Petrov, M.P., and Davydenko, B.E. (1985). *Opt. and Quantum Electronics.* **17**, 393–397.

Kuzin, E.A., Petrov, M.P., and Spirin, V.V. (1986). *Pisma v Zh. Tekh. Fiz.* **12**, 406–409 (in Russian). English transl. in *Sov. Tech. Phys. Lett.*

Lin, C., Stolen, R.H., and Cohen, L.C. (1977). *Appl. Phys. Lett.* **31**, 97–99.

Pantell, R.H., and Puthoff, H.E. (1969). "Fundamentals of Quantum Electronics." Wiley, New York.

Petrov, M.P., and Kuzin, E.A. (1982). *Pisma v Zh. Tekh. Fiz.* **8**, 729–732 (in Russian). English transl. in *Sov. Tech. Phys. Lett.*

Petrov, M.P., and Kuzin, E.A. (1983). *Fiz Tverd. Tele.* **25**, 334–338 (in Russian). English transl. in *Sov. Phys. Solid State.*

Petrov, M.P. and Kuzin, E.A. (1985). Preprint of A.F. Ioffe Physical Technical Institute, No 975, Leningrad.

Petrov, M.P., and Kuzin, E.A. (1985). *Acta Polytechnica Scandinavica* **Ph– 150**, 254–257.

Shen, Y.-R. (1984). "The Principles of Nonlinear Optics." Wiley, New York.

Smith, S.D. (1986). *Appl. Opt.* **25**, 1550–1564.

Stolen, R.H., Ippen, E.P., and Tynes, A.R. (1972). *Appl. Phys. Lett.* **20**, 62–64.

Stolen, R.H. (1979). *Fiber and Integrated Optics* **3**, 21–51.

Tang, C.L. (1966). *J. of Appl. Phys.* **37**, 1945–1955.

3.

Fundamental Physical Limitations of the Photorefractive Grating Recording Sensitivity

R.V. Johnson* and A.R. Tanguay, Jr.

Optical Materials and Devices Laboratory
Departments of Electrical Engineering and Materials Science
and Center for Photonic Technology
University of Southern California
University Park
Los Angeles, California

Contents

1. Introduction 60
2. Factors Contributing to the Photorefractive Sensitivity 63
3. The Grating Recording Efficiency 68
4. Representative Grating Recording Efficiency Calculations 95
5. Conclusions 98
   Acknowledgments 99
   References 99

* Current affiliation: Crystal Technology, Inc., 1060 E. Meadow Circle, Palo Alto, CA 94303

59

1.

Introduction

A number of inherent inefficiencies exist in the photorefractive recording of grating structures due to the nature of the photoexcitation and charge transport processes. These inefficiencies can be quantified by postulating highly idealized photoexcitation and charge transport models that yield optimum (quantum limited) space charge field distributions, assuming a photoexcitation constraint of no more than one mobile charge per incident photon. By comparing such highly idealized photorefractive recording models with more realistic models, the fundamental origins of several such inherent inefficiency factors can be identified and their magnitudes estimated. In this manner, the grating recording efficiencies of photorefractive materials can be directly compared with the fundamental physical limitations imposed by quantum constraints.

In this chapter, we will establish the absolute quantum efficiency of the photorefractive grating recording process by deriving the optimum idealized photorefractive recording model subject to such quantum constraints. A more realistic photoexcitation and charge transport model applicable to numerous currently investigated real time photorefractive materials will then be examined in depth, with emphasis on a comparison with the characteristics of the optimum quantum limited model. This realistic charge transport model, based on the extensive previous work of numerous authors, is presented in such a manner as to illustrate its statistical nature and to provide a physically intuitive interpretation of its principal attributes.

Of all of the parameters that seek to quantify the absolute or relative performance of photorefractive materials, one of the most important is the photorefractive sensitivity (von der Linde and Glass, 1975; Micheron, 1978; Glass, 1978; Gunter, 1982; Yeh, 1987a and 1987b; Glass et al., 1987; Valley and Klein, 1983). This key parameter is typically defined in theoretical analyses either as the refractive index modulation obtained in writing a uniform grating of fixed spatial frequency per unit absorbed recording energy density (energy per unit volume) (von der Linde and Glass, 1975; Micheron, 1978; Glass, 1978; Gunter, 1982; Glass et al., 1987; Valley and Klein, 1983), or as the inverse of the recording energy density required to achieve a specified value of the diffraction efficiency for a uniform grating of fixed spatial frequency in a material of given thickness (Valley and Klein, 1983; Huignard and Micheron, 1976). Alternatively, for purposes of experimental measurement, the photorefractive sensitivity may be specified as the inverse of the recording energy density required to reach a given fraction of the saturation diffraction efficiency of a particular material (Gunter, 1982; Amodei and Staebler, 1972). The photorefractive sensitivity, and the fundamental physical limitations that apply to it, are of current significant interest because they establish the maximum reconfiguration rate of volume holographic optical elements (VHOEs) (von der Linde and Glass, 1975; Tanguay, 1985) at constant average optical input power. The maximum reconfiguration rate of VHOEs is in turn important for applications ranging from massively parallel interconnections in optical processing and computing systems (Tanguay, 1985) to the development of the photorefractive incoherent-to-coherent optical converter (PICOC) (Kamshilin and Petrov, 1980; Shi et al., 1983; Marrakchi et al., 1985).

A number of factors contribute to the various photorefractive sensitivities characteristic of photoconductive, electrooptic materials. One such factor is the photogeneration quantum efficiency, which represents the number of photogenerated mobile charge carriers per photon absorbed from the recording beam(s). A second factor is the charge transport efficiency, which is a measure of the degree to which the average photogenerated mobile charge carrier contributes to the forming space charge grating after separation from its original site by means of drift and/or diffusion and subsequent trapping. The magnitude of the space charge field generated by a given space charge grating is inversely proportional to the dielectric permittivity ϵ of the photorefractive material, which thus contributes a third factor to the grating recording sensitivity. A fourth factor describes the perturbation of the local index ellipsoid (dielectric tensor at optical frequencies) that results from a given space charge field through the electrooptic (Pockels or Kerr) effect. And finally, a fifth factor pertains to the physical optics inherent in the readout process, whereby the diffraction efficiency and polarization properties of the readout beam are derived directly from the index ellipsoid modulation.

In addition, several other physical quantities factor into an evaluation of the photorefractive sensitivity, including the wavelength of the recording illumination (to convert the number of absorbed photons into an equivalent energy), the absorption coefficients of the material at the wavelengths of both the recording and readout beams (to correct for the fractional absorbance of the recording beams and the fractional transmittance of the readout beam), and the magnitude of the applied voltage (which significantly alters the sensitivity characteristics for certain materials by changing the nature of the dominant charge transport mechanism from the diffusion regime to the drift regime).

In previous treatments of the photorefractive sensitivity and its associated limits, all of the abovementioned factors have been addressed to some degree, though not necessarily within a single unified treatment, or even within a consistent set of constraints, assumptions, and approximations. Such a unification is also beyond the scope of the present work. In this chapter, we present the results of a study in which we have approached the photorefractive sensitivity issue from a somewhat different perspective: that of the *absolute quantum efficiency* of the photorefractive grating recording process. As such, we attempt to answer an oft-stated but as yet unanswered question as to the origin of the apparent insensitivity of photorefractive grating recording, particularly in comparison with the relatively high sensitivities characteristic of electrooptic spatial light modulators that utilize a similar combination of photoconductive charge separation and electrooptic modulation in the same single crystal materials (Tanguay, 1985).

In order to provide a quantitative metric that does in fact have a fundamental physical limitation, we define herein the *grating recording efficiency* of a photorefractive recording model or configuration as the magnitude of the space charge field produced by a fixed number of photogenerated mobile charge carriers at a given spatial frequency, normalized by the maximum quantum limited space charge field that can be produced by the same number of photogenerated carriers. This metric thus effectively combines the notions of a photogeneration efficiency and a charge transport efficiency, and it provides an estimate of the fundamental quantum efficiency of the photorefractive grating recording process as determined by the particular photoexcitation and charge transport mechanism invoked.

In order to fully utilize the concept of the grating recording efficiency, we first calculate the maximum quantum limited space charge field that can be produced by a fixed number of photogenerated mobile charge carriers, assuming optimum photoexcitation and redistribution (transport) functions. We then calculate the grating recording efficiencies that describe several important limiting cases with selected idealized photoexcitation and redistribution functions. This in turn allows for the definition of a baseline case against which more realistic charge transport models can be compared. Examination of a particular charge transport model as a test case then indicates several other generically applicable factors that act to further decrease the grating recording efficiency in various recording configurations. These results allow the above analysis to be conveniently utilized for a wide range of applications of current technological interest.

The organization of the remainder of this chapter is as follows. A brief summary of the origin, material dependence, and implications of the several parameters that affect the photorefractive grating recording sensitivity is provided in the following section (Section 2). Alternative models of the photorefractive recording process are defined in Section 3, and the appropriate grating recording efficiencies are presented therein for each case. Assumptions and limitations common to all of the models are discussed in Section 3.1. Idealized photogeneration and charge transport models are defined and analyzed in Section 3.2, and more realistic models based upon the analyses of Young et al. (1974) and Moharam et al. (1979) in the initial stages of recording before significant space charge field amplitudes evolve, and of Kukhtarev (1976) for temporal evolution with small modulation depths of the illumination profile, are discussed and analyzed in Section 3.3. Representative grating recording efficiency calculations are presented in Section 4 for several common materials and applications in order to illustrate the effect of the quantum inefficiency factors on the overall quantum efficiency of photorefractive recording. Finally, conclusions drawn from the above analyses are discussed in Section 5.

2.
Factors Contributing to the Photorefractive Sensitivity

In this section, each of the five factors outlined in the introduction that collectively determine the photorefractive sensitivity is briefly discussed, in order to provide a suitable context for the derivation of the quantum limited grating recording efficiency as presented in the following section. It should perhaps be emphasized at the outset that although each of the primary factors considered herein affects at least one of the aforementioned alternative photorefractive sensitivity parameters, not all of the factors enter into each defined parameter.

In the context of photorefractive grating recording, the photogeneration quantum efficiency is related to the fraction of the incident photon flux that generates mobile charge carriers free to participate in subsequent charge transport and trapping processes. For a given recording wavelength, several distinct photoexcitation processes can contribute to the total absorption coefficient. In most commonly considered models of the photorefractive effect, the dominant process is the photogeneration of free carriers from deep donor or acceptor states, such that only one sign mobile carrier (either an electron or a hole) is liberated for each photoevent. In wavelength regions of significant photoconductivity, a second important process is the creation of electron-hole pairs (as well as excitons in certain materials and material structures) by means of band-to-band transitions. Examples of photoinduced transitions that are not likely to contribute to the photorefractive effect, and hence tend to reduce the photogeneration quantum efficiency, are intersubband absorptions, intraionic level promotions, quantum well interlevel excitations, and photochromic charge transfer exchanges. Since each contributing process will in general be characterized by its own charge transport efficiency (discussed below), it is most appropriate to assign separate photogeneration quantum efficiencies not only to each charge carrier type, but also to each distinct photoproduction origin (or photoexcitation channel).

The inherent absorptive inefficiency implied by a finite thickness photorefractive medium also affects the overall photogeneration quantum efficiency. In the case of a thin crystal (such that $\alpha d \ll 1$, in which α is the absorption coefficient at the recording wavelength and d is the crystal thickness), only a small fraction $(= \alpha d)$ of the recording beam intensity is absorbed and hence has an opportunity to participate in the photorefractive process. In a thicker crystal, for which the thickness may be optimized for maximum saturation diffraction efficiency, the absorbed fraction is $[1 - e^{-\alpha d}]$ if only the entrance surface of the photorefractive medium is allowed to achieve saturation. In this case the recorded grating will exhibit an exponential nonuniformity throughout the crystal thickness that will decrease the maximum achievable diffraction efficiency. If the entire crystal is exposed to saturation, the photogeneration quantum efficiency will be further reduced by a factor of order $e^{-\alpha d}$. Finally, the effects of reflection at both front and rear crystal surfaces reduce the fraction of incident photons that contribute to the formation of a given grating component and, hence, also reduce the effective quantum efficiency. For a crystal thickness optimized for maximum saturation diffraction efficiency with equal write and read wavelengths, and for indices of refraction typical of common photorefractive materials, the combined effects of absorption of the recording beams, absorption of the readout beam, and reflection losses (assuming uncoated surfaces) on the photorefractive sensitivity is approximately an order of magnitude.

An additional effect that acts to reduce the photogeneration quantum efficiency is the constraint imposed indirectly by the nature of the photoexcitation distribution. As we shall demonstrate in the next section, the sinusoidal intensity interference pattern generated by two coherent recording beams is not the optimum (quantum limited) photoexcitation distribution function.

Perhaps the most critical factor that determines the photorefractive sensitivity is the charge transport efficiency, in that this quantity, above all others, exhibits the greatest degree of variation among commonly investigated photorefractive materials. The charge transport efficiency quantifies the degree to which the average photoproduced charge carrier contributes to the forming space charge grating following photoexcitation, charge transport, and subsequent recombination or trapping. Charge transport in the refractory oxides, as well as in the compound semiconductor family, is a statistical process in which the net result of a given photoinduced event may be to increase, decrease, or leave unchanged the magnitude of the space charge modulation at the fundamental grating frequency.

The statistical nature of the charge transport process can be subsumed in the standard band transport treatment (Young et al., 1974; Moharam et al., 1979; Kukhtarev et al., 1976, 1979), or made explicit as in the hopping conduction model (Feinberg et al., 1980); both approaches lead to essentially equivalent results (Feinberg et al., 1980; Jaura et al., 1986). The charge transport efficiency is strongly affected in photorefractive materials by the dominant conduction mechanism (diffusion and/or drift in an externally applied field), and by the ratio of the average displacement of a photoexcited carrier (before recombination or trapping) to the grating spacing. In both the drift and diffusion regimes, the average displacement depends primarily on the mobility-lifetime product of the photoexcited species. As such, separate charge transport efficiencies should be assigned to each carrier type. A significant net charge transport efficiency will be realized only if there is a net differential in the carrier displacement and trapping process.

It should be noted that there are several situations that can yield vanishing charge transport efficiencies, even with large photogeneration quantum efficiencies. For example, in a single donor/single trap model, if the initial Fermi level is more than $10 \; k_B T$ or so above the un-ionized donor level, no substantial charge rearrangement is possible due to the unavailability of ionized donors (traps) outside the regions of significant photoexcitation. Likewise, if the initial Fermi level is more than $10 \; k_B T$ or so below the un-ionized donor level, only band-to-band photoexcitations can contribute with nonvanishing photogeneration quantum efficiencies, which again is likely to yield negligible charge transport efficiency unless the mobilities and/or lifetimes are significantly different, or unless operation in the drift regime is engendered by employing an externally applied electric field.

The space charge grating that results from the combination of photoexcitation and charge transport processes in turn gives rise to a modulation of the local electric field at the same spatial frequency through the first Maxwell equation:

$$\nabla \cdot [\epsilon \mathbf{E}(x)] = \frac{\rho(x)}{\epsilon_0}, \tag{3.1}$$

in which $\mathbf{E}$ is the total electric field at each point in space x, ϵ is the dielectric permittivity tensor, ρ is the local space charge amplitude, and ϵ_0 is the dielectric permittivity of free space. Note that the magnitude of the space charge field derived from a given space charge grating amplitude is inversely proportional to the grating wave vector, as implied by the differential relationship expressed in Eq. (3.1). The tensor character of ϵ is important to note, as many photorefractive materials (particularly the ferroelectric oxides) exhibit marked dielectric anisotropy. Hence, space charge gratings oriented in different directions within the same crystal can give rise to quite large variations in the resultant space charge field. Note further that the magnitude of the space charge field scales inversely with a diagonal component of the dielectric permittivity for a given space charge grating oriented along a principal dielectric axis of the crystal. Thus, materials with large dielectric constants (such as $BaTiO_3$ and SBN) require correspondingly large space charge amplitudes in order to produce an internal electric field modulation of given amplitude.

In the types of photorefractive materials considered herein, the index of refraction is a function of the local electric field. This dependence can arise from a number of electrorefractive effects, including among others the linear electrooptic (Pockels) effect, the quadratic electrooptic (Kerr) effect, the Franz-Keldysh effect, and the quantum confined Stark effect (Chemla et al., 1985). In some materials, notably multiple quantum well structures in compound semiconductors, more than one such electrorefractive effect can contribute simultaneously to the establishment of the resultant index perturbation. For our purposes herein, we consider only the linear electrooptic effect, in which the change in the dielectric impermeability tensor $\mathbf{B}$ (the inverse of the dielectric tensor ϵ) is linear in the electric field:

$$\Delta B_{ij} = \Delta(\epsilon^{-1})_{ij} = r_{ijk} E_k, \tag{3.2}$$

in which the Einstein summation rule is implied, and in which r_{ijk} is the third rank tensor representing the electrooptic coefficient (Kaminow, 1974). As shown in Eq. (3.2), the tensor nature of the electrooptic effect implies a dependence of the effective index of refraction on the orientation of the grating within the crystal, as well as on the direction of propagation of the readout beam and its polarization. Since in general one can derive an effective electrooptic coefficient for a given experimental configuration, Eq. (3.2) may be rewritten in the form

$$\Delta n_{\text{eff}}(x) = -\tfrac{1}{2} n_0^3 r_{\text{eff}} E(x) \tag{3.3}$$

in which the x coordinate is taken parallel to the grating wave vector, $\Delta n_{\text{eff}}(x)$ is the effective index modulation resulting from the combination of the space charge field and the readout configuration, and n_0 is the corresponding unperturbed index at the wavelength of the readout beam.

In discussions of the photorefractive sensitivity, it is of considerable value to combine the effects of the previous two factors, since it has been shown that for a wide range of common photorefractive materials, the ratio $n_0^3 r_{\text{eff}}/\epsilon$ exhibits considerably reduced variation compared with that of each parameter separately (Glass et al., 1984; Glass, 1984). This is indicative of the general observation that materials with large static polarizabilities typically also exhibit concomitantly large perturbations of the dielectric tensor at optical frequencies in response to low frequency applied (or internal) electric fields.

Once the magnitude of the index perturbation is established, the resultant diffraction efficiency can be directly determined from the thickness (and uniformity) of the grating, the grating wave vector, the readout wavelength, and the corresponding absorption coefficient. Provided that the grating structure is sufficiently thick to assure diffraction in the Bragg regime and that the phase and amplitude distortions associated with self-diffraction effects can be neglected (Kukhtarev et al., 1979; Marrakchi et al., 1987), the diffraction efficiency is given by (Kogelnik, 1969)

$$\eta = \exp\left(\frac{-\alpha d}{\cos \theta_{\text{B}}}\right) \sin^2\left(\frac{\pi \Delta n d}{\lambda \cos \theta_{\text{B}}}\right), \tag{3.4}$$

in which θ_{B} is the Bragg angle. The first term in this expression denotes the inherent inefficiency associated with finite absorption at the readout wavelength, while the second term derives from the grating-modulation-induced diffraction process. Since for suitably small values of the argument $\pi \Delta n d / \lambda \cos \theta_{\text{B}}$ the diffraction efficiency scales as the square of both the index modulation and the grating thickness, this photorefractive sensitivity factor is inherently nonlinear and must be utilized with considerable caution.

Until this point in the discussion, we have assumed implicitly that the grating recording exposures and spatial frequencies employed have been large enough and small enough, respectively, to keep the photorefractive recording process outside the additional limitations imposed by quantum statistical fluctuations. For the recording of photorefractive gratings at very high spatial frequencies and at very low grating recording exposures, several additional factors will come into play, including statistical fluctuations in the photogeneration process, corresponding fluctuations in the charge transport and trapping processes that yield a locally inhomogeneous charge distribution with spatial frequency components near that of the grating wave vector, and concomitant variations in the direction and magnitude of the local space charge field. These additional factors may act to further reduce the overall photorefractive sensitivity.

3.
The Grating Recording Efficiency

As defined in the introduction (Section 1), the grating recording efficiency of a given photorefractive recording model or configuration is the ratio between the magnitude of the space charge field at a given spatial frequency produced by a fixed number of photogenerated mobile charge carriers, and the maximum quantum limited space charge field that can be produced by the same number of photogenerated carriers. The grating recording efficiency is introduced as a useful metric that effectively compares the photogeneration and charge transport efficiencies of any given model with the optimum quantum limited case, and as such provides an estimate of the overall fundamental quantum efficiency of the photorefractive grating recording process. Note that since the grating recording efficiency is normalized, any effect of the dielectric permittivity tensor in establishing the magnitudes of the space charge fields cancels out. Hence the grating recording efficiency may be equivalently defined directly in terms of the space charge grating amplitudes or in terms of the space charge fields for a dielectric constant of unity.

In this section, idealized photogeneration and charge transport models are postulated and analyzed in order to determine the maximum quantum limited space charge amplitude that can be produced by a fixed number of photogenerated mobile charge carriers at a given spatial frequency. The grating recording efficiencies of several such idealized models are then calculated to form a set of baseline cases against which the corresponding efficiencies of more realistic photorefractive recording models can be directly compared. For one such model, that of a single mobile charge species transported between a single type of donor site and its associated (ionized) trap sites, several factors are identified that contribute to the grating recording efficiency and that are particularly illustrative of the fundamental limitations on the photorefractive sensitivity inherent in the model.

3.1. Constraints Common to Alternative Models of Photorefractive Recording

The idealized photogeneration and charge transport models defined herein are abstractions of a more realistic model that has been studied by many authors and has been analyzed in considerable detail by Kukhtarev et al. (1976, 1979), and as such these models share key assumptions concerning quantum recording limitations and implications of the readout process. For simplicity, we confine our attention herein to a version of the model characterized by a single mobile charge species, and a single type of donor site with associated un-ionized donor and ionized donor (trap) states, although more intricate models have been proposed for particular materials sytems [e.g., the existence of mobile holes as well as electrons in lithium niobate (Orlowski and Kratzig, 1978) and barium titanate (Strohkendl et al., 1986), or the existence of multiple trap levels in bismuth silicon oxide (Attard and Brown, 1986; Valley, 1986)].

Four principal material species are considered in the single mobile charge/single trap level model, as diagrammed in Fig. 3.1. The mobile charge species (usually electrons) has number density $n(x, t)$ and is represented by the symbol e^- in Fig. 3.1. It is assumed that negligible densities of these mobile charges exist under dark conditions; essentially all mobile charges are created by photoionization of donors. In this model, *donors* and *traps* are assumed to be different valence states of the same impurity atom (e.g., iron in lithium niobate) or lattice defects, as diagrammed in Fig. 3.2. The total number of such impurity ions or defects is distributed uniformly throughout the crystal at potential donor sites. A donor is converted into a trap (ionized donor), simultaneously with the creation of a mobile charge, by photogeneration; conversely, a mobile charge is removed from the conduction band, and a trap is converted into a donor, by recombination (Fig. 3.2). The sum of the number densities of donors and ionized donors is denoted by N_D, which is therefore the total density of potential donor sites and is assumed to be constant in space and time. If the number density of ionized donors is taken to be $N_D^+(x, t)$, then the number density of (un-ionized) donors is $[N_D - N_D^+(x, t)]$. In Fig. 3.1, the donors are represented by the symbol O and the traps are represented by the symbol $+$. A fourth material species is needed in this model to ensure charge conservation, as the density of ionized donors $N_D^+(x, t)$ frequently exceeds the density of mobile charges $n(x, t)$ by several orders of magnitude. This fourth species, with number density N_A, has traditionally been called an *acceptor*, but is also called a *charge compensation site* herein and is represented in Fig. 3.1 by the symbol $-$. The charge compensation sites are electrically negative with respect to the donors and are presumed to be negatively charged impurity ions or lattice defects incorporated during the crystal growth process. The density N_A is assumed to be constant in space and time, and is further assumed to be numerically equal to $N_D^+(x, t = 0)$, the concentration of ionized donors in equilibrium. In point of fact, the only requirement for charge compensation is that the product of the charge compensation site density and the effective number of negative charges on each be equal to $N_D^+(x, t = 0)$.

It is instructive to consider the relative densities of these various species. Consider, for example, a crystal of bismuth silicon oxide ($Bi_{12}SiO_{20}$). Typ-

Fig. 3.1.

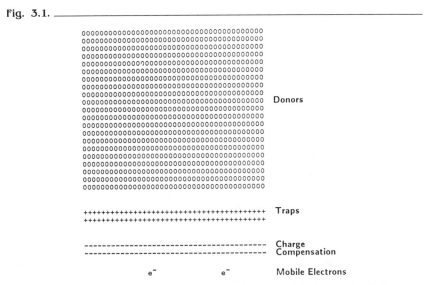

Schematic representation of the single mobile charge/single trap level photorefractive recording model, indicating both the uniform distributions and the relative densities of the four principal material species involved prior to grating recording.

Fig. 3.2.

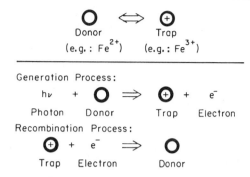

Schematic representation of the single active species photorefractive recording model, indicating the electron photogeneration (and recombination) processes involved in the transformation of donors into traps (and traps into donors).

ical concentrations of donors, charge compensation sites, and mobile charges under reasonable optical intensities are of order 10^{19} cm^{-3}, 10^{16} cm^{-3}, and no more that 10^{12} cm^{-3}, respectively (Peltier and Micheron, 1977; see also Hou et al., 1973). (The number density of electrons under dark conditions for typical crystals of bismuth silicon oxide is entirely negligible.) Thus, $N_D \gg N_D^+ \simeq N_A \gg n$. A number of other photorefractive media exhibit similar proportionalities. For these materials, the total space charge density $\rho(x, t)$ is given by

$$\rho(x, t) = e[N_D^+(x, t) - n(x, t) - N_A] \approx e[N_D^+(x, t) - N_A]. \quad (3.5)$$

The local density of ionized donors N_D^+ can be spatially redistributed under the influence of inhomogeneous photogeneration, as shown by comparing Figs. 3.1 and 3.3. This redistribution occurs as follows. A photon is absorbed by a donor, converting the donor into a trap (ionized donor) and generating a mobile charge carrier. The mobile charge carrier is transported some distance through the photorefractive medium due to drift and/or diffusion, and it is subsequently captured by a trap thus generating another donor. If we choose to follow a particular electron, the entire process can be viewed as a simple exchange between equivalent donor sites of a donor state with an ionized donor (or trap) state.

As a final note, the space charge profile $\rho(x, t)$ might evolve into a highly distorted profile with respect to the distribution of incident illumination because of nonlinearities inherent in the recording process. However, since the grating readout is typically performed deep within the Bragg regime, at most

Fig. 3.3.

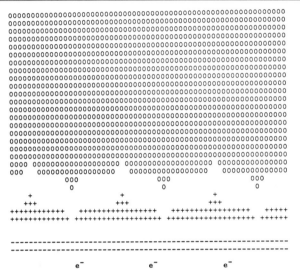

Schematic representation of the single mobile charge/single trap level photo-refractive recording model, indicating the spatial redistribution of the four principal material species following grating recording. Note that the *sum* of the donor and trap densities is space-invariant. The symbols identifying each species are given in Fig. 3.1.

a very limited range of spatial frequencies is effective in diffracting the read-out light. Thus only one spatial harmonic of the space charge field is of interest, which is assumed herein to be the fundamental harmonic.

In summary, the photorefractive recording model studied by Kukhtarev and all idealized photogeneration and charge transport abstractions considered in the following analysis share these basic assumptions: a) only a finite amount of space charge $[N_D^+(x, t = 0) = N_A]$ exists for generating the space charge electric field, b) this space charge can be spatially redistributed under the influence of an illumination pattern, c) no more than one mobile charge is generated for each absorbed photon of the illumination beam, and d) only the fundamental spatial harmonic of the space charge is effective in the holographic readout process. The photorefractive recording model and the idealized models differ, however, in the details of the photogeneration and charge transport processes, as discussed next.

3.2. Idealized Photogeneration and Charge Transport Models

The grating recording efficiency comprises three successive physical processes: photogeneration, charge transport, and trapping. In order to determine the maximum quantum limited space charge field (at unity dielectric constant) that can result from a fixed number of photogenerated mobile charges, we investigate four idealized photogeneration and charge transport models, as defined below.

The photogeneration process is controlled by the recording illumination profile. Two alternative profiles are considered herein, a periodic comb function and a sinusoidal function. The comb illumination profile $I_C(x)$, as shown in Fig. 3.4, is defined by

$$I_C(x) = I_{C0} \, \text{comb}\left(\frac{x}{\Lambda_G}\right) \Rightarrow I_{C0} \sum \delta\left(p + \frac{x}{\Lambda_G}\right), \qquad (3.6)$$

in which the arrow $\Rightarrow$ indicates that the desired function asymptotically approaches a sequence of Dirac delta functions, i.e., a series of intensity peaks with spatial extent small compared with the spatial period Λ_G. Unlike a mathematical delta function, however, the intended comb peaks are assumed to be large enough to overlap a reasonable number of donor sites. Note that the periodic comb function does not correspond to any normal recording configuration. This is acceptable for purposes of this analysis because the maximum quantum limited space charge field at unity dielectric constant is intended to define an upper limit against which more realistic models might

Fig. 3.4.

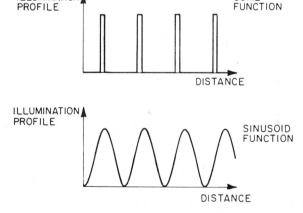

Schematic representation of the two principal illumination profiles (comb and sinusoid functions) utilized in the idealized photogeneration and charge transport models. The comb function is illustrated with finite width to incorporate a given number of donors at a predetermined donor density.

be compared. The sinusoid illumination profile $I_S(x)$ of unity modulation depth is defined by

$$I_S(x) = I_{S0}\left[1 + \cos\left(\frac{2\pi x}{\Lambda_G}\right) \right],$$ (3.7)

in which Λ_G is the spatial period of the illumination profile. To compare these two illumination profiles, the same photon flux is assumed; that is, the scaling parameters I_{S0} and I_{C0} are adjusted such that the following normalization integral is satisfied:

$$\int I_S(x)\, dx = \int I_C(x)\, dx,$$ (3.8)

from which we derive the relation that $I_{S0} = I_{C0} \equiv I_0$. In the idealized photogeneration models, all photons in the illumination profile are assumed to be absorbed and to generate mobile charge carriers.

Two alternative models of charge transport and trapping are also considered: half wavelength translation, and randomization (Figs. 3.5 and 3.6). In the half wavelength translation process shown schematically in Fig. 3.5, each electron is assumed to translate precisely half the grating period of the illumination profile before capture, without diffusive blooming of the elec-

Fig. 3.5. _____

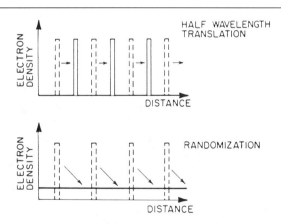

Schematic representation of the two principal charge redistribution mechanisms (half wavelength translation and randomization) utilized in the idealized photogeneration and charge transport models, for the case of comb illumination. A single mobile charge species (electrons) is assumed for purposes of illustration.

Fig. 3.6.

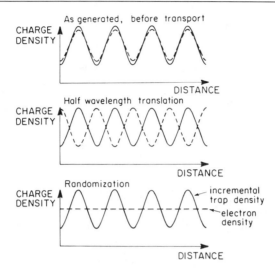

Schematic representation of the two principal charge redistribution mechanisms (half wavelength translation and randomization) utilized in the idealized photogeneration and charge transport models, for the case of sinusoidal illumination.

tron cloud. In the analysis that follows, it will be shown that half wavelength translation corresponds to the quantum limited charge transport process, giving rise to the maximum grating recording efficiency. The second idealized transport and capture process to be considered herein is complete randomization, as shown schematically in Fig. 3.6, in which the photogenerated electrons are assumed to redistribute randomly until they exhibit no spatial variation in density, and only then are recaptured by local traps. The randomization model is intended to represent a more realistic charge transport model; even so, this model corresponds to an *upper* bound on realizable charge transport efficiencies, as shown in the next section.

Combination of the two photogeneration models and the two charge transport and trapping models produces four alternative idealized recording models for comparison (Fig. 3.7), which will hereinafter be identified as the bipolar comb, the monopolar comb, the transport-efficient sinusoid, and the baseline sinusoid. Each of the four combinations will be considered in turn. Grating recording efficiencies are calculated for these four combinations in Section 3.2.1, and the corresponding space-charge-field saturation behavior is considered in Section 3.2.2.

Fig. 3.7.

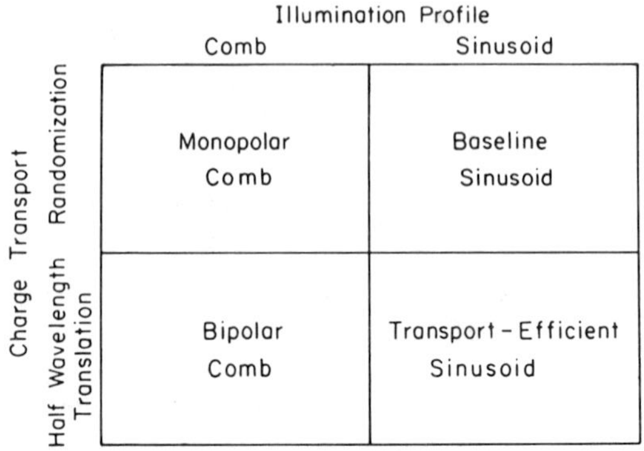

Matrix representation of the four idealized photogeneration and charge transport models, as derived from the principal illumination profiles and charge transport mechanisms.

3.2.1. Idealized Grating Recording Efficiencies

The bipolar comb results from a periodic comb illumination function combined with a half wavelength translation. The resulting space charge density $\rho(x)$ induced by this illumination and transport combination is a periodic comb function superimposed on a periodic comb function of opposite sign shifted by half of a grating wavelength, as shown in Fig. 3.8. For a given peak photogenerated charge density ρ_0 (proportional to $I_0 t$, in which t is the exposure time), the resultant space charge distribution $\rho(x)$ is given by

$$\rho(x) = \rho_0\left[\mathrm{comb}\left(\frac{x}{\Lambda_G}\right) - \mathrm{comb}\left(\frac{1}{2} + \frac{x}{\Lambda_G}\right)\right]. \tag{3.9}$$

This space charge profile $\rho(x)$ can be readily integrated [see Eq. (3.1)] to yield a space charge field $E(x)$ that is a square pulse train (Fig. 3.8). The first spatial harmonic component, E_1, defined by

$$E_1 = 2\Lambda_G^{-1} \int E(x) \sin\left(\frac{2\pi x}{\Lambda_G}\right) dx, \tag{3.10}$$

has a magnitude of

$$E_1 = 4e \frac{\rho_0}{\epsilon\epsilon_0 K_G}, \tag{3.11}$$

in which $K_G = 2\pi/\Lambda_G$ is the wave vector of the illumination profile.

Fig. 3.8.

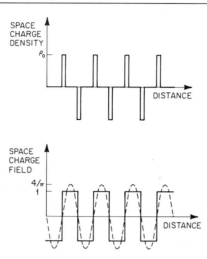

Space charge density and field profiles for the bipolar comb distribution. The first spatial harmonic of the space charge field is represented by the dashed curve and is scaled to the magnitude of the total space charge field.

The monopolar comb commands interest because it can support the highest space charge field before saturation due to limited ionized trap density, as discussed in the next section. The monopolar comb results from a periodic comb illumination function combined with electron randomization. The resulting space charge profile $\rho(x)$ induced by this illumination and transport combination is a periodic comb function superimposed on a uniform background of opposite charge, as shown in Fig. 3.9. The resulting charge distribution is represented by

$$\rho(x) = \rho_0 \left[\text{comb}\left(\frac{x}{\Lambda_G}\right) - 1 \right]. \tag{3.12}$$

The corresponding space charge field exhibits a sawtooth profile (Fig. 3.9), and the magnitude E_1 of its first spatial harmonic is

$$E_1 = 2e \frac{\rho_0}{\epsilon \epsilon_0 K_G}. \tag{3.13}$$

The transport-efficient sinusoid results from a sinusoidal illumination profile combined with a half wavelength translation, as shown schematically in Fig. 3.10, leading to a charge density $\rho(x)$ given by

$$\rho(x) = 2\rho_0 \cos\left(\frac{2\pi x}{\Lambda_G}\right) \tag{3.14}$$

and a first spatial harmonic field component E_1 of

$$E_1 = 2e\,\frac{\rho_0}{\epsilon\epsilon_0 K_G}. \tag{3.15}$$

The transport-efficient sinusoid combination is included for completeness, but is not emphasized because it is neither realistic nor does it correspond to any upper bound of grating recording efficiency or saturation performance.

The baseline sinusoid, although seemingly artificial, is of very pronounced interest because it represents an asymptotic upper bound on the grating recording efficiency predicted by more realistic recording models, as discussed in Section 3.3 below. The baseline sinusoid results from a sinusoidal illumination profile combined with randomization of the electron distribution. The resulting space charge distribution exhibits a sinusoidal

Fig. 3.9.

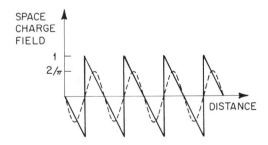

Space charge density and field profiles for the monopolar comb distribution. The first spatial harmonic of the space charge field is represented by the dashed curve and is scaled to the magnitude of the total space charge field.

Fig. 3.10.

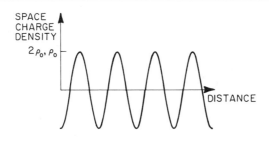

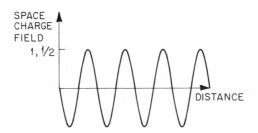

Space charge density and field profiles for the transport-efficient (first scale values) and baseline sinusoid (second scale values) distributions. The space charge fields are scaled to the magnitude of the transport-efficient case.

profile, as does the corresponding space charge field, as shown in Fig. 3.10. The charge density is given by:

$$\rho(x) = \rho_0 \cos\left(\frac{2\pi x}{\Lambda_G}\right), \tag{3.16}$$

corresponding to a first spatial harmonic field component E_1 of

$$E_1 = e\,\frac{\rho_0}{\epsilon\epsilon_0 K_G}. \tag{3.17}$$

As can be seen from the analysis above, the bipolar comb photogeneration/charge transport combination generates the maximum quantum limited space charge field at unity dielectric constant, and hence provides the normalization constant required for evaluation of the grating recording efficiencies of both idealized and realistic photorefractive recording models. Physically, this optimum combination of photogeneration and charge transport results from the maximum possible average separation of the positive and negative charge distributions, as well as from the fact that the amplitude of the first harmonic of a square wave exceeds the amplitude of the square wave itself.

The grating recording efficiencies for the four idealized photorefractive grating recording combinations are shown in Table 3.1. The most quantum-efficient recording occurs for the bipolar comb, which therefore is assigned a grating recording efficiency of unity. The next most efficient configurations are the monopolar comb and the transport-efficient sinusoid, which both yield a grating recording efficiency of 0.5. The least efficient configuration is the baseline sinusoid, with a grating recording efficiency of 0.25. As we shall show later, the efficiency of the baseline sinusoid is an asymptotic upper limit of more realistic recording models. Table 3.2 gives the relative photorefractive grating recording sensitivities for these four cases in terms of diffraction efficiency per unit incident photon flux, assuming low diffraction efficiencies such that the efficiency is proportional to the square of the space charge field component E_1. Note that by this measure the sensitivity of the baseline sinusoid is degraded by a factor of 16, over an order of magnitude, compared with the quantum limit represented by the bipolar comb charge distribution function.

3.2.2. Space Charge Saturation for the Idealized Models

Not only is the photorefractive recording sensitivity of concern, but also saturation limitations of the space charge field occurring because of limited ionized trap density. Consider, for example, the bipolar comb example shown in Fig. 3.8. The regions of positive space charge grow by the photoexcitation of neutral donors, which converts them into positively ionized donors (traps) and generates mobile electrons. The electrons are removed from this region by the various transport processes, leaving behind the positively ionized donors. As will be shown later, it is these regions of net positive space charge that primarily contribute to the buildup of the space charge field. The regions of negative space charge grow by the reverse process, i.e., by capturing mobile electrons at local ionized donor sites to form neutral donors. In pho-

TABLE 3.1

Grating Recording Efficiencies of the Various Idealized Models

Bipolar comb	1.0
Monopolar comb	0.5
Transport-efficient sinusoid	0.5
Baseline sinusoid	0.25

TABLE 3.2

Relative Diffraction Efficiencies of the Various Idealized Models

Bipolar comb	1.0
Monopolar comb	0.25
Transport-efficient sinusoid	0.25
Baseline sinusoid	0.0625

torefractive crystals that initially are in quasi-thermodynamic equilibrium, the density of donors typically far exceeds the density of ionized donors, which implies that the regions of negative space charge will saturate first. This corresponds to the complete conversion of all ionized donors into neutral donors at the peaks of the negative space charge distribution, resulting in the local complete cancellation of $N_D^+(x, t = 0) = N_A$, as shown schematically in Fig. 3.11.

The bipolar comb combination exhibits by far the most rapid charge saturation at the lowest space charge field of the four combinations considered herein, because for this combination the electrons after transport are concentrated into a very small volume, with a correspondingly small number

Fig. 3.11.

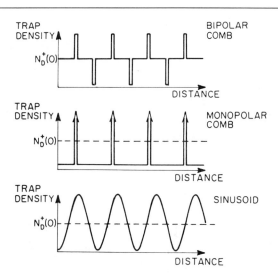

Saturation of the space charge modulation for the bipolar comb, monopolar comb, and sinusoid charge distributions as a result of the finite available trap density. An initially uniform trap density of $N_D^+(0)$ is assumed prior to photogeneration and charge redistribution.

of ionized donors available to capture these electrons. Conversely, the monopolar comb combination exhibits the slowest saturation at the highest space charge field because the electrons are uniformly distributed throughout the volume of the photorefractive medium and, hence, can be captured by all of the ionized donors. The saturation characteristics of the sinusoidal combinations are intermediate between the bipolar and the monopolar combinations.

The relative photorefractive grating recording sensitivities (grating recording efficiencies) and saturation characteristics of these four photogeneration/charge transport combinations are schematically diagrammed in Fig. 3.12. The photosensitivities are indicated by the initial linear slopes and the saturation by the final space charge field levels. The space charge field is plotted here in units of E_q, which is defined as $eN_A/\epsilon\epsilon_0 K_G$ (Amodei, 1971). (This expression is valid when the density of charge compensation sites N_A is much smaller than the total density of potential donor sites N_D.) Note that the saturation level for the bipolar comb should really be much closer to the horizontal axis; it has been overstated for clarity of illustration.

Having calculated the grating recording efficiencies and saturation fields for these four highly idealized cases, we now proceed to compare these ideal

Fig. 3.12.

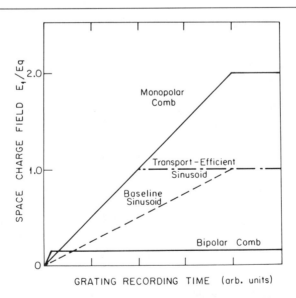

GRATING RECORDING TIME (arb. units)

Space charge field as a function of grating recording time, showing the initial linear growth (phtorefractive sensitivity) and subsequent saturation regimes.

results with more realistic photogeneration and charge transport models in the next two sections.

3.3. Realistic Recording Models

The idealized photorefractive recording models discussed above allow the effects of the photogeneration profile and charge transport process on the grating recording efficiency to be assessed relative to the fundamental quantum limits. We now examine a more realistic model applicable to a wide range of commonly investigated photorefractive media, which exhibits an overall efficiency degraded from that of the baseline sinusoid case presented above by several additional factors. In this model, the photogeneration profile is assumed to be sinusoidal, and the effects of the photogeneration quantum efficiency, absorption coefficients, and reflection losses are assumed to be space-invariant efficiency factors and hence can be directly incorporated in any estimate of the photorefractive grating recording sensitivity. Another major factor is an inherent inefficiency in the charge transport process; this inefficiency is studied in Section 3.3.1 using analytical solutions derived by Young et al., (1974; see also Moharam et al., 1979), which are valid in the initial recording interval before significant space charge fields have evolved. A related factor derives from the reduced recording sensitivity exhibited as the space charge field approaches its steady state limit. This is studied in Section 3.3.2 using analytical solutions derived by Kukhtarev (1976) that describe the temporal evolution of the space charge field in the limit of very low illumination profile modulation depths. Recording configurations that generate low modulation depths are inherently inefficient, as most of the photons in the illumination contribute a uniform background photocurrent, and only a fraction of the incident intensity contributes to the spatial structure of the image. The modulation depth, therefore, is also a factor that reduces the photorefractive grating recording sensitivity. However, low modulation depths are necessary in certain recording techniques for enhancing the space charge field in the steady state limit, such as the running grating process discussed in Section 3.3.3.

3.3.1. Initial Recording Sensitivity

To determine the existence of degraded charge transport efficiency, the idealized recording models discussed in Section 3.2 must be compared with more realistic charge transport solutions, such as those given by Young et al. (1974; see also Moharam et al., 1979). Under normal recording conditions, the coupled photorefractive recording equations are nonlinear, making analytical solutions difficult or impossible to derive. However, a significantly simplified analysis can be utilized during the initial recording period, which enables analytical solutions to be derived at least for certain illumination profiles. These analytical solutions are well worth studying for the physical insight they furnish into the charge transport process.

The analytical simplification described above derives from a linearization of the recording equations, in which two recording parameters, the total electric field and the ionized donor (trap) density, remain essentially constant throughout space during the initial recording interval (Young et al., 1974; Moharam et al., 1979). This assumes that the photorefractive crystal is initially in quasi-thermodynamic equilibrium, i.e., with a spatially uniform distribution of ionized donors $N_D^+(x, t = 0) = N_A$, and that the trap density remains essentially constant throughout this initial recording interval.

The analytical solutions that exist in this regime have typically emphasized recording with sinusoidal illumination profiles. While such a profile corresponds closely with typical experimental situations and simplifies the mathematics, the physics of the transport process is somewhat obscured in comparison with an alternative illumination profile, that of a very narrow slit, which can be viewed as an approximation of a Dirac delta function. Typical trapped electron density profiles obtained in response to a narrow slit illumination profile are shown in Fig. 3.13 for the cases of diffusion-only transport (top illustration), drift-only transport (middle illustration), and one particular combination of drift and diffusion processes (bottom illustration); the derivation of these figures is described below. These figures emphasize several important features of a more realistic transport analysis. The transport mechanism is inherently a random process, with a spread in characteristic transport lengths associated with a corresponding spread in charge carrier lifetimes. Useful parameters for characterizing the transport processes are the average transport lengths L_E for drift-induced transport and L_D for diffusive transport, defined as (Young et al., 1974; Moharam et al., 1979)

$$L_E = \mu\tau E_0 , \qquad (3.18)$$

and

$$L_D = (D\tau)^{1/2} = \left(\frac{k_B T}{e}\right)^{1/2} (\mu\tau)^{1/2} , \qquad (3.19)$$

in which μ is the mobility of the charge carriers, E_0 is the applied bias electric field, τ is the charge carrier lifetime, D is the diffusion coefficient

Fig. 3.13. _____

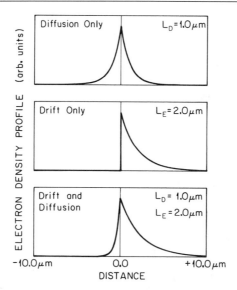

Typical trapped electron density profiles obtained in response to a narrow slit illumination profile. The average transport lengths L_D for diffusive transport and L_E for drift-induced transport are defined in the text.

for the charge carriers, k_B is Boltzmann's constant, T is the crystal temperature, and e is the charge of an electron. Einstein's relation between the diffusion coefficient and the mobility has been used in Eq. (3.19). Note that in both cases the transport lengths are functions of the $\mu\tau$ product.

For the diffusion-only case, the electron spread is symmetrical, which introduces no net phase shift in the photorefractive response to any arbitrary illumination profile. For the drift case, as well as for the combined drift/ diffusion case, the electron distribution is skewed to one side by the presence of an applied bias field, which does in fact introduce a phase shift when recording particular illumination profiles, as shown in Fig. 3.13.

Now consider an illumination profile $I(x)$ that is sinusoidal and of the form

$$I(x) = I_0[1 + m \cos(K_G x)], \qquad (3.20)$$

in which m is the modulation depth of the light profile and K_G is the wave vector associated with the interference pattern. For such an illumination profile, Young et al. (1974; see also Moharam et al., 1979) have derived expressions for the growth of the space charge field during the initial recording interval. When transport is dominated by diffusion, the initial growth of the first harmonic component E_1 of the space charge field is expressed by

$$E_1 = m\left[\frac{teg_0}{\epsilon\epsilon_0 K_G}\right]\left[\frac{K_G^2 L_D^2}{1 + K_G^2 L_D^2}\right], \tag{3.21}$$

in which g_0 is the photogeneration rate and t is the time relative to the initiation of grating recording. The initial growth when drift transport dominates is expressed by

$$E_1 = m\left[\frac{teg_0}{\epsilon\epsilon_0 K_G}\right]\left[K_G L_E(1 + K_G^2 L_E^2)^{-1/2}e^{i\phi}\right], \tag{3.22}$$

in which the phase shift ϕ is defined by

$$\tan\phi = K_G L_E. \tag{3.23}$$

The first bracketed term $[teg_0/\epsilon\epsilon_0 K_G]$ in Eqs. (3.21) and (3.22) corresponds to the grating recording efficiency predicted by the baseline sinusoid model (with $\rho_0 = teg_0$), as discussed in Section 3.2. This represents the upper bound on achievable recording sensitivity. The second bracketed terms in Eqs. (3.21) and (3.22) correspond to an additional charge transport inefficiency inherent in more realistic models of photorefractive recording, the subject of this section. This transport inefficiency factor is plotted as a function of increasing transport length in Fig. 3.14 for diffusion-only transport and in Fig. 3.15 for drift-only transport. Recall that these curves apply only during the initial recording interval, before significant space charge has accrued. Later recording will be characterized by a lower transport efficiency because of the presence of the space charge field. Note in Figs. 3.14 and 3.15 that the charge transport efficiency asymptotically approaches its maximum value in the limit of very long transport lengths, as intuitively expected, although even in this limit the maximum recording sensitivity is that of the baseline sinusoid, not that of the transport-efficient sinusoid.

The reason that the recording sensitivity only reaches the baseline sinusoid level in this limit is best understood by considering the spatial modulation profile of the mobile charge density $n(x)$. Analytical expressions for the modulation depth of the mobile charge density can be readily derived from the same analysis that led to Eqs. (3.21) and (3.22) (Young et al., 1974; Moharam et al., 1979), for times sufficiently long compared with the mobile carrier lifetime so that the mobile charge density represents a quasi-steady-state distribution, and also sufficiently short so as to remain in the initial recording regime. In the diffusion-only case, the mobile charge density is

Fig. 3.14.

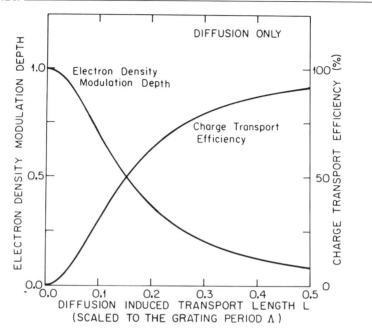

Electron density modulation depth and charge transport efficiency as a function of the diffusion-induced transport length, in the diffusion-only regime.

$$n(x) = \tau g_0 \left[1 + m_e(K_G L_D) \cos\left(\frac{2\pi x}{\Lambda_G}\right) \right],$$ (3.24)

in which τ is the mobile carrier lifetime and in which the modulation depth $m_e(K_G L_D)$ is given by

$$m_e(K_G L_D) = \frac{m}{1 + K_G^2 L_D^2}.$$ (3.25)

Note that this charge distribution has the least efficient possible phase for building up a space charge field. Recall from the discussion in Section 3.2.1 that the optimum phase of the mobile charge profile is a 180° phase shift with respect to the incident illumination profile, allowing the space charge field contribution of the mobile charge after subsequent trapping to add to the contribution of the excess positively charged trap profile produced by the photogeneration process. Here, however, the mobile charge profile is aligned coincident with the illumination and with the excess positively charged

Fig. 3.15.

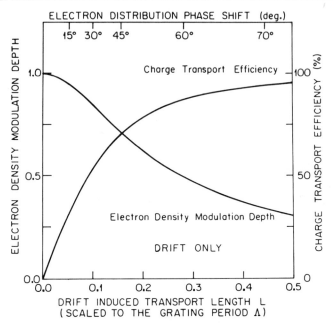

Electron density modulation depth and charge transport efficiency as a function of the drift-induced transport length, in the drift-only regime. The resultant phase shift of the mobile electron distribution is shown at the top of the figure.

trap profiles. As a consequence, when a mobile charge is captured, it removes one of the incremental photogenerated traps, thereby reducing the overall space charge profile. A net space charge field can then accrue in the diffusion-dominated transport case only by partially randomizing the mobile charge distribution, corresponding to a reduction in the modulation depth $m_e(K_G L_D)$. Note in Fig. 3.14 that the rise in charge transport efficiency with increasing transport length $K_G L_D$ is coincident with a reduction of the mobile charge modulation depth, as expected. Optimum charge transport efficiency occurs when the mobile charge profile has been completely randomized, which, according to Eq. (3.25), occurs in the limit $L_D \gg \Lambda_G$.

Similarly, for drift-dominated transport, the mobile charge profile has a modulation depth of

$$m_e(K_G L_E) = \frac{m}{(1 + K_G^2 L_E^2)^{1/2}} \tag{3.26}$$

and a phase shift of ϕ, as given by Eq. (3.23). The charge transport efficiency, mobile charge modulation depth, and phase shift of the mobile charge profile with respect to the incident illumination are plotted in Fig. 3.15 as a function of the transport length $K_G L_E$ for drift-dominated transport, which is in turn proportional to the applied bias field E_0. For short transport lengths, the phase shift is close to $0°$, which as pointed out above is the least efficient phase for building a space charge field, and the modulation depth m_e exhibits its maximum value of m, the modulation depth of the illumination profile. For longer transport lengths, the mobile charge profile phase shifts away from $0°$, but is always less than $90°$, and hence always degrades the net space charge profile. The modulation depth m_e similarly decreases with increasing charge transport length. The most efficient charge transport occurs for very large transport lengths, $K_G L_E$, for which the mobile charge profile has become completely randomized.

The reason that the phase of the mobile charge profile never exceeds a $90°$ phase shift for drift-dominated transport (and that the phase is always $0°$ for diffusion-dominated transport) can perhaps best be appreciated from Fig. 3.13, which shows the mobile charge profile that is generated in response to a narrow slit (i.e., very tightly focused) illumination profile. The profiles shown in Fig. 3.13 can be derived by Fourier decomposing the Dirac delta function of the illumination profile into an equivalent set of spatial harmonics, applying Eqs. (3.25) and (3.26) to find the mobile charge profile in response to each spatial frequency and then performing an inverse Fourier transform. But the profiles shown in Fig. 3.13 are also intuitively reasonable. Diffusion tends to broaden the mobile charge density symmetrically about the location of an illumination region, whereas drift tends to pull the mobile charges to one side. In addition, note that the mobile charge distribution resulting from any arbitrary illumination profile can be derived by convolving the illumination profile with the appropriate distribution shown in Fig. 3.13 (which can be considered to be a blur function). Because of the monotonically decreasing shape of these blur functions, no phase shift in excess of $90°$ is feasible.

Thus we find that the baseline sinusoid model represents an upper bound on the grating recording efficiency predicted by the single mobile charge species/single donor/single trap photorefractive recording model.

3.3.2. Temporal Approach to Steady State

In addition to the charge transport efficiency factor just discussed, two additional factors must be considered when evaluating any realistic recording situation. One factor pertains to the saturation in temporal growth of the space charge field, resulting in a reduced growth rate as the field approaches its steady state limit. The second factor pertains to the modulation depth m of the illumination profile, which is often chosen to be small to enable enhanced recording techniques, as discussed in the next section.

The reduction in sensitivity of the recording process as the space charge field approaches its steady state limit can be assessed from analytic solutions that have been derived by Kukhtarev (1976). Typical solutions are shown in Fig. 3.16 for a variety of bias fields, E_0, scaled to the maximum possible field, E_q, due to limited ionized trap density (discussed in Section 3.2.2). These curves were generated based upon typical charge mobility-lifetime product ($\mu\tau$) parameters for bismuth silicon oxide ($Bi_{12}SiO_{20}$; BSO), as given in Table 3.3. (A bias field to saturation field ratio of 10:1 is unphysical for several photorefractive materials such as bismuth silicon oxide, requiring exceptionally high bias fields and/or spatial frequencies, but is nonetheless included for generality.) Note that in all cases shown the time needed to

Fig. 3.16.

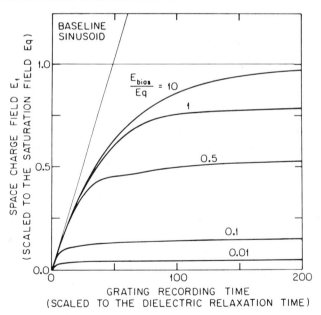

Temporal approach of the first harmonic of the space charge field E_1 to its steady state limit with applied field as a parameter for $Bi_{12}SiO_{20}$, assuming a stationary illumination profile with small modulation depth m.

TABLE 3.3

Material Parameters Assumed in the Calculations

	$Bi_{12}SiO_{20}$	$BaTiO_3$	Units
Mobility-lifetime product $\mu\tau$	15	0.5	$\mu m^2/V$
Trap density N_A	1×10^{16}	2×10^{16}	cm^{-3}
Dielectric constant ϵ	56	168 (ϵ_{33})	
Index of refraction n_0	2.5	2.4	
Electrooptic coefficient r_{ij}	5 (r_{41})	80 (r_{33})	pm/V
$n_0^3 r_{eff}/\epsilon$	1.4	6.8	pm/V

(After Valley and Klein, 1983, and references cited therein)

reach saturation is approximately a factor of two longer than that predicted by the baseline sinusoid idealized transport model.

Due to the fact that the analytical solutions for temporal evolution derived by Kukhtarev (1976) are valid only for small modulation depths m of the illumination profile, such solutions describe low recording efficiency situations in which the majority of the photons in the illumination beam contribute a uniform photocurrent and only a small fraction of the photons convey the spatial structure in the image profile. This point is emphasized in Fig. 3.17, in which numerical solutions of the photorefractive equations are presented, showing the temporal evolution of the first spatial harmonic component of the space charge field for various modulation depths m. These solutions have been produced by the authors using numerical techniques discussed by Moharam et al. (1979) but applied to the full set of photorefractive equations proposed by Kukhtarev (1976).

In Fig. 3.17, a crystal of bismuth silicon oxide illuminated by a 300 cycle/mm sinusoid has been assumed. Note in this figure the slight oscillations that can be observed in the temporal evolution. The strength of these oscillations is directly dependent on the charge mobility-lifetime product, $\mu\tau$; the curves in Fig. 3.17 correspond to the material and configuration parameters as listed in Table 3.3. It should be noted that a wide variation in mobility-lifetime products has been reported, even for crystals with nominally the same composition (Lesaux et al., 1986).

Note also in Fig. 3.17 that the highest space charge fields are associated with the highest illumination profile modulation depths, a regime for which the time-dependent analytical solutions derived by Kukhtarev are no longer applicable. Furthermore, to first order the resultant space charge field E_1, both in the initial recording regime as well as in saturation, is directly proportional to the modulation depth parameter m.

Fig. 3.17. _____

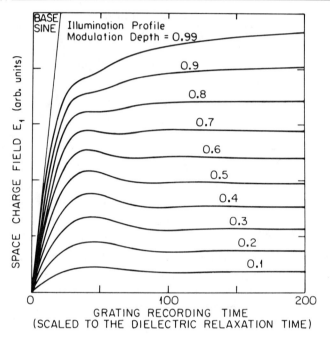

Increase in saturation space charge field with increasing modulation depth for $Bi_{12}SiO_{20}$, showing transition from linear to nonlinear recording regimes.

3.3.3. Enhanced Recording Techniques

The recording configuration just considered assumes a stationary illumination profile and a constant applied bias field (for brevity, hereinafter called the *stationary illumination technique*). Space charge fields with much higher steady state limits can be obtained by either of two alternative nonstationary recording configurations: One technique is to translate the illumination profile with respect to the photorefractive crystal (hereinafter referred to as the *running grating technique*) (Huignard and Marrakchi, 1981; Stepanov et al., 1982; Valley, 1984; Refregier et al., 1985), and the second technique is to periodically reverse the direction of the applied bias field (the *alternating field technique*) (Stepanov and Petrov, 1985). These techniques do not improve the rate at which space charge builds up with time under constant illumination intensity, compared with the stationary illumination/constant field recording configuration.

The running grating technique, in particular, was chosen for study herein, both to illustrate enhanced photorefractive recording concepts and because it is commonly employed to provide significant amplification of weak images. This technique can be studied by a combination of analytical solutions that are valid in the linearized regime of very small modulation depths and by numerical solutions for larger image modulations.

The relative advantage of the running grating technique is summarized in Fig. 3.18, which has been derived from the analytical solutions of Valley (1984) and Refregier et al. (1985) in the limit of small illumination profile modulation depths. A grating spatial frequency of 110 cycles/mm and parameters typical of bismuth silicon oxide have been assumed in the solutions shown in Fig. 3.18. The spatial frequency is chosen to be 110 cycles/mm, rather than 300 cycles/mm, because the enhancement of the steady state space charge field is maximized for this grating frequency, assuming material parameters for $Bi_{12}SiO_{20}$ as given in Table 3.3. Note that the steady state limit of the space charge field is in fact increased by the running grating technique relative to that obtained with a stationary grating, but that the

Fig. 3.18.

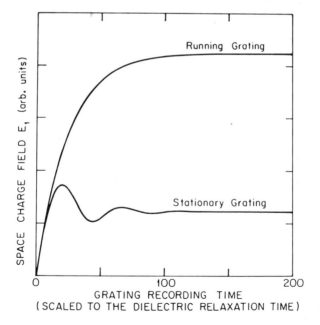

Temporal evolution of the space charge field, comparing the cases of stationary and running gratings for $Bi_{12}SiO_{20}$ in the low modulation limit.

initial recording sensitivities are asymptotically equal. The initial growth of the space charge field continues to be bounded by a combination of quantum limitations and charge transport inefficiencies, as described above. Furthermore, the additional factor of two reduction in sensitivity observed on approach to saturation obtains for both solutions.

The magnitude of the steady state space charge field is necessarily quite small in the linearized regime for which the analytical solutions apply, as the field is proportional to the modulation depth m of the illumination profile, which must be kept small to ensure accurate analytical solutions. Larger space charge fields require larger illumination modulation depths, which in turn result in eventual nonlinear saturation of the space charge field itself. Numerical solutions have been generated by the authors to explore the onset of this field saturation, with typical results as shown in Fig. 3.19, again assuming the nominal $Bi_{12}SiO_{20}$ material parameters listed in Table 3.3. Note that the saturation of the steady state field occurs at quite modest values of the modulation depth, which is consistent with the experimental observations reported by Refregier et al. (1985). Thus the running grating technique proves to be most effective for amplifying weak images, but not for recording large space charge fields. For recording the largest fields, stationary illumination is preferred.

Fig. 3.19.

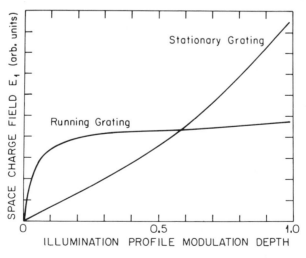

Steady state space charge field as a function of modulation depth for $Bi_{12}SiO_{20}$, comparing the cases of stationary and running gratings.

4.
Representative Grating Recording Efficiency Calculations

In order to illustrate the above concepts, we proceed in this section to consider the several factors that contribute to the overall grating recording efficiency for two different types of materials and for two different types of applications. The materials considered are bismuth silicon oxide ($Bi_{12}SiO_{20}$, or BSO) and barium titanate ($BaTiO_3$); the principal material parameters assumed in the estimates are listed in Table 3.3, based upon a set of values utilized in previous related analyses by Valley and Klein (1983). The two applications considered are those of reconfigurable holographic interconnections and the amplification of weak images.

Let us first consider a reconfigurable holographic interconnection implemented in bismuth silicon oxide. For simplicity, we assume that only one grating with a spatial frequency of 300 cycles/mm is recorded in the crystal. To achieve maximum diffraction efficiency, the modulation depth of the recording beams should be as large as possible; ideally, $m = 1$. Also, a bias electric field is typically applied to crystals of $Bi_{12}SiO_{20}$ to enhance the photosensitivity; a field of 6 kV/cm is typical, implying a drift transport length L_E from Eq. (3.18) of 9 μm, assuming the mobility-lifetime product given in Table 3.3. For a 300 cycle/mm grating frequency, this implies an (L_E/Λ_G) ratio of about 2.7, and from Fig. 3.15 we see that this corresponds to essentially 100% charge transport efficiency in the initial stages of recording.

The recording efficiency for a $Bi_{12}SiO_{20}$ interconnect, compared with the ideal (i.e., bipolar comb) quantum efficiency limit, is listed in Table 3.4. Three factors are considered in this and subsequent tables. The first is the

TABLE 3.4

Representative Grating Recording Efficiency Calculation: Reconfigurable Interconnection Drift Recording in Bismuth Silicon Oxide

Modulation depth = 1.0	
300 cycles/mm grating frequency	
Space charge efficiency factors:	
Baseline sinusoid/bipolar comb	0.25
Charge transport (to saturation)	0.5
Modulation depth factor	1.0
Grating recording efficiency	0.125
Diffraction efficiency derating factor	0.016

25% efficiency factor that applies between the baseline sinusoid and bipolar comb cases, a factor that is common to all recording configurations considered in this section. The second factor is the charge transport efficiency, comparing actual recording performance to that of the baseline sinusoid case. The $Bi_{12}SiO_{20}$ interconnect is assigned a 50% charge transport efficiency to account for the factor of two increase in recording energy (photon flux) estimated to reach saturation, as shown in Fig. 3.16 and as discussed in Section 3.3.2. The final factor is the modulation depth, which we have assumed to be unity for a reconfigurable interconnect. Thus the total grating recording efficiency, in terms of the magnitude of the space charge field generated per unit photon flux, compared with ideal quantum efficient recording, is only about 12.5% for a $Bi_{12}SiO_{20}$ interconnection. This gives a diffraction efficiency derating factor of only 1.6% (assuming a diffraction efficiency that is proportional to the square of the space charge field).

As a second example, consider image amplification in $Bi_{12}SiO_{20}$ using a running grating enhanced recording technique. We will again assume a 110 cycle/mm grating spatial frequency (see Section 3.3.3) and a bias field of 6 kV/cm applied to the $Bi_{12}SiO_{20}$ crystal. However, the modulation depth must be reduced from 100% to approximately 10% to achieve the peak space charge enhancement in saturation provided by the running grating recording technique, as shown in Fig. 3.19 and as discussed in Section 3.3.3. For our calculations, we chose a modulation depth equal to 10%, implying a corresponding reduction in the quantum efficiency of the recording process; i.e., most of the photons must supply the pump beam, with comparatively few photons in the signal beam containing signal information. Thus the total quantum efficiency for image amplification, shown in Table 3.5, is an order of magnitude lower than that given in Table 3.4 for the reconfigurable in-

TABLE 3.5

Representative Grating Recording Efficiency Calculation: Two-Wave Image Amplification
Running Gratings in Bismuth Silicon Oxide

Modulation depth = 0.1	
110 cycles/mm grating frequency	
Space charge efficiency factors:	
Baseline sinusoid/bipolar comb	0.25
Charge transport (to saturation)	0.5
Modulation depth factor	0.1
Grating recording efficiency	0.0125
Diffraction efficiency derating factor	0.00016

terconnection. Correspondingly, the diffraction efficiency derating factor is two orders of magnitude lower for this case than for the case of the reconfigurable interconnection and nearly four orders of magnitude less efficient than the absolute quantum limitation.

As a final example, consider a reconfigurable interconnection in barium titanate, with grating recording efficiency as shown in Table 3.6 for the case of recording by diffusion transport only. Because of the large electrooptic coefficient in barium titanate, only very modest space charge fields, typically a fraction of the diffusion field for a 300 cycle/mm grating, are needed to achieve peak diffraction efficiencies in crystals of reasonable size. Hence diffusion transport often proves to be sufficient in this material in order to generate experimentally useful diffraction efficiencies. Unfortunately, two factors work against the high electrooptic coefficient in barium titanate. One is the concomitantly high dielectric constant, which from Maxwell's first equation implies that a considerable amount of space charge must be moved to achieve a modest space charge field. As mentioned in the introduction, the combined material parameter $(n_0^3 r_{eff}/\epsilon)$, which is a measure of the amount of optical index modulation per unit space charge, proves to be surprisingly constant from material to material (Glass et al., 1984; Glass, 1984). Based upon this measure alone, barium titanate proves to be modestly superior to bismuth silicon oxide, as shown in Table 3.3.

The second, and far more serious, factor degrading grating recording efficiency for diffusion recording in barium titanate is its low mobility-lifetime product $\mu\tau$, which is almost two orders of magnitude lower than that for bismuth silicon oxide, implying a significantly degraded charge transport efficiency. The diffusion transport length L_D predicted by Eq. (3.19) is of order 35 nm, based upon the mobility-lifetime product $\mu\tau$ given in Table

TABLE 3.6

Representative Grating Recording Efficiency Calculation: Reconfigurable Interconnect Diffusion Recording in Barium Titanate

Modulation depth = 1.0	
300 cycles/mm grating frequency	
Space charge efficiency factors:	
Baseline sinusoid/bipolar comb	0.25
Charge transport (to saturation)	0.002
Modulation depth factor	1.0
Grating recording efficiency	0.0005
Diffraction efficiency derating factor	2.5×10^{-7}

3.3. Assuming a 300 cycle/mm grating, this implies by Eq. (3.21) a charge transport efficiency factor of order 0.004. We include an additional factor of 0.5 in Table 3.6 to account for the additional photon flux required to reach saturation, as indicated in Fig. 3.16 and by the discussion in Section 3.3.2. Thus we find that the grating recording efficiency for diffusion recording in barium titanate is some 250 times less than that for drift recording in bismuth silicon oxide, in terms of space charge generated per unit incident photon.

Thus we have considered representative examples of several different materials, transport mechanisms and efficiencies, and recording applications. We find that, even in the most efficient grating recording configurations, a significant inefficiency still exists between the absolute quantum limits and actual performance.

5.
Conclusions

In this chapter, we have considered a number of the fundamental physical limitations that constrain the potential performance of photorefractive materials. In particular, we have described several idealized photogeneration and charge transport models in terms of the grating recording efficiency, and we have identified one such model (the bipolar comb) as the absolute quantum limit against which other such models may be compared. The bipolar comb model generates the maximum possible fundamental harmonic of the space charge field at unity dielectric constant for a given number of photoexcited mobile charge carriers. A second idealized model, the baseline sinusoid, provides an upper bound for the grating recording efficiency of a more realistic photorefractive grating recording model involving a single mobile charge carrier and a single donor/single trap photorefractive center. This upper bound was shown to be a factor of four less efficient in generating a given space charge field than the quantum limitations imply for an optimum photogeneration distribution and perfectly efficient charge transport. An additional factor of two accrues from the nonlinearity of the grating recording process observed as the space charge field nears saturation. The combination of absorption and reflection losses in typical photorefractive recording configurations (without antireflection coatings) contributes approximately one order of magnitude to the inefficiency of grating recording and readout relative to the incident photon flux. Hence, the usual photorefractive recording configuration exhibits an overall sensitivity that is approximately two orders of magnitude less than that achievable in the quantum limit. This results in roughly four orders of magnitude reduction in the corresponding diffraction efficiency per incident photon. These considerations explain to a certain degree why photorefractive recording has proven to be relatively insensitive as compared with distinct but related mechanisms of spatial light modulation.

Perhaps far more important, however, are the implications of the above analysis for the conceptual design and technological implementation of optimized grating recording media that operate far closer to the quantum limits. For example, the bipolar comb illumination profile is not necessarily as unphysical as it may at first seem, and it can be closely approximated by the utilization of stratified volume holographic optical elements (Johnson and Tanguay, 1988) for beam formation. This approach is perhaps most appropriate for the generation of a grating of given spatial frequency, as in the photorefractive incoherent-to-coherent optical converter (Marrakchi et al., 1985). As a second example, the factor of two inherent in the approach to saturation can be avoided by seeking photorefractive materials of near unity charge transport efficiency and high electrooptic figures of merit, such that experimentally suitable diffraction efficiencies can be obtained well within the linear recording regime. As a final example, the inefficiency implied by surface reflection losses can be dramatically reduced, even over the broad spectrum of angles and wavelengths characteristic of photorefractive recording, by the design and incorporation of appropriate antireflection coatings (Karim et al., 1988).

Acknowledgments

This research was supported in part by the Defense Advanced Research Projects Agency (through the Office of Naval Research and the Air Force Office of Scientific Research), the Air Force Office of Scientific Research, the Army Research Office, and the Joint Services Electronics Program.

References

Amodei, J.J. (1971). "Analysis of transport processes during holographic recording in insulators," *RCA Review* **32,** 185–198.
Amodei, J.J., and Staebler, D.L. (1972). "Holographic recording in lithium niobate," *RCA Review* **33,** 71–93.

Attard, A.E., and Brown, T.X. (1986). "Experimental observations of trapping levels in BSO," *Appl. Opt.* **25**(18), 3253–3259.

Chemla, D.S., Miller, D.A.B., and Smith, P.W. (1985). "Nonlinear optical properties of GaAs-GaAlAs multiple quantum well material: Phenomena and applications," *Opt. Eng.* **24**(4), 556–564.

Feinberg, J., Heiman, D., Tanguay, A.R. Jr., and Hellwarth, R.W. (1980). "Photorefractive effects and light-induced charge migration in barium titanate," *J. Appl. Phys.* **51**(3), 1297–1305.

Glass, A.M. (1978). "The photorefractive effect," *Opt. Eng.* **17**(5), 470–479.

Glass, A.M. (1984). "Materials for optical information processing," *Science* **226**, 657–662.

Glass, A.M., Johnson, A.M., Olson, D.H., Simpson, W., and Ballman, A.A. (1984). "Four-wave mixing in semi-insulating InP and GaAs using the photorefractive effect," *Appl. Phys. Lett.* **44**(10), 948–950.

Glass, A.M., Klein, M.B., and Valley, G.C. (1987). "Fundamental limit of the speed of photorefractive effect and its impact on device applications and material research: Comment," *Appl. Opt.* **26**(16), 3189–3190.

Gunter, P. (1982). "Holography, coherent light amplification, and optical phase conjugation with photorefractive materials," *Phys. Rep.* **93**, 199–299.

Hou, S.L., Lauer, R.B., and Aldrich, R.E. (1973). "Transport processes of photoinduced carriers in $Bi_{12}SiO_{20}$," *J. Appl. Phys.* **44**(6), 2652–2658.

Huignard, J.P., and Marrakchi, A. (1981). "Coherent signal beam amplification in two-wave mixing experiments with photorefractive $Bi_{12}SiO_{20}$ crystals," *Opt. Commun.* **38**(4), 249–254.

Huignard, J.P., and Micheron, F. (1976). "High-sensitivity read-write volume holographic storage in $Bi_{12}SiO_{20}$ and $Bi_{12}GeO_{20}$ crystals," *Appl. Phys. Lett.* **29**(9), 591–593.

Jaura, R., Hall, T.J., and Foote, P.D. (1986). "Simplified band transport model of the photorefractive effect," *Opt. Eng.* **25**(9), 1068–1074.

Johnson, R.V., and Tanguay, A.R. Jr. (1988). "Stratified volume holographic optical elements," *Opt. Lett.* **13**(3), 189–191.

Kaminow, I.P. (1974). "An Introduction to Electrooptic Devices," Academic Press, New York.

Kamshilin, A.A., and Petrov, M.P. (1980). "Holographic image conversion in a $Bi_{12}SiO_{20}$ crystal," *Sov. Tech. Phys. Lett.* **6**(3), 144–145.

Karim, Z., Garrett, M.H., and Tanguay, A.R. Jr. (1988). "A bandpass AR coating design for bismuth silicon oxide," *Tech. Digest* 1988 Annual Meeting of the Optical Society of America, Santa Clara, California.

Kogelnik, H. (1969). "Coupled wave theory for thick hologram gratings," *Bell Syst. Tech. J.* **48**(9), 2909–2947.

Kukhtarev, N.V. (1976). "Kinetics of hologram recording and erasure in electrooptic crystals," *Sov. Tech. Phys. Lett.* **2**(12), 438–440.

Kukhtarev, N.V., Markov, V.B., Odulov, S.G., Soskin, M.S., and Vinetskii, V.L. (1979). "Holographic storage in electrooptic crystals," *Ferroelectrics* **22,** 949–964.

Lesaux, G., Launay, J.C., and Brun, A. (1986). "Transient photocurrent induced by nanosecond light pulses in BSO and BGO," *Opt. Commun.* **57**(3), 166–170.

von der Linde, D., and Glass, A.M. (1975). "Photorefractive effects for reversible holographic storage of information," *Appl. Phys.* **8,** 85–100.

Marrakchi, A., Johnson, R.V., and Tanguay, A.R. Jr., (1987). "Polarization properties of enhanced self-diffraction in sillenite crystals," *IEEE J. Quantum Electron.* **QE-23**(12), 2142–2151.

Marrakchi, A., Tanguay, A.R. Jr., Yu, J., and Psaltis, D. (1985). "Physical characterization of the photorefractive incoherent-to-coherent optical converter," *Opt. Eng.* **24**(1), 124–131.

Micheron, F. (1978). "Sensitivity of the photorefractive process," *Ferroelectrics* **18,** 153–159.

Moharam, M.G., Gaylord, T.K., Magnusson, R., and Young, L. (1979). "Holographic grating formation in photorefractive crystals with arbitrary electron transport lengths," *J. Appl. Phys.* **50**(9), 5642–5651.

Orlowski, R., and Kratzig, E. (1978). "Holographic method for the determination of photo-induced electron and hole transport in electro-optic crystals," *Solid State Comm.* **27**(12), 1351–1354.

Peltier, M., and Micheron, F. (1977). "Volume hologram recording and charge transfer process in $Bi_{12}SiO_{20}$ and $Bi_{12}GeO_{20}$," *J. Appl. Phys.* **48**(9), 3683–3690.

Refregier, Ph., Solymar, L., Rajbenbach, H., and Huignard, J.P. (1985). "Two-beam coupling in photorefractive $Bi_{12}SiO_{20}$ crystals with moving grating: Theory and experiments," *J. Appl. Phys.* **58**(1), 45–57.

Shi, Y., Psaltis, D., Marrakchi, A., and Tanguay, A.R. Jr. (1983). "Photorefractive incoherent-to-coherent optical converter," *Appl. Opt.* **22**(23), 3665–3667.

Stepanov, S.I. and Petrov, M.P. (1985). "Efficient unstationary holographic recording in photorefractive crystals under an external alternating electric field," *Opt. Commun.* **53**(5), 292–295.

Stepanov, S.I., Kulikov, V.V., and Petrov, M.P. (1982). "Running holograms in photorefractive $Bi_{12}SiO_{20}$ crystals," *Opt. Commun.* **44**(1), 19–23.

Strohkendl, F.P., Jonathan, J.M.C., and Hellwarth, R.W. (1986). "Hole-electron competition in photorefractive gratings," *Opt. Lett.* **11**(5), 312–314.

Tanguay, A.R. Jr. (1985). "Materials requirements for optical processing and computing devices," *Opt. Eng.* **24**(1), 2–18.

Valley, G.C. (1984). "Two-wave mixing with an applied field and a moving grating," *J. Opt. Soc. Am. B* **1**(6), 868–873.

Valley, G.C. (1986). "Simultaneous electron/hole transport in photorefractive materials," *J. Appl. Phys.* **59**(10), 3363–3366.

Valley, G.C., and Klein, M.B. (1983). "Optimal properties of photorefractive materials for optical data processing," *Opt. Eng.* **22**(6), 704–711.

Yeh, P. (1987). "Fundamental limit of the speed of photorefractive effect and its impact on device applications and material research," *Appl. Opt.* **26**(4), 602–604.

Yeh, P. (1987). "Fundamental limit of the speed of photorefractive effect and its impact on device applications and material research: Author's reply to comment," *Appl. Opt.* **26**(16), 3190–3191.

Young, L., Wong, W.K.Y., Thewalt, M.L.W., and Cornish, W.D. (1974). "Theory of formation of phase holograms in lithium niobate," *Appl. Phys. Lett.* **24**(6), 264–265.

4.

Biopolymers for Real-Time Optical Processing

Vladimir Yu. Bazhenov, Marat S. Soskin
Victor B. Taranenko, and Mikhail V. Vasnetsov

Institute of Physics, Academy of Sciences of the Ukrainian SSR
Kiev, USSR

Contents

1. Introduction. 103
2. Sensitized Gelatin 105
    2.1   Real-Time Holography. 106
    2.2   Nonlinear Planar Waveguides 111
3. Materials Based on Bacteriorhodopsin. 118
    3.1   Biochrom Films 121
    3.2   Purple Membrane Suspensions 133
4. Conclusion 139
    Acknowledgements 140
    References 141

1.

Introduction

In the field of real-time optical processing of information based on the principles of nonlinear optics and holography (e.g., image processing, switching, logic, phase conjugation), a key role belongs to recording materials, and each application requires its own specialized class of materials (Auston et al., 1987). There are certain properties of biopolymers that make them attractive materials for real-time optical processing. Biopolymer photoresponses may include mechanisms that are either reversible or nonreversible in character. The photoresponse of some biopolymers arise from cooperative rather than from intrinsic intramolecular reaction to light. There is a very high degree of flexibility in the fabrication of biopolymer materials. They can be formed as bulk materials, as films, as waveguides, etc.

The interest in biopolymers and biomolecules has grown during the past several years due mainly to an extremely attractive proposal to create, on their basis, devices capable of performing functions of some computer elements and having extraordinarily small dimensions measured in nanometers (the dimensions of molecules). This new and exciting field of investigation has been called bioelectronics or molecular electronics (e.g., Robinson, 1983; Carter, 1984; Davydov, 1986). Research in this field is in the early stage of development and for the present far from the practical realization of potential biological systems. Nevertheless investigations of the simplest processors and of memory elements based on biopolymers are being intensively developed in many laboratories all over the world.

It has been well known for over 100 years that certain biological colloids such as gelatin, egg albumen, fish glue, casein, and other materials sensitized by dichromates become photosensitive (Kozar, 1865). The best results from a practical point of view were obtained with dichromated gelatin, which was successfully used for permanent optical information storage. During the last few years, dichromated gelatin has been used as a recording material for real-time optical processing operations like image subtraction, edge enhancement, image recognition, etc. (e.g., Calixto and Lessard, 1984). This has stimulated investigations on the mechanisms of real-time recording in dichromated gelatin films (e.g., Bazhenov et al., 1982a; Newell et al., 1985). Other sensitizers of gelatin films have been utilized, which gave more stable real-time characteristics (Gladden, 1980; Bazhenov et al. 1986a) and made them sensitive to the state of polarization of the recording beam (Kakichashvili and Shaverdova, 1967; Calixto et al. 1985). The very high thermal nonlinearity of gelatin film gave the possibility of creating effective nonlinear waveguides, by means of which optical bistability and spatial hysteresis have been realized (Bazhenov et al., 1986b, 1986c).

Among the reversible photochemically sensitive biopolymers suitable for real-time processing, the most investigated are chlorophyll-protein (Shuvalov, 1985) and retinal-protein (Vsevolodov, 1985) complexes. The chlorophyll-protein complexes are responsible for the photosynthesis in plants, whilst the retinal-protein complexes provide the photoreception in animals as well as the photosynthesis in some microorganisms. Bacteriorhodopsin, (Stoeck-enius et al., 1979), which belongs to the retinal-protein complex, is very promising as a recording material for real-time processing. Depending on the preparation procedure, these materials have a very wide range of pho-toresponse time from 100 sec down to 10 psec, and an extremely high spatial resolution limited by the dimensions of the molecules. Moreover, they are sensitive to the state of polarization of the recording light, due to photoin-duced anisotropy, and are effectively controlled by means of an external influence such as an electric field, temperature, etc.

It is the purpose of this chapter to review the work devoted to sensitized gelatin (Section 2) and materials based on bacteriorhodopsin (Section 3), to describe the properties and the mechanisms of their photoresponses, and to give some demonstrations of their applications for the real-time optical pro-cessing of information.

2.
Sensitized Gelatin

Gelatin is obtained from collagen, a protein contained in animal tissue and bones. By means of digestion in hot water, the collagen molecules are bro-ken into polypeptide chains of the amino acids that constitute gelatin. A sensitizer such as ammonium dichromate dispersed in the gelatin matrix acts to form a crosslink bond between the carboxylate groups of neighboring gelatin chains after exposure by actinic light in the blue spectral range (Mey-erhofer, 1977). This bond gives rigidity to the gelatin. In the initial stage of dichromated gelatin (DCG) investigations, the difference in the solubility of the exposed (hardened) and unexposed areas of film was used for optical information recording in the form of relief images in photographic and print-ing applications. Later Shankoff (1968) proposed the use of chemically pre-hardened DCG film with a thickness of 5–20 μm as a holographic material for optical information processing. According to this method, the exposed DCG film is treated in two liquids: water and isopropyl alcohol. This method generated a great interest in the recording and the permament storage of optical information as well as in the fabrication of holographic optical ele-ments (e.g., Chang and Leonard, 1979; Soskin and Taranenko, 1984) due to the high diffraction efficiency and signal-to-noise ratio of the material.

Calixto and Lessard (1984) have used undeveloped DCG film for the pur-poses of real-time optical processing operations like image subtraction, edge enhancement, and image recognition. More stable and reproducible results were obtained on gelatin film sensitized by bis azido compounds (Gladden, 1980; Bazhenov et al., 1986a). Then it was shown (Kakichashvili and Shaverdova, 1967; Calixto et al., 1985) that gelatin film sensitized by a mixture of dichromate and malachite green dye became sensitive to the polarization of a recording beam due to photoinduced anisotropy. Finally, a reversible thermo-optical recording in a gelatin nonlinear waveguide was used (Bazhenov et al., 1986b, 1986c) for the realization of optical bistability and spatial hysteresis.

2.1. Real-time Holography

It is well known that undeveloped DCG film has a photochromic effect, that is, the film changes color under illumination by actinic light. As mentioned above, this effect has been applied for real-time holographic recording (Fig. 4.1). The reason for the DCG film color change is a photoinduced chemical reaction, which, however, sometimes contains a dark reaction stage essentially dependent on the relative humidity of the surrounding atmosphere. Moreover, for a high water content in DCG film the photochromic process is accompanied by a change of the gelatin network structure. Let us consider the influence of these factors on the real-time properties of gelatin films sensitized by ammonium dichromate or by bis azido compounds.

2.1.1. Dichromated Gelatin

In the initial state, a DCG film contains hexavalent chromium ions Cr^{6+}, which are reduced to some lower ionization state after absorption of light

Fig. 4.1. ──

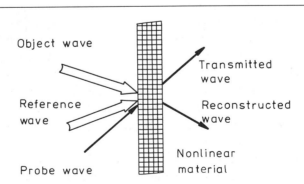

Diagram for real-time holographic recording.

in the blue band. The details of the photoinduced chemical processes taking place in DCG film during exposure are poorly understood. Nevertheless, it is well known that in the final stage chromium ions are trivalent Cr^{3+}, which are thought to form crosslink bonds between neighboring gelatin chains (Meyerhofer, 1972). Under illumination by actinic light a change of the DCG film absorption band takes place (e.g., Bazhenov et al., 1982b), leading to a change in the absorption coefficient $\Delta\kappa$ and is accompanied by a change of the refractive index Δn. This means that in a holographic experiment (Fig. 4.1), a mixing-type hologram is recorded that has a complex transmittance

$$T(x) = \exp(-A) \exp\left[(A + i\Phi) \cos\left(\frac{2\pi x}{\Lambda}\right) \right], \qquad (4.1)$$

where $A = (\pi/\lambda) \Delta\kappa\, h$, $\Phi = (\pi/\lambda) \Delta n h$, h is the DCG film thickness, λ is the wavelength of light in a vacuum, Λ is the grating spacing, and x is the axis in the direction of modulation.

To determine the dependence of the magnitude and sign of the ratio Φ/A on the water content in DCG film, a self-imaging method was used (Bazhenov et al., 1982a, 1983). The distance between the holographic grating and the first self-imaging plane Z_1 is determined by the ratio Φ/A according to the formula

$$Z_1 = \left(\frac{\Lambda^2}{\lambda}\right)\left[1 + \left(\frac{1}{\pi}\right) \operatorname{arctg}\left(\frac{-\Phi}{A}\right) \right]. \qquad (4.2)$$

The experimental dependence of the normalized distance $\bar{Z}_1 = Z_1 \lambda/\Lambda^2$ on the water content in DCG film W is shown in Fig. 4.2a. From this figure and in accordance with Eq. (4.2) it can be inferred that at $W = 0$ (dehydrated film) the sign of the ratio Φ/A is dependent on the wavelength of the probe beam: $\Phi/A > 0$ for a wavelength of 633 nm (He-Ne laser) and $\Phi/A < 0$ for a wavelength of 442 nm (He-Cd laser). Taking into consideration that after exposure the absorption coefficient of DCG film increased practically in the whole visible spectrum (Bazhenov et al., 1982b), this means that $\Delta n > 0$ at 633 nm and $\Delta n < 0$ at 442 nm.

The estimation of Δn has been made using experimental data about dehydrated DCG film absorption spectrum changes during exposure. The initial film absorption spectrum was approximated by two Lorentz bands with a maximum at 270 nm and at 360 nm, respectively. The absorption spectrum of the exposed film was represented by the sum of the nonreacted sensitizer band and the photoproduced one (Fig. 4.3). The calculations carried out by

Fig. 4.2.

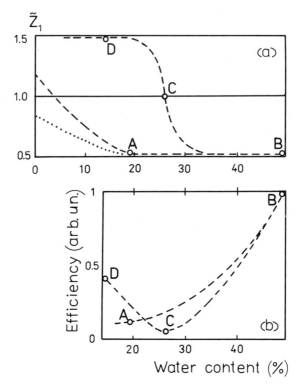

Normalized distance between a holographic grating in DCG film and the first self-imaging plane (a), and the diffraction efficiency of this grating (b) as functions of water content in the DCG film. The probe beam wavelengths are 442 nm (. . .) and 633 nm (---).

Bazhenov et al. (1982a) showed that $\Delta n = 0$ (pure absorption-type grating) for $\lambda = 500$ nm independently of the quantity of photoreacted sensitizer. Then $\Delta n < 0$ for $\lambda < 500$ nm and, vice versa, $\Delta n > 0$ for $\lambda > 500$ nm, which corresponds to the data of the self-imaging experiment for $W = 0$ (Fig. 4.2a). Thus in dehydrated DCG film, a mixture-type hologram is recorded having a photochromic origin.

For dehydrated DCG film the time dependence of the diffraction efficiency was measured using a configuration for real-time processing (Fig. 4.1). The recording beams had a wavelength of 488 nm (argon-ion laser), and the probe beam had a wavelength of 633 nm (He-Ne laser). The result of the measurement is shown in Fig. 4.4, curve $W = 0$. It is necessary to

Fig. 4.3.

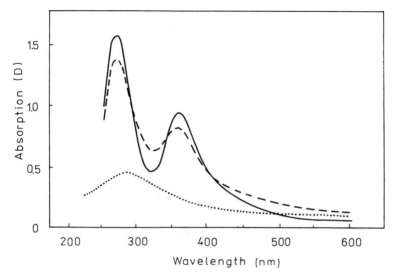

Absorption bands of unexposed (——) and exposed (---) DCG film as well as of photochemical product (. . .).

Fig. 4.4.

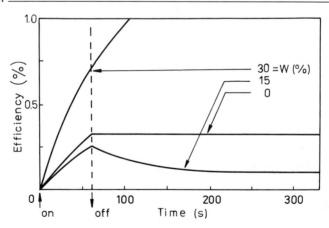

Diffraction efficiency of a holographic grating in a DCG film at 633 nm versus time, for different water contents W in film. Recording beams are turned on (↑) and turned off (↓).

underline that in this case the diffraction efficiency of the grating remains constant after turning off the recording beams. Consequently in a dehydrated DCG film, the dark reaction processes are practically absent.

When W is increased up to approximately 15%, the grating becomes of pure phase type (Fig. 4.2a, point A). For these conditions, the diffraction efficiency of the grating decreases after turning off the recording beams (Fig. 4.4, curve $W = 15\%$). This means that dark reaction processes begin. In this case the real-time properties of DCG film are determined by several simultaneous processes: The film absorption band changes due to the dark chemical reactions, the water content decreases in exposed areas because water is expended in chemical reactions, and the water content increases in exposed areas due to water absorption from the surrounding atmosphere and from unexposed areas.

A further increase of W brings about the appearance of processes similar to those that take place when exposed DCG film is washed in water. The chemical reactions are stopped and crosslink bonds are formed. Simultaneously the gelatin film swells due to the high concentration of water. Therefore, after turning off the recording beams, the diffraction efficiency of the grating continues to rise with the same speed as under exposure (Fig. 4.4, curve $W = 30\%$). In this case it is necessary to take into account the change of the film thickness Δh because of the spatially periodic swelling of the gelatin film, which gives rise to the phase modulation

$$\Phi = \left(\frac{\pi}{\lambda}\right)[\Delta nh + \Delta h(n - 1)]. \tag{4.3}$$

As for the diffraction efficiency dependence on W, it increases smoothly (Fig. 4.2b, A $\rightarrow$ B) provided that W is increased, whereas it has quite different behavior when the DCG film is dehydrated, that is, when W falls (Fig. 4.2b, B $\rightarrow$ C $\rightarrow$ D). It is then interesting to see that the grating remained of the phase type with $\Delta n < 0$ independently of the probe-beam wavelength when W was increased (Fig. 4.2a, A $\rightarrow$ B), but the modulation amplitude Δn proved to change its sign when the film was dehydrated (Fig. 4.2a, B $\rightarrow$ D). At first sight this is rather surprising. However, more detailed measurement (Bazhenov et al., 1983) showed that after the first cycle A $\rightarrow$ B $\rightarrow$ C $\rightarrow$ D (Fig. 4.2) an irreversible change in the bulk structure of the gelatin network took place: Just after exposure (Fig. 4.2, point A) the film surface was plane, whereas at the end of the cycle (Fig. 4.2, point D) the relief had appeared, with the film thickness reaching its maximum in the exposed areas. All further cycles D $\rightarrow$ C $\rightarrow$ B $\rightarrow$ C $\rightarrow$ D are reversible.

2.1.2. Gelatin with Bis Azido Compounds

Real-time recording in gelatin with bis azido compounds (BAC) was performed by Bazhenov et al. (1986a) using a water-soluble salt of 4,4'-bis azido stilbene-2,2'-disulfonic acid. Under exposure by actinic light, the aromatic group (ArN_3) of the compound is disintegrated, with the formation of a free biradical nitrene (ArN:) and nitrogen molecule (N_2). Biradical nitrene in the singlet state is able to react with active groups of gelatin in the following way

$$ArN_3 \xrightarrow{h\nu} ArN: + N_2,$$

$$ArN: + H-C\equiv \rightarrow Ar(NH)-C\equiv.$$

Nitrene in the triplet state can react in another way, but the final chemical product is the same.

After the absorption of two light quanta, a bisazido compound can form from a crosslink bond between neighboring gelatin chains. The lifetimes of both states are very short: 10^{-9} sec for the singlet state and 10^{-4} sec for the triplet. The hardening of gelatin therefore takes place practically without any change of the gelatine structure. Moreover, the same reasoning leads to the absence of the dark chemical reactions.

As for DCG film, photoinduced chemical reactions give rise to a change of the BAC film optical absorption and refractive index, which allow the grating to be tested during its recording. The dependence on time of the diffraction efficiency tested at a wavelength of 633 nm using a He-Ne laser, for a BAC film exposed at a wavelength of 325 nm using a He-Cd laser, is shown in Fig. 4.5. As expected, the diffraction efficiency of the grating remained practically constant after turning off the recording beams. Measurements of the exposed BAC film surface with a high-resolution interferometer showed that it remained practically plane, even if the film was treated in water and then dried.

2.2. Nonlinear Planar Waveguides

Nonlinear waveguides (Stegeman, 1982) can be widely used in optical processing systems as bistable and logic elements (Abraham and Smith, 1982). Theoretical analysis (Bosacchi and Narducci, 1983; Vincent et al., 1985; Montemayor and Deck, 1985, 1986) has shown the advantages of nonlinear planar waveguides achieving a one-dimensional spatial compression of the incident beam (10^2–10^3), leading to a proper increase of light intensity in the waveguide and an increase of the nonlinear phase shift due to the longitudinal light propagation in the waveguide layer.

Fig. 4.5.

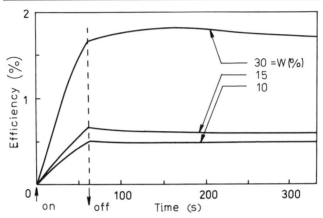

The same as in Fig. 4.4 for a holographic grating in BAC.

Using the method described by Brandes et al. (1969), it is possible to produce a high optical quality gelatin layer that can be used as a waveguide. Moreover, the thermal nonlinearity of the gelatin layer proves to be -5×10^{-4} degrees^{-1} and is closer to that of a liquid than to that of a solid. A nonlinear waveguide can therefore be produced on the basis of a gelatin layer, and self-action can be accomplished using available CW lasers.

Let us consider a nonlinear waveguide with one-sided leakage (Fig. 4.6). When the incident beam excites the waveguide modes, the beam reflected from the waveguide undergoes a change of amplitude, phase, and polarization. This transformation of the reflected beam is determined by the interference of the unperturbed and of the leaky waves (Fig. 4.6). If the leakage is strong enough, the guided wave has a short propagation length in comparison with the transverse size of the incident beam, and the beams therefore overlap well. The amplitude and the phase of the guided wave and hence of the reflected beam depend on detuning from the waveguide resonance. When the waveguide layer has optical nonlinearity, it causes self-consistent changes of the guided wave resonance conditions, thus giving rise to different self-action effects.

2.2.1. Optical Bistability

Bazhenov et al. (1986b) formed a gelatin layer having a thickness of 5 μm and an absorption of 1.5 cm^{-1} (due to layer saturation by an optically firm

Fig. 4.6. _____

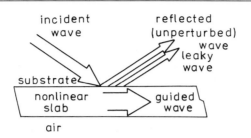

Light waves in a planar waveguide with one-sided leakage.

dye) on a prism substrate, which ensured strong optical coupling with the gelatin waveguide. The zero-order TM waveguide mode was excited by an unfocused beam from an argon-ion laser with a wavelength of 488 nm. The incident beam angular detuning from the waveguide resonance was varied over a range of several milliradians.

Measurements have demonstrated three self-action regimes depending on the angular detuning from the wavelength resonance (Fig. 4.7). It is interesting that when proper experimental conditions for optical bistability are fulfilled, and the nonlinear waveguide is switched into the second stationary state, a small dark spot appears on the reflected beam cross section, which is then transformed into an asymmetric dark ring (Fig. 4.8). The area of this ring is rather small, and the contrast of the averaged switching characteristic is therefore not high (Fig. 4.7, curve 3). Such a transformation of the beam transversal profile indicates that the switching wave appears and propagates in the nonlinear planar waveguide. This switching wave possesses considerable spatial asymmetry in comparison with one observed in a nonlinear Fabry-Perot cavity (e.g., Apanasevich et al., 1985).

A theoretical analysis of the nonlinear planar waveguide with thermal nonlinearity has shown that the transmission of thermal perturbation into the neighboring regions of the layer is done by means of isotropic thermoconductivity and unidirectional propagation of the light through the layer. The simultaneous action of these two processes gives rise to the asymmetry of the switching wave profile.

2.2.2. Spatial Hysteresis

The switching wave propagation depends on the light intensity distribution in the waveguide layer and therefore can be controlled by changing the in-

Fig. 4.7.

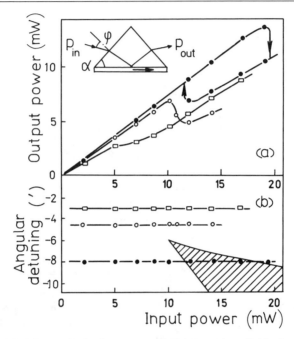

Steady-state response (output power vs. input power) available for nonlinear planar waveguide: reflected beam power stabilization (□), differential amplification (o), and optical bistability (●). In (b) the set of experimental parameters is presented. (The bistability region is shaded.)

cident beam intensity profile. In an experiment conducted by Bazhenov et al. (1986c), a shadow region (0.15 mm) on the illuminated part of a non-linear waveguide was created that crossed the switching wave. When the switching wave penetrated through this shadow region, a spatial (transversal) hysteresis was observed (Fig. 4.9). This effect is due to the nonlinear variations of a temperature barrier in the shadow region of the guide layer. When the switching wave overcomes the temperature barrier the shadow region proves to be in a "switched-on" state and the barrier decreases, thus providing a new steady state of the system. It is accompanied by the vanishing of the shadow in the reflected beam (see Fig. 4.9).

It should be emphasized that both steady states observed in this experiment correspond to the switched-on state of the nonlinear waveguide and

Fig. 4.8. _____

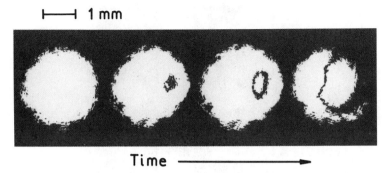

⊢——⊣ 1 mm

Time ————————————————▶

Kinetics of the reflected-beam intensity profile demonstrating the propagation of the switching wave. The left side corresponds to the beginning of the illuminated region of the guide layer.

differ only in the spatial configuration of a switched-on region of the waveguide.

2.2.3. Autowave Processes

Distributed nonlinear systems can undergo different transients connected with the propagation of autowaves (Rozanov, 1981, 1983; Moloney, 1985; Firth and Galbright, 1985). There are autowave processes that do not change the stationary state of the system, but that provide the propagation of dynamic perturbations in the nonlinear medium. Such processes are promising for the transmission and processing of information in optically controlled computing systems.

A nonlinear planar waveguide is a convenient system for the realization of such transient processes, because the maximum of the intensity distribution can be shifted forward with respect to the nonlinear perturbation, and hence a moving force for the nonlinear perturbation appears. Analysis of the light intensity and of the temperature spatial distributions shows that it is possible to make the propagation speeds of the forward and the backward fronts of the switching wave equal. If a nonlinear planar waveguide is illuminated by a plane light wave, the autowaves can propagate without changing shape.

Fig. 4.9. _____

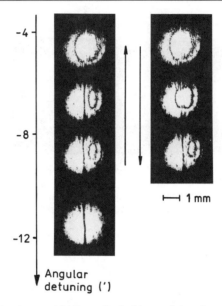

Spatial hysteresis observed in the reflected beam intensity profile. Angular detuning was smoothly decreased (↑) and then increased (↓).

This transient process was experimented with using the gelatin waveguide described above. The incident beam of an argon-ion laser (output 100 mW) was expanded by a prism telescope. Its intensity and angle of incidence were chosen just near a "switch-off" point of the bistability region in order to avoid steady-state switching. The excitation of autowaves was performed by an additional beam from a pulsed light source having a duration of 0.1 sec. It was focused on a spot with a diameter of 30 μm at the beginning of the illuminated waveguide layer. The unidirectional propagation of the nonlinear perturbation through the waveguide layer without capture of the switched-on state was observed (Fig. 4.10). The change of the autowave transverse size during its propagation is connected with the nonuniform (Gaussian) intensity distribution in the incident beam, leading to a speed unbalance for the forward and backward fronts of the switching wave.

2.2.4. Transformation of Phase and of Polarization

Analysis of the switching process in the nonlinear planar waveguide indicates that the transverse spatial modulation of the reflected beam phase is

Fig. 4.10.

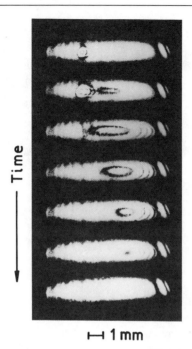

⊢⊣ 1 mm

Kinetics of the reflected-beam intensity profile demonstrating the unidirectional propagation of an autowave.

characterized by a sharp phase shift of 2π on the wavefronts of the switching wave (Bazhenov et al., 1986d). The existence of the phase shift has been confirmed experimentally using a twin-wave interferometer with a nonlinear planar waveguide in one of its paths (Fig. 4.11).

If the conditions for excitation of the TE and TM modes are different, the phase modulation gives rise to a transformation of polarization of the reflected beam. In this case it is necessary for the incident beam to have both s and p polarization components. Such a polarization transformation was accomplished using the linear gelatin waveguide described above. The gelatin layer proved to be optically anisotropic due to a unidirectional deformation induced at the stage of the gelatin layer preparation. Measurements (Bazhenov et al., 1986d) have shown that the anisotropy of the gelatin layer refractive index is about 0.003, and therefore the TE and TM mode

Fig. 4.11.

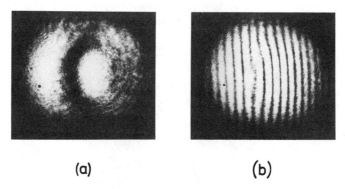

(a)   (b)

Phase modulation over the reflected beam cross section measured by a twin-wave interferometer. The reference beam is turned off (a) and on (b).

excitation angles differ by 20 milliradians. Moreover, the self-action effects for the TE mode proved to be practically absent for the range of intensity used. This can be explained by compensation of the nonlinear variations caused by simultaneous changes of the layer thickness and refractive index. In the experiment, considerable variations of the polarization were observed over the reflected beam cross section.

3.
Materials Based on Bacteriorhodopsin

Bacteriorhodopsin was found in the so-called purple membrane of extreme halophilic bacteria, *Halobacterium halobium* (e.g., Stoeckenius et al., 1979) and became the subject of intensive investigations by biologists, chemists, and physicists. It was determined that the purple membrane is composed of a single species of protein, bacteriorhodopsin, and lipids. Purple membranes perform an extremely important function in halobacteria. They convert solar energy into an electrochemical positive ion gradient across the membrane. This function of light-energy conversion belongs to bacteriorhodopsin molecules that are embedded in purple membranes and are arranged in a two-dimensional crystalline lattice of the space group P_3.

Bacteriorhodopsin contains a chromophore, one molecule of retinal bound to a lysine residue that has a strong absorption band around 570 nm (bR570). Optical excitation of bacteriorhodopsin produces a photochemical cycle of a complex series of intermediates (Fig. 4.12) that is accompanied by a positive ion transfer process from the interior of the bacteria to the outside. Each intermediate state throughout the photocycle is defined by an absorption band and corresponds to a certain conformation of the protein (Lozier and Niederberger, 1977).

The purple membrane fragments can be easily extracted from the halobacteria, and the main properties of the bacteriorhodopsin prove to be preserved in the isolated purple membranes. This circumstance enables the fabrication of different recording materials based on bacteriorhodopsin. The following materials are, or may be, suitable for real-time optical processing:

(1) *Purple membranes dispersed in a solid-state polymer matrix such as gelatin or polyvinyl alcohol.* This material was elaborated in the Biophysical Institute of Academy of Sciences of USSR, Pushchino, and was called biochrom film (e.g., Vsevolodov, 1985; Vsevolodov et al., 1986). It has a relaxation time ranging from 0.1 sec to 100 sec, depending on the preparation procedure, and it is used for real-time holography (Burykin et al., 1985). Biochrom films have the dynamic Weigert effect (or photoinduced anisotropy), allowing non-Fourier optical processing, like image subtraction, edge enhancement, con-

Fig. 4.12. _____

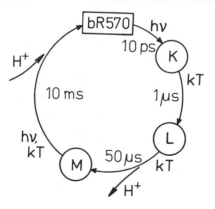

The photocycle of bacteriorhodopsin.

trast reversal, etc. to be performed, as well as recording real-time polarization holograms (Vsevolodov et al., 1984).

(2) *Purple membranes immobilized in gel-state polymer matrix.* This material has practically the same properties as the solid-state film biochrom, except for the relaxation time, which is about 10 msec, and the possibility of fabricating samples having thicknesses of more that 1 mm with a rather high optical quality.

(3) *A thin layer of purple membranes precipitated on a glass substrate.* The layer has an electrochromic effect: The color of the layer is changed when an electric field of the order of 10^5 V/cm is applied to the layer (Maksimychev et al., 1985). This effect is enhanced in oriented purple membrane layers obtained be means of electrolytic precipitation of purple membrane fragments on electroconductive substrates. In this layer, membrane planes are parallel to the substrate surface. The photocycle time proves to be dependent on the magnitude and on the sign of the applied electric field. This gives the possibility of controlling the duration of the optical information storage. In addition, conversely, under illumination a potential difference of up to 10 V is created between the opposite sides of the layer of oriented purple membranes.

(4) *Purple membranes at low temperatures.* It has been shown (Lozier and Niederberger, 1977; Balashov, 1985) that at low temperatures, thermal reactions are inhibited, whereas the photoreaction is enabled and bacteriorhodopsin becomes a two-component photoreversible system. The primary photoproduct (Fig. 4.12, intermediate K) is stable at liquid nitrogen temperatures, where it can be photochemically converted back to the initial state bR570. Thus upon actinic illumination at $-196°C$ a photostationary-state mixture of bR570 and K is produced. Subsequent illumination by red light completely regenerates the original-state bR570. This property is very promising for optical memories and logical elements, taking into consideration that the time transition bR570 $\rightarrow$ K is about 10 psec. At the temperature of $-50°C$ the photocycle is interrupted in the state of intermediate M (see Fig. 4.12). Subsequent illumination by blue light returns the molecules into the original-state bR570. This makes optical processing possible using two beams with different wavelengths (green and blue).

(5) *Aqueous suspensions of purple membrane fragments.* The material is of high optical quality and easily controllable thickness and concentration. It has been successfully used for pulsed holography (Savransky et al., 1985). When the concentration of the purple membranes is increased, their mobility is decreased due to the aggregation process. This allows the use of available CW lasers for holographic recording. Moreover, it has been shown by Bazhenov et al. (1987) that at concentrations of about 5×10^{-4} mol/liter an additional recording process having a diffusional origin takes place. It leads to a more effective holographic recording than the photochromic recording taking place in an immobilized purple membrane. Moreover, it is possible to control optical anisotropy of the suspension by means of an extremely low-strength electrical field of 10–100 V/cm due to the electroinduced orientation of purple membrane fragments.

(6) *Purple membrane crystalline materials.* A further increase of suspension concentration leads to a complete loss of the membrane mobility and to the formation of a polycrystal. It is very promising material due to an extremely high concentration of bacteriorhodopsin.

3.1. Biochrom Films

In the initial state biochrom films have an absorption band with a maximum at 570 nm. Under illumination by actinic light in the green-red spectral range, they are bleached (Fig. 4.13), and when light is turned off they spontaneously return to the initial state. The relaxation time τ depends on the film preparation procedure and varies in a very wide range from 0.1 sec up to 100 sec and sometimes even more. Additional illumination by blue light accelerates the regeneration of the film initial state.

Real-time recording on biochrom film is due to the reversible photochemical transformation of the bacteriorhodopsin molecules (Fig. 4.12), hence it has a photochromic origin (Tomlinson, 1975). As mentioned above, light absorption initiates the photochemical process in bacteriorhodopsin, leading to its deionization. The deionizated bacteriorhodopsin (intermediate M) has an absorption band in the violet spectrum with a maximum at 410 nm. When a positive ion is joined to the deionized molecule, it returns to the initial state.

The photostationary-state distribution of bacteriorhodopsin molecules between the two forms (bR570 and M) in the simplest approximation is determined by the following balance equation:

Fig. 4.13.

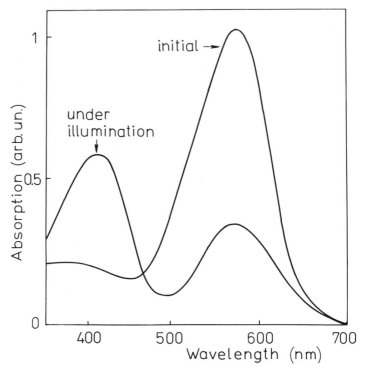

Biochrom film absorption band.

$$\sigma_1 I_1 N_1 = \left(\sigma_2 I_2 + \frac{1}{\tau} \right) N_2, \tag{4.4}$$

where σ_1 and σ_2 are the cross sections of photoinduced transitions bR570 $\rightarrow$ M and M $\rightarrow$ bR570, respectively; I_1 and I_2 are the intensities of the green-red and blue light, respectively; and N_1 and N_2 are the concentrations of bacteriorhodopsin molecules in the original (bR570) and intermediate (M) states, respectively. It is assumed that $N_1 + N_2 = N_o$, where N_o is the total concentration of bacteriorhodopsin molecules.

3.1.1. Photoinduced Anisotropy

A biochrom film is isotropic in its initial state, because bacteriorhodopsin molecules are, in general, randomly distributed about the axis normal to the plane of the glass substrate. When the biochrom film is excited by linearly polarized light it becomes anisotropic (Vsevolodov et al., 1984). Dichroism and birefringence are induced (Fig. 4.14). The magnitude and sign of the induced anisotropy are dependent on the actinic light intensity and wavelength (Fig. 4.15). When the actinic light is turned off the film returns to its initial isotropic state. The time of anisotropy erasure is approximately equal to the relaxation time of the intermediate M.

This effect can be explained by photoselective bleaching of the biochrom film: Only these bacteriorhodopsin molecules whose transition dipole moments for absorption lie in or near the direction of the electric field of the actinic light are bleached due to the transition $bR570 \rightarrow M$. It is sufficient to take into account that the cross sections σ_1 and σ_2 in Eq. (4.4) are dependent on the angles ϕ_1 and ϕ_2 between the transition dipole vector and the electric field vector of actinic light:

Fig. 4.14.

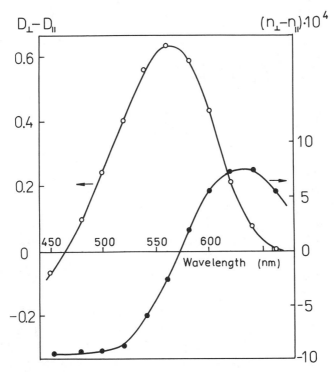

Photoinduced dichroism $(D_\perp - D_\parallel)$ and birefringence $(n_\perp - n_\parallel)$ in a biochrom film as a function of wavelength.

Fig. 4.15.

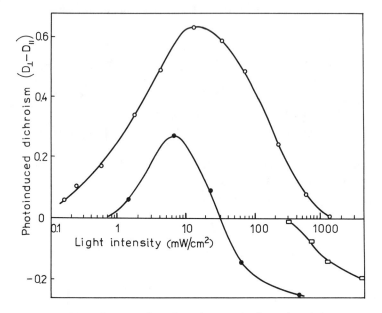

Dependence of the biochrom film dichroism on the intensity of linearly polarized light measured at 570 nm with wavelengths 442 nm ($\square$), 458 nm ($\bullet$), and 633 nm (o).

$$\sigma_1 = \sigma_{1\parallel} \cos^2 \phi_1 + \sigma_{1\perp} \sin^2\phi_1, \qquad (4.5)$$

$$\sigma_2 = \sigma_{2\parallel} \cos^2\phi_2 + \sigma_{2\perp} \sin^2\phi_2,$$

where $\sigma_\parallel$ and $\sigma_\perp$ are the molecule cross sections for the light polarized parallel and perpendicular to the molecule axis, respectively.

Taking into account that when $I_1 = I_2 = I$ in Eq. (4.4), it can be concluded that positive macroscopic dichroism takes place in the spectral range where $\sigma_2 = 0$ and $\sigma_{1\parallel} > \sigma_{1\perp}$. This corresponds to the green-red region of the spectrum where bacteriorhodopsin molecules in the state bR570 oriented parallel to or near the polarization plane of actinic light ($\phi_1 \approx 0$) are bleached (Fig. 4.15, curve for 633 nm). In the violet region of the spectrum, the molecular dichroism of bR570 has the opposite sign, that is, $\sigma_{1\parallel} < \sigma_{1\perp}$. Therefore the transition bR570 → M is more probable for molecules having $\phi_1 \approx 90°$. In this spectral range, $\sigma_{2\parallel} > \sigma_{2\perp}$, and hence the intermediate M with $\phi_2 \approx 0$, undergoes the transition M → bR570 with maximum speed. As a result, a negative macroscopic dichroism takes place (Fig. 4.15, curve for 442 nm). It is interesting that illumination by light in the spectral range just near the isosbestic point (458 nm), where $\sigma_{1\parallel} > \sigma_{1\perp}$, $\sigma_{2\parallel} > \sigma_{2\perp}$, and $\sigma_{1\parallel} > \sigma_{2\perp}$ gives rise to a macroscopic dichroism that changes its sign depending on the intensity of actinic light (Fig. 4.15), curve for 458 nm).

In full accordance with this consideration it can be shown that the simultaneous action of two mutually perpendicular polarized beams with different wavelengths, one in the red region and the other in the blue, must enhance the induced dichroism that has been confirmed experimentally (Vsevolodov et al., 1984) using a He-Ne laser (633 nm) and a He-Cd one (442 nm). In this case the induced dichroism was increased by 20–30% in comparison with the single wavelength beam action.

The photoinduced dichroism of biochrom films can be used for real-time non-Fourier processing such as image substraction, contrast reversal, etc., in accordance with the methods developed by Jonathan and May (1979a, 1979b) Todorov et al. (1985), and Calixto et al. (1985). To demonstrate that feasibility, we have used the experimental setup illustrated in Fig. 4.16. The biochrom film was inserted between crossed polarizers. The anisotropy was induced by two incoherent mutually perpendiculiar polarized beams from a He-Ne laser (633 nm) that were expanded and passed through the transparencies O_1 and O_2 and then superimposed on the film. The planes of polarization of the beams were oriented at 45° with respect to the axes of the polarizers P_1 and P_2. The probe beam had a wavelength of 570 nm, for which the photoinduced birefringence is equal to zero and dichroism reaches its maximum value (Fig. 4.14). Thus two images O_1 and O_2 having mutually perpendicular polarizations are superimposed on the biochrom film.

Fig. 4.16. ——————————————————————————————————————

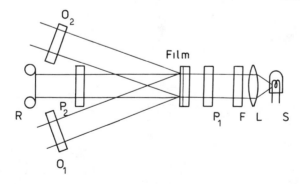

Experimental configuration used for real-time non-Fourier image processing on biochrom film: S, white light source; L, lens; F, filter; P_1 and P_2, crossed polarizers; O_1 and O_2, transparencies; R, recorder.

The resulting dichroism is induced only in those regions of the film where the image intensities are different. Therefore the identical parts of the images are seen as dark, and only the nonidentical regions of the images appear bright because the film is observed through crossed polarizers. This means that in this case subtraction of those images takes place. Examples of this operation for binary transparencies are shown in Fig. 4.17. When in the setup of Fig. 4.16 anisotropic phase transparencies are used instead of amplitude transparencies, the transmittance of the system becomes spatially modulated, depending on the polarization variations caused by the anisotropic transparencies O_1 and O_2 (Fig. 4.18). Another example of non-Fourier processing is the image contrast reversal that is observed when the polarizer P_2 is rotated from its crossed position (Fig. 4.19). This operation is based on the angular rotation of the plane of polarization of the probe beam transmitted through the dichroic parts of the film.

3.1.2. Polarization Four-Wave Mixing

Because the biochrom film photoresponse is anisotropic, it is possible to record both usual intensity-type real-time holograms (with the recording beams

Fig. 4.17. _____

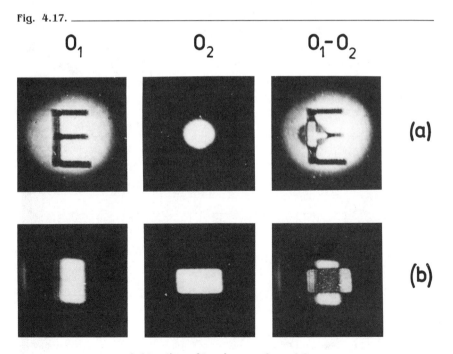

Subtraction of two images O_1 and O_2.

Fig. 4.18. _____

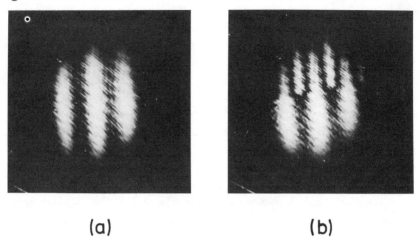

(a)   **(b)**

Spatial modulation of the transmitted probe beam using phase anisotropic transparencies: (a) O_1, quartz wedge; (b) at the top O_1, quartz wedge, and O_2, gyrotropic element.

having the same polarizations) and polarization-type holograms (with mutually orthogonal polarizations of the recording beams). An important peculiarity of biochrom films resides in the equality of these hologram diffraction efficiencies as well as both transmission- and reflection-type hologram diffraction efficiencies (Vsevolodov et al., 1986). These properties give rise

Fig. 4.19. _____

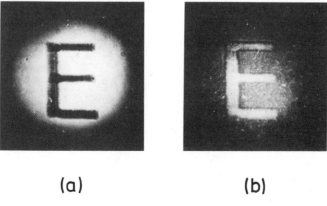

(a)   **(b)**

Contrast reversal.

to interesting regimes of polarization four-wave mixing such as polarization-preserving phase conjugation (Zeldovich and Shkunov, 1979; Martin et al., 1980) and the controlling of phase-conjugated wave polarization.

Analysis (Korchemskaya et al., 1987) has shown that when elementary holograms have the same diffraction efficiencies, a complete phase conjugation takes place in the configuration of quasilongitudinal four-wave mixing (Fig. 4.20). This means that for a signal wave C_3 with a randomly non-uniform polarization over the wavefront, the reflected wave C_4 in every point over its wavefront has the same polarization ellipse as in the proper point of a signal wave, but their electric field vectors are rotated in opposite directions in a laboratory coordinate system, that is, $C_4 \sim C_3^*$.

Korchemskaya et al. (1987) used biochrom film in an experiment of quasilongitudinal polarization four-wave mixing (Fig. 4.20). The experiment was carried out with variable parameters of the pump beams C_1 and C_2: polarization, intensity, and mutual coherence. The state of polarization of the signal wave C_3 was modulated over its wavefront by means of a quartz wedge. Compensation of the polarization distortions of the signal wave through the quartz wedge is seen to take place (Fig. 4.21) due to a complete phase-polarization conjugation based on the anisotropic nonlinearity of the biochrom film. A complete phase-polarization conjugation was realized under the following conditions:

(1) The pump beams C_1 and C_2 were circularly polarized, and their electric field vectors were rotated in opposite directions. Only transmission-type holograms were recorded because C_2 was chosen to be incoherent with respect to C_1 and C_3. The diffraction efficiencies of the intensity-type and polarization-type holograms proved to be equal in this case (Fig. 4.22).

Fig. 4.20. ———————————————————————————————————————

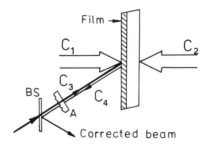

Scheme for the correction of polarization distortions with four-wave mixing.

Fig. 4.21.

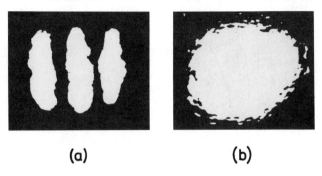

(a)   **(b)**

Complete phase-polarization conjugation. Signal (a) and corrected (b) beams observed through the polarizer.

(2) C_1 and C_2 were linearly polarized and their planes of polarization were mutually parallel. Only transmission-type holograms were recorded, as in (1). If the intensity of interacting waves was high enough to saturate the biochrom film, the diffraction efficiencies of the intensity- and polarization-type holograms became very close to each other (Fig. 4.22).

(3) C_1 and C_2 had an arbitrary elliptical polarization, and their electric field vectors were rotated in opposite directions. All interacting beams were coherent, and hence both transmission-and reflection-type holograms were recorded. In this case the diffraction efficiencies of proper transmission-type (both intensity- and polarization-type) and reflection-type (both intensity- and polarization-type) holograms were equal due to the absence of diffusion processes in the immobilized purple membranes of biochrom films.

Thus, due to the fact that the biochrom film nonlinearity is anisotropic and saturable in character, it was possible to realize those various cases of complete phase-polarization conjugation (1)–(3) using a single recording material. All these properties are explained in the framework of the above-mentioned model of the photoselective bleaching of biochrom films (Section 3.1.1).

Deviations from conditions (1)–(3) lead to the appearance of "wrong" polarization components in the reflected wave C_4: C_4 contains a component of polarization orthogonal to the conjugated component of polarization. This enables control of the state of polarization of the reflected beam C_4. For

Fig. 4.22. _____

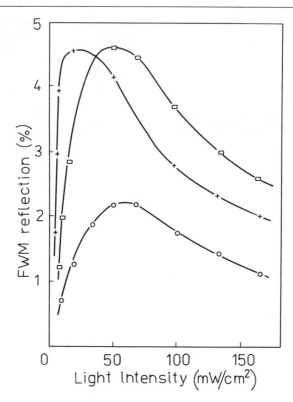

Four-wave mixing reflection coefficient versus light intensity in biochrom film
waves. All waves are linearly polarized: The signal wave is parallel (+) and perpendicular (o) to the pump-wave polarization plane. All waves are circularly polarized (□).

example, let the pump beam parameters be the same as in (2) except for
their planes of polarization, which are not parallel, but mutually perpendicular. In this case the polarization distortions of the reflected wave are dou-
bled (Fig. 4.23). If in condition (1) the direction of rotation of the electric
field of C_2 is changed, the reflected wave parameters become essentially
different from those of (1). First, the reflection coefficient (the ratio of intensities of the reflected and signal beams) becomes highly dependent on
the state of polarization of the signal wave C_3, dropping to zero if C_3 has a
circular polarization of opposite sign to that of the pump beams. The conjugate component of polarization in C_4 is then practically completely absent,
and only the perpendicular component of polarization is present in this case.

Fig. 4.23.

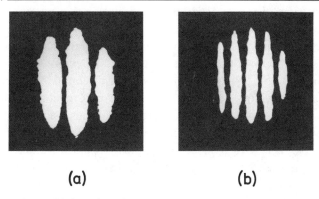

(a)   (b)

Doubling of polarization distortions. The signal beam (a) and reflected beam passed through the quartz wedge (b) as observed through the polarizer.

3.1.3. Nonlinear Transformation of Polarization

Photochromic materials are practically unused in nonlinear interferometers such as Fabry-Perot cavities because the background absorption of the material increases the cavity losses, and the saturable character of the optical nonlinearity limits the nonlinear phase shift. Nevertheless, due to the fact that the optical nonlinearity of photochromic materials such as biochrom film is anisotropic in character, there are additional possibilities for the realization of self-action effects in nonlinear interferometers. Some other kinds of polarization self-action effects have been considered (Kitano et al., 1981; Cecchi et al., 1982; Adonts et al., 1984; Dykman and Tarasov, 1985).

Let us consider the passive Fabry-Perot cavity filled with biochrom film. The long wavelength side of the film absorption band is preferable because of comparatively low background absorption and a high nonlinear phase shift. Analysis shows that if the intensity of an elliptically polarized beam incident on a nonlinear Fabry-Perot cavity is varied, a transformation of the polarization of the transmitted beam takes place. The same result is obtained if the intensity of the incident beam is fixed while the cavity base is varied. The interaction between the strong and the weak components of the polarization ellipse (the orthogonal axes of the electric field ellipse) inside the cavity, through the nonlinear anisotropy, leads to an increase of the feedback efficiency for the weak component (the semiminor ellipse axis). Simultaneously the feedback efficiency for the strong component (the semimajor ellipse axis) is decreased because of the film saturation. Calculations indicate that to reach bistability in this case, the cavity fineness can be three times lower than that in a cavity with an isotropic nonlinearity.

The experimental realization of this polarization self-action effect was performed using a passive Fabry-Perot cavity filled with biochrom film having a thickness of 50 μm (Bazhenov et al., 1985). The ellipticity of the incident beam from a He-Ne laser (633 nm) was chosen to be 0.53, which gave the maximum polarization self-action effect. The experimental results for the output of the anisotropic nonlinear interferometer (intensity of the weak and strong components, ellipticity and azimuth) versus the cavity base are shown in Fig. 4.24. The cavity fineness was only 7, and therefore the bistable regime was not reached. Nevertheless, the self-action of the weak component is seen to be increased in comparison with that of the strong component. The self-action effect is sharper for the light polarization than for the light

Fig. 4.24. ───

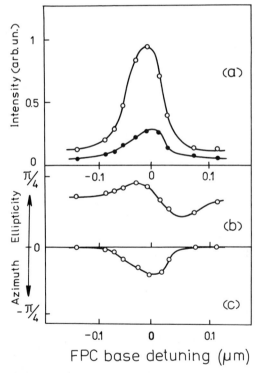

Polarization self-action depending on the base detuning of a Fabry-Perot cavity filled with biochrom film. In (a), (o) and (●) correspond to the strong and weak components of the output beam polarization.

intensity (Fig. 4.24). The experimental results thus confirm the existence of an additional mechanism of feedback for the weak component of polarization.

3.2. Purple-Membrane Suspension

As mentioned above, there are several factors that make an aqueous suspension of purple membranes of halobacteria a promising material for real-time processing. First of all, it has high optical quality and low scattering. The relaxation time of the intermediate M (see Fig. 4.12) in suspension is about 10 msec at room temperature, and it can be reduced by means of blue-light illumination. This allows optical processing with the frequency of television standards. Finally, it is easy to vary the thickness of the sample as well as the concentration of purple-membrane fragments. When the concentration of the suspension is increased, membrane aggregation takes place. This leads to a decrease of the mobility of the purple-membrane fragments, and therefore holographic recordings can be performed with available CW lasers. Moreover, it has been shown by Bazhenov et al. (1987) that in concentrated suspensions an additional efficient recording process having the nature of a diffusion took place. A further increase of concentration leads to the appearance of oriented areas having transverse dimensions of 1 mm or more. These oriented areas of clusters then undergo immobilization, and a polycrystal is formed with an extremely high bacteriorhodopsin concentration.

3.2.1. Real-Time Holography

The mobility of purple membranes in a suspension causes the erasure of a holographic grating because of a diffusion process. The steady-state spatial modulation amplitude of the unbleached bacteriorhodopsin molecules ΔN therefore becomes dependent on the holographic grating spacing Λ according to the formula

$$\Delta N = \frac{\sigma N_0 I_0 m}{\dfrac{4\pi^2 D}{\Lambda^2} + \dfrac{1}{\tau}}, \qquad (4.6)$$

where σ is the cross section of the photoinduced transition bR570 $\rightarrow$ M, m is the contrast of the interference pattern, I_o is the light intensity, N_o is the total molecular concentration of the bacteriorhodopsin molecules, D is the coefficient of the Brownian diffusion of purple-membrane fragments, and τ is the relaxation time (transition M $\rightarrow$ bR570). Our measurements have shown that the diffusional erasing of a holographic grating took place for a grating spacing of 0.3 μm. This allows the estimation of D using Eq. (4.6), giving a value of the order of 10^{-9} cm^{2}s^{-1}. The kinetics of holographic grating writing and erasing for an aqueous suspension concentration of 1.3×10^{-4} mol/liter is shown in Fig. 4.25b. It can be seen that the grating erasure time is determined quite well by the intermediate M relaxation time. Moreover, additional measurements have shown that the grating erasure time did not change for a wide range of grating spacings (0.4–50 μm), as well as the steady-state diffraction efficiency, for a fixed intensity of the recording beams.

Quite different properties were observed for a concentrated aqueous suspension (6×10^{-4} mol/liter) (Bazhenov et al., 1987). First of all, the holographic recording became more efficient and dependent on the grating spacing (Fig. 4.26). From the kinetic characteristic (Fig. 4.25a) it can be seen that the holographic grating has two components: a fast component (the abrupt parts of the curve, Fig. 4.25a) and a slow one (the smooth parts of the curve, Fig. 4.25a). The fast component is described rather well by the above-mentioned (Section 3.1) photochromic model based on the spectral transitions of bacteriorhodopsin. According to this model the diffraction efficiency is

Fig. 4.25.

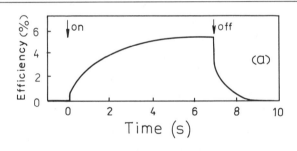

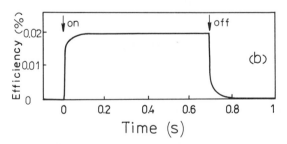

Kinetics of the diffraction efficiency of a holographic grating in an aqueous suspension of purple membranes with concentrations: (a) 6×10^{-4} mol/liter and (b) 1.3×10^{-4}.

Fig. 4.26.

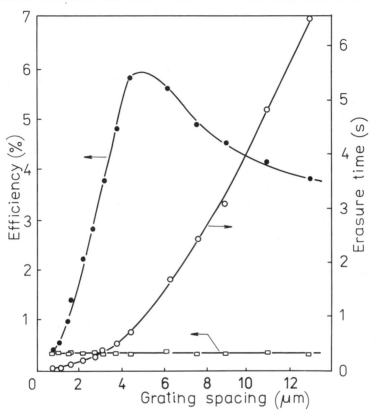

Diffraction efficiencies of the fast (□) and slow (●) components of a holographic grating recorded in a concentrated purple-membrane suspension and erasure time of the slow component (o) versus the grating spacing.

proportional to the second power of the photochromic molecule concentration. Then the diffraction efficiency and the erasure time are independent of the grating spacing. All these properties were observed in the experiment (Fig. 4.25 and Fig. 4.26). As to the slow component of the holographic grating, the reverse is true: Its diffraction efficiency and erasure time are highly dependent on the grating spacing. This indicates the existence of an additional effective process for real-time holographic recording in a concentrated suspension of purple membranes.

For the qualitative description of this process we have assumed the existence of photoinduced increase of the purple-membrane mobility. It is well known that in a concentrated suspension the interaction between neighboring membrane fragments becomes essential, and an aggregation takes place that leads to a decrease of the mobility of the purple-membrane fragments. Under different physical perturbations, like ultrasound, temperature, and others, the purple-membrane mobility is increased. We have assumed that light exerted the same influence on the purple-membrane mobility. In a holographic experiment the light intensity is spatially modulated. In the regions of maximum light intensity the purple membranes acquire high mobility, and due to mutual diffusion they reach the regions of minimum light intensity, where they spontaneously transform into the original state with low mobility. Thus a spatial redistribution of the purple-membrane concentration takes place, and a holographic grating is formed.

The simplest model of that process is the following: Under illumination the aggregated purple membranes undergo a transition from the original state 1 with a comparatively low diffusion coefficient D_1 to a photoinduced state 2 with a high diffusion coefficient D_2. It is assumed that the optical properties of both these states are the same and that the spatial modulation amplitude of the purple-membrane concentration is low in comparison with the total concentration of purple membrane. Analysis shows that the steady-state amplitude of spatial modulation of a bacteriorhodopsin-molecule concentration (which is proportional to the purple-membrane concentration) is determined by

$$\Delta N = \frac{\sigma_{12} N_0 I_0 m}{\frac{4\pi^2 D_2}{\Lambda^2} + \frac{1}{\tau_{21}}} \left(1 - \frac{D_2}{D_1} \right), \qquad (4.7)$$

where σ_{12} is the cross section of the photoinduced transition (state 1 → state 2) and τ_{21} is the relaxation time (state 2 → state 1). The other symbols are the same as in Eq. (4.6). If $D_2 \gg D_1$, the erasure time of the slow component τ_e is given by

$$\tau_e = \frac{\Lambda^2}{4\pi^2 D_1}. \qquad (4.8)$$

Note that the second power dependence of the erasure time of the slow component on the grating spacing predicted by Eq. (4.8) was observed in an experiment (Fig. 4.26). Then according to Eq. (4.7) the dependence of the diffraction efficiency, which is proportional to ΔN^2, on the grating spacing has two parts: an abrupt rise for small Λ and saturation at $\Lambda \geq 2\pi \sqrt{D_2 \tau_{21}}$. This is in qualitative agreement with experimental data (Fig. 4.26).

From Eq. (4.7) it can be inferred also that when $D_2 > D_1$ the modulation amplitude has a negative sign ($\Delta N < 0$), that is, the bacteriorhodopsin concentration reaches its minimum value in the area of maximum light intensity. This has been confirmed experimentally. A cuvette with a concentrated suspension of purple membranes was placed in the focusing beam of a He-Ne laser (633 nm) where the intensity spatial distribution has a Gaussian shape. A defocusing nonlinear lens was induced, which had a relaxation time of 200 sec, which corresponds to the diffusion time. This means that the refraction index of the suspension reached its minimum value on the center of the Gaussian spot. This is in complete agreement with Eq. (4.7). Thus the bacteriorhodopsin concentration was redistributed between the bright and dark regions due to the photoinduced increasing of the aggregated purple-membrane mobility and the diffusion.

Similar considerations can be carried out for the rotational motion of a purple membrane, taking into account that the bacteriorhodopsin molecules in a purple-membrane disk are aligned. When the suspension is excited by linearly polarized light, the only aggregated membranes that increase their mobility are those whose total transition dipole moments lie in or near the polarization plane of the excited light (similar to the photoselection model, see Section 3.1.1). The photoexcited purple membranes, having high mobility, are then rotated due to rotational diffusion and spontaneously transform into the original state, having a comparatively low mobility. The orientational function of the purple membrane thereby becomes asymmetrical, and macroscopic anisotropy is induced.

For measuring the photoinduced anisotropy, the cuvette with a concentrated suspension of purple membrane was introduced between crossed polarizers and was illuminated by a linearly polarized beam from a He-Ne laser (633 nm). The polarization plane of the actinic beam was oriented at an angle of 45° with respect to the axes of the polarizers. The probe beam had the same wavelength as the actinic beam. The intensity of the transmitted probe beam, which is proportional to the magnitude of the photoinduced anisotropy, was measured. The experimental results are shown in Fig. 4.27, from which it can be concluded that the photoinduced anisotropy has two components (fast and slow) of opposite signs. The fast component proved to be photochromic in character (see Section 3.1). As to the slow component, we assumed that it was connected with the above process of photoinduced increase of rotational mobility. Analysis shows that this process leads to a partial orientation of the aggregated purple membranes, with the membrane planes perpendicular to the plane of polarization of the actinic light.

Fig. 4.27.

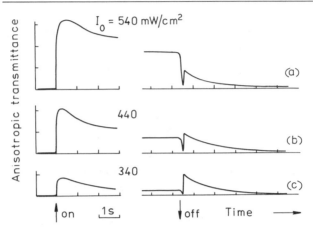

Kinetics of a probe beam transmitted through crossed polarizers filled with a purple-membrane suspension. Linearly polarized actinic light with intensities of (a) 540, (b) 440, and (c) 340 mW/cm² is turned on (↑) and off (↓).

Note that the chromophores are oriented at an angle of approximately 20° with respect to the membrane plane (Stoeckenius et al., 1979). This means that in order to explain the opposite sign of the slow component with respect to that of the fast component, it is necessary to assume that the refractive index in the purple-membrane plane is less than that in the perpendicular direction. This was confirmed in our experiment on electroinduced anisotropy (see Section 3.2.2).

3.2.2. Electro-Optical Effects

As mentioned in Section 3.2, an electric field applied to an aqueous suspension led to the orientation of purple membranes. Due to this effect, oriented and immobilized layers of purple membranes were obtained that could be used as elements for light-electricity transformations. It has been demonstrated by Keszthelyi (1982) that a small direct current electric field (~20 V/cm) is enough to align a large quantity of the purple-membrane fragments perpendicular to the electric field, due to a large permanent electric dipole moment oriented perpendicular to the purple-membrane plane. The value of the permanent dipole moment was determined to be of 140 D per protein (Kimura et al., 1981). Orientation of the purple-membrane fragments can also be attained by means of an alternating electric field with a frequency greater than 100 Hz, because of the induced dipole moment.

By measuring the electroinduced dichroism in the suspension, it has been shown that the permanent and induced dipoles of a purple membrane are mutually perpendicular, that is, in an alternative electric field, the purple-membrane fragments tend to align themselves parallel to the electric field. The electroinduced orientation of the purple-membrane fragments in suspension was determined from linear dichroism measurements, taking into account that chromophores are oriented with the angle of approximately 20° to the membrane plane.

In an experiment, we have measured the electroinduced birefringence in the purple-membrane suspension. A direct current electric field of 15 V/cm was applied to the suspension. The state of polarization of the transmitted probe beam was changed when an electroinduced orientation was established. The linearly polarized probe beam became elliptically polarized in the whole visual spectrum after the electric field was turned on. By measuring the ellipticity and the direction of rotation of the electric field of the light, it was determined that $n_\parallel > n_\perp$ ($n_\parallel$ and $n_\perp$ are the refractive indices for polarizations parallel and perpendicular to the direction of the electric field, respectively). It is well known that in this case the induced dichroism has the opposite sign, that is $\kappa_\parallel < \kappa_\perp$ ($\kappa_\parallel$ and $\kappa_\perp$ are the absorption coefficients for polarized light). This means that the refractive index for the polarization parallel to the purple-membrane plane is less than that for the polarization in the perpendicular direction. This confirms the conclusion made from the photoinduced anisotropy experiment (Section 3.2.1). Moreover, the erasure time for electroinduced birefringency proved to be the same as that for the slow component of the photoinduced anisotropy (Fig. 4.27).

4.
Conclusion

We have tried to illustrate the main advantages of the best-known biopolymer materials, sensitized gelatin and materials based on bacteriorhodopsin, which are favorable for optical processing tasks; no attempt was made to review the vast amount of work devoted to other organic materials. There are several reasons for the importance of the biopolymers discussed in this chapter, which are briefly summarized below.

(1)   They have an extremely wide flexibility for the fabrication of various recording materials, which gives the possibility of forming bulk materials (both solid-state and liquid), films, waveguides, etc.

(2)   They allow optical processing operations in a very wide range of time scales from 10^2 sec down to 10^{-11} sec (see Section 3). As mentioned above, at the temperature of liquid nitrogen, bacteriorhodopsin becomes photoreversible between two stationary states with a very short switching time of about 10 psec. This property is promising for the creation of optical high-speed erasable memories and logical elements.

(3)   They allow performance of bit-by-bit or holographic recording with an extraordinary high spatial resolution, limited by the light wavelength, rather than by material structural element dimensions. It is expected that on the basis of purple membranes of halobacteria an optical memory with a capacity of 10^9 bits/cm^2 will be created in the near future.

(4)   Because of their high sensitivity in the visible spectrum, it is possible to use available CW lasers. For semiconductor lasers operating in the near infrared, chlorophyll-protein complexes are thought to be the most suitable.

(5)   The effect of photoinduced anisotropy (or the dynamic Weigert effect) enables performance of real-time polarization recording.

(6)   There is a possibility of controlling the process of optical recording by means of external influences such as electric or magnetic fields, temperature, etc.

In addition to the materials discussed here, there are many other biopolymer systems, including so-called Langmuir-Blodgett multilayer films with different molecules in different layers, that are especially attractive. Much work is still needed in the field of biopolymer materials. Nevertheless, recent results indicate that there are areas of real-time optical processing in which biopolymers seem to offer real and practical solutions.

Acknowledgments

The authors are grateful to N.N. Vsevolodov for his helpful discussions, and to N.M. Burykin and E.Ya. Korchemskaya for their assistance in various experiments.

References

Abraham, E., and Smith, S.D. (1982). *Rep. Progr. Phys.* **45**, 815–885.

Adonts, G.G., Jotyan, G.P., and Kanetsyan, E.G. (1984). *Kvantovaya Elektronika* **11**, 1152–1155 (in Russian). English transl. in *Sov. J. Quantum Electron.*

Apanasevich, S.P., Karpushko, F.V., and Sinitsyn, G.V. (1985). *Kvantovaya Elektronika* **12**, 387–390 (in Russian). English transl. in *Sov. J. Quantum Electron.*

Auston, D.H., Ballman, A.A., Bhattacharya, P., Bjorklund, G.J., Bowden, C., Boyd, R.W., Brody, P.S., Buruham, R., Byer, R.L., Carter, G., Chemla, D., Dagenais, M., Dohler, G., Efron, U., Eimerl, D., Feigelson, R.S., Feinberg, J., Feldman, B.J., Garito, A.F., Garmire, E.M., Gibbs, H.M., Glass, A.M., Goldberg, L.S., Gunshor, R.L., Gustafson, T.K., Hellwarth, R.W., Kaplan, A.E., Kelly, P.L., Leonberger, F.J., Lytel, R.S., Majerfeld, A., Menyuk, N., Meredith, G.R., Neurgaonkar, R.S., Peyghambarain, N.G., Prasad, P., Rakuljic, G., Shen, Y.-R.. Smith, P.W., Stawatoff, J., Stegeman, G.I., Stillman, G., Tang, C.L., Temkin, H., Thakur, M., Valley, G.C., Wolff, P.A., and Woods, C. (1987). *Appl. Opt.* **26**, 211–234.

Balashov, S.P. (1985). *In*: "Photosensitive Biological Complexes and Optical Information Recording." (G.R. Ivanitskii, ed.), Academy of Sciences USSR, Pushchino, pp. 49–67 (in Russian).

Bazhenov, V.Yu, Burykin, N.M., Vasnetsov, M.V., Soskin, M.S., and Taranenko, V.B. (1982a). *Ukrainskii Fiz. Zh.* **27**, 1018–1022 (in Russian).

Bazhenov, V.Yu., Burykin, N.M., Vasnetsov, M.V., Volkov, S.V., Soskin, M.S., and Taranenko, V.B. (1982b). *Ukrainskii Fiz. Zh.* **27**, 30–36 (in Russian).

Bazhenov, V.Yu., Burykin, N.M., Vasnetsov, M.V., Soskin, M.S., and Taranenko, V.B., (1983). *Avtometriya*, **5**, 3–9 (in Russian). English transl. in *Automatic Monitoring and Measuring*.

Bazhenov, V.Yu., Vsevolodov, N.N., Dukova, T.V., Soskin, M.S., and Taranenko, V.B., (1985). *In*: "Photosensitive Biological Complexes and Optical Information Recording." (G.R. Ivanitskii, ed.), Academy of Sciences USSR, Pushchino, pp. 123–129 (in Russian).

Bazhenov, V.Yu., Berezin, I.V., Burykin, N.M., Eremeev, N.L., Kazanskaya, N.F., Soskin, M.S., and Taranenko, V.B., (1986a). *Ukrainskii Fiz. Zh.* **31**, 193–195 (in Russian).

Bazhenov, V.Yu., Soskin, M.S., and Taranenko, V.B. (1986b). *Zh. Tekh. Fiz.* **56**, 788–790 (in Russian). English transl. in *Sov. Phys.-Tech. J.*

Bazhenov, V.Yu., Soskin, M.S., and Taranenko, V.B., (1986c). *Kvantovaya Elektronika* **13**, 2325–2328 (in Russian). English transl. in *Sov. J. Quantum Electron.*

Bazhenov, V.Yu., Soskin, M.S., and Taranenko, V.B., (1986d). *Kvantovaya Elektronika* **13**, 245–247 (in Russian). English transl. in *Sov. J. Quantum Electron.*

Bazhenov, V.Yu., Soskin, M.S., and Taranenko, V.B. (1987). *Pisma v Zh. Tekh. Fiz* **13**, 918–922 (in Russian). English transl. in *Sov. Tech. Phys. Lett.*

Bosacchi, B., and Narducci, L.M. (1983). *Opt. Lett.* **8**, 324–326.

Brandes, R.G., François, E.E., and Shankoff, T.A., (1969). *Appl. Opt.* **8**, 2346–2348.

Burykin, N.M., Dukova, T.V., Korchemskaya, E.Ya., Soskin, M.S., Taranenko, V.B., Vsevolodov, N.N. (1985). *Opt. Commun.* **54**, 68–70.

Calixto, S., and Lessard, R.A. (1984). *Appl. Opt.* **23**, 1989–1994.

Calixto, S., Solano, C., and Lessard, R.A. (1985). *Appl. Opt.* **24**, 2941–2947.

Carter, F.L. (1984). *J. Phys. D.* **10**, 175–194.

Cecchi, S., Giusfredi, G., Petriella, E., and Salieri, P. (1982). *Phys. Rev. Lett.* **49**, 1928–1931.

Chang, B.J., and Leonard, C.D. (1979). *Appl. Opt.* **18**, 2407–2417.

Davydov, A.S. (1986). "Solitons in Bioenergetics." Naukova Dumka, Kiev, USSR (in Russian).

Dykman, M.I., and Tarasov, G.G. (1985). "Tech. Dig. XII Nat. Conf. Nonlinear Optics, Moscow 1985," pp. 311–312 (in Russian).

Firth, W.J., and Galbraith, I. (1985). *IEEE J. Quantum Electron.* **QE–21**, 1399–1403.

Gladden, J.W. (1980). *Appl. Opt.* **19**, 1537–1540.

Jonathan, J.M.C., and May, M. (1979a). *Opt.Commun.* **28**, 30–34.

Jonathan, J.M.C., and May, M. (1979b). *Opt. Commun.* **28**, 295–299.

Kakichashvili, Sh.D., and Shaverdova, V.G. (1967). *Opt. i Spektrosk.* **41**, 525–528 (in Russian). English transl. in *Opt. and Spectrosc.*

Keszthelyi, L. (1982). *Methods in Enzymology* **88**, 287–297.

Kimura, Y., Ikegami, A., Ohno, K., Saigo, S., and Takeuchi, Y. (1981). *Photochem and Photobiol.* **33**, 435–439.

Kitano, M., Jabuzaki, J., and Ogawa, T. (1981). *Phys. Rev. Lett.* **46**, 926–929.

Korchemskaya, E.Ya., Soskin, M.S., and Taranenko, V.B. (1987). *Kvan-

tovaya Elektronika **14,** 714–721 (in Russian). English transl. in *Sov. J. Quanum Electron.*

Kozar, J. (1965). "Light Sensitive Systems," Wiley, New York.

Lozier, R.H., and Niederberger, W. (1977). *Federation Proceedings* **36,** 1805–1909.

Maksimychev, A.V., Lukashov, E.P., Kononenko, A.A., Timashov, S.F., and Chekulaeva, L.N. (1985). *In*: "Photosensitive Biological Complexes and Optical Information Recording." (G.R. Ivanitskii, ed.), Academy of Sciences USSR, Pushchino, pp. 152–156, (in Russian).

Martin, G., Lam, L.K., and Hellwarth, R.W. (1980). *Opt. Lett* **5,** 185–187.

Meyerhofer, D. (1972). *RCA Rev.* **33,** 110–130.

Meyerhofer, D. (1977). *In*: "Holographic Recording Materials." (H.M. Smith, ed.). Springer-Verlag, Berlin, pp. 75–99.

Moloney, J.V. (1985). *IEEE J. Quantum Electron.* **Q-21,** 1393–1398.

Montemayor, V.J., and Deck, R.T. (1985). *J. Opt. Soc. Am. B.* **2,** 1010–1013.

Montemayor, V.J., and Deck, R.T. (1986). *J. Opt. Soc. Am. B.* **3,** 1211–1220.

Newell, J.C., Solymar, L., and Ward, A.A. (1985). *Appl. Opt.* **24,** 4460–4466.

Robinson, A.L. (1983). *Science* **220,** 940–942.

Rozanov, N.N. (1981). *Zh. Eksp. Teor. Fiz.* **53,** 47–53 (in Russian). English transl. in *Sov. Phys. -JETP.*

Rozanov, N.N. (1983). *Opt. i Spektrosk* **55,** 658–659 (in Russian). English transl. in *Opt. and Spectrosc.*

Savransky, V.V., Tkachenko, N.V., and Chukhaev, V.I. (1985). *In*: "Photosensitive Biological Complexes and Optical Information Recording," (G.R. Ivanitskii, ed.), Academy of Sciences USSR, Pushchino, pp. 106–109 (in Russian).

Shankoff, T.A. (1968) *Appl. Opt.* **7,** 2101–2105.

Shuvalov, V.A. (1985). *In*: "Photosensitive Biological Complexes and Optical Information Recording," (G.R. Ivanitskii, ed.), Academy of Sciences USSR, Pushchino, pp. 167–171 (in Russian).

Stegeman, G.I. (1982). *IEEE J. Quantum Electron.* **QE–18,** 1610–1619.

Soskin, M.S., and Taranenko, V.B. (1984). *Proc. SPIE* **473,** 276–279.

Stoeckenius, W., Lozier, R.H., and Bogomolni, R.A. (1979). *Biochem. Biophys. Acta* **505,** 215–278.

Todorov, T., Nikolova, L., Stoyanova, K., and Tomova, N. (1985). *Appl. Opt.* **24,** 785–788.

Tomlinson, W.J. (1975). *Appl. Opt.* **14,** 2456–2467.

Vincent, P., Paraire, N., Nevier, M., Koster, A., and Reinish, R. (1985). *J. Opt. Soc. Am. B.* **2,** 1106–1116.

Vsevolodov, N.N., Dukova, T.V., Korchemskaya, E.Ya., Soskin, M.S., and Taranenko, V.B. (1984). *Ukrainskii Fiz. Zh.* **29,** 1120–1122 (in Russian).

Vsevolodov, N.N. (1985). *In*: "Photosensitive Biological Complexes and Optical Information Recording," (G.R. Ivanitskii, ed.), Academy of Sciences USSR, Pushchino, pp. 98–106 (in Russian).

Vsevolodov, N.N., Ivanitskii, G.R., Soskin, M.S., and Taranenko, V.B. (1986). *Avtometriya* **2,** 41–48 (in Russian). English transl. in *Automatic Monitoring and Measuring.*

Zeldovich, B.Ya., and Shkunov, V.V. (1979). *Kvantovaya Elektronika* **6,** 629–631 (in Russian). English transl. in *Sov. J. Quantum Electron.*

5.

Diode Lasers in Optical Computing

Valentin N. Morozov

P.N. Lebedev Physical Institute
USSR Academy of Sciences
Moscow, USSR.

Contents

1. Introduction. 145
2. Basic Characteristics of Diode Lasers 146
3. Generation of Short Pulses by Diode Lasers 150
4. Recording and Reconstruction of Fourier Holograms with Diode-Laser
   Radiation 154
   4.1. Basic Configurations for Holographic Storage 160
5. Diode Lasers in Correlation Systems 161
6. Integration of Holograms with Optical Waveguides 169
7. Optical Logic Gates on Diode Lasers 174
8. Integration of Diode Lasers with Electronic Circuits 179
9. Conclusion 185
   References 186

1.

Introduction

Optical computing requires sufficiently powerful and bright sources of radiation characterized by a small size and by a highly effective transformation of pumping energy into coherent radiation. Analysis of these incomplete conditions leads to the conclusion that diode or injection lasers provide the best choice in terms of power consumption and size. To these advantages one should also add that for analog optical operations, such as image reconstruction from holograms, matched filtering, etc., their coherence is adequate. Optical computing requires highly nonlinear bistable logic elements that may be built around diode lasers. Moreover, as these lasers may be integrated on chips with electronic control circuits, photodiodes, etc., integrated optoelectronic circuits that execute various logic and arithmetic operations may be designed around them. This brush treatment of diode lasers reveal that they provide a unique optical computing facility and possibly will underlie the components of future high-performance optical computers. The present paper discusses basic applications of diode lasers in optical computing.

2.
Basic Characteristics of Diode Lasers

The most popular lasers now are GaAlAs/GaAs and GaInAsP/InP lasers radiating at 0.85 and 1.3 μm, respectively. Coherent radiation is generated by the recombination of electrons and holes in the p-n junction under direct current. The feedback may be implemented by means of reflection from a) crystal internal facets; b) periodic structures realized in the semiconductor; or c) external mirrors. These methods each have their own merits and specific areas of application. Lasers with crystal-facet-based cavities are the most extensively used. Figure 5.1 shows a buried heterostructure laser with an active area 300 μm long, 1–2 μm wide, and 0.1 μm thick. Outside the area, current is limited by blocking layers. Output power is upper-limited by the ability to sink the heat generated from internal resistance and from nonradiating processes, as well as by the maximum light flux power that can be withstood by the mirrors. The ohmic resistance of the structures usually is of the order of several ohms. The maximum output power has been experimentally found to be equal to 10 mW per micron of radiating surface width. The threshold current ranges from 2.5 to 100 mA, with a typical value lying between 20 and 50 mA.

Solid-state laser threshold currents are exponentially dependent on the temperature according to the following empirical formula:

$$I = I_0 \exp \frac{T}{T_0},$$

Fig. 5.1.

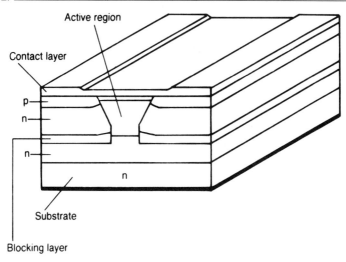

Active region

Contact layer

p

n

n

n

Substrate

Blocking layer

Basic structure of a buried-heterostructure diode laser.

where T is the operating temperature, usually room temperature. Continuous output power varies form several milliwatts to several hundred milliwatts. The output radiation is horizontally polarized and has 30° and 70° angular divergence in the horizontal and vertical planes, respectively. The lifetime of current lasers emitting at 0.85 and 1.3 μm is determined by the configuration rather than by imperfections of the crystal itself and is at least 100,000 hours. The reliability of such lasers is steadily improving.

Threshold currents must be reduced in order to integrate lasers with electronic components and to maximize the efficiency of "current-to-light" conversion in order to improve the heat sinking.

These problems are largely solved through multi-quantum-well (MQW) based lasers. The active area of GaAs-based MQW lasers consists of several 50- to 100-Å thick layers of GaAs separated by GaAlAs as barrier layers of about the same thickness. The MQW lasers have smaller threshold currents, higher quantum effectiveness, and less temperature dependence on the threshold current.

Computations with two-dimensional space-time light modulators require high-power diode lasers (Elion and Morozov, 1984). Power may be increased by the coherent addition of radiation from several lasers integrated within a common semiconductor structure. With diffraction coupling of in-

Fig. 5.2. _____

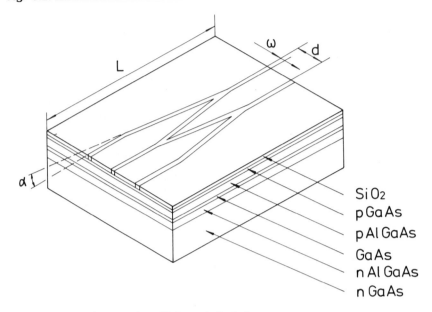

SiO2
pGaAs
pAlGaAs
GaAs
nAlGaAs
nGaAs

A multielement diode laser array.

dividual lasers, fixed-phase relations may be established between the fields
of adjacent elements. This may provide higher power, a considerably nar-
rowed divergence in the heterojunction plane, and a better spectrum
stabilization.

A multielement laser is diagrammed in Fig. 5.2. The maximum power
produced by a row of 40 radiators in the continuous mode at room temperature was 2.6 W with a divergence an order of magnitude narrower than
that of a single laser. If lasers are spaced sufficiently far apart and radiate
independently of each other, then each element may be controlled independently of the others. This individually addressable row may be used as an
element of communication channel switches. Data processing systems require laser arrays that may be implemented, for instance, with lasers radiating orthogonally to the p-n junction plane. Radiation orthogonal to the
p-n junction plane may be output with periodic lattices (Bragg reflectors) as
well.

Basic characteristics of the GaAlAs/GaAs injection lasers are summarized
in Table 5.1 (Suematsu, 1985).

TABLE 5.1

Output Properties of GaAlAs/GaAs Diode Lasers

GaAlAs/GaAs	Wavelength (microns)	Typical Power (mW)	Maximum Power (mW)	Quantum Efficiency (%)	Device Efficiency (%)	T_o (°C)	I_{th} (mA)
Laser diode	0.85	5–10	200	50–70	45		4.5
Quantum well LD	0.85		200	80	40	120–150	2.5
Phased array LD	0.85		2600	60		200	

$\gamma = 10^9/s$

c/γ

3. _____

Generation of Short Pulses by Diode Lasers

Short pulses of light are required for optical communications and for switching of optical logic elements. Optical communications requires a bandwith of several gigahertz, and logic elements can be switched by picosecond or even shorter pulses. A controlled generation of light pulses with a duration of 30–100 psec and a frequency of 1–10 GHz can be provided by high-frequency modulation of the injection current. One-psec light pulses can be generated by means of various mode-locking techniques.

The high-frequency modulation of diode laser radiation intensity has been extensively experimented, with results described by a simple theoretical model relying upon the following rate equations:

$$\frac{dP}{dt} = \frac{\partial G}{\partial N}(N - N_t)P - \frac{P}{\tau_{ph}} + \eta\frac{N}{\tau_s} \qquad (5.1)$$

$$\frac{dN}{dt} = \frac{J}{ed} - \frac{N}{\tau_s} - \frac{\partial G}{\partial N}(N - N_t)P,$$

where N is the electron density, N_t is the electron density at which gain in an active medium is zero, P is the photon density in a cavity, J is the injection current, d is the active area thickness, τ_s is the spontaneous carrier lifetime, τ_{ph} is the photon lifetime in a cavity, $\partial G/\partial N$ is the differential gain, e is the electron charge, and η is the portion of spontaneous radiation getting into the laser modes. Analysis of Eq. (5.1) reveals that the transition to the stationary state is accompanied by a relaxational intensity pulsation with frequency

$$f_0 = \frac{1}{2\pi}\sqrt{\frac{\partial G}{\partial N}\frac{P_0}{\tau_{ph}}}. \qquad (5.2)$$

where P_0 is the stationary power generated.

Often used is another formula of the transient pulsation frequency

$$f_0 = \frac{1}{2\pi}\sqrt{\frac{\beta - 1}{\tau_s\tau_{ph}}}, \qquad (5.3)$$

where $\beta = J/J_{th}$ is the current excess over the threshold value.

Figure 5.3 depicts a typical transient of laser radiation intensity under a stepwise increase of the injection current. The characteristic frequency of pulsation is $\sim f_0$, and τ_s is its decay time. If a periodic component ΔJ

Fig. 5.3.

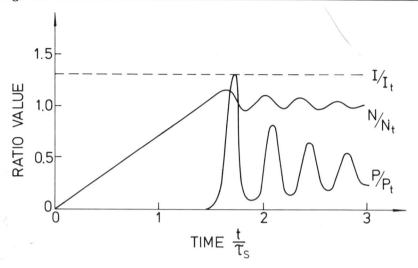

Transient processes in a diode laser at step current switching—numerical calculation.

$\cos 2\pi ft$ is added to the constant injection current, the output modulation intensity will be periodically modulated as well. Figure 5.4 shows the depth of laser intensity modulation versus the modulation frequency that characterizes resonance at the coincidence of the UHF current modulation frequency and f_0. There are three ways to increase the resonance frequency f_0: Increase the photon density in the cavity, decrease the lifetime τ_{ph}, and increase the differential gain.

The resonance frequency f_0 as a function of the square root of power for decreased resonator length and increased degree of active domain doping level is plotted in Fig. 5.5. The figure shows that the frequency may be controlled by technological means and shifted to 20 GHz or even higher. The equivalent laser electrical circuit consists of a capacitor and a resistance connected in parallel. The impact of its RC constant on the modulation bandwith is estimated to be appreciable at modulation frequencies over 15 GHz (Lau and Yariv, 1985). The majority of studies on diode-laser high-frequency modulation consider the case where the depth of modulation of the laser intensity is essentially below one. To minimize the error probability for digital/optical transmission of binary sequences, it is desirable to have 100% modulation depth. However, for deep modulation, the situation is disadvantageous, because each pumping pulse affects the parameters of the

Fig. 5.4.

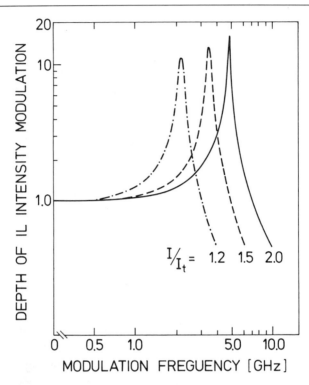

Intensity depth modulation as a function of frequency modulation.

light pulse resulting from the next current pulse and relaxation oscillations distort the light pulse profile with respect to that of the pumping current pulse. The resonance frequency f_0 depends on the depth of the radiation intensity modulation and decreases with its growth. In this case, it is safe to say that pulse-code modulation provides a 5-GHz bandwidth and in the near future 10 GHz may be expected.

Different methods of mode locking are used for the generation of light pulses shorter than 1 psec. As diode lasers are typically 200–400 μm long, the distance between neighboring axial modes is very large—about 100–200 GHz. Laser mode synchronization and the detection of the resulting pulses is a complicated problem that has not yet been resolved. The first step is this direction is mode locking in external resonator lasers, where the intermode distance diminishes to 1–10 GHz because of the longer resonator. This allows active synchronization of the laser external resonator through

Fig. 5.5.

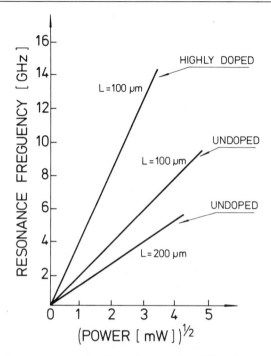

Resonance frequency as a function of power for different cavity lengths and doping levels.

periodic modulation of the pumping current with a frequency close to the intermode distance. The method of collision mode locking provides the best emitted pulse duration. It relies upon the interaction of two opposite pulses in a nonlinear absorber. The coherent addition of pulses in a nonlinear absorber forms a nonstationary periodic lattice that favors more compression of the light pulses than passive mode locking. Figure 5.6 shows an experimental setup for colliding mode synchronization in a laser consisting of two amplifying areas 200 μm long and one absorbing (nonpumped) area 40 μm long situated in the diode center symmetrically to the amplifying areas. The effectiveness of the nonpumped area as a nonlinear absorber was estimated through the hysteresis of the power-current characteristic. To excite mode locking, a 710.5 MHz AC signal corresponding to a 21-cm long resonator is input to one of the amplifying areas.

Autocorrelation functions of light pulses obtained under mode synchronization are plotted in Fig. 5.7. If the currents I_1 and I_2 differ, active-passive

Fig. 5.6.

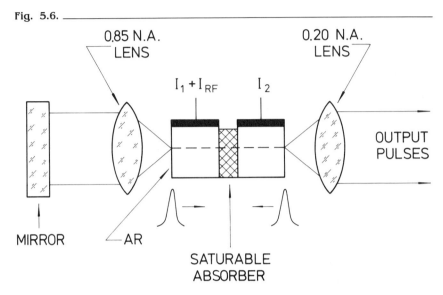

Setup for colliding mode-locking experiments.

mode locking occurs. Figure 5.7a shows a typical correlation function. The half-width of the amplitude autocorrelation peak is 6 psec, which corresponds to a 3-psec pulse having the shape of a one-sided exponent. The lateral maxima are 15 psec from the central one. The separation is equal to the time of a double passage between the diode facets. With a symmetrical diode, pumping colliding pulse synchronization occurs. The correlation maxima follow with a period twice as small, equal to 7.5 psec, which implies that in the resonator bounded by the diode facets two pulses exist. Taking into account the instrumental resolution, the length of the light pulses is 0.8 psec, which is four times less than that provided by active-passive synchronization at the same pumping level (Vasiliev et al., 1986). The average laser radiation power was about 5 mW, with the power of a single supershort pulse being 1–2 W. After optimization of the setup shown in Fig. 5.6, pulses 0.2–0.3 psec long might be expected with powers up to 10 W.

4.
Recording and Reconstruction of Fourier Holograms with Diode-Laser Radiation

Holography studies have used gas lasers radiating in the visible range because of their high coherence and polarization, and because of the avail-

Fig. 5.7.

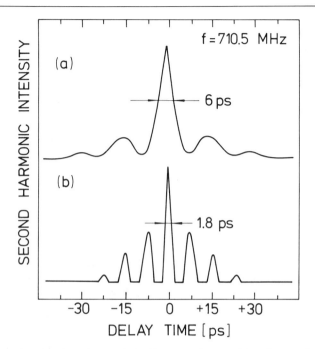

Autocorrelation functions for mode-locking experiments: (a) active-passive mode locking, (b) colliding mode locking.

ability of high-resolution photographic materials sensitive to the visible light spectrum. As it has turned out, gas lasers do not allow the design of economical, compact, and fast data processing devices because of the high-voltage power supplies, large size, low effectiveness, and difficulty of modulation. Use of the same type of lasers for both the recording and the reconstruction of holograms is one of the conditions for attaining the highest memory capacity for optical data-processing devices. Therefore, holograms used in diode-laser-based devices for data processing and storage must be recorded with diode-laser radiation as well.

The major requirements on infrared sensitive photographic materials for hologram recording may be formulated as follows. The material should be sufficiently sensitive in order to relax the requirements on exposure time and on vibration resistance, and to avoid the effects of optical inhomogeneities caused by air flowing through the light beam. For hologram recording by diode laser radiation, the energy sensitivity of a photographic material may be defined as follows:

$$E = \frac{\alpha \tau P}{S},$$

where α is the coefficient of energy transmission from the laser to the material, τ is the exposure time, S is an effective hologram area, and P is the laser radiation power. Assuming that $\alpha = 10^{-2}$, $S = 1$ mm^2, $\tau = 0.1$ sec, and $P = 5$ mW, we obtain that $E = 5 \times 10^{-6}$ J/mm^2. Taking into account the spatial separation of the zero-order wave and of the reconstructed image, the maximum spatial frequency for recording a hologram array is

$$\nu_{max} = \frac{3\left(\dfrac{D}{f}\right)}{\lambda \sqrt{1 + \left(\dfrac{D}{f}\right)^2}}.$$

From this expression, the maximum spatial frequency depends on the relative objective aperture D/f and on the wavelength of light. For $D/f = 0.5$ and $\lambda = 0.9$ μm, $\nu_{max} = 1490$ mm^{-1}, i.e., the photographic material resolution should be over 1500 lines/mm. In addition to the above requirements, a material must be easy to produce, require no special processing, and undergo little lateral deformation of the photographic layer, which causes aberrations and shifts of the reconstructed image elements. The creation of photographic materials with sensitivities of the order of 10^{-6} J/mm^2 and with resolutions of over 1500 mm^{-1} for the near-infrared range of the spectrum is a rather involved technological problem. This is because the sensitivity may be enhanced in this case only through large concentrations of sensitizers at increased temperatures, which results in larger emulsion grains. Special methods of emulsion synthesis and stabilization have enabled new infrachromatic materials I-880G (USSR) with an average size of AgBr microcrystals equal to 0.06 μm and with a maximum spectral sensitivity at 0.88 μm.

The relative spectral sensitivity of the layers of I-880G is plotted in Fig. 5.8. The maximum diffraction efficiency η_{max} of holograms recorded with plane waves was 32% for an exposure equal to approximately 9×10^{-6} J/mm^2. For spatial frequencies close to 1500 mm^{-1}, the transfer characteristic (the ratio of the diffraction efficiency to its maximum value) dropped to 0.5, i.e., the resolution of the photographic material was over 1500 mm^{-1}. Due to the small size of the active area and to astigmatism of the wavefront, the diode-laser beam divergence is much higher than that of gas lasers and is

Fig. 5.8. ————————————————————————————————

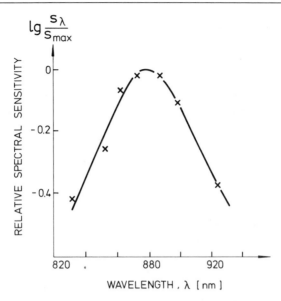

Spectral sensitivity of a J-880-G photoplate.

different along and across the p-n junction. This presents some difficulties
for the transmission of energy from the laser to a storage medium. The optical setup for hologram recording by a single-mode diode laser is not significantly different from that using gas lasers. However, it is difficult to
obtain high radiation power in a single mode: At high powers the spectrum
is always multimodal. The simultaneous generation of only two adjacent
axial modes of close intensities reduces the coherence length to about ΔL
< 300 μm. The temporal coherence length ΔL for radiation with a spectrum
bandwidth Δv may be approximated as follows:

$$\Delta L \sim \frac{c}{\Delta v} \sim \frac{2l}{m},$$

where l is the laser diode length and m is the number of excited axial modes.
For $l = 300$ μm and $m = 6$, the temporal coherence length is about 100
μm. Hence, in order to record holograms with multimode radiation, the
optical path differences between the object and the reference beams must be
aligned within an accuracy of 10–50 μm.

Figure 5.9 demonstrates an optical setup for recording a Fourier hologram
that is appropriate for lasers having either high or low temporal coherence.

Fig. 5.9.

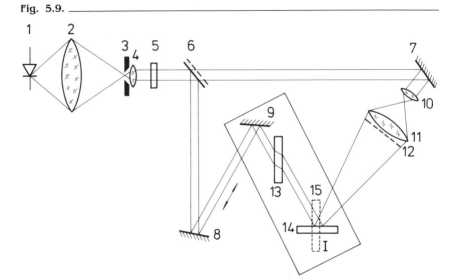

Experimental installation for writing holograms with a diode laser. 1, IL; 2, lens; 3, pinhole; 4, microobjective; 5, cylindrical lens; 6, beam splitter; 7, 8, and 9, mirrors; 10 and 11, optical systems; 12, data matrix; 13 and 15, glass plates; and 14, photoplate.

By mechanical movement of mirror 8 in the direction of the arrow, the contrast of the interference pattern was maximized, and plane-parallel plate 13 was used for compensation of the optical path difference. Figure 5.10 shows a real image reconstructed with a diode laser from holograms having a 1-mm diameter recorded on I-880G plates. The pictures in Figs. 5.10a and 5.10b are reconstructed from holograms recorded by multimode and by single-mode diode lasers, respectively. For multimode lasers, the bit density was 0.7×10^3 bits/mm^2 and the diffraction efficiency was 10%. For single-mode lasers, they were 4×10^3 bits/mm^2 and about 15%, respectively. By using optics with higher numerical apertures, the bit density may be further improved.

Data-processing systems require rows and matrix arrays of holograms. Analysis reveals that holograms with identical parameters must be recorded by single-mode lasers because the coherence length of diode laser radiation should be at least 1–100 mm depending on the particular optical arrangement.

An optical system for recording hologram row arrays is shown in Fig. 5.11. The reference beam scanned the surface of the photographic material

Fig. 5.10a.

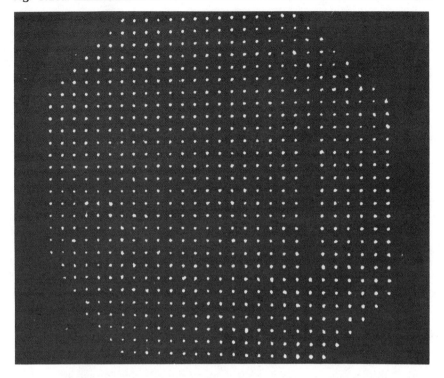

Reconstructed real image written with a multimode diode laser.

due to movement of mirror 8. A Fourier transform of the data matrix was generated in plane 16 by the lens-raster system, and moving aperture 15 limited the sizes of the object and of the reference beams to the hologram size. Holograms were recorded where the aperture and the reference beam coincided. A row of 32 Fourier holograms with areas of 1 mm² and a 1.5 mm step has been recorded. The holograms were reconstructed by 10^{-7}-sec diode-laser pulses. Figure 5.12 shows real images reconstructed from holograms in the array. Figure 12a shows the image from one hologram, and Fig. 5.12b shows superimposed images reconstructed simultaneously from the central and the two end holograms. As can be seen, both the quality and the coincidence of images are quite satisfactory. The images of Fig. 5.12 may be read out by a matrix of photodetectors and input into an optical data-processing system (Kalashnikov et al., 1980).

Fig. 5.10b.

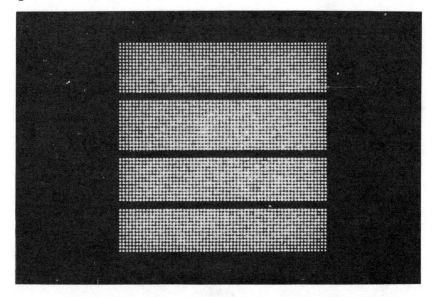

Reconstructed real image written with a single-mode diode laser.

4.1. Basic Configurations for Holographic Storage

Optical computations require optical memories for the storage of two-dimensional images from computation programs and algorithms, tabulated functions, vector arrays, etc. A holographic memory allows the parallel input of two-dimensional images into a data-processing system. Consider first the energy relations. If η is the hologram diffraction efficiency, α is the energy loss in the optics due to beam collimation, W_p is the sensitivity of one element of an array of silicon photodetectors, N is the number of bits in a reconstructed image, and τ is the data access time; then the laser power P is

$$P = \frac{W_p N}{\alpha \eta \tau}.$$

For $\eta = 0.2$, $\alpha = 0.5$, and $W_p = 10^{-13}$ J, a 50-mW laser can support an input image of 5×10^3 bits in 100 nsec. The data input rate in this case is 5×10^{10} bits/sec. These figures are average and quite realistic.

Figure 5.13 shows a holographic memory built around a diode laser array and a one-dimensional acousto-optics deflector. A desired address is chosen

Fig. 5.11.

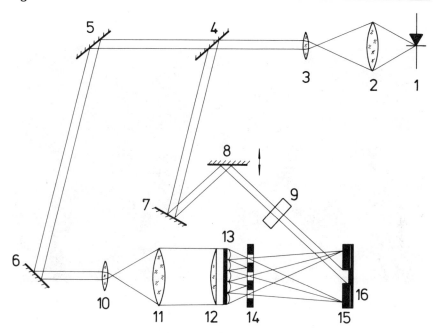

Experimental installation for recording an array of holograms. 1, diode laser; 2, 3, 10, 11, and 12, optical systems; 13, lens raster; 4, 5, 6, 7, and 8, mirrors; 9, attenuator; 15, diaphragm; and 16, photoplate.

in the horizontal direction by switching on the appropriate laser in a row, and in the vertical direction by deflecting the beam by the appropriate angle. A holographic memory using a matrix array of lasers is shown in Fig. 5.14. The system with a mechanically positioned carrier in Fig. 5.15 may be used for the long-term storage of large data arrays.

5.
Diode Lasers in Correlation Systems

Analog optical data processing may be carried out by means of both coherent and incoherent light. Each of these methods has its own merits and disadvantages, and addresses certain classes of applications. The coherent methods are more flexible and allow the processing of a wide class of two-dimensional complex functions defined by distributions of light-field amplitudes

Fig. 5.12.

a)   b)

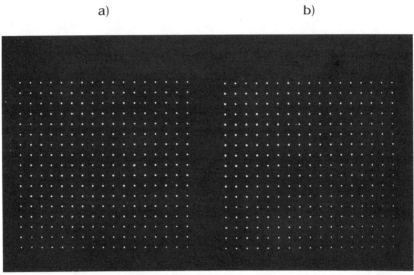

(a) Real images reconstructed with a diode laser from a single hologram. (b) Superimposed images, reconstructed from the 1st, 16th, and 32nd holograms in an array.

Fig. 5.13.

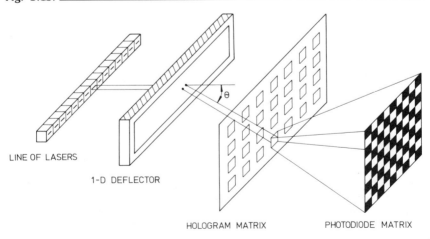

Diagram of a holographic memory on a 1-D array of lasers.

Fig. 5.14. ————————————————————————————————————

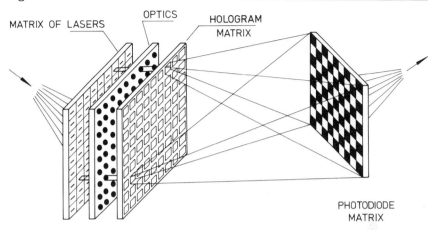

Diagram of a holographic memory on a 2-D array of diode lasers.

and phases. Coherent systems, however, are more involved and more sensitive to mechanical actions and impose stricter requirements on the cosmetic quality of optical elements and light sources. The design of incoherent systems for optical processing is simpler. However, their application is mostly confined to the processing of real positive functions, and special techniques are required to process bipolar functions.

Fig. 5.15. ————————————————————————————————————

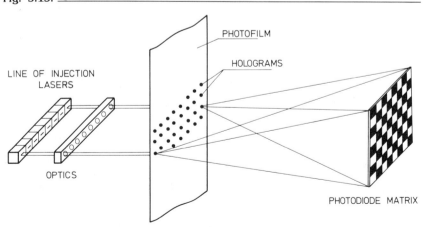

Mass memory on diode lasers with a film cartridge.

Coherent analog systems address four basic groups of optical computations: spectral analysis, spatial filtering, correlation analysis, and integral transformations.

In fact, any physical source is partially coherent, and the same diode laser may radiate either coherent or incoherent light, depending on the injection current. Therefore, in order to estimate the capabilities of diode-laser-based analog data-processing systems, a general discussion of optical processing systems with sources of arbitrary coherence is necessary. The coherent properties of electromagnetic fields are described in terms of the mutual coherence function

$$\Gamma(R_1, R_2, \tau) = \langle V_1(t + \tau)V_2^*(t) \rangle,$$

where $V_1(t)$ and $V_2(t)$ are analytical signals at spatial points R_1 and R_2, and the parentheses stand for averaging over a time interval much greater than the light period. For $\tau = 0$, the values of the mutual coherence function define the intensities at the points R_1 and R_2, i.e., $\Gamma(R_1, R_1, 0) = I_1$ and $\Gamma(R_2, R_2, 0) = I_2$.

Partially coherent radiation may be also characterized by the mutual spectral density $G(R_1, R_2, \nu)$

$$G(R_1, R_2, \nu) = \begin{cases} \int_{-\infty}^{+\infty} \Gamma(R_1, R_2, \tau)e^{2\pi \iota \nu \tau} \, d\tau & \nu \geq 0 \\ 0 & \nu < 0 \end{cases}$$

and $\Gamma(R_1, R_2, \tau)$, correspondingly, by

$$\Gamma(R_1, R_2, \tau) = \int_0^\infty G(R_1, R_2, \nu)e^{-2\pi \iota \nu \tau} \, d\nu.$$

Both functions are equivalent as a description of partially coherent radiation, but $G(R_1, R_2, \nu)$ is preferable for the analysis of the influence of the coherence on the performance of optical data-processing systems.

The law of mutual spectral density propagation relating the function values $G(R_1, R_2, \nu)$ in the observation plane with those in the source plane Q_1, Q_2 is known (Born and Wolf, 1964). Here, $R_1 = (x_1, y_1)$ and $R_2 = (x_2, y_2)$ are the Cartesian coordinates of points in the observation plane, and $Q_1 = (\rho_1, \phi_1)$ and $Q_2 = (\rho_2, \phi_2)$ are those in the source plane. The application of the van Cittert-Zernike theorem to the calculation of multicomponent optical processing systems comprising lenses, spatial light modulators, filters, holograms, etc. runs into significant difficulties. If one passes to the symbolic coordinates

$$\bar{x}_1 = x_1, \qquad \bar{x}_2 = ix_2, \qquad \bar{x}_3 = y_1, \qquad \bar{x}_4 = iy_2,$$

the task becomes much simpler. In the new notation, the vectors $\mathbf{x}$ and $\boldsymbol{\rho}$ will be regarded as vectors with the following components:

$$\mathbf{x}(\bar{x}_1, \bar{x}_2, \bar{x}_3, \bar{x}_4) = \mathbf{x}(x_1, ix_2, y_1, iy_2) \tag{5.4}$$

$$\boldsymbol{\rho}(\bar{\rho}_1, \bar{\rho}_2, \bar{\rho}_3, \bar{\rho}_4) = \boldsymbol{\rho}(\rho_1, i\rho_2, \phi_1, i\phi_2).$$

The law of mutual spectral density propagation becomes

$$G_x(\mathbf{x}, \nu) = - \frac{1}{\lambda^2 r^2} \int G_\rho(\boldsymbol{\rho}, \nu) e^{ik(\mathbf{x}-\boldsymbol{\rho})^2/2r} d\boldsymbol{\rho}, \tag{5.5}$$

where $r \approx r_1 \approx r_2$, and r_1 and r_2 are the distances between the pairs of points Q_1, R_1 and Q_2, R_2, respectively. The law of mutual spectral density propagation given in the form of Eq. (5.5) is representable as a convolution

$$G_x(\mathbf{x}, \nu) = G_\rho(\mathbf{x}, \nu) \otimes h_r(\mathbf{x}, \nu). \tag{5.6}$$

This allows the propagation of the mutual spectral density in free space to be considered as the propagation of a four-dimensional signal through a linear invariant system with a function $h_r(\mathbf{x}, \nu) = -1/\lambda^2 r^2 \exp ik\mathbf{x}^2/2r$ having the meaning of an impulse response for the mutual spectral density. If the transfer function $H_r(\boldsymbol{\omega}, \nu)$ is defined as usual, that is, as the Fourier transform of the impulse response

$$H_r(\boldsymbol{\omega}, \nu) = \int_{-\infty}^{+\infty} h_r(\mathbf{x}, \nu) e^{-i\boldsymbol{\omega}\cdot\mathbf{x}} d\mathbf{x},$$

then

$$H_r(\boldsymbol{\omega}, \nu) = e^{-ir\omega^2/2k}, \tag{5.7}$$

and the Fourier transforms of the mutual spectral densities in the source and in the observation planes are related by

$$\mathscr{F}\{G_x(\mathbf{x}, \nu)\} = \mathscr{F}\{G_\rho(\boldsymbol{\rho}, \nu)\} H_r(\boldsymbol{\omega}, \nu). \tag{5.8}$$

This means that in the symbolic system of coordinates chosen in Eq. (5.4), the design procedure for a partially coherent optical data-processing system is formally the same as that for a corresponding coherent linear system. In doing so, the mutual spectral density $G(\mathbf{x}, \nu)$ should be taken as the equivalent of the complex field amplitude $\mathscr{E}(x, y)$, and the function $T(\mathbf{x}) = t(x_1, y_1) t^*(x_2, y_2)$ should be employed instead of the amplitude transmission coefficients $t(x, y)$ of the optical elements.

Fig. 5.16.

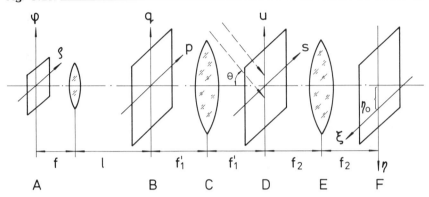

Optical matched filtering system. A, light source plane; B, input object plane; C and E, Fourier transform lenses; D, matched filter plane; and F, correlation plane.

An optical correlator configuration shown in Fig. 5.16 contains a source with a mutual spectral density function $G(\rho, \nu)$ in plane A, an object with an amplitude transmission function $t_2(\rho, q)$ in plane B, a matched filter with a transmission $t_1(\rho, q)$ in plane D, lenses with a focal distance f for Fourier transmission in planes C and E, and the result of correlation is recorded in plane F. The mutual spectral density function corresponding to the cross-correlation function in plane F may be determined through the above technique

$$G_\zeta^*(\zeta, \nu) = -\{T_2(\zeta)G_\rho(\zeta, \nu)\} \times T_1(\zeta), \qquad (5.9)$$

where $\times$ and $*$ denote correlation and complex conjugation, respectively. The function $G_\rho(\zeta, \nu)$ is expressed here in terms of the mutual spectral density $G_\rho(\rho, \nu)$ in the source plane using a collimating lens with focal length f' and propagation in free space to plane B. It was assumed in the derivation of Eq. (5.9) that $f_1 = f_2$ and that a matched filter with a transmission $t_1(\rho, q)$ is recorded with a laser having a perfect spatial and temporal coherence. It is assumed also that a laser of the same wavelength is used for both hologram recording and correlation.

Using Eq. (5.9) one may compute the effect of the laser spatial and temporal coherence on the shape of the correlation signal in the matched filtering configuration. Figure 5.17 shows the effect of the laser spectrum width on the shape of the correlation peak in the output plane of the correlator in Fig. 5.16. The light intensity in the correlation plane is the vertical axis, and the normalized coordinate in the correlation plane $\Psi = a\eta/\lambda f$ (where a is the diameter of the holographic matched filter and η is one of Cartesian coordinates in the correlation plane) is the horizontal axis. The graphs are normalized so that the total radiation power is the same for different widths of source spectra. In the output plane, the width of the correlation peak along η depends only on $\alpha = T/\tau$, where $T = a \sin \vartheta / \lambda c$, ϑ is the angle of the reference beam incident on the matched filter, and $\Delta \nu = 1/\tau$ is the spectrum bandwidth of the light. The parameter α is also representable as $\alpha = R \Delta\lambda / \lambda$, where $R = a \sin \vartheta / \lambda$ is the resolution of a diffraction grating having a diameter a with a line spacing $\lambda / \sin \vartheta$. For $\alpha \leq 1$, the relative width of the laser spectrum is less than the inverse of the resolution of the diffraction grating equivalent to the filter, and the spread of the correlation peak is small because of the limited coherence length. For $\alpha > 1$, the correlation peak width increases approximately linearly with the spectrum width. The laser spectrum width may thus limit the spatial resolution in the correlator output

Fig. 5.17.

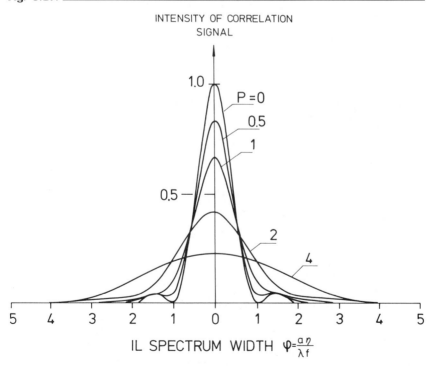

Dependence of the correlation peak intensity on the spectrum of diode lasers; different curves correspond to $\alpha = T/\tau = 0$; 0.5; 1; 2; and 4.

plane. Variations of the laser wavelength cause signal shifts in the correlation plane.

In order to investigate the effect of the diode-laser spatial coherence on
the shape of the correlation signal, one may assume that the source is quasimonochromatic, i.e., $\alpha < 1$. In this case, the mutual intensity can be substituted for the mutual spectral density $G_\rho(\zeta, \eta)$ in Eq. (5.9) and

$$\Gamma_\zeta(\zeta) = - [T_2(\zeta)\Gamma_\rho(\zeta)] \times T_1(\zeta), \qquad (5.10)$$

from which two well-known limiting cases follow. For coherent radiation,
$\Gamma_\rho(\rho) = 1$, and we have $I(\zeta, \eta) = |t_2(\zeta, \eta) \times t_1(\zeta, \eta)|^2$ in a coherent optical
correlator. For incoherent radiation, $\Gamma_\rho(\rho) = \delta(\rho_1 - \rho_2)\delta(q_1 - q_2)$, and we
have $I(\zeta, \eta) = |t_2(\zeta, \eta)|^2 \times |t_1(\zeta, \eta)|^2$ in a Lohmann correlator.

The result is generally dependent on both the mutual intensity in the input
plane $\Gamma_\rho(\rho)$ and on the amplitude transmission coefficients $t_1(\rho, q)$ and $t_2(\rho, q)$.
For a particular mutual intensity function, the influence of the degree of
spatial coherence on the shape of the correlation signal and other properties
of the correlator may be determined from Eq. (5.10) in a manner similar to
the calculation result shown in Fig. 5.17. As an example, Fig. 5.18 shows
theoretical and experimental graphs of the relative correlation peak intensity

Fig. 5.18. _____

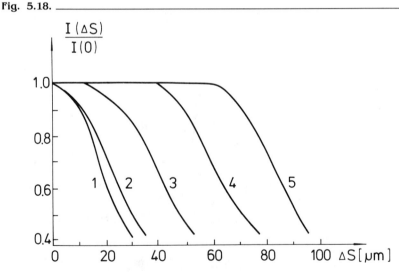

Dependence of the relative correlation intensity peak $I(\Delta S)/I(0)$ on the matched
filter shift ΔS for different emitting region sizes L of diode lasers. $1 - L = 10$
μm; $2 - L = 20$ μm; $3 - L = 40$ μm; $4 - L = 60$ μm; and $5 - L = 80$ μm.

versus the lateral filter shift for various areas of diode-laser radiation surface. Experiments with narrow radiation areas (BH structures) and with rows of lasers (simulating spatially noncoherent radiation) have demonstrated that the correlation signal quality does not differ from that obtained with He-Ne laser ilumination (Elkhov et al., 1982; Morozov, 1973; Zolotarev et al., 1982).

6.
Integration of Holograms with Optical Waveguides

It is interesting to consider the feasibility of integrating optical waveguides with holograms to perform various functions such as beam focusing or switching, correlation analysis, etc. Since integrated optical modulators, switches, and deflectors are characterized by high speed and small control voltages, such integration could improve the functional capabilities of integrated optical circuits in the optical computing environment. If diode lasers are used as light sources, small-size multifunctional data processing circuits become feasible.

Figure 5.19 shows the diagram for recording waveguide holograms of two-dimensional objects. In this particular case, holograms were recorded with a wavelength $\lambda = 0.44$ μm. Thin layers (less than 0.5 μm) of As_2S_3 semiconductor were deposited on planar waveguides produced in glass by means of ion exchange. Processing by selective etching resulted in thin-relief holograms. The recording was designed to compensate for the aberrations caused by reconstructing with diode-laser radiation. The reconstruction setup is diagrammed in Fig. 5.20. An image reconstructed with a diode laser from a waveguide hologram is shown in Fig. 5.21. Diffraction efficiencies of the Fourier and Fraunhofer holograms were about 30% and 60%, respectively.

For recording waveguide holograms, diode lasers are of course preferable. However, the lack of sufficiently sensitive waveguide-compatible recording media presents a serious problem. Therefore, computer holograms made by electron-beam processing followed by etching of an appropriate resist deposited on the waveguide surface should be preferred.

Figure 5.22 shows a correlator for one-dimensional signals that is based on waveguide holograms (Morozov and Putilin, 1987). The lens L_2 Fourier transforms an input $f(x)$ into the hologram plane. This signal wave is coupled by means of an input grating. Two pseudorandom 20-bit binary se-

Fig. 5.19. _____

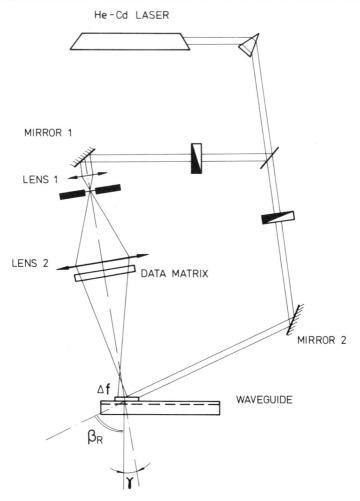

Experimental setup for waveguide hologram recording.

quences were recorded on the hologram. Figure 5.23 shows images of the
pseudorandom sequences reconstructed from the hologram, and Figs. 5.24a
and 5.24b show the autocorrelation function of the upper sequence and the
cross-correlation function of both sequences. The actual autocorrelation peak
was 9 dB, as compared with a 12-dB estimated value. The discrepancy is
caused by scattering in the waveguide and by aberrations of the input grating

Fig. 5.20.

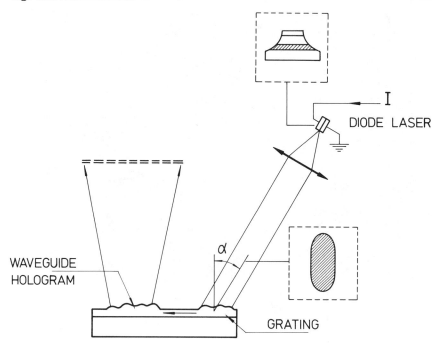

I

DIODE LASER

α

WAVEGUIDE
HOLOGRAM

GRATING

Reconstruction of waveguide holograms with a diode laser.

and of the hologram. In physical devices, information may be input by a row of modulators and the correlation signal may be sensed by a row of photodetectors, thus making the correlator structure planar.

Waveguide holograms may be used for optical communications in LSI circuits. The distribution of clock signals by an optical circuit consisting of waveguide holograms and lasers radiating short light pulses with an IC clock frequency is possible, as illustrated in Fig. 5.25. The light from waveguide holograms is output through the substrate and sensed by photodetectors. The laser light passes through several holograms and reconstructs individual pictures that may be either alike or different. Several objectives are thus accomplished, such as 100% percent use of the light energy, reduction of aberrations, and elimination of diode-laser frequency chirping effects on the reconstructed picture quality at high-frequency modulation. This allows an increase in the IC area or operation concurrently with multiple ICs.

Fig. 5.21.

Image reconstructed from a waveguide hologram with a diode laser; diffraction efficiency of hologram ≃ 50%.

Fig. 5.22.

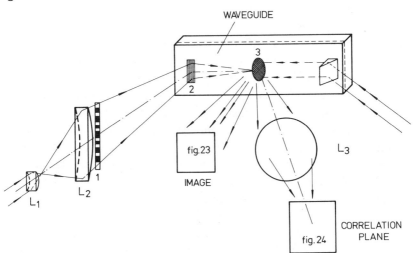

Matched filtering with waveguide holograms. L_1, L_2, and L_3, lenses; 1, input signal $f(x)$; 2, grating coupler; 3, waveguide hologram; and 4, read-out beam.

Fig. 5.23. _____

Images reconstructed from a hologram of binary random signals.

Fig. 5.24. _____

a)

b)

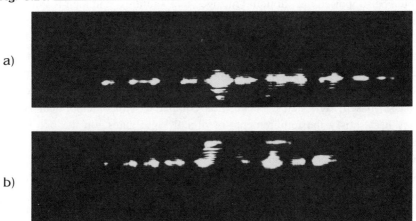

(a) Autocorrelation signal of upper sequence in Fig. 5.23. (b) Cross-correlation peak of two random signals in Fig. 5.23.

Fig. 5.25. _____

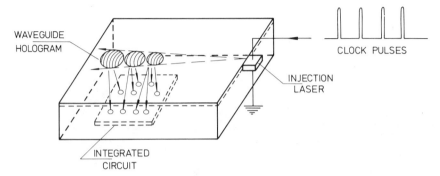

Example of a waveguide hologram application to the clock frequency distribution on an integrated circuit.

7.
Optical Logic Gates on Diode Lasers

Diode-laser-based optical logic gates were proposed by Basov as early as 1965 and were implemented soon after (Basov, 1965; Basov et al., 1969a, 1969b, 1969c, 1972). At that time, continuous operation of diode lasers could be supported only at liquid nitrogen temperatures, and their technology was in its initial stage. It is quite natural that the majority of designers did not regard diode-laser-based logic favorably. The development of laser technology and the improvement of diode-laser properties took 20 years. It was largely motivated by the need to introduce diode lasers into fiber communication lines and video disc systems. It now seems reasonable to turn again to laser-based logic gates, because as compared with other optical gates, they best satisfy the requirements of digital logic gates, on the one hand, and they allow integration with electronic control circuits and photodiodes within the same crystal, on the other.

During all the history of digital technology, the performance of electronic logic elements has been improving with respect to speed and power consumption as well as with respect to the level of integration. A similar trend exists in the field of diode lasers and logic gates built around them. The power dissipated by a laser may be estimated as

$$P_s = P_e - P_0 = IU(1 - \eta),$$

where P_s is the power dissipated as heat, P_e is the electrical supply power, P_0 is the output radiation power, I is the current flowing through the laser,

U is the p-n junction voltage, and η is the efficiency of "current-to-light" conversion. Assuming, in accordance with the data of Table 5.1, that $I = 2$ mA, $\eta \simeq 0.5$, and $U \simeq 1$ V, we obtain that $P_s \simeq 1$ mW. This approximate dissipation power estimated for a single laser is close to the mean dissipation power of existing TTL and ECL gates. For a clock frequency of 5 GHz, the switching energy is 2×10^{-13} J, which is also close to the typical values of electronic circuits. These estimates have improved over recent years by more than one order of magnitude and are not yet final.

Optical logic gates are built around a bistable double-section diode laser (D^2), as shown in Fig. 5.26. It consists of two galvanically isolated areas placed one behind the other within a common cavity with a common waveguide. Each part of D^2 has its own ohmic contact, which enables independent variation of currents injected into them. D^2 is an optical counterpart of an electronic trigger, i.e., a bistable device. Generation in D^2 is described as follows:

$$\frac{dP}{dt} = [G_1(N) + \gamma G_2(M)]P - \frac{1}{\tau_{ph}} P \qquad (5.11)$$

$$\frac{dN}{dt} = \frac{J_1}{ed} - \frac{N}{\tau_s} - G_1(N)P$$

$$\frac{dM}{dt} = \frac{J_2}{ed} - \frac{M}{\tau_s} - G_2(M)P,$$

where P is the photon density; N and M are electron concentrations in the first and second parts of D^2, respectively; γ is the ratio of the length of the first part to that of the second; $G_1(N)$ and $G_2(M)$ are gains in both parts; and the rest of the notations are the same as in Eq. (5.1). Analysis of Eq. (5.11) allows one to draw the following conclusions. In conventional lasers the gain monotonically decreases with the increase of radiation intensity P due to the saturation of gain, and, on the contrary, in D^2 the total gain $G(P) = G_1(P) + \gamma G_2(P)$ may grow with intensity. It follows from Eq. (5.11) that

$$\frac{dG(P)}{dP} = - \left[G_1 \frac{\partial G_1}{\partial N} \tau_N + \gamma G_2 \frac{\partial G_2}{\partial M} \tau_M \right], \qquad (5.12)$$

where

$$\tau_N^{-1} = \tau_s^{-1} \left[1 + \frac{\partial G_1(N)}{\partial N} P \right] \quad \text{and} \quad \tau_M^{-1} = \tau_s^{-1} \left[1 + \frac{\partial G_2(M)}{\partial M} P \right].$$

Fig. 5.26.

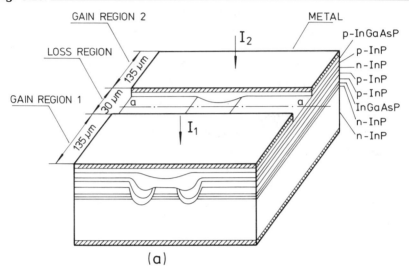

(a)

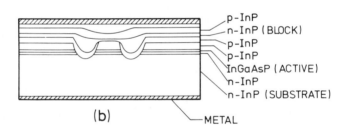

(b)

Construction of bistable laser diode (D^2).

From Eq. (5.12), the bistable mode exist for $dG(P)/dP > 0$ only if one part absorbs radiation, that is, if $G_2 < 0$, for example. When the number of photons increases, the rate of absorbtion decreases more than the gain. The total gain therefore grows at first with the field and then drops due to the saturation. The threshold curve in the plane I_1, I_2, where the threshold conditions of self-excitations are met, is defined by the following condition:

$$G_1(P = 0) + \gamma G_2(P = 0) \geq 1/\tau_{\text{ph}}.$$

The threshold curve for D^2 and the solution of Eq. (5.12) are plotted in Fig. 5.27 as 1-1 and 2-2 curves, respectively. Above 1-1, the threshold

Fig. 5.27. _____

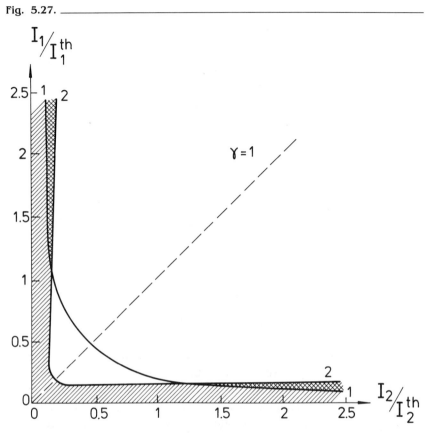

Current plane for D^2: curve 1-1, threshold condition for laser action; curve 2-2, bistable region. In the double-dashed region D^2 operates in a bistable mode.

conditions are obeyed, and within the double-shaded area, the bistability condition is met. The bistable D^2 have a hysteresis dependence on the generated power versus the injection current: Generation occurs stepwise at certain currents and ceases at smaller injection currents. The hysteresis curve of D^2 output power is shown in Fig. 5.28.

By varying the injection currents J_1 and J_2, one can change the current range ΔJ_2 where the hysteresis loop exists. In this range, switching from the mode of spontaneous radiation to that of stable coherent radiation may be triggered by a small current, which on the average comes up to several percent of the total injection current. The D^2 device is an analog of the electronic transistor in that small changes of the current in the absorbing part

Fig. 5.28.

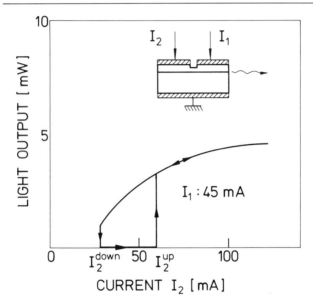

Hysteresis loop in D^2.

or a small intensity optical pumping delivered into this part causes a significant change in the power of emitted coherent radiation. The ability of D^2 to be in two stable states, and the small level of signals required to switch it from one state into another, make it an attractive basis for the design of optical logic gates. Figure 5.29 shows one of the first laser GaAs integrated circuits functioning as a half-adder (Nishizawa, 1967). Fan-in and fan-out of logic elements are important characteristics because they define the number of other elements that may be connected to the input or output of a given element without violating normal operating conditions. The load-carrying capacity of electronic gates is as follows: Fan-out ranges from 10 to 30 and fan-in is 10. Generally, fan-in and fan-out characterize the complexity of circuits that may be constructed with those elements. For optical logic gates, signal fan-in and fan-out is rather a challenge because by spreading a signal the power of each information pulse is proportionally reduced. Since it is desirable that optical logic elements be switched by standard pulses having certain powers, one runs into the problem of designing optical power amplifiers. The design of optical power amplifiers integrated with logic elements is an important but insufficiently explored subject. Numerous problems are eliminated by integrating logic elements with photodiodes where

Fig. 5.29.

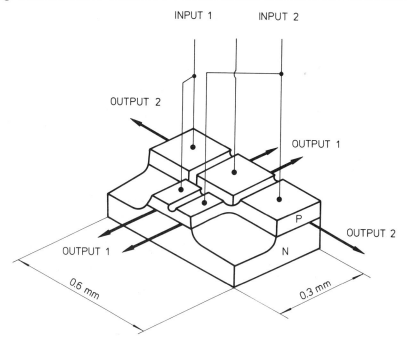

Logic gates on diode-laser functioning as a half-adder.

input optical control signals are transformed into electrical ones controlling logic elements. The current-to-light transition delays are minimal due to the constant injection current fed into the amplifying part of D^2. The control power is also minimal due to the fact that D^2 radiation is controlled by modulating the current flowing into its absorbing part. Some possible versions of electrical connections in a D^2 + photodiode system are diagrammed in Fig. 5.30. The constant injection current into the amplifying part is marked with an asterisk.

8.
Integration of Diode Lasers with Electronic Circuits

The strategy of designing components for optical computing must draw upon the experience accumulated by electronic technology. Logic components for

Fig. 5.30.

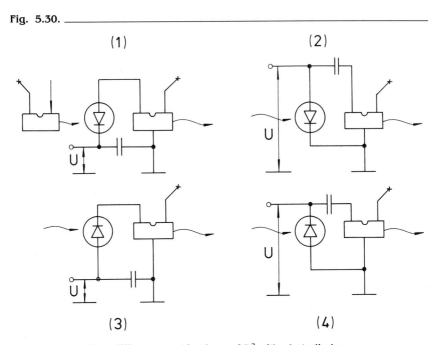

Four different combinations of D^2 with photodiodes.

Fig. 5.31.

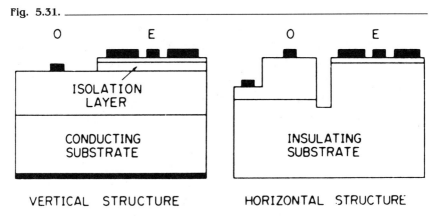

Two methods of integration of optoelectronic and electronic components on a chip.

Fig. 5.32.

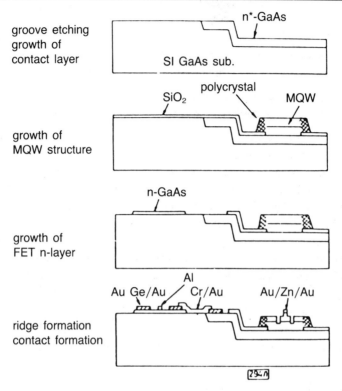

groove etching
growth of
contact layer

growth of
MQW structure

growth of
FET n-layer

ridge formation
contact formation

Example of the formation of MQW laser with MESFET structures.

optical computing should enable integration into a single integrated circuit. A set of logic gates should include capability for negation and amplification. There is an optical data processing configuration with two-dimensional space-time light modulators where the signal energy is increased up to a standard level at the expense of the energy of the external coherent source. Electronic signal inverters and amplifiers integrated in the same chip with optical elements provide an alternative approach, which has become an independent research field covered by numerous reviews (Forrest, 1985; Wada et al., 1986). The first GaAlAs/GaAs laser was integrated with a transistor as early as 1978 (Lee et al., 1978), and the structural complexity and the degree of integration are ever increasing. The design of effective integrated optoelectronic circuits faces the following problems that are under study today:

- The production of pure $A^{III}B^V$ (GaAs, InP) semiconductors with a small number of defects and sufficient area

- The interfacing of optical and electronic components that are often made in layers of different nature and require high-resolution photolithography with several micron steps between the layers

- Heat emission by diode lasers; the dependence of their properties on temperature require circuits having a high heat resistance

- The optical decoupling of circuit areas containing light sources from those with light-sensitive devices such as photodetectors or field-effect transistors.

The problem of diode-laser mirrors is solved through the local manufacture of laser mirrors directly on the semiconductor wafer by means of different types of selective etching (chemical, ion, etc.) or through using lasers where the feedback is realized by means of, for instance, distributed feedback rather than by mirrors. Both approaches give good results.

Two basic structures, vertical and horizontal (Figs. 5.31a, 5.31b), are used for the integration of optical and electronic components. With the vertical structure, epitaxial layers for optical and electronic components are sequentially grown on a conductive substrate and electrically decoupled by an isolating sublayer. In the horizontal structure, optical and electronic components are grown on a nonconductive substrate. A common conductive layer in the vertical structures may result in capacitive coupling of the electronic components; this type of circuit is therefore used with a small degree of

Fig. 5.33.

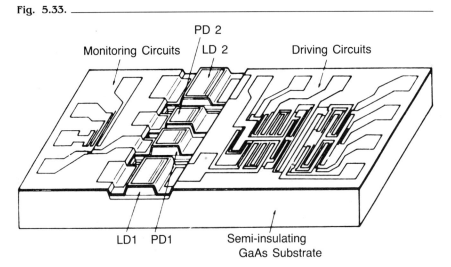

Example of integration of IL, photodiodes, and electronics.

integration. In the horizontal structures using semi-isolating substrates, the current is parallel to the substrate surface and there is no capacitive coupling at all. The production of such an optoelectronic circuit is more complicated, however, because high steps and mesas are required on the substrate. GaAs doped by chromium with a specific resistance of 10^8 ohm cm is used for semi-isolating substrates.

Figure 5.32 shows the production sequence of a MQW laser with a su-

Fig. 5.34. _____

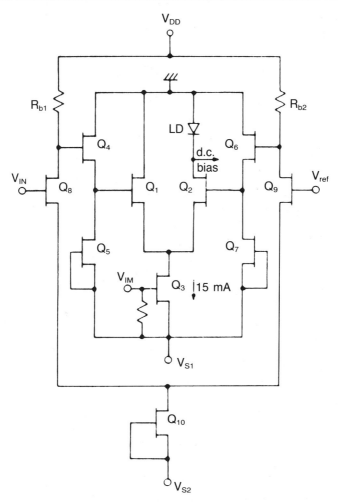

Electronic representation of the integrated optoelectronic module of Fig. 5.33.

Fig. 5.35.

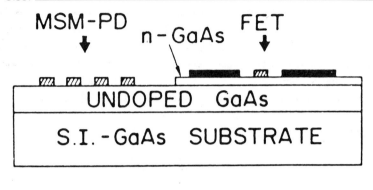

Metal-semiconductor-metal array of photodiodes integrated on a GaAs substrate.

Fig. 5.36.

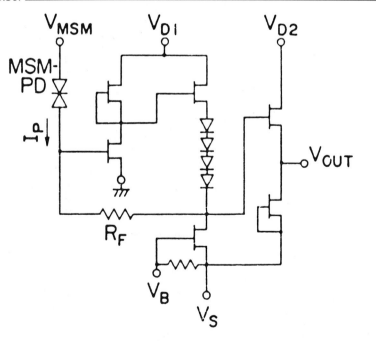

Electronic diagram of a photodiode array and electronic components.

perlattice structure of the active area and a metal-Schottky field-effect transistor (MESFET). A step is first etched in the semi-isolated substrate of GaAs that is then filled with n^+ GaAs in order to produce a contact layer. A MQW heterostructure is produced through a SiO_2 mask, and then an n layer of field-effect transistor is grown and the technological steps, wells, and contact layers are formed.

Integration of lasers, photodetectors, and electronic control circuitry is exemplified by Fig. 5.33, and the equivalent electrical circuit is shown in Fig. 5.34 (Tanaka, 1985). MESFET and resistor-based electronic circuits are produced by ion implantation. Rows of photodetectors integrated with preamplifiers have been implemented. Figures 5.35 and 5.36, respectively, show the design and the electrical diagram of the photodetectors. The photodetectors are based on metal-semiconductor-metal structures, and the amplifier is built with MESFET transistors. The photodetectors change the conductivity of the illuminated semiconductor; they are simple in design and compatible with FET technology. Their rate of change is 0.2 amps/watt and their response time is below 300 psec. The spread of channel sensitivities is less than 10%. In all, 52 components have been integrated into one chip.

9.
Conclusion

The broad treatment of the capabilities of diode lasers demonstrates that they provide a unique vehicle for optical computing enabling high-speed communication between the units of an optical computer, the generation of ultrashort light pulses, the switching of optical logic gates, the design of holographic memories, the storing of two-dimensional pictures, correlation analysis, optical intra-LSI circuit communication, and the design of logical elements. Last but not least, such lasers may be integrated on the same chip with traditional electronic elements. The advent of integrated circuits having optical inputs and outputs would be a decisive step towards high-performance optical computers. Those integrated circuits would join together the advantages of optical computing with the advanced technology of the electronic industry.

The design of LSI circuits with optical inputs and outputs, and connections to optical systems, would lead to merging the philosophies of electronic and optical computers into a single whole having the merits of both.

References ───────────────────────────────────

Basov, N.G. (1965). *Usp. Fiz. Nauk* **85**, 585–598 (in Russian). English transl. in *Sov. Phys.-Usp.*

Basov, N.G., Morozov, V.N., Nikitin, V.V., and Semenov, A.S. (1969a). "Proc. No. 14 Joint Conf. on Lasers and Opto-Electronics," Southhampton, U.K., Suppl. Vol., p. 7.

Basov, N.G., Morozov, V.N., Nikitin, V.V., and Samoilov, V.D. (1969b). "Proc. No. 14 Joint Conf. on Lasers and Opto-Electronics," Southhampton, U.K., Suppl. Vol., p. 17.

Basov, N.G., Morozov, V.N., Nikitin, V.V., and Samoilov, V.D. (1969c). *Radiotekh. i. Elektronika* **14**, 1623–1633, (in Russian). English transl. in *Radio Engng. Electronic Phys.*

Basov, N.G., Culver, W.H., and Shah, B. (1972). *In:* "Laser Handbook," (F.T. Arecchi and E.O. Schulz-Dubois, eds.), Vol. 2, North-Holland, Amsterdam, pp. 1649–1693.

Born, M., and Wolf, E. (1964). "Principles of Optics," Pergamon, New York.

Elion, H.A., and Morozov, V.N. (1984). "Optoelectronic Switching Systems in Telecommunications and Computers," Marcel Dekker, New York.

Elkhov, V.A., Zolotarev, A. I., Morozov, V.N., and Popov, Yu.N. (1982). *Avtometriya* **5**, 60–63 (in Russian). English transl. in *Automatic Monitoring and Measuring.*

Forrest, S.R. (1985). *J. Lightwave Technol.* **LT-3**, 1248–1263.

Kalashnikov, S.P., Molochev, V.I., Pilipovich, V.A., Popov, Yu.M., Semenov, G.I., and Shmatin, S.G. (1980). *Kvantovaya Elektron.* **7**, 1826–1827 (in Russian). English transl. in *Sov. J. Quant. Electron.*

Lau, K., and Yariv A. (1985). *IEEE J. Quant. Electron* **QE-21**, 121–138.

Lee, C.P., Margalit, S., Ury, I., and Yariv, A. (1978). *Appl. Phys. Lett.* **32**, 806–807.

Morozov, V.N. (1973). *Kvantovaya Elektron.* **5**, 5–13 (in Russian). English transl. in *Sov. J. Quant. Electron.*

Morozov, V.N., and Putilin, A. (1987). Proc. OFC-I00C-87, Reno, Nevada, TuQ41.

Nishizawa, J. (1967). *Electronics* **40**, 117.

Suematsu, Y. (1985). *Phys. Today* **38**(5), 32–39.

Tanaka, T. (1985). Technical Digest OFC-OFC-85, San Diego, California, TuC2, p. 30.

Vasiliev, P., Morozov, V.N., Popov, Yu.N., and Sergeev, A. (1986). *IEEE J. Quant. Electron.* **QE-22,** 149–152.

Wada, O., Sakuzai, T., and Nakagami, T. (1986). *IEEE J. Quant. Electron.* **QE-22,** 805–821.

Zolotarev, A.I., Morozov, V.N., Popov, Yu.N., and Semenov, G.I. (1982). *Avtometriya* **5,** 58–61 (in Russian). English transl. in *Automatic Monitoring and Measuring.*

6.

Array Optoelectronic Computers

Pyotr E. Tverdokhleb

Institute of Automation and Electrometry
Siberian Branch of the USSR Academy of Sciences
Novosibirsk, USSR

Contents

1. Introduction. 189
2. Optoelectronic Computer Structure 191
3. Optical Preprocessor 193
4. Microoperations of the Optical Preprocessor 201
    4.1. Logic Multiplication of Vectors 202
    4.2. Data Structure Rearrangement 203
    4.3. Summary of Section 4 210
5. Photoelectronic Parallel Processor 210
6. Logic Data Processing 213
    6.1. Data Array Definition and Standard Search Problems 213
    6.2. Generalization of Search Problems 217
7. Data Search in an Array Computer 219
8. Summary. 220
    References 220

1. Introduction

New inventions have always given birth to new discoveries. This well-known scientific fact has wonderfully been reaffirmed in the field of optical array computing.

Optical Processing and Computing
ISBN 0-12-064470-3

189

At least two important events have happened in this field during the last 10 to 15 years, events that have raised considerable interest in optical computing all over the world:

(1) A new class of analog optical systems intended specifically for the performance of matrix algebra operations has appeared. The impulse response in this kind of system depends on the position of the input point source, so they are referred to as *space variant,* as opposed to optical space-invariant correlators.

(2) On the basis of new possibilities offered by space-variant systems, architectures of matrix-vector and matrix-matrix optical processors have been proposed for spectral analysis of images by arbitrary orthogonal bases, solutions of sets of linear equations, parallel analog-digital data processing, Kalman filtering, etc. The field of potential applications of optical computing has thus considerably increased.

The results of research activities in these areas are described in Goodman (1981), Rhodes and Sawchuk (1981), Casasent (1984), Rhodes and Guilfoyle (1984), Athale and Lee (1984), and in other publications. The authors present the principles for building coherent and incoherent space-variant optical systems, pay much more attention to the architecture of pipeline (systolic) processors, and give algorithms for the solutions of the above problems. For the majority of cases, peripheral electronic systems are supposed to be the source of the data being processed in this type of processor.

The aim of this paper is to draw the attention of researchers to the unique multichannel switching capabilities of matrix-matrix optical systems and also to the potential application of such systems to the solution of nonarithmetical problems, such as simple or complex associative searching and data structure rearrangement. To this end we describe an array electronic computer structure for the processing of large digital data arrays. This computer includes a parallel optical memory, an optical preprocessor, and a photoelectronic parallel processor. The novelty in our approach resides in the optical system for triple-matrix multiplication used as a preprocessor.

Consider the case where an unerasable page-oriented optical memory is a source of data to be processed. Data input to the preprocessor is parallel-sequential: parallel within a page of $N \times N$ bits, and sequential in that page after page is input with a clock cycle T. Because the page has N vectors (rows or columns) with the length of N bits, the preprocessor is intended for parallel processing operations: logic multiplication, rearrangement, shift, multiplexing, masking, and the shuffling of vectors. The photoelectronic parallel processor continues logic processing of the elements of the optical image ($N \times N$ pixels) arriving from the preprocessor output.

The chapter summarizes the results of studies carried out by the author and his coworkers from 1972 to 1984. The optical systems for triple-matrix multiplication were built by us during 1971–1978 (Krivenkov et al., 1975; Krivenkov et al., 1976; Mikhlayev et al., 1978; Gofman et al., 1978). The feasibility of multichannel associative searches in such systems was experimentally demonstrated in 1976–1978 (Tverdokhleb, 1981a). The optical computer structure with an architecture of the type *memory-preprocessor-processor* was proposed in 1981 (Tverdokhleb, 1981b; Tverdokhleb, 1982). The feasibility of parallel data structure rearrangement was first demonstrated in the publications mentioned above. Parallel algorithms for simple and for complex associative searching are described in Vanyushev et al. (1984).

2.
Optoelectronic Computer Structure

The block diagram of the computer shown in Fig. 6.1 consists of a parallel optical memory (POM), an optical preprocessor (OP), a photoelectronic parallel processor (PPP), and a control unit (CU). The image of a binary page

Fig. 6.1.

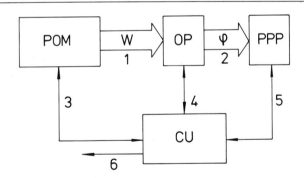

Diagram of an optoelectronic computer. POM, parallel optical memory; OP, optical preprocessor; PPP, photoelectronic parallel processor; CU, control unit; W, input binary image taken from POM; Φ, input preprocessed image; 1 and 2, optical channels; 3, 4, and 5, electronic channels; and 6, output electronic signal.

W from the POM is fed to the OP input via parallel channel 1 and then the transformed data go to the PPP via parallel optical channel 2. The operating instructions for the computer units are fed from the CU via electronic parallel-sequential channels 3, 4, and 5. The results of the final processing are generated in the PPP, and then they are fed through channel 5 to the CU and to the output channel 6.

A POM must have a large information capacity and a fast data page access. An unerasable holographic memory of 1 Gbit served as the POM in our experiments (Tverdokhleb, 1979), with a page format W of 32×32 bits.

An optical system is used as an OP, which carried out an integral transformation of the form

$$\Phi = A \times B \times C, \tag{6.1}$$

where A, B, and C are $N \times N$ matrices with real elements. The elements of the matrix Φ of Eq. (6.1) are calculated according to the algorithm of triple-matrix multiplication and are proportional to the values

$$\phi_{\eta\xi} = \sum_{i=1}^{N} \sum_{j=1}^{N} a_{\eta i} b_{ij} c_{j\xi}, \tag{6.2}$$

where $a_{\eta i}$, b_{ij}, and $c_{j\xi}$ are elements of the matrices A, B, and C.

It is assumed below that the matrix C of Eq. (6.1) is an information matrix or, in other words, that $C = W$. The matrices A and B then determine the nature of the transformation of the page W.

The PPP consists of an arrray of $N \times N$ identical processing cells (SIMD architecture). As can be seen from Fig. 6.2a, each cell has its own photodetector, which allows the simultaneous input of all the elements of the image Φ to the PPP. In the simplest case the PPP can perform a photoelectronic transformation of the elements of the image Φ, a comparison with a threshold (binary quantization), and a row reading of the elements. As Fig. 6.2b shows, each cell includes a photodetector and three MOS transistors (Tr_1 is a reset switch, Tr_2 is an address switch, and Tr_3 is a control transistor). In our more complicated case, each of the PPP cells contains two additional single-digit memory elements (flip-flops) with rearrangeable input logic elements. The structure and the logic operations of such a cell are discussed in Section 5.

The PPP cells have common supply, bias, and control lines. The results of processing are read out row by row. For this purpose the processor contains addressing lines AL_1-AL_N and output data lines DL_1-DL_N.

Fig. 6.2.

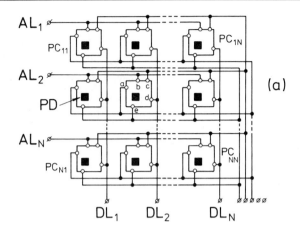

(a)

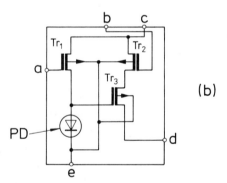

(b)

Structure of a photoelectronic parallel processor: (a) an array of processing cells and (b) structure of one cell. AL_i, addressing lines; PC_{ij}, information matrix of a processor transformation; DL_j, output data lines; PD, photodetector; Tr_1, Tr_2, and Tr_3, MOS transistors; and a, b, c, d, and e, input and output ports of one cell.

3.
Optical Preprocessor

A few optical systems that do the transformations of Eq. (6.1) are known (Krivenkov et al., 1976; Mikhlayev et al., 1978; Gofman et al., 1978). One of these is shown in Fig. 6.3 (Mikhlayev et al., 1978).

Fig. 6.3.

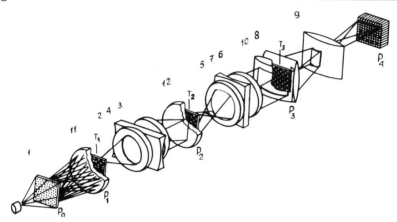

Block diagram of a lens raster optical system for array processing. A, B, and C, matrices introduced to the system with transparencies T_1, T_2, and T_3 in the planes P_1, P_2, and P_3, respectively; 1, incoherent extended light source; 2, 3, and 4, spherical, cylindrical, and lens raster objectives for the projection of columns of the matrix [A] in the x direction; 5, 6, and 7, similar objectives for projecting rows of the matrix [B] in the y direction; 8, 9, and 10, sphero-cylindrical objectives integrating in the x and y directions; 11 and 12, spherical objectives; and [Φ], output matrix in the P_4 plane.

The values from the matrices A, B, and C are input into the system using the transparencies T_1, T_2, and T_3 in the planes P_1, P_2, and P_3, respectively. The system consists of an incoherent extended light source 1, a unit for projecting columns of matrix A along the x coordinate (spherical and cylindrical lenses 2, 3, and 4), a unit for projecting rows of matrix B along the y coordinate (elements 5, 6, and 7), an integrating-projecting unit (cylindrical lenses 8, 9, and 10), and the spherical lenses 11 and 12. The light distribution corresponding to elements of the matrix Φ is reproduced in the plane P_4. In Fig. 6.4, where a simple diagram of the OP is shown, we explain the process of transformation of light beams.

Let one of the light-modulating cells of the transparency T_1 with coordinates $x_1 = i_0 \Delta x_1$ and $y_1 = \eta_0 \Delta y_1$ [where Δx_1 and Δy_1 are distances between the light-modulating cells along the x and y axes and $(i_0 \eta_0)$ is the cell number] be in state 1 ("transparent"). A divergent light beam will then propagate in the interval P_1-P_2. Passing through the unit 2-4-3 it takes the form of a light strip localized on the column of the transparency T_2 with a coordinate $x_2 = -x_1 = -i_0 \Delta x_2$. In the interval P_2-P_3 the image of the column

Fig. 6.4. _____

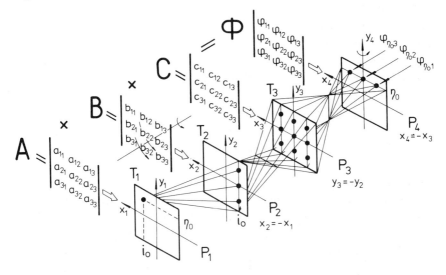

Operational diagram of an optical preprocessor. A, B, and C, matrices with real elements displayed on the T_1, T_2, and T_3 transparencies in the P_1, P_2, and P_3 planes, respectively; Φ, triple matrix multiplication product in the P_4 plane.

of matrix B formed behind the transparency T_2 is broadcast along the x co-ordinate and is projected (inverted) onto the plane P_3 along the y coordinate. All columns of the transparency T_3 are illuminated with this image. Since the transmittance of the light-modulating cells of the transparency T_3 correspond to the elements of matrix $C = W$, the output image is proportional to the result of an element-by-element multiplication of matrix W. The image obtained at the output of the transparency T_3 in the interval P_3-P_4 is integrated along the y coordinate and projected (inverted) onto the plane P_4 along the x coordinate. The result of the transformation is reproduced in the plane P_4 in the form of a light strip localized on the row with a coordinate $y_4 = \eta_0 \Delta y_4$. It can be easily seen that the light energy on the elements of this row is proportional to the scalar product of the i_0^{th} column of matrix B by the corresponding columns of matrix C, that is,

$$\phi(-\xi \Delta x_4) = \sum_{j=1}^{N} b_{i_0 j} c_{j\xi}, \qquad \xi = 1, 2 \ldots, N. \qquad (6.3)$$

Note the main characteristics of the optical system under consideration. The process of formation of light beams in the system is accompanied by inversion of the coordinate axes: x_1 in the interval P_1-P_2, y_2 in the interval P_2-P_3, and x_3 in the interval P_3-P_4. The transformation realized by the system therefore corresponds to Eq. (6.1) when the elements of the matrices A, B, and C are arranged on the transparencies as shown in Fig. 6.4. Consequently, the input of data does not change the arrangement of elements of matrices A and C on transparencies T_1 and T_3; on the other hand, the arrangement of elements of matrix B on transparency T_2 changes. The same change can be achieved by a 180° rotation of matrix B about the right diagonal. Figure 6.4 also shows the arrangement of the matrix Φ' elements, that is, the light intensity distribution at the system output. The elements of matrices Φ' and Φ can be matched by a 180° rotation of matrix Φ' about the vertical axis.

Property 1. The light beams from the elements of the i_0^{th} column of transparency T_1 are made to coincide on the column of transparency T_2 with the number $i = -i_0$, see Fig. 6.5. This means that the same scalar product in Eq. (6.3) can be obtained when any of the elements of i_0^{th} column of T_2 changes to state 1. The only difference for different elements is that the

Fig. 6.5. _____

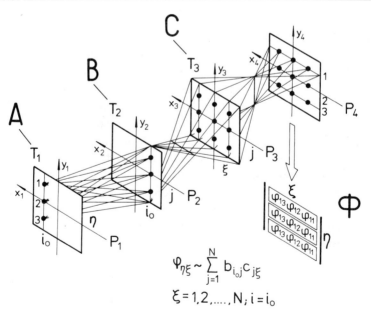

$$\varphi_{\eta\xi} \sim \sum_{j=1}^{N} b_{i_0 j} c_{j\xi}$$

$$\xi = 1, 2, \ldots, N;\ i = i_0$$

Operational diagram of the optical preprocessor of Fig. 6.4 with one column input.

result of the calculations with Eq. (6.3) is imaged on different rows in plane P_4. If η is the number of the element turned on, the result is imaged on the row of the output plane with the number η. If all elements of the i_0^{th} column are turned on, the result of Eq. (6.3) is replicated on all rows of the output plane.

Property 2. The light beams formed by the elements of the ηth row of transparency T_1 in plane P_2 are spatially separated in such a way that they illuminate all the columns of transparency T_2, see Fig. 6.6. This allows calculation in parallel of the scalar products of all the columns of matrix B by all the columns of matrix C. N^2 results of Eq. (6.3) are spatially matched in plane T_4 on row number η.

Property 3. The light beams formed by the elements of the left and right diagonals of transparency T_1 also make it possible to illuminate all the columns of transparency T_2 and, as in Property 2, to calculate N^2 scalar products of the columns of matrix B by the columns of matrix C. As Fig. 6.7 shows, the difference is that these results are spatially separated and appear on N rows of the output plane.

Fig. 6.6.

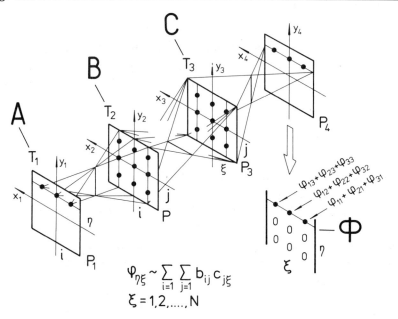

$$\varphi_{\eta\xi} \sim \sum_{i=1}^{} \sum_{j=1}^{} b_{ij}\, c_{j\xi}$$
$$\xi = 1,2,....,N$$

Operational diagram of the optical preprocessor of Fig. 6.4 with one row input.

Fig. 6.7. ──

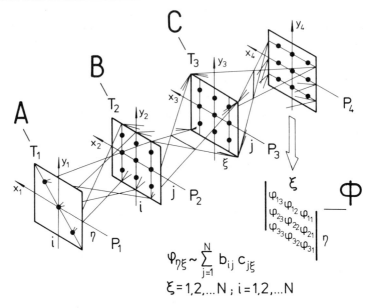

Operational diagram of the optical preprocessor of Fig. 6.4 with one, left or right, diagonal input.

Let us estimate the OP resolution using the basic diagram of Fig. 6.8 (Tverdokhleb, 1979). As compared to the diagram in Fig. 6.3, the sphero-cylindrical unit 2-4-3 is replaced by conditional cylindrical (0_c) and spherical (0_s) lenses. Their equivalent focal lengths are equal to

$$f_c = \frac{f f_1}{f - 2f_1} \quad \text{and} \quad f_{sp} = \frac{f}{2} \,,$$

where f and f_1 are focal lengths of the spherical (2 and 3) of the cylindrical (4) lenses. A similar operation is done with the spherical-cylindrical unit 5-7-6. The filament lamp and the diffuser are represented in the diagram by an extended source in plane P_0. The beam path is shown for the case when a point with coordinates (y_1, x_1) in plane P_1 is in state 1.

If the geometrical parameters of the optical system are chosen starting from the conditions

$$d_1 = d_2 = d_4 = f, \quad d_8 = \frac{f f_1}{f + f_1} \,,$$

$$d_3 = d_9 = \frac{f f_1}{f - f_1}, \quad d_6 = d_7 = \frac{f^2}{2f_1},$$

$$\Delta_1 = 0, \quad \text{and} \quad \Delta_2 = \frac{f^2}{f_1},$$

then the system provides transfer of point y_1 from plane P_1 to P_4 with a $1:1$ magnification. Point x_1 is transferred to plane P_4 with defocusing. Since defocused beams of all of the points on the x_1 axis overlap in plane P_4, the system responds to a change in the y_1 coordinate of a point (Properties 1 and 3), and it does not respond to a change in the x_1 coordinate of the same action (Property 2).

The light beams are severely limited when projected from plane P_3 (where transparency T_3 with a minimum size of the element Δy_3 is placed) to plane P_4. The light beams are limited in the x direction by the size of aperture D of objective 9 in Fig. 6.3 and 0_4 in Fig. 6.8. This means that the dimensions of the projected element in plane P_4 are equal to

$$\Delta y_4 = 2 \frac{\lambda f^2 N_3}{f_1 L} \quad \text{and} \quad \Delta x_4 = \frac{\lambda f^2}{f_1 D}, \tag{6.4}$$

Fig. 6.8. _____

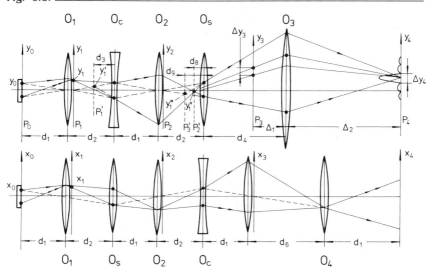

Resolution assessment in an optical preprocessor. 0_1 and 0_2, spherical objectives; 0_s and 0_c, spherical and cylindrical objectives, respectively; 0_3 and 0_4, cylindrical objectives; P_o, plane of an extended white light source; P_1, P_2, and P_3, input data planes; and P_4, output data plane.

where λ is the average wavelength of the incoherent source, N_3 is the number of rows on transparency T_3, and L is the linear size of the operating field.

Let $N_1 = L/(\Delta y_4)$ be the number of rows on transparency T_1. Taking into account Eq. (6.4) we have

$$N_1 N_3 = \frac{1}{2\lambda} \left(\frac{f_1}{f}\right)\left(\frac{L}{f}\right) L = \text{constant.} \tag{6.5}$$

It follows from Eq. (6.5) that the product of the number of rows on transparencies T_1 and T_3, for fixed geometrical parameters of the optical system, is a constant value, which is proportional to the product of the relative focal length of cylindrical lenses 4 and 7 in Fig. 6.3, the angular aperture L/F, and the size of its operational field. For instance, if N_1 is some arbitrary value, then N_3 should be determined from Eq. (6.5).

The number of resolvable elements along the x_4 axis of the system is given by

$$N_4 = \frac{L}{\Delta x_4} = \frac{1}{\lambda} \left(\frac{f_1}{f}\right)\left(\frac{L}{f}\right) D. \tag{6.6}$$

Taking into account Eqs. (6.5) and (6.6), the number of resolvable elements at the system output is equal to

$$N_1 N_4 = \frac{1}{2\lambda^2 N_3} \left(\frac{f_1}{f}\right)^2 \left(\frac{L}{f}\right)^2 LD. \tag{6.7}$$

For $N_3 = 100$, $\lambda = 0.5 \ 10^{-3}$ mm, $L = 20$ mm, $D = 40$ mm, $f_1/f = \frac{1}{4}$, and $L/f = \frac{1}{7.5}$, it follows from (6.7) that $N_1 N_4 \approx 100 \times 100$. Therefore, relatively large images can be processed in the OP.

The feasibility of the OP implementation has been proven by the construction of experimental models of such devices (Krivenkov et al., 1976; Mikhlayev et al., 1978; Gofman et al., 1978; Tverdokhleb, 1981a). Binary images of matrices A, B, and C were generated as phototransparencies. Figure 6.9 shows gray-level images with a 32×16 matrix (a) and a 32×32 matrix (b), observed in the output OP plane. In the models the magnifications of the images along the x and y axes were different.

As part of a computer, the OP would function as an optical system consisting of an optically controlled transparency (PROM; FOTOTITUS; MDSDM, that is, a metal-dielectric-semiconductor-dielectric-metal type structure; etc.) in plane P_3 and electrically controlled transparencies in planes P_1 and P_2. The optically controlled transparency is connected via a parallel channel to the optical memory and serves as an intermediate memory register

Fig. 6.9.

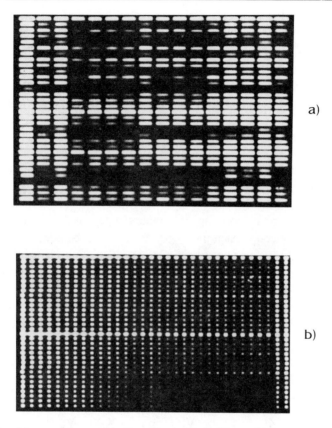

a)

b)

Gray-level images observed in the output plane of the optical preprocessor; (a) 32 × 16, and (b) 32 × 32 matrices.

that helps to input the content of matrix $C = W$ to the OP. Matrices A and B are generated with electrically controlled transparencies. In this case, the data are fed from the computer control unit.

4.

Microoperations of the Optical Preprocessor

An OP doing transformations of the form of Eq. (6.1) is well suited for the performance of two important and practical operations: the multichannel logic multiplication of binary vectors or words and the rearrangement of data structures in the pages W.

Let us explain the meaning and technique of such operations.

4.1. Logic Multiplication of Vectors

The logic multiplication of binary vectors X and Y is equal to the number of noncoincident bits in the words X and Y and is expressed by the Hamming distance

$$d = \text{dist}(X, Y). \tag{6.8}$$

If $X = Y$, then $d = 0$. If $X \neq Y$, then $d > 0$. The larger the number of bits that differ in the words X and Y, the larger is the distance d. The coincidence of corresponding bits is calculated by the rules of modulo 2 addition.

Let the word X be given in inverted binary code (i.e., as $\bar{X}$) and the word Y in direct binary code. Then the words $\bar{X}$ and Y can be generated on transparencies T_X and T_Y so that a pair of light-modulating elements will correspond to each of the bits. Figure 6.10 shows the possible values of bits $\bar{x}_k$ and y_k, and the corresponding states of a pair of light-modulating elements on the transparencies T_X and T_Y. The method of coding binary variables used here is known as paraphrase.

Fig. 6.10. _____

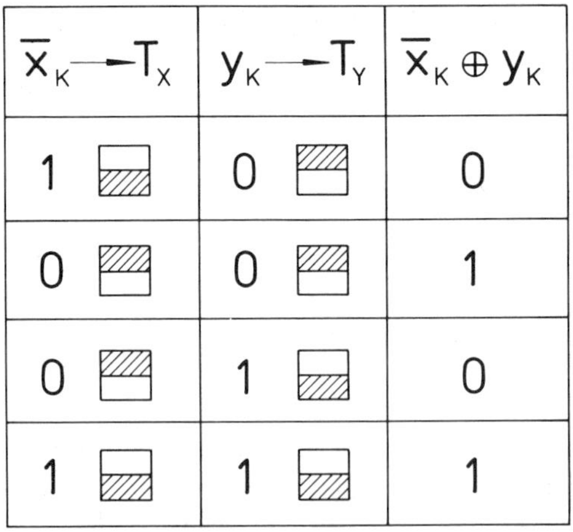

$\bar{X}_K \!-\! T_X$	$y_K \!-\! T_Y$	$\bar{X}_K \oplus y_K$
1	0	0
0	0	1
0	1	0
1	1	1

Possible values of bits in words x_k (inverted) and y_k, and the resulting states of a pair of light-modulating elements.

For simplicity let $\bar{X} = \bar{x}_k$, and $Y = y_k$. Matching an optical image of bit $\bar{x}_k$ and an image of bit y_k we obtain a modulation of the light beam transmitted through transparencies T_X and T_Y, which follows the rule of modulo 2 addition.

Logic multiplication of multidigit words is performed in a similar manner. An image of word $\bar{X}$ on transparency T_X is matched optically with an image of word Y on transparency T_Y. For $X = Y$ the transmitted light fluxes are equivalent and the Hamming distance is zero. When X differs from Y even in one binary digit, the transmitted light flux has a nonzero value.

The OP can do parallel logic multiplication of N vectors with N bits in each vector. This follows from the fact that the OP does a multichannel scalar product of words; thus N paraphase-coded binary words can be given on columns of transparencies T_2 and T_3. The operation is realized when $C = W$ and $A = I$ in Eq. (6.1) (I is a unit matrix), and when the binary words b_i (rows of the matrix B) are given in inverted paraphase code, while the binary words w_ξ (columns of matrix W) are in direct paraphase codes. Then

$$\Phi = I \times \bar{B} \times W, \qquad (6.9)$$

where $\bar{B}$ and W are matrices with paraphase-coded elements $\bar{b}_{ij}$ and $w_{j\xi}$.

The principle of multichannel logic multiplication of binary vectors in the OP is illustrated in Fig. 6.11.

The matrices I, $\bar{B}$, and W have sizes of 3×3. The state of transparency T_1 corresponds to a unit matrix. Paraphase images of the words $\bar{b}_i$ and w_ξ are shown on transparencies T_2 and T_3, with digits of the words b_i running upwards and digits of the words w_ξ downwards. Illumination of plane P_2 with linear light beams formed by diagonal elements of transparency T_1 results in the transfer of paraphase images of the words $\bar{b}_i$ to the plane P_3, inverted along the y axis and replicated along the x axis. Hence, each of the images of the words $\bar{b}_i$ is projected on each of the images of the words w_ξ; the sequence of digits of the words w_ξ and $\bar{b}_i$ is the same. The product of matrices $\bar{B}$ and W is shown in plane P_4. Since $b_1 = w_3$ and $b_3 = w_1$, there is no light flux on elements 13 and 31 in plane P_4 ($\phi_{13} = \phi_{31} = d = 0$). Other pairs of the words b_i and w_ξ differ from one another. Therefore, the light flux is nonzero on other elements of plane P_4.

4.2. Data Structure Rearrangement

The role and the importance of operations for data structure rearrangement in computing are described in Kagan and Kanevsky (1973).

The data to be rearranged are N binary vectors on the rows of page W.

Fig. 6.11.

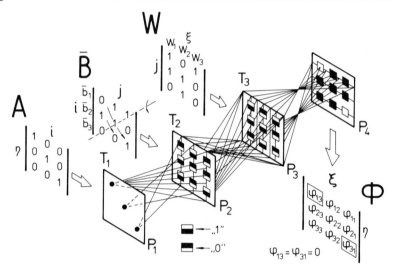

Operational diagram for multichannel logic multiplication of binary vectors in an optical preprocessor.

Hence the rearrangement of the data structure of this page is necessary for integrating bits with the same address in original vectors that belong to a group of N binary vectors. Below the principal types of each microoperations and their performance in the OP are described.

4.2.1. Transfer of Page W to the Output

It follows from Eq. (6.1) that for $C = W$ and $A = B = I$ we have $\Phi = W$. Figure 6.12 illustrates this operation in the OP. The state of transparencies T_1 and T_2 with diagonal elements turned on corresponds to the content of matrices A and B; and the state of transparency T_3 to that of matrix W. As the light beams pass through transparencies T_2 and T_3, rows of image W are read and simultaneously transferred (inverted along the x axis) to the rows of plane P_4. Due to the inversion, the arrangement of the elements of matrix Φ is as shown in Fig. 6.12.

4.2.2. Masking of Individual Rows

This operation can be performed for $C = W$, $A = I$, and $B = \bar{I}$; where $\bar{I}$ is a unit matrix with some of its diagonal elements b_{ii} equal to zero. Let $\bar{I}$ differ from I by one of the elements b_{ij}, for which $i = i_0$, $j = i_0$ being zero.

Fig. 6.12. _____

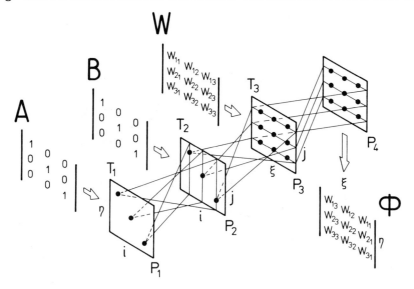

Operational diagram for transferring page W to the output of an optical preprocessor.

It follows from Eq. (6.1) that all the rows of image W will be generated on the rows of matrix Φ, except for row w_{i_0}. In the general case, the elements b_{ij} for which $i, j = i_0, i_1, \ldots \leq N$ can take on zero values. All the rows of image W will be generated in matrix Φ, except for the rows numbered $\eta = i_0, i_1, \ldots$. The order of rows in matrix Φ corresponds to the order of the rows being read in image W.

Figure 6.13 illustrates this microoperation. Because in matrix B the element $b_{22} = 0$, row W_2 on page W is masked. Thus the row numbered $\eta = i_0 = 2$ is zeroed in the output image.

4.2.3. Transfer of an Arbitrary Row or a Preset Combination of Rows

Consider the simplest case $C = W$, $A = I$, and let the elements of matrix B satisfy the condition

$$b_{ij} = \begin{cases} 1, & \text{for } i = i_0, \ j = j_0 \\ 0, & \text{otherwise.} \end{cases} \tag{6.10}$$

It follows from Eq. (6.1) that the $\eta = i_0^{\text{th}}$ row of matrix Φ will be generated on the $j = j_0^{\text{th}}$ row of matrix W.

Fig. 6.13. ──

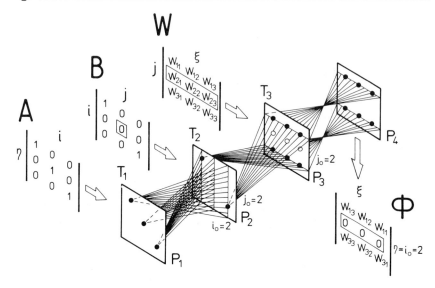

Operational diagram for masking of individual rows in page W in an optical preprocessor.

The above microoperation is realized in the OP as shown in Fig. 6.14. Since at $i = i_0 = 2$ and $j = j_0 = 1$, the element $b_{ij} = 1$, the corresponding light-modulating cell on transparency T_2 changes to state 1. A row of the image numbered $j = j_0 = 1$ is read with a linear light beam generated by the OP and transferred to the row of matrix Φ with a number $\eta = i_0 = 2$.

In general, a few elements of matrix B can take on unit values, i.e.,

$$b_{ij} = \begin{cases} 1, & \text{for } i = i_0, i_1, \ldots \\ & \quad\; j = j_0, j_1, \ldots \\ 0, & \text{for } i \neq i_0, i_1, \ldots \\ & \quad\; j \neq j_0, j_1, \ldots \end{cases} \qquad (6.11)$$

From Eq. (6.1) the $j_0, j_1, \ldots$ −th rows of page W will be reproduced on the $i_0, i_1, \ldots$ −th rows of matrix Φ.

4.2.4.   Multiplexing of Rows

Let $C = W$ and let the elements of matrices A and B satisfy the conditions

$$b_{ij} = \begin{cases} 1, & \text{for } i = i_0, j = j_0 \\ 0, & \text{otherwise} \end{cases} \qquad (6.12)$$

Fig. 6.14. _____

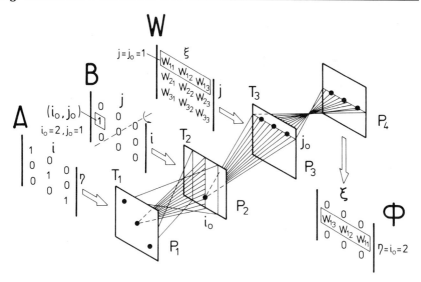

Operational diagram for transferring an arbitrary row of matrix W to matrix Φ.

$$a_{\eta i} = \begin{cases} 1, & \text{for } i = i_0 \\ 0, & \text{otherwise.} \end{cases}$$

From Eq. (6.1) the j_0^{th} row of image W is multiplexed on all the rows of matrix Φ.

Figure 6.15 corresponds to the case where $i = i_0 = $ 2nd column on transparency T_1 and the element $j = j_0 = 1$ on transparency T_2 are changed to state 1. The row $j = j_0 = 1$ of image W is then read with three linear light beams superimposed in plane P_3. These beams are spatially separated in the gap P_3-P_4 of the OP. As a result, we obtain three identical inverted rows $j_0 = 1$ of page W. It is clear that when the element $a_{\eta_0 i}$ of column $i = i_0$ is zero, the multiplexed image W of the $j_0 = 1$ row is absent on row $\eta = \eta_0$ of matrix Φ.

4.2.5. A Single-Coordinate Shift

The rows of page W can be shifted downwards by τ fixed positions for $C = W$, $A = I$, and values of matrix B elements chosen as follows

$$b_{i'j} = \begin{cases} 1, & \text{for } i' = i + \tau, j = i \\ 0, & \text{otherwise,} \end{cases} \tag{6.13}$$

Fig. 6.15. _____

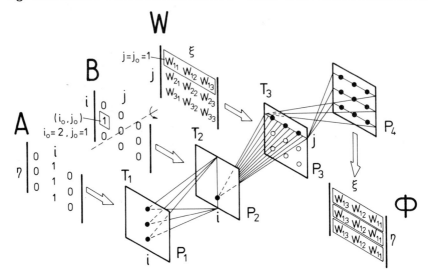

Operational diagram for the multiplexing of an arbitrary row of matrix W in matrix Φ.

where $\tau = 0, 1, 2, \ldots$ is a parameter of the shift. Then, it follows from
Eq. (6.1) that the τ upper rows of matrix Φ become zero, while the remaining $N - \tau$ rows are occupied by the $N - \tau$ first rows of page W. The
remaining τ rows of page W will be outside matrix Φ. When the values of
the elements of matrix B are chosen according to the condition

$$b_{i'j'} = \begin{cases} 1, & \text{for } i' = i, \; j' = i + \tau \\ 0, & \text{otherwise,} \end{cases} \qquad (6.14)$$

then according to Eq. (6.1), page W will be shifted by τ rows upwards with
respect to the rows of matrix Φ.

   Figure 6.16 illustrates the microoperation of shift. The original 5×5
matrices are used here. The values of matrices A and B, and the light beams
formed by the OP, correspond to a shift of page W by $\tau = 2$ rows upwards.
The dots and broken rows in the figure indicate the positions of unit elements
of matrix B that provide a shift of page W by $\tau = 0, 1, 3, 4$ positions
upwards and downwards. The position of the unit elements correspond to
the conditions of Eqs. (6.13) and (6.14).

Fig. 6.16. _____

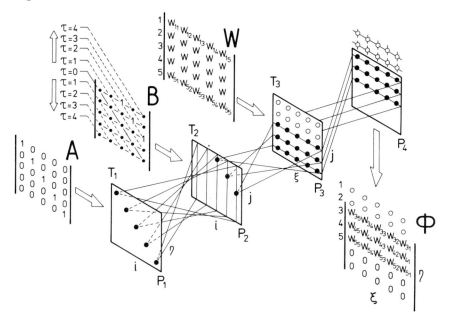

Operational diagram for a single-coordinate shift.

4.2.6. A Cyclic Single-Coordinate Shift

The cyclic shift differs from that described above because the rows of page W that lie outside matrix Φ as the shift occurs are not lost but are imaged on the zeroed rows of matrix Φ. This can be achieved when $A = I$, $C = W$, and when the elements of matrix B are chosen as follows:

$$b_{i'j'} = \begin{cases} 1, & \text{for } i' = i + \tau, \quad j' = i \quad \text{and} \\ & \text{for } i' = s, \quad j' = (N - \tau) + s, \\ & \text{and } s = 1, 2, \ldots, \tau. \\ 0, & \text{otherwise} \end{cases} \qquad (6.15)$$

for a downward shift and

$$b_{i'j'} = \begin{cases} 1, & \text{for } i' = i, \quad j' = i + \tau \quad \text{and} \\ & \text{for } i' = (N - \tau) + s, \; j' = s, \\ & \text{and } s = 1, 2, \ldots, \tau. \\ 0, & \text{otherwise} \end{cases} \qquad (6.16)$$

for an upward shift.

Fig. 6.17. _____

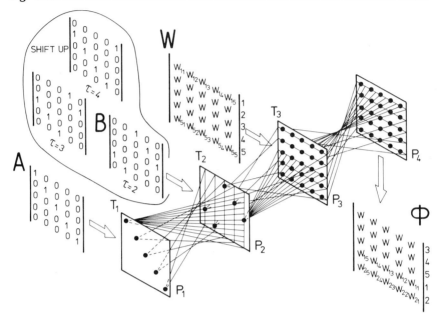

Operational diagram for a cyclic single-coordinate shift of rows of matrix W in matrix Φ.

Figure 6.17 illustrates an example of a cyclic shift by $\tau = 2$ positions upwards. The rows 3, 4, and 5 of page W are shifted to the rows 1, 2, and 3 of matrix Φ, respectively, while rows 1 and 2 of page W are shifted to rows 4 and 5 of the output matrix. The values of matrix B that enable a cyclic shift of the page W by $\tau = 3$ and 4 positions are also given in Fig. 6.17.

4.3.   Summary of Section 4

The OP can be used in array computers for multichannel associative storage (see operations in Section 4.1) or as a programmable optical data switch (see operations in Section 4.2).

5. _____
Photoelectronic Parellel Processor

The PPP shown in Fig. 6.2a is a uniform microelectronic structure consisting of a matrix of $N \times N$ identical photosensitive processing cells (PC).

Fig. 6.18. _____

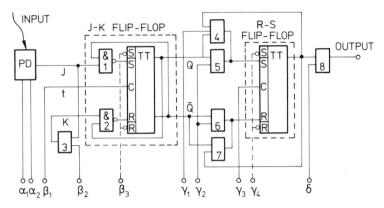

Block diagram of the PPP cell, which performs addition, multiplication, and modulo 2 addition. PD, photodetector; J–K and R–S flip-flops, single-digit memory registers; 1 and 2, NAND logic elements; 4–8, AND logic elements; α, β, γ, and δ, inputs of control signals. Detailed description in Section 5.

Figure 6.18 shows a schematic circuit of the cell for three logic operations: addition, multiplication, and modulo 2 addition. It includes a photodetecting element (PD) composed of a photodetector, a thresholder, switching transistors, etc; and two single-digit memory registers, that is, J–K and R–S flip-flops with input logic elements. NAND logic elements are denoted by the numbers 1 and 2, AND elements by the numbers 4–8. The optical input and the electronic output of the cell are also shown in Fig. 6.18. The cell includes control inputs α, β, γ, and δ for signals: α_1—erase the optical recording in PD;α_2—write the PD content to the J–K flip-flop; β_1—clock the J–K flip-flop operation; β_2—change the J–K flip-flop to T flip-flop; β_3—erase the recording in the J–K flip-flop (set to 0); γ_1—enable logic multiplication microoperation; γ_2—write the content of the J–K flip-flop to the R–S flip-flop; γ_3—clock the R–S flip-flop operation; γ_4—erase the recording in the R–S flip-flop (set to 0); and δ—read the R–S flip-flop content to the CU. Each microoperation performed by the cell has its own control inputs. The rules for changing the J–K and R–S flip-flops are given in Tables 6.1 and 6.2, respectively (Feng, 1974).

The transformation of one pixel of the gray-level image Φ to a binary one and the subsequent inversion of the result is ensured by an appropriate selection of the PD circuit.

Let the J–K flip-flop of the cell be in state a $Q(t - 1) = 0$ or 1 as a

TABLE 6.1

t			
J	K	$Q(t)$	Notes
0	0	$Q(t-1)$	Storage
0	1	0	Reset "0"
1	0	1	Reset "1"
1	1	$\bar{Q}(t-1)$	Inversion

result of the input to the PPP of the previous image. As the next image is input to the PPP at a time t, there are two possibilities:

- 0 (J = 0, K = 0) is fed from the PD to the J–K flip-flop input. The flip-flop does not change.

- 1 (J = 1, K = 0) is fed from the PD to the J–K flip-flop input. $Q(t) = 1$, independently of the previous state.

All the results for logic addition are thus fulfilled ($0 + 0 = 0$, $0 + 1 = 1$, $1 + 0 = 1$, $1 + 1 = 1$).

The microoperation of modulo 2 addition is accomplished by setting the J–K flip-flop to a count mode. For this, a unit signal is applied to the β_2 bus input. Hence, two combinations can be generated at the flip-flop inputs: 11—when a 1 comes from the PD output, and 00—when a 0 comes. In the first case the flip-flop changes from the previous state (0 or 1) to the inverse state, i.e., $Q(t) = \bar{Q}(t-1)$. In the second case it does not change, i.e., $Q(t) = Q(t-1)$. The binary sequence arriving to the flip-flop input is therefore processed by the rule of modulo 2 addition ($0 + 0 = 0$, $0 + 1 = 1$, $1 + 0 = 1$, $1 + 1 = 0$).

The R–S flip-flop and logic elements 4 and 7 perform logic multiplication in a cell, providing $\gamma_1 = 1$. In this case there are no signals through the elements 5 and 6.

TABLE 6.2

t			
R	S	$Q(t)$	Notes
0	0	$Q(t-1)$	Storage
1	0	0	Reset "0"
0	1	1	Reset "1"
1	1	—	Forbidden

Let the R–S flip-flop state be 1 at time $(t - 1)$. Then, at $Q(t) = 1$ the R–S flip-flop inputs at time t are S = 1 and R = 0; and at $Q(t) = 0$ they are S = 0, R = 1. In the first case the R–S flip-flop retains its state 1; whereas in the second, it changes to 0. Now, let the R–S flip-flop be 0 at a time $(t - 1)$. Then, with either output of the J–K flip-flop, that is $Q(t)$ = 1 or 0, the R–S flip-flop inputs are S = 0 and R = 0. The flip-flop does not change. Thus the contents of the J–K and R–S flip-flops are processed by the rules of logic multiplication ($0 \times 0 = 0$, $0 \times 1 = 0$, $1 \times 0 = 0$, $1 \times 1 = 1$).

As the cell accomplishes any microoperation, the R–S flip-flop content is read by sending one unit signal to the control input δ.

The PPP inputs α, β, γ are common for all cells. The input δ in connected to the address bus, the output to the data bus.

The cell includes 26 logic elements and a photodetecting element. Each element consists of three transistors, and known types of photodetecting elements contain three transistors, in addition to a photodetector. The total number of transistors in the cell is about 80–90. The PPP can be implemented as in integrated (integrated-hybrid) microcircuit.

6.
Logic Data Processing

The principle of computing in an array computer can be illustrated by problems of simple and complex searches in a data array (Vanyushev *et al.*, 1984).

6.1. Data Array Definition and Standard Search Problems

A disordered array of digital data characterizing a set of $G \gg N$ similar objects (for example, organic compounds) can be simply represented as a table of number features. The first figure in the table represents an ordinal number of an object in the given set, the second figure its numerical feature (e.g., melting point or molar weight).

A data page is output from the optical memory, combines the numerical features of a subset of N objects, and has the form of an array

$$W = \|w_{ij}\bar{w}_{ij}\|, \tag{6.17}$$

where the jth bit of the feature w_i is imaged in direct w_{ij} and inverted $\bar{w}_{ij}$ forms in such a way that 1 conforms to 10, and 0 conforms to 01. The

TABLE 6.3

Number	Feature	Matrix W				
1	21	10	01	10	01	10
2	26	10	10	01	10	01
3	6	01	01	10	10	01
4	14	01	10	10	10	01
5	19	$\rightarrow$	10	01	01	10	10
6	23	10	01	10	10	10
7	4	01	01	10	01	01
8	11	01	10	01	10	10
9	17	10	01	01	01	10
10	19	01	10	01	01	10

dimension of an array in Eq. (6.17) is $N \times N$. As an example, Table 6.3 represents the numerical features of a subset of 10 objects and shows the form of array W for a binary paraphase coding of 10 features. G/N is the total number of pages needed for the storage of a full data array.

Let us consider the methods of processing the content of a page W, assuming that other pages are processed in a similar way.

Method 1. Search for numbers of the objects whose features match or mismatch the prescribed feature l. The problem can be solved by matching a binary word l to all the words w_i ($i = 1, 2, \ldots, N$) on page W. When the word l is given in an inverted paraphase code, i.e., $\bar{l} = \{\bar{l}_1 l_1 \bar{l}_2 l_2 \ldots \bar{l}_{N/2} l_{N/2}\}$, the group matching represents the calculation of a set of logic functions

$$\phi_i = \overset{N/2}{\underset{j=1}{\mathbf{V}}} (w_{ij} \bar{l}_j + \bar{w}_{ij} l_j), \qquad i = 1, 2, \ldots, N, \qquad (6.18)$$

where $\mathbf{V}$ denotes the operation of logic addition. If the bits of the compared words are equal ($l = w_i$), then $\phi_i = 0$. If they are not equal ($l \neq w_i$), then $\phi_i = 1$. For example, let $l = \{10\ 01\ 01\ 01\ 10\}$ and page W have the form as shown in Table 6.3. Computing the set of functions ϕ_i of Eq. (6.18), the object numbered 4 ($\phi_4 = 0$) satisfies the condition for matching features.

It can easily be shown that the transform in Eq. (6.18) is equivalent to the matrix equation

$$|\phi_i| = |\bar{l}_j l_j| \times \|w_{ij} \bar{w}_{ij}\|^{\mathrm{T}}, \qquad (6.19)$$

where $l_j l_j$ ($j = 1, 2, \ldots, N/2$) is a row vector formed from the bits of the feature l, $\|w_{ij} \bar{w}_{ij}\|^{\mathrm{T}}$ is a transposed $(N/2) \times N$ matrix W, and $|\phi_i|$ ($i = 1, 2, \ldots, N$) is a row vector of computed results.

Method 2. Search for object numbers whose features are greater or less than a prescribed feature l. In this case we find a set of logic functions of the form

$$f_i = \bigvee_{q=1}^{Q} \phi_{iq} = \bigvee_{q=1}^{Q} \bigvee_{j=1}^{N/2} (w_{ij}\bar{l}_{jq} + \bar{w}_{ij}l_{iq}), \qquad i = 1, 2, \ldots, N, \quad (6.20)$$

where q is the current iteration number, l_{iq} and $\bar{l}_{iq}$ are direct and inverted values of the ith digit of the word l_q, known as an inquiry word.

A series of Q inquiry words can be obtained by analyzing the word l at each iteration. When one searches for objects whose features are greater than the feature l, the first significant bit of the 0 value is found in the binary word l. This bit changes to 1; while the other bits to the right are masked. The masked bit conforms to a combination of 00. The obtained word l_1 can be used in searching for numbers of objects with units in more significant nonmasked bits of the word l. This can be done by calculation from Eq. (6.18). The result of the search is stored. At the second iteration the previously changed bit of the word l is restored to the initial state and the next bit of 0 value is searched for. As before, this bit changes to 1, while those bits to the right are masked. The generated word l_2 is used in Eq. (6.18) to search for the next group of objects with unity in the last nonmasked bit and matched to all the most significant bits of the words w_i. According to Eq. (6.20), the result of the search at the second iteration is added (by the rules of logic addition) to the result of the previous addition. The process of formation of inquiry and search words in subsequent steps is similar to that described above. Obviously, the number of iterations in this case is smaller than the number of bits in word l.

Inquiry words in the search for numbers of objects whose features are less than the preset feature l are formed in an analogous way but with a successive change from 1 to 0.

The function f_i is equal to 1 when the word w_i satisfies the conditions for the type of search: $w_i > l$ or $w_i < l$. The function f_i is equal to 0 when the condition of the search is not fulfilled.

Tables 6.4 and 6.5 represent inquiry words for features $l = 2, 13$ and 28 in paraphase code. The inquiry words are formed by the rules described above. Table 6.4 corresponds to a search when $w_i > l$, and Table 6.5 to that when $w_i < l$. Masked bits are denoted by 00. Let $l = 13$. Having done the search in page W (Table 6.3) objects 1, 2, 4, 5, 6, and 9 satisfy the condition $w_i > l$, and objects 3, 7, 8, and 10 satisfy the condition $w_i < l$.

Method 3. The search for numbers of objects whose features are in the interval $[l_H, l_B]$. This type of search is often used for sorting. It allows find-

TABLE 6.4

l	2					13					28				
l_q	01	01	01	10	01	01	10	10	01	10	10	10	10	01	01
l_1	10	00	00	00	00	10	00	00	00	00	10	10	10	10	00
l_2	01	10	00	00	00	01	10	10	10	00	10	10	10	01	10
l_3	01	01	10	00	00	—					—				
l_4	01	01	01	10	10	—					—				
Q			4					2					2		

TABLE 6.5

l	2					13					28				
l_q	01	01	01	10	01	01	10	10	01	10	10	10	10	01	01
l_1	01	01	01	01	00	01	01	00	00	00	01	00	00	00	00
l_2	—					01	10	01	00	00	10	01	00	00	00
l_3	—					01	10	10	01	01	10	10	01	00	00
Q			1					3					3		

ing objects whose features satisfy the conditions $w_i > l_H$ and $w_i < l_B$, respectively. This can be done by the formation of two series of inquiry words from the binary words l_H, l_B, and the subsequent calculation of the set of functions in Eq. (6.20) for each of the series. The set of objects within the prescribed interval of features can be calculated by determining the values of the functions

$$f_i^{(H,B)} = f_i^H \wedge f_i^B, \qquad i = 1, 2, \ldots, N, \qquad (6.21)$$

where $\wedge$ denotes the operation of digit-by-digit logic multiplication. The function $f_i^{(H,B)} = 1$ for $l_H < w_i < l_B$ and $f_i^{(H,B)} = 0$ when the relation is not fulfilled.

For example, let us make a search among the 10 objects of Table 6.3. Objects with the numbers 3, 7, 8, and 10 that fall within the interval are given in Tables 6.4 and 6.5.

From the above analysis one may conclude that the principal points of the search are:

(1) The operation of logic vector-matrix multiplication of Eq. (6.19), which allows matching of feature l to the content of page W. The vector ϕ results from the computation.

(2) The operation of inversion of the vector components ϕ.

(3) The operation of logic addition of the vector components ϕ_q ($q = 1, 2, \ldots Q$) of Eq. (6.20), which allows integration of the results of the search for sequential iterations. The vector f results from the computation.

(4) The operation of logic multiplication of the vectors f^H and f^B of Eq. (6.21), which provides the result of a search that satisfies two conditions.

6.2. Generalization of Search Problems

The array computer that includes an OP can carry out simultaneous and independent searches for N predetermined features l_k. The search techniques considered in Section 6.1 can therefore be done in parallel.

6.2.1. Match (Mismatch) Search

When each of the binary features l_k is given in inverted paraphase code, the multichannel match (mismatch) search requires the calculation of a matrix expression

$$\Phi = L \times W^T, \tag{6.22}$$

where

$$L = \left\| \begin{matrix} \bar{l}_{11}l_{11} & \cdots & \bar{l}_{N/21}l_{N/21} \\ \vdots & & \vdots \\ \bar{l}_{1k}l_{1k} & \cdots & \bar{l}_{N/2k}l_{N/2k} \\ \vdots & & \vdots \\ \bar{l}_{1N}l_{1N} & \cdots & \bar{l}_{N/2N}l_{N/2N} \end{matrix} \right\| \tag{6.23}$$

is a matrix, whose rows are composed of binary features l_k, $k = 1, 2, \ldots,$ N, and

$$\Phi = \left\| \begin{matrix} \phi_{11} & \cdots & \phi_{1N} \\ \vdots & & \vdots \\ \phi_{k1} & \cdots & \phi_{kN} \\ \vdots & & \vdots \\ \phi_{N1} & \cdots & \phi_{NN} \end{matrix} \right\|$$

is an $N \times N$ matrix. The comparison of the word l_k to the words (columns) of the transposed matrix W are given on the kth row of that matrix, that is, $w_i = l_k$ when $\phi_{ki} = 0$ and $w_i \neq l_k$ when $\phi_{ki} = 1$.

6.2.2.   Greater Than (Less Than) Search

This type of search is performed in Q iterations. A matrix of Eq. (6.23) is composed of inquiry words l_{kq}, $k = 1, 2, \ldots, N$, at the qth iteration, and a value of the matrix Φ_q is found from Eq. (6.22). The matrix

$$P = \bigvee_{q=1}^{Q} \bar{\Phi}_q \qquad (6.24)$$

is formed by the disjunction of the inverted matrices $\bar{\Phi}_q$ generated at each of the iterations. This is the final result of the search. The element $p_{ki} = \bigvee_{q=1}^{Q} \bar{\phi}_{kiq} = 1$ or 0, depending on whether vector w_i satisfies the condition $w_i > l_k$ or $w_i < l_k$. Matrix P has a structure such that the results of matching the feature l_k to all the columns w_i of matrix W^T are arranged on its kth row.

6.2.3.   Between Limits Search

The problem is generalized for sorting the objects by $m = N$ intervals at a time $[l_1^H, l_1^B], \ldots, [l_N^H, l_N^B]$. The boundaries of the intervals can overlap. Sorting by N intervals as well as sorting by one interval (see Section 6.1) can be done in three steps.

At the first step objects whose features satisfy conditions $w_i > l_1^H, \ldots$, $w_i > l_N^H$ are found. This can be done by an algorithm for a multichannel *greater than* search. The matrix P^H generated according to Eq. (6.24) is stored.

At the second step the objects whose feature satisfy conditions $w_i < l_1^B$, $\ldots$, $w_i < l_N^B$ are found. In this case we speak about an algorithm for a *less than* search. The matrix P^B is computed according to Eq. (6.24).

Finally, at the third step the matrix

$$P = P^H \wedge P^B \qquad (6.25)$$

is computed, where the element $p_{ki} = p_{ki}^H \wedge p_{ki}^B$ is equal to 1, when w_i falls within the interval $[l_k^H, l_k^B]$, and it is equal to 0, when w_i is outside the interval. It follows that whether any object belongs to the interval $[l_k^H, l_k^B]$ can be determined by readout of the values of the kth row of matrix P.

$2Q$ $(Q \leq N/2)$ iterations are required for solving this problem by a multichannel technique. For comparison, it should be mentioned that the problem can be solved in $2NQ$ iterations by a common technique (see Section 6.1).

7.

Data Search in an Array Computer

Data processing in an array computer is carried out by a combined operation of OP and PPP. Let $C = W^T$, $B = L$, and $A = I$. The computer OP then functions as a multichannel associative storage and the PPP as a main logic processor. The processing algorithm depends on the character of the search task.

In case of a match (mismatch) search the OP performs the transformation of Eq. (6.22), and the PPP (a layer of photoreceiving elements) performs the photoelectronic transformation, the binary quantization, and the inversion of the components of matrix Φ. The result from the processing of matrix Φ are stored in the layer of J–K flip-flops.

The problem of a *greater than (less than)* search (see Section 6.2.2) can be solved in $Q \leq N/2$ sequential iterations. At each iteration the OP performs transformation (6.22), and the PPP (a layer of J–K flip-flops) performs transformation (6.24), which is equivalent to an element-by-element logic addition of matrices $\bar{\Phi}_q$, $q = 1, 2, \ldots, Q$. A binary matrix P is the result of the processing; the values of its components are stored in the layer of J–K flip-flops.

Finally, the search algorithm in an interval (see 6.2.3) requires the following operations to be performed:

(1) Find a value of matrix P^H through realization of a *greater than* search algorithm. The result obtained is transferred in parallel from the layer of J–K flip-flops to the layer of R–S flip-flops. The content of the J–K flip-flop layer is then erased.

(2) Find a value of matrix P^B (the J–K flip-flop layer) through a *less than* search algorithm.

(3) Do the transformation of Eq. (6.25) by the process of parallel transfer of the J–K flip-flop contents to the R–S flip-flop layer. A binary matrix P is the result of the processing; the values of its components are stored in the R–S flip-flop layer.

A system cycle T of a computer operation includes the input time and the processing of a page W image in the OP, in addition to the input time and the processing of an image Φ in the PPP. During this period, the computer carries out more than $2N^2$ scalar product operations (OP) and more than N^2

elementary logic operations (PPP). The computer productivity π can be approximately evaluated from the formula $\pi \sim 2N^2/T$ operation/sec, assuming that a scalar product of vectors of length $N/2$ is more powerful than the operation of element-by-element logic processing. The computer productivity $\pi = (0.4 - 1) \times 10^9$ operation/sec, when $N = 100$, and $T = 20$ μs to 50 μs.

The creation of a computer with a cycle time of the order of 20–50 μs is considered feasible, judging by the results of studying high-speed optically controlled structures of the type MD_1SD_2M. In particular, from Sikharulidze (1980) we know that the write-erase time is 20 μs in a PLZT ferroelectric ceramic structure (dielectric D_2). An energy of 10^{-9}–10^{-8} J/cm^2 with a wavelength $\lambda = 0.9$ μs was required to control the structure. An analogous structure described by Belyaev et al. (1980) demonstrated a write-ease time of 50 μs. A warm liquid-crystal layer (S effect) served as a dielectric D_2. A voltage of the order of 100 V was required. This data indicates that the creation of fast optically controlled transparencies for the OP is probably feasible.

The creation of fast electrically controlled transparencies based on, e.g., multichannel acousto-optical light modulators, also seems feasible. Input speeds can reach 100–400 Mbit/sec or more.

8.
Summary

An array optoelectronic computer is a flexible and multifunctional device for associative digital data processing. This is achieved due to the optical preprocessor associated with a parallel operation of triple matrix multiplication included in the computer. Depending on the task to be solved, the preprocessor can function as a multichannel associative storage or as a programmable parallel data switch. There are physical and technical premises for the creation of a search computer that performs 10^9 operation/sec.

References

Athale, R.A., and Lee, J.N. (1984). *Proc IEEE* **72**, 931–941.

Belyaev, V.V., Vasil'ev, N.A., Kompanets, I.N., Matsveiko, A.A., Parfenov, A.V., and Popov, Yu.M. (1980). *Pisma v Zh. Tekh. Fiz.* **6**, 845–847 (in Russian). English transl. in *Sov. Tech. Phys. Lett.*

Casasent, D. (1984). *Proc. IEEE* **72,** 831–849.

Feng, T.-Y. (1974). *IEEE Trans. Comp.* **C-23,** 309–318.

Gofman, M.A., Kibirev, S.F., Krivenkov, B.E., Tverdokhleb, P.E., and Chugui, Yu.V. (1978). *In:* "Optical Information Processing," (E.S. Barrekette, G.W. Stroke, Yu.E. Nesterikhin, and W.E. Kock, eds.), Plenum, New York, pp. 305–316.

Goodman, J.W. (1981). *In:* "Optical Information Processing," (S.H. Lee, ed.), Springer, Berlin, pp. 235–260.

Kagan, B.M., and Kanevsky, M.M. (1973). "Digital Computers and Systems," Energiya, Moscow (in Russian).

Krivenkov, B.E., Tverdokhleb, P.E., and Chugui, Yu.V. (1975). *Appl. Opt.* **14,** 1829–1934.

Krivenkov, B.E., Mikhlayev, S.V., Tverdokhleb, P.E., and Chugui, Yu.V. (1976). *In:* "Optical Information Processing," (Yu.E. Nesterikhin, G.W. Stroke, and W.E. Kock, eds.), Plenum, New York, pp. 203–217.

Mikhlayev, S.V., Tverdokhleb, P.E., and Chugui, Yu.V. (1978). *Opt. i Spektrosk.* **44,** 383–388 (in Russian). English transl. in *Opt. & Spectrosc.*

Rhodes, W.T., and Sawchuk, A.A. (1981). *In:* "Optical Information Processing," (S.H. Lee, ed.), Springer, Berlin, pp. 69–110.

Rhodes, W.T., and Guilfoyle, P.S. (1984). *Proc. IEEE* **72,** 820–830.

Sikharulidze, D.G. (1980). "Space-Time Light Modulation in Structures of MDS Type Electrooptical Material," Candidate's Degree Dissertation, Tbilisi State University, Tbilisi (in Russian).

Tverdokhleb, P.E. (1979). *Avtometriya* **1,** 117–120 (in Russian). English transl. in *Automatic Monitoring and Measuring.*

Tverdokhleb, P.E. (1981a). *Avtometriya* **1,** 19–29 (in Russian). English transl. in *Automatic Monitoring and Measuring.*

Tverdokhleb, P.E. (1981b). *Avtometriya* **3,** 17–26 (in Russian). English transl. in *Automatic Monitoring and Measuring.*

Tverdokhleb, P.E. (1982). *In:* "Optoelectronic Image Processing Techniques," (S.B. Gurevich and G.A. Gavrilov, eds.), Nauka, Leningrad, pp. 3–12.

Vanyushev, B.V., Volkov, A.V., Gibin, I.S., Dombrovskii, V.A., Dombrovskii, S.A., Mantush, T.N., Pen, E.F., Pechurkin, V.I., Polivanov, V.A., Potapov, A.N., Tverdokhleb, P.E., Chernyshev, A.I., and Chernyshev, L.F. (1984). *Avtometriya* **3,** 19–26 (in Russian). English transl. in *Automatic Monitoring and Measuring.*

7.

Optical Matrix
Computations

Mustafa A.G. Abushagur

Department of Electrical and Computer Engineering
University of Alabama in Huntsville
Huntsville, Alabama

H.J. Caulfield

Center for Applied Optics
University of Alabama in Huntsville
Huntsville, Alabama

Contents

1. Introduction 224
2. Linear Algebra 225
   2.1 Preliminaries/Notation 225
   2.2 Computational Complexity 227
   2.3 Accuracy 228
   2.4 Operations 231
3. Optical Computations 231
   3.1 Vector-Matrix Multiplications 232
   3.2 Matrix-Matrix Multiplication 234
   3.3 The Bimodal Optical Computer 234
4. Summary 247
   References 247

1.

Introduction

The data-processing capabilities of coherent and incoherent analog optical systems are remarkable. Optical analog processors are parallel in nature and have a large space-bandwidth product. This, in turn, makes the optical analog processors capable of performing a huge amount of operations with a very high speed. This is demonstrated very clearly by the Fourier transform computer, the positive lens that performs two-dimensional Fourier transforming with the speed of light (Goodman, 1967).

A great effort has been directed towards increasing the flexibility of optical systems. The search has been for developing general systems that can perform a variety of operations instead of being restricted to a specific operation. Cutrona (1965) suggested a simple vector matrix multiplier. Multiplication of two matrices by coherent optical techniques was proposed by Heinz et al. (1970) and was demonstrated experimentally by Jablonowski et al. (1972) for the simple case of 2×2 matrices. An alternative method for matrix-matrix multiplications was introduced by Tamura and Wyant (1977). Shneider and Fink (1975) introduced an incoherent method for the matrix-matrix multiplication. Krivenkov et al. (1976), and later Bocker (1984), described an incoherent method for multiplying 3 two-dimensional matrices together. A very important method for multiplying a vector by a matrix has been introduced by Bocker (1974) and by Bromley (1974), and an improved version was later described by Monahan (1975). More recently, attention has been focused on optical architectures for performing matrix operations using systolic, engagement, and outer-product approaches. (Goodman et al., 1978; Caulfield and Rhodes, 1981; Caulfied et al., 1981, 1984a, 1984b; Guilfoyle, 1983, 1984; Bocker et al., 1983a, 1983b; Athale and Collins, 1982; Rhodes and Guilfoyle, 1984; Athale and Lee, 1984; Goutzoulis, 1984; Casasent, 1984).

Our purpose in this chapter is to review some of the basic activities in the field of optical matrix computations. We will concentrate more on our work in this area. No attempt will be made to summarize all the research that has been done in this area.

In Section 2 of this chapter we will review some of the basics of linear algebra, problem complexities, solution algorithms, accuracy of the solution, and linear algebra operations. In Section 3 we review some of the basic optical matrix computations, which will lead us to introduce the bimodal optical computer. Application of the bimodal optical computer to solving systems of linear equations and eigenproblems will be discussed.

2.
Linear Algebra

2.1.   Preliminaries/Notation

An operator $O[\cdot]$ is said to be linear if

$$O[x_1 + x_2] = O[x_1] + O[x_2].$$

In linear algebra the linear operations are matrix operations. In this chapter we will use lower-case English letters for vector symbols: $\mathbf{a}$, $\mathbf{b}$, $\mathbf{x}$, ... Vectors are viewed as columns of scalars

$$\mathbf{a} = \begin{bmatrix} a_1 \\ a_2 \\ \vdots \\ a_M \end{bmatrix}. \tag{7.1}$$

We write $(\mathbf{a})$-transpose as

$$\mathbf{a}^T = [a_1 \quad a_2 \quad \dots \quad a_M]. \tag{7.2}$$

Matrices are represented by capital letters:

$$A = \begin{bmatrix} a_{11} & a_{12} & \dots & a_{1M} \\ \vdots & & & \\ a_{N1} & a_{N2} & \dots & a_{NM} \end{bmatrix}. \tag{7.3}$$

From time to time we will view the matrix as a collection of vectors, e.g.,

$$A = \begin{bmatrix} a_{11} & a_{12} & & a_{1M} \\ \vdots & \vdots & \dots & \vdots \\ a_{N1} & a_{N2} & & a_{NM} \end{bmatrix} \tag{7.4}$$

$$= [\mathbf{a}_1 | \mathbf{a}_2 | \dots | \mathbf{a}_M],$$

or

$$A = \begin{bmatrix} a_{11} & a_{12} & \dots & a_{1M} \\ & \vdots & & \\ a_{N1} & a_{N2} & \dots & a_{NM} \end{bmatrix} \tag{7.5}$$

$$A = \begin{bmatrix} \propto_1^T \\ \vdots \\ \propto_N^T \end{bmatrix}.$$

An inner product of two vectors is dimension reducing

$$\mathbf{a}^{\mathrm{T}}\mathbf{b} = a_1b_1 + a_2b_2 + \ldots + a_M\mathbf{b}_M .\qquad(7.6)$$

The outer product of two vectors is dimension increasing

$$\mathbf{a}\mathbf{b}^{\mathrm{T}} = \begin{bmatrix} a_1b_1 & a_1b_2 & \ldots & a_1b_N \\ a_2b_1 & a_2b_2 & \ldots & a_2b_N \\ \vdots & & & \vdots \\ a_Mb_1 & a_Mb_2 & & a_Mb_N \end{bmatrix}.\qquad(7.7)$$

Three levels of linear algebraic operations must be distinguished. First, there are elementary operations such as a_1b_1 or $a_1 + b_2$. The a_i's may be non-negative, real, or complex. Second, there are matrix operations such as

$$A\mathbf{x},\qquad(7.8)$$

$$\mathbf{x} + \mathbf{y},\qquad(7.9)$$

$$\mathbf{a}^{\mathrm{T}}\mathbf{b},\qquad(7.10)$$

$$AB,\qquad(7.11)$$

or even strings such as

$$AB C\mathbf{x} + D\mathbf{y}.\qquad(7.12)$$

Third, there is problem solution. This is the real payoff. Many problems are of the form

$$A\mathbf{x} = \mathbf{b}.\qquad(7.13)$$

If A and $\mathbf{b}$ are given, we seek $\mathbf{x}$. If $\mathbf{x}$ is exactly determinable, this is the classic "N equations with N unknowns" problem. If $\mathbf{x}$ is overdetermined (more equations than unknowns), this is linear curve fitting, usually solved in terms of the normal equations (least squares). If $\mathbf{x}$ is underdetermined (more variables than equations), we often seek to make it determined by adding constraints. Linear constraints lead to linear programming, etc. If we know $\mathbf{x}$ and $\mathbf{b}$ and seek A we arrive at the classic problem of linear neural network design. Other problems of interest are the

- eigenvalue problem (find the $\mathbf{e}_i$, λ_i pairs satisfying

$$A\mathbf{e}_i = \lambda_i\mathbf{e}_i).\qquad(7.14)$$

- matrix inversion (find the matrix A^{-1} such that,

$$A^{-1}A = I),$$

where

$$I = \begin{bmatrix} 1 & & 0 \\ & \cdot & \\ & & \cdot \\ 0 & & 1 \end{bmatrix}, \qquad \text{and}$$

• singular value decomposition (express A as

$$A = \alpha_1 \mathbf{u}_1 \mathbf{v}_1^T + \ldots + \alpha_N \mathbf{u}_N \mathbf{v}_N^T, \tag{7.15}$$

with the minimum number of terms and with

$$\mathbf{u}_i^T \mathbf{u}_j = \mathbf{v}_i^T \mathbf{v}_j = \delta_{ij}) . \tag{7.16}$$

Note that processes (e.g., $A\mathbf{x}$) are made up of elementary operations, while algorithms for problem solutions are made up of processes.

2.2. Computational Complexity

While the processes can be performed in various ways, the results are always the same. This is not so of algorithms. Errors in problem posing as well as errors in carrying out the processes cause errors in the final answers. Algorithm design involves complex tradeoffs between convenience, cost, etc. and accuracy; that is, the most accurate algorithms are often the most "costly," in some sense of that word.

One component of cost is resource complexity. Our resources are time, space, etc. While we can often trade off one of these against the other, there is a conserved price to be paid to do a calculation. We often refer to the price scaling law as the computational complexity. For instance, unless you are a skilled algorithmecist, it will take you N^3 adds and N^3 multiplies to multiply two $N \times N$ matrices. We say that the computational complexity is of the order of N^3 or, simply, $O(N^3)$. Algorithms have been designed that do this process with approximately $O(N^{2.5})$ complexity. All operations that are $O(N^x)$ are said to be of polynomial complexity. All other problems are said to be exponential.

The study of computational complexity, nondeterministic polynomial (*NP*) problems, the *NP = P* problem, the *NP* complete problem, etc. are beyond our goals here. What we do want to note is

1. computational complexity is a good measure of "the price to be paid,"
2. for each problem there is a (generally unknown) minimum complexity,
3. complexity varies with the algorithm, and
4. (not illustrated here) it is often effective to solve high-complexity problems with inexact (heuristic) approximations of far lower complexity.

The one note we wish to make on complexity is to note that heuristic algorithms require in-process decisions. While these decisions can often be made optically, they may come to dominate the optical process time by requiring conversion of signal format.

A final note on complexity is simply an elaboration of observation (1) above. Often we can do an $0(N^P)$ problem with temporal complexity $0(1)$ simply by using $0(N^P)$ components in parallel. We can always do the problem with temporal complexity $0(N^P)$ using only $0(1)$ complexity. The trick is to share complexity optimally (in some problem-dependent sense) between component complexity and temporal complexity. This can be done by proper choice of "algotecture" and/or by appropriate partitioning (Caulfield *et. al*, 1984).

Another major component of "cost" is format conversion. Each time we convert optical information either into a new format and back again or into electronic information and back again, we pay a huge price. We conclude that a useful design principle for the optical algorithmecist is: minimize or (better) eliminate format conversions.

Algorithms may be classified in many ways. One useful classification is "iterative" versus "direct." For the determinate $A\mathbf{x} = \mathbf{b}$ problem, the most famous good (accurate) method is Gaussian elimination, with or without "pivoting." Pivoting, selection of the next variable to be eliminated in an optical fashion, leads to very good accuracy. These methods are determinate in that we know ahead of time precisely how many operations must be performed to achieve the final result. Pivoting is a typical result-dependent adaptation that almost inevitably requires the conversions just mentioned. This is a problem so common as to be worthy of being termed fundamental to optical computing. The most accurate algorithms lead to the most (undesirable) conversions.

Iterative algorithms apply the same operation over and over until the desired accuracy is achieved or until convergence fails (blowup, oscillation). This simplicity often allows us to minimize or even eliminate conversions. They are, in that sense, ideal for optical implementation. In general, however, they are less accurate than direct algorithms. Again, the optical algorithmecist must make tradeoffs.

2.3. Accuracy

It is convenient to represent the accuracy of such multielement entities as vectors and matrices with a single number. To that end, we introduce the concept of the "norm," $\|\cdot\|$.

The p-order vector norm is

$$\|\mathbf{a}\|_p = [|a_1|^P + |a_2|^P + \ldots + |a_M|^P]^{1/P.} \qquad (7.17)$$

Only three norms are ever seriously studied.

The order-1 norm

$$\|\mathbf{a}\|_1 = |a_1| + \ldots + |a_M| \qquad (7.18)$$

is fairly simple to calculate and is a fair measure of how all of the components contribute. By way of contrast, the infinity norm

$$\|\mathbf{a}\|_\infty = \underset{i}{\text{MAX}} \; [|a_i|] \qquad (7.19)$$

is also easy to calculate but directs attention to only one component.

The order-2 or Euclidean norm is so common that the subscript is often dropped. Thus

$$\|\mathbf{a}\| = [|a_1|^2 + \ldots + |a_M|^2]^{1/2}. \qquad (7.20)$$

Having defined a vector norm, we can define a matrix norm

$$\|A\|_q = \frac{\|A\mathbf{x}\|_q}{\|\mathbf{x}\|_q}. \qquad (7.21)$$

Those readers familiar with eigenvalue theory will see immediately that

$$\|A\| = \sqrt{\mu_{\text{MAX}}}, \qquad (7.22a)$$

where $\sqrt{\mu_{\text{MAX}}}$ is the maximum absolute value eigenvalue of $A^H A$ where A^H is the conjugate transpose of A (Young and Gregory, 1973). For symmetrical A,

$$\|A\| = \sqrt{\mu_{\text{MAX}}} = |\lambda|_{\text{MAX}}. \qquad (7.22b)$$

$$\|A^{-1}\| = \sqrt{\mu_{\text{MIN}}} = |\lambda|_{\text{MIN}}. \qquad (7.23)$$

These observations will become important shortly.

Returning the the $A\mathbf{x} = \mathbf{b}$ problem, we can see that there are two ways to define the error in an approximate solution $\mathbf{x}_a$. We could use the value

$$e_1 = \|A\mathbf{x}_a - \mathbf{b}\|_q. \qquad (7.24)$$

If we knew the true solution $\mathbf{x}_t$, we could use

$$e_2 = \|\mathbf{x}_a - x_t\|_q. \qquad (7.25)$$

Note that e_2 is a more stringent measure than e_1, because e_1 could be driven to zero with $\mathbf{x} \neq \mathbf{x}_t$ by error calculation. On the other hand, in many problems e_1 is operationally adequate. This is a vitally important observation that

makes "accurate" solutions by optical computing far more feasible than pur-
ists (users of the e_2 criterion) often grant.

We now cite without proof some important results from the analysis of
e_2 accuracy. These involve a number called the *condition number of the
matrix*, often written as cond(A) or $\chi(A)$. By definition,[1]

$$\text{cond}(A)_q = \|\mathbf{A}\|_q\|A^{-1}\|_q \geq \frac{|\lambda|_{\text{MAX}}}{|\lambda|_{\text{MIN}}}. \tag{7.26}$$

We see that cond(A) > 1. Often cond(A) $>> 1$. The condition number of
a matrix is fixed but not the condition number of a problem. By reformu-
lating the problem we can often state it in such a way that its condition
number is smaller (Westake, 1975). This is called *preconditioning* and we
consider it vital computing.

Posing the problem inaccurately by writing $\mathbf{b} + \delta\mathbf{b}$ instead of $\mathbf{b}$, the resulting *exact* equation is

$$\text{from which } A(\mathbf{x} + \delta\mathbf{x}) + \mathbf{b} = \delta\mathbf{b}, \tag{7.27}$$

$$\delta\mathbf{x} = A^{-1}\delta\mathbf{b}. \tag{7.28}$$

Applying any norm $\|.\|$ and using the triangle inequality

$$\|\delta\mathbf{x}\| \leq \|A^{-1}\|\|\delta\mathbf{b}\| \tag{7.29}$$

and

$$\|\mathbf{b}\| \leq \|A\|\|\mathbf{x}\|; \tag{7.30}$$

dividing, we get

$$\frac{\|\delta\mathbf{x}\|}{\|\mathbf{x}\|} \leq \|A\|\|A^{-1}\|\frac{\|\delta\mathbf{b}\|}{\|\mathbf{b}\|} \tag{7.31}$$

We recall

$$\chi(A) = \|A\|\|A^{-1}\| \tag{7.32}$$

is the condition number of A. With somewhat more difficulty, we can show
(for a posing error in A, that is, for an inability to represent A exactly),

$$\frac{\|\delta\mathbf{x}\|}{\|\mathbf{x} + \delta\mathbf{x}\|} \leq \chi(A)\frac{\|\delta A\|}{\|A\|}. \tag{7.33}$$

---

[1]Other definitions of the condition number do exist, as, e.g., the Van Neumann condition
number $P(A) = |\lambda|_{\text{MAX}}/|\lambda|_{\text{MIN}}$ (Westake, 1975).

Thus $\chi(A)$ is a multiplier of $\|\delta b\|/\|b\|$ or $\|\delta A\|/\|A\|$, which gives $\|\delta x\|/\|x\|$. Unfortunately

$$\chi(A) > 1, \qquad (7.34)$$

for all matrices. For an ill-conditioned matrix

$$\chi(A) \gg 1. \qquad (7.35)$$

2.4. Operations

Matrix-vector multiplication can be done by inner products. Thus

$$A\mathbf{x} = \begin{bmatrix} \boldsymbol{\alpha}_1^T \\ \vdots \\ \boldsymbol{\alpha}_M^T \end{bmatrix} \mathbf{x} = \begin{bmatrix} \boldsymbol{\alpha}^T \quad \mathbf{x} \\ \vdots \\ \boldsymbol{\alpha}_M^T \quad \mathbf{x} \end{bmatrix}, \qquad (7.36)$$

$$A\mathbf{b} = \begin{bmatrix} \mathbf{a}_1^T \\ \vdots \\ \mathbf{a}_M^T \end{bmatrix} [\mathbf{b}_1 | \ldots | \mathbf{b}_N] \qquad (7.37)$$

$$= \begin{bmatrix} \mathbf{a}_1^T \mathbf{b}_1 & & \mathbf{a}_1^T \mathbf{b}_N \\ & \cdots & \\ \mathbf{a}_M^T \mathbf{b}_1 & \cdots & \mathbf{a}_M^T \mathbf{b}_N \end{bmatrix}$$

or, by outer product,

$$AB = [\mathbf{a}_1 | \ldots | \mathbf{a}_M] \begin{bmatrix} \boldsymbol{b}_1^T \\ \vdots \\ \boldsymbol{b}_M^T \end{bmatrix}. \qquad (7.38)$$

3.
Optical Computations

In this section we review the implementation of the basic matrix operations optically. Then we introduce the theory of our bimodal optical computer (BOC). The applications of the BOC to solving a system of linear equations (determined, overdetermined, and underdetermined) and in determining the eigenvalues and eigenvectors of a matrix are also discussed.

3.1. Vector-Matrix Multiplications

One of the first operations in linear algebra that has been implemented optically is the vector-matrix multiplication. This operation can be achieved
by representing the vector **x** by an array of light-emitting diodes (LEDS),
where each LED represents one element of the vector **x**, then the light beam
illuminated by the LEDs expand horizontally, as shown in Fig. 7.1. The
matrix A is represented by an optical mask, then the light from each LED
element illuminates the corresponding row of the optical mask. The light
emerging from each column of the optical mask of the matrix A is collected
vertically to illuminate one element of the photodiode array. The output of
the photodiode array will represent the vector **b**, where

$$A\mathbf{x} = \mathbf{b}. \tag{7.39}$$

This system is capable of multiplying very large size vectors and matrices.
The limitation on the size is influenced by the electro-optic devices and the
medium on which the matrix mask will be written. The other advantage of
the system is the speed of the operation. Since the system operates in parallel, then the size of the matrix will not impose any limitations on the speed
of the operation. The disadvantage of the system is its low accuracy. Analog
optical processors, because of their analog nature, have low accuracy. So
the accuracy of the vector-matrix operation shown above can be achieved
within 2% or 3%.

The other problem that has to be solved is the representation of a complex
number in the system, since optical intensities can have zero or positive

Fig. 7.1.

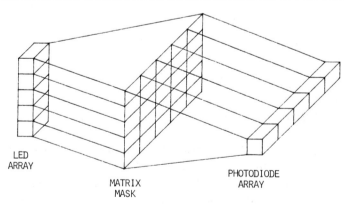

LED
ARRAY

MATRIX
MASK

PHOTODIODE
ARRAY

Incoherent vector-matrix multiplier.

values only. This can be solved by using the three-component decomposition of the complex number (Goodman and Woody, 1977). Any complex number z can be uniquely decomposed in terms of the phasors $\text{Exp}(j0)$, $\text{Exp}(j2\pi/3)$, and $\text{Exp}(j4\pi/3)$ as

$$z = x_0 e^{j0} + x_1 e^{j2\pi/3} + x_2 e^{j4\pi/3}, \qquad (7.40)$$

where x_0, x_1, and x_2 are real numbers. The vectors $\mathbf{x}$, $\mathbf{b}$ and the matrix A can be expressed as

$$\mathbf{x} = x_0 e^{j0} + \mathbf{x}_1 e^{j2\pi/3} + \mathbf{x}_2 e^{j4\pi/3} \qquad (7.41a)$$

$$\mathbf{b} = \mathbf{b}_0 e^{j0} + \mathbf{b}_1 e^{j2\pi/3} + \mathbf{b}_2 e^{j4\pi/3} \qquad (7.41b)$$

$$A = A_0 e^{j0} + A_1 e^{j2\pi/3} + A_2 e^{j4\pi/3}, \qquad (7.41c)$$

where the vector components and the matrix elements are all nonnegative and real quantities. This technique of representing complex numbers will increase the size of the LED array by a factor of three and the matrix mask by a factor of nine.

To avoid this increase in the number of LEDs and photodiodes color-multiplexing was introduced by Psaltis et al., (1979). In the color-multiplexing technique, as shown in Fig. 7.2, each phasor is represented by an LED emitting in an unoverlapping spectrum from the other two. The output from the matrix mask is passed through a grating for the purpose of demultiplexing.

Fig. 7.2.

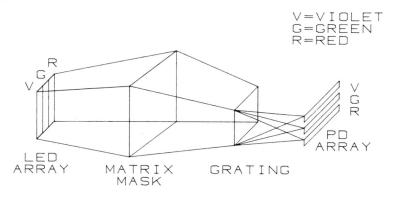

Color-multiplexed optical processor.

3.2. Matrix-Matrix Multiplication

The second basic linear algebra operation is the matrix-matrix operation. Matrix-matrix operation can be implemented optically in many different ways (Bocker, 1984; Bakarat, 1987). One way of doing this is by using the vector-matrix multiplier shown in Fig. 7.1. Let A and B be $N \times K$ and $K \times M$ matrics, and let C be their product. This operation can be written as

$$AB = C, \qquad (7.42)$$

$$A[\mathbf{b}_1|\mathbf{b}_2|\dots|\mathbf{b}_M] = [\mathbf{c}_1|\mathbf{c}_2|\dots|\mathbf{c}_M]. \qquad (7.43)$$

To do this operation using the vector matrix-multiplier we write $\mathbf{b}_1$ on the LED array and read the vector $\mathbf{c}_1$ on the photodiode array and then we keep feeding one column of B and read one column of C. In M cycles we can achieve the matrix-matrix multiplication operation.

Now by being able to do the basic operation in linear algebra, namely, vector-matrix and matrix-matrix multiplications optically, we can solve many linear algebra problems. In the following section we present an optical hybrid system capable of solving systems of linear equations, matrix inversion, eigenvalue problems, as well as other linear and nonlinear problems.

3.3. The Bimodal Optical Computer

Solving systems of linear equations and determining the eigenvalue and the eigenvectors are only a few of the challenging problems faced by the numerical computations. These problems do arise in solving many physical problems, as in solving partial differential equations, signal extrapolations, phased-array radars, image enhancement, etc. In most of these cases the size of the matrices involved are very large. Solving a system of linear equations and determining eigenvalues and eigenvectors for large matrices is time consuming because of the computation complexity. Digital computers revolutionized this field because of the fast execution of number-crunching operations. However, still solving a problem with a matrix of 1000×1000 elements takes a few seconds, which, by today's standards, is a long time.

Optics, by its inherent parallelism and speed, seems to present a natural choice for solving this class of problems. Analog optics is very attractive for optical information processing and computing. As shown in Fig. 7.1, in the vector-matrix multiplier all the elements of the vector are processed at the same time. At almost the same time that we write $\mathbf{x}$, we do read $\mathbf{b}$. If the optical path length between the input and output planes is 3 cm, the whole operation of the vector-matrix operation can be done in less than 100 psec. For $N = 1000$, the number of operations needed to perform $Ax = \mathbf{b}$ is $0(10^6)$. Hence, the speed of the processor is $0(10^{-16})$ sec/operation. This illustrative example gives a sense of the speed of the analog optics in performing linear algebra operations. Unfortunately this high speed of operations is combined with a low accuracy, which is the nature of all the analog systems.

Analog optics is very fast but inaccurate. On the other hand, digital electronics is very accurate but not as fast as analog optics. Utilizing the advantages of both analog optics and digital electronics can be achieved in a "compromise" hybrid system: a system that slows down the processor speed but in return increases the accuracy substantially.

The bimodal optical computer (BOC) introduced by Caulfield et al. (1986) is based on this idea of combining the speed of analog optics and the accuracy of digital electronics.

In the following subsections we will show how to solve some of the basic linear algebra problems using the BOC.

3.3.1. Solving a System of Linear Equations

Consider an $N \times N$ matrix A, and $N \times 1$ vectors $\mathbf{x}$ and $\mathbf{b}$. Let A and $\mathbf{b}$ be given. We would like to solve the system of equations

$$A\mathbf{x} = \mathbf{b} \tag{7.44}$$

for the vector $\mathbf{x}$. This can be solved by analog optics techniques. The relaxation method introduced by Cheng and Caulfield (1982) can be used to solve Eq. (7.44) for $\mathbf{x}$. Consider the hybrid system shown in Fig. 7.3. Assume an initial value for the solution $\mathbf{x}$ and write it using the LEDs. Then the vector $\mathbf{x}$ is multiplied by the matrix A. The resultant vector $\mathbf{y}$ is compared with $\mathbf{b}$ by a difference amplifier. This difference is fed back to correct $\mathbf{x}$. This process of multiplying the new value of $\mathbf{x}$ with A and comparing $\mathbf{y}$ to $\mathbf{b}$ continues until the difference between $\mathbf{y}$ and $\mathbf{b}$ becomes zero. Then the value of $\mathbf{x}$ will converge to the solution of Eq. (7.44).

For a positive definite matrix A a convergence to the solution always exists. To achieve a nonnegative definite matrix, we can multiply Eq. (7.44) from the left by the Hermitian A^H of A. The new matrix $A^H A$ is non-negative definite. We will show later that the increase in condition number this causes need not affect convergence and that we can solve the equations even if $A^H A$ is singular.

This method in solving a system of linear equations is very rapid. Its speed

Fig. 7.3.

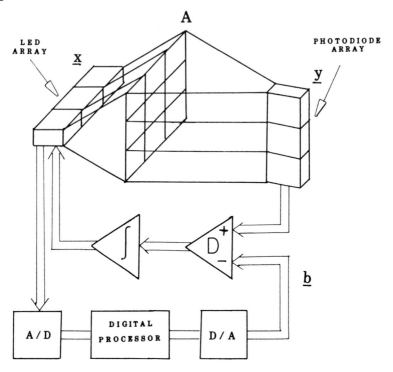

Block diagram for the bimodal optical computer (BOC) for solving the system of linear equations $Ax = b$.

is limited only by the speed of the electro-optics devices and on the feedback electronics, which can be in the picosecond range.

Let us consider now the accuracy of the system. In writing both A and x on the optical mask (it can be a photographic film or a spatial light modulator) and the LED array, a considerable amount of error will exist because of the nature of these analog devices. In addition, reading the vector b on the photodiode array cannot be done exactly. Therefore, the system in Fig. 7.3 did not solve the system in Eq. (7.44) but instead the system given by

$$A_0 x_0 = b_0 , \tag{7.45}$$

where the subscript zeros indicate inaccuracies in the optics and electronics. The solution x_0 of Eq. (7.45) can be refined to get the vector x using the following algorithm:

(1) Solve the system in Eq. (7.45) using the analog optical processor for $\mathbf{x}_0$.

(2) Store the solutions $\mathbf{x}_0$ to a high accuracy with the digital processor. Use a dedicated digital processor to calculate the residue

$$\mathbf{r} = \mathbf{b} - A\mathbf{x}_0 = A(\mathbf{x} - \mathbf{x}_0) = A\Delta\mathbf{x}. \qquad (7.46)$$

(3) Use the optical analog processor to solve the new system of linear equations

$$A_0\mathbf{y}_0 = s\mathbf{r}_0, \qquad (7.47)$$

where $\mathbf{y} = s\Delta\mathbf{x}$ and s is a "radix," or scale factor, chosen to make good use of the dynamic range of the system.

(4) Use the digital processor to refine the solution $\mathbf{x}_0$ for $\mathbf{x}_1$:

$$\mathbf{x}_1 = \mathbf{x}_0 + \Delta\mathbf{x}. \qquad (7.48)$$

If the refined solution $\mathbf{x}_1$ is accurate enough, terminate the iterations. Otherwise, return to (2), (3), and (4) for a more refined solution. The system, which implements the algorithm outlined above, is shown in Fig. 7.3.

The convergence and speed of the solution for the system of linear equations is studied and reported by Abushagur and Caulfield (1986a, 1987a) and Caulfied and Abushagur (1986). The convergence of the iterative solution depends on two main factors. The first is the condition number of the matrix A_0, $\chi(A_0)$: The smaller condition number is, the faster it will converge. The second is the error involved in reading and writing A, $\mathbf{x}$, and $\mathbf{b}$ using electro-optic devcies. The higher the accuracy in representing these parameters, the faster the convergence will occur.

The condition number of the matrix is a critical factor in the convergence of the solution. In representing the matrix A by an optical mask, an error will be added to it. The inaccuracies in representing the matrix A changes the values of the matrix elements a_{ij}'s. These variations in the matrix elements change the condition number of the matrix. Let us represent the mask's matrix A_0 in the following form

$$A_0 = A + E, \qquad (7.49)$$

where E is an error matrix. The error matrix E is generated using Gaussian statistics, with standard deviation, σ_E.

The effect of the error matrix E on the condition number of the optical mask's matrix is demonstrated in Fig. 7.4. In Fig. 7.4a, a matrix A with a condition number of 60 is considered. The coefficients of the matrix are normalized such that the maximum a_{ij} is equal to unity. The condition num-

Fig. 7.4.

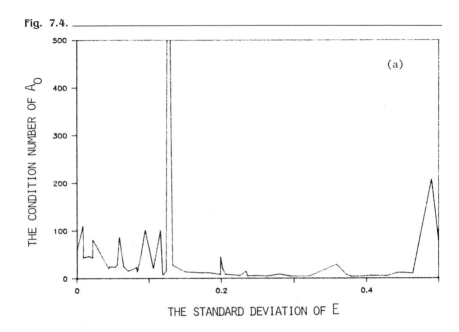

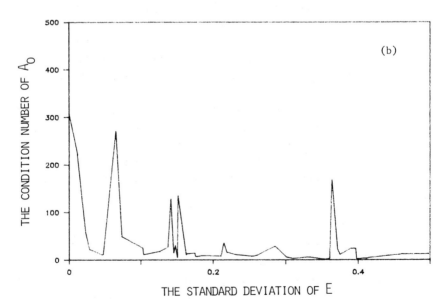

The condition number of the matrix's mask $\chi(A_o)$, as a function of σ_E, for (a) $\chi(A) = 60$, and (b) $\chi(a) = 300$.

ber of A_0 plotted as a function of the standard deviation of the error matrix, σ_E. The condition number of the matrix A_0 tends to decrease by the increase of σ_E, especially for large σ_E. In Fig. 7.4b, a matrix A with condition number 300 (ill-conditioned) is considered. The condition number decreased significantly throughout the range considered of σ_E. Thus, if A is an ill-conditioned matrix, the mask's matrix can very well be a better-conditioned one. Of course, in this case when we solve the system give in Eq. (7.45) A_0 will be different from the original A. Hence, we solve a better-conditioned system for the approximate solution x_0, and then we refine using the algorithm outlined above.

Now, let us consider the effect of the condition number on the convergence of the solution. The condition number is the determining factor in the accuracy of the solution of the system of equations, as given by Eq. (7.32). Hence, for a matrix with a large condition number, the first iteration of the solution with a limited accuracy computer will be highly inaccurate. This leads to the result that the larger the condition number, the larger number of iterations needed for the convergence of the solution. To demonstrate this result, we ran a computer simulation of the bimodal optical computer. The simulated BOC is used to solve a system of linear equation with a 16-bit resolution. The matrix A, was generated randomly using Gaussian statistics. An error matrix E, with an error of 1% of that of the maximum coefficient of the matrix A, was then added to A to generate A_0, as in Eq. (7.49). An error of 1% was also used in reading x_0 and in writing b_0. In each case we computed the condition numbers of the matrix and its mask. The number of iterations required for convergence of the solution to the specified accuracy was determined for each case. The iterations were terminated if they exceeded 25 or $\|r^{(k+1)}\|/\|r^{(k)}\| > 1$, which is the condition for the solution divergence. The number of iterations, N_I, required for convergence of the solution with 16-bit accuracy is plotted as a function of the condition number $\chi(A_0)$ in Fig. 7.5. In these experiments it is clear that the number of iterations increases with the increase of the condition number.

The condition number, as shown above, is one of the determining factors for the number of iterations required for convergence of the solution of the system of equations. It is also shown in Fig. 7.4 that the condition number of the optical mask's matrix decreases by the increase of the standard deviation of the error matrix E.

The influence of the standard deviation of the error matrix, E, on the convergence of the solution is shown in Fig. 7.6. The number of iterations, N_I, increases with the increase of σ_E. This decrease in the convergence rate

Fig. 7.5. ————————————————————————————————

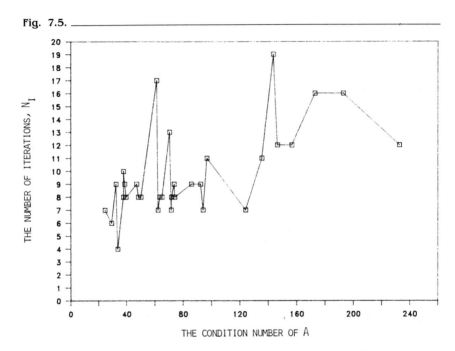

The number of iterations, N_I, is plotted as a function of the condition number of the matrix A.

is expected, because for large σ_E's the matrix A_0 is quite different from A. The important result demonstrated in Fig. 7.6 is that even with an error up to 50% in writing matrix A in the optical mask, convergence is still achieved.

This result is very important in realizing this algorithm by analog optics. In representing matrix A by an optical mask, an error will always exist. An error of 1% is quite hard to achieve in this representation using our current technology. In the present state-of-the-art technology an accuracy of 2% to 3% in writing matrix A is within our reach. This accuracy does not sacrifice the convergence of the solution.

The above results show that the bimodal optical computer can solve a system of linear equations with very high accuracy. This accuracy can be achieved using I/O devices that have limited accuracy. Digital computers are capable of achieving high accuracy solutions for all the cases considered above. Thus, what is the real advantage of introducing this new class of computers? Speed is what we are after. An analysis of the speed of the BOC shows that for it to be faster than the digital computer, the following condition should be satisfied (Abushagur and Caulfield, 1987a)

Fig. 7.6. _____

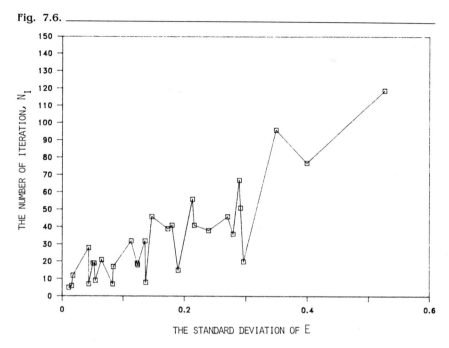

The number of iterations, N_I, is plotted as a function of the standard deviation, σ_E, of the error matrix.

$$A_p A_I \gg 1, \qquad\qquad (7.50)$$

where

$$A_p = \frac{2[N^3/6) + N^2(1 - K) - NK]}{K}, \qquad (7.51)$$

$$A_I = \frac{T_{DI}}{T_{AI}}, \qquad\qquad (7.52)$$

$$K = I_O/I_D, \qquad\qquad (7.53)$$

N = the size of the matrix, I_O = the number of iterations needed for the convergence of the solution to the specified accuracy using the BOC, I_D = the number of iterations needed for the convergence of the solution using the digital computer, T_{DI} = the time required to perform one digital operation, and T_{AI} = the time required to solve $A_0 x_0 = b_0$ using the analog processor.

The speed advantage depends on the size of the matrix, N, and the speed of the electronic and electro-optic devices used in the BOC. The factor A_p is plotted in Fig. 7.7 as a function of N for a set of values of K. It is quite clear that A_p is very large $0(10^5)$ for moderately large values of N.

The values of T_{DI} and T_{AI} can be compared using approximate values and current data:

$$T_{AI} \simeq 2 \; \mu\text{sec}, \tag{7.54}$$

$$T_{DI} \simeq 1 \; \mu\text{sec for a microcomputer}, \tag{7.55}$$

and

$$T_{DI} \simeq 1 \; \text{nsec for a CRAY2}. \tag{7.56}$$

The factor $A_p A_I$ is plotted in Fig. 7.8 as a function of N using the data given by Eqs. (7.54) and (7.56). The advantage in speed is very large and the condition of Eq. (7.50) is satisfied for $N > 50$.

This advantage in speed of the BOC over the existing digital computer makes it a very attractive computing machine and shows the potential of this class of hybrid systems.

Fig. 7.7. ⎯⎯⎯⎯⎯⎯⎯⎯⎯⎯⎯⎯⎯⎯⎯⎯⎯⎯⎯⎯⎯⎯⎯⎯⎯⎯⎯

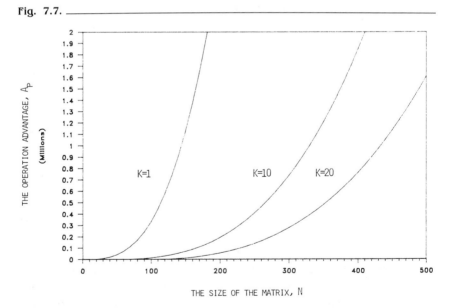

The operation advantage, A_p, in Eq. (7.51) as a function of the size of the matrix, N for $K = 1$, 10, and 20.

Fig. 7.8.

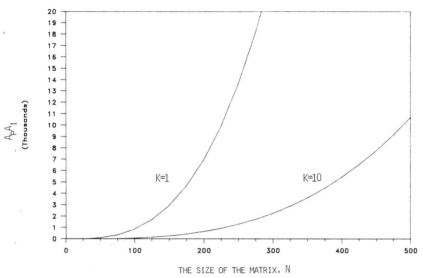

THE SIZE OF THE MATRIX, N

The factor $A_p A_l$ is plotted as a function of the size of the matrix, N, for $K = 1$ and 10.

3.3.2. Eigenvalue Problems

Determining the eigenvalues and the corresponding eigenvectors is another basic problem of linear algebra. The eigenvalue determinations are often performed by iterative methods using digital computers. Several methods were proposed for solving this class of problems using optical techniques (Caulfield et al., 1981; Caulfield and Gruninger, 1981) that suffer from potential accuracy problems.

In this section we introduce a new method to determine the eigenvalues and their corresponding eigenvectors using the BOC (Abushagur and Caulfield, 1986b). The accuracy of the solution is equivalent to that of the floating-point processors.

For an $N \times N$ matrix A the eigenvalues and the eigenvectors are given by

$$A\mathbf{e}_i = \lambda_i \mathbf{e}_i, \qquad i = 1, 2, \ldots, N, \tag{7.57}$$

where λ_i's are the eigenvalues of the matrix A and $\mathbf{e}_i$'s are the corresponding eigenvectors. In this method, we consider the case where the eigenvalues are all positive and not equal, i.e.,

$$\lambda_1 > \lambda_2 > \ldots > \lambda_n > 0. \tag{7.58}$$

There are many methods for determining the eigenvalues of a matrix. One of the powerful methods is the inverse iteration method (Wilkinson, 1965). This method is outlined as follows:

(1) Assume an initial value for the eigenvalue $\lambda_i = q_i$ and an eigenvector $\mathbf{z}^{(0)}$. The assumption for the initial value of the eigenvalue can be done using the Gershgorin circle theorem.

(2) Then solve the system of linear equations

$$(A - q_i I)\mathbf{y}^{(p+1)} = \mathbf{z}^{(p)}, \qquad p = 0, 1, 2, 3, \ldots \tag{7.59}$$

where

$$\mathbf{z}^{(p+1)} = \frac{\mathbf{y}^{(p+1)}}{\left\|\mathbf{y}^{(p+1)}\right\|_\infty}, \tag{7.60}$$

$\|\cdot\|_\infty$ is the infinite norm, and I is the identity matrix. As

$$p \to \infty, \qquad \mathbf{y}^{(p)} = \mathbf{e}_i \qquad \text{and} \qquad \frac{1}{\left\|\mathbf{y}^{(p)}\right\|_\infty} = \lambda_i - q_i. \tag{7.61}$$

Of course other norms will work, but the infinite norm is very easy to calculate.

The time-consuming operation in this method is solving the system of linear equations in Eq. (7.59) for $\mathbf{y}^{(p+1)}$. This system of equations can be solved using the bimodal optical computer (BOC) very rapidly relative to electronics, especially for large N. The algorithm that will be used for determining the eigenvalues and the eigenvectors using the BOC is as follows:

(1) Assume a value for q_i and $\mathbf{z}^{(0)}$ using the digital processor.

(2) Solve the linear system of equations

$$(A - q_i I)\mathbf{y}^{(1)} = \mathbf{z}^{(0)} \tag{7.62}$$

for $\mathbf{y}^{(1)}$ using the BOC.

(3) Compute the norm dv$\mathbf{y}^{(1)}\|_\infty$ and $\mathbf{z}^{(1)}$ using a dedicated digital processor.

(4) If $\left\|\mathbf{y}^{(1)}\right\|_\infty - \left\|\mathbf{y}^{(0)}\right\|_\infty \leq \epsilon$, where ϵ is the error acceptable in computing the eigenvalues and the vectors, then stop the iterations; otherwise go back to step (2).

In this algorithm we use the analog optics to compute an approximate solution for the system of the linear equation, which is then refined using the digital processor. This refined solution has digital computer accuracy but is determined much more quickly.

To get a quantitative idea of the speed advantage in solving these problems using the BOC over the digital computer, let the time required for joint one iteration of the procedure outlined above using the digital computer be $T_D \cdot T_D$, as given by Abushagur et al. (in press):

$$T_D = \left(\frac{7n^3}{4}\right) T_{D1}. \tag{7.63}$$

The time required to do the same algorithm using the BOC is

$$T_0 = [T_{A1} + 2n(n + 2)T_{D1}]I_0. \tag{7.64}$$

For a clear advantage in speed for the BOC over the digital computer we need to satisfy the following condition:

$$T_D \gg T_0 \tag{7.65}$$

or

$$A_{PE}A_I \gg 1,$$

where A_I is given by Eq. (7.52) and

$$A_{PE} = \frac{[7n^3/4 - 2n(n + 1)I_0]}{I_0}. \tag{7.66}$$

Using Eqs. (7.54) and (7.56)

$$A_{PE} \gg 2000.$$

This condition can be satisfied for all $M \geq 25$ and $N \geq 50$ for $I_0 = 1$ and $I_0 = 10$, respectively. The advantage in speed increases rapidly by the increase of the size of the matrix N.

3.3.3. Systems with Ill-Conditioned and Singular Matrices

In Section 3.3.1 we considered systems of linear equations with well-conditioned matrices. If the matrix A of the system $A\mathbf{x} = \mathbf{b}$ is singular (i.e., its determinant is equal to zero) or near singular (ill conditioned), this sytem will not be solved using the conventional methods, because the inverse of A does not exist or can not be calculated accurately. In this case, usually, the least squares solution is determined using either the singular-value-decomposition or other standard techniques (Johnson, 1982).

In our case, using the BOC, we still can solve this class of problems using the same method used for the well-conditioned system Abushagur et al. (1987b). In the BOC we can not represent matrix A exactly on an optical mask, but A can be represented by A_0 as given by Eq. (7.49). A_0 will not

TABLE 7.1

Convergence behavior of 10×10 matrices of ranks 9 and 1 for various additive errors. N_1 is the number of iterations required to achieve $\|\mathbf{r}_{Ni}\| = 0$ to within 16 bits. The ratio of $\|\mathbf{r}_2\|/\|\mathbf{r}_1\|$ gives another measure of convergence (or divergence indicated by D) rate. We have used the infinity norm for convenience.

			10×10, Rank $= 9$		10×10, Rank $= 1$	
σ_E	σ_b	σ_x	N_1	$\|\mathbf{r}_2\|/\|\mathbf{r}_1\|$	N_1	$\|\mathbf{r}_2\|/\|\mathbf{r}_1\|$
0	0	0	1		1	
0	1.E-6	0	4	0.5585	D	5.1E+26
1.E-6	1.E-6	0	1	3.4E-6	1	8.9E-7
0	1.E-6	1.E-6	D	2.3273	D	6.7E+26
1.E-6	1.E-6	1.E-6	1	9.2E-4	1	1.2E-5
0	.01	0	D	1.0000	D	2.4E+64
1.E-6	.01	0	4	2.2E-2	2	2.9E-3
0	.01	.01	D	1.1953	D	1.2E+31
1.E-6	.01	.01	9	2.1E-1	5	6.9E-2
1.E-4	.01	.01	7	1.7E-1	4	3.6E-3
.01	.01	.01	8	2.5E-1	5	1.3E-1
.05	.01	.01	11	2.4E-1	4	2.0E-1
.10	.01	.01	18	7.2E-1	4	8.6E-2

be singular, and the condition number of A_0 is very small compared to that of A (which is infinity for the singular matrix), and the solutions will converge in few iterations, even much faster than that for a matrix A with $\chi(A_0)$ $\cong 10^4$. When a matrix is singular it has infinitely many solutions. The solution obtained by the BOC for the system is a solution, which can be different for different noise matrices. The same is applicable for systems with near-singular matrices in which the solution converges very rapidly. We have tested systems with condition numbers in the range of 10^6 to 10^8 and they still achieve convergence in less than 10 iterations to a solution with 16 bits of resolution. In Table 7.1, the results of a computer simulation for the BOC in solving systems of equations with singular matrices are given. The matrices considered here are 10×10 with ranks 9 and 1, respectively. The effect of the error in $\mathbf{b}$, $\mathbf{x}$, and A on the convergence rate is shown. Thus, if there is an error in writing $\mathbf{b}$, the solution diverges, but by adding an error to matrix A, a convergence to a solution will occur. This technique is very remarkable and is not limited to the use in the BOC but can be applied to the digital computer by replacing A by an inaccurate matrix A_0 and using it to find an approximate solution, which can be refined using the algorithm that is outlined in Section 3.4.1.

Additionally, this technique is used to solve over determined and under-determined systems by making the rectangle matrix A in a square one, S, by adding zeros to missing coefficients. S will be singular but it can be solved using the BOC technique.

4.
Summary

In this chapter we have presented a brief review of linear algebra. Computational complexity is discussed with relation to computational algorithms. Optical implementations of the basic linear algebra operations are reviewed with emphasis on more recent and practical techniques. The bimodal optical computer (BOC) is presented. It is shown that the nature of the BOC as an optical-hybrid processor enables it to solve linear algebra problems with high accuracy without much sacrifice of the analog optics speed. Finally, the applications of the BOC to solving singular and ill-conditioned systems is presented. This technique will enable the BOC and optical matrix computations, in general, to solve a great variety of practical problems.

References

Abushagur, M.A.G., and Caulfield, H.J. (1986a). "Highly precise optical-hybrid matrix processor," (D. Pape, ed.), *Proc. SPIE* **639, 63**.

Abushagur, M.A.G., and Caulfield, H.J. (1987a). "Speed and convergence of bimodal optical computers," *Opt. Eng.* **26, 22**.

Abushagur, M.A.G., and Caulfield, H.J. (1986b). "Solving eigenvalue problems using the bimodal optical computer," *JOSA A* **3, 23**.

Abushagur, M.A.G., Caulfield, H.J., Gibson, P.M., and Habli, M. (1987b). "Superconvergence of hybrid opto-electornic processors," *Appl. Optics* **26,** 4906–4907.

Athale, R.A., and Collins, W.C. (1982). "Optical matrix-matrix multiplier based on outer product decomposition," *Appl. Optics* **21, 2089–2090**.

Athale, R.A., and Lee, J.N. (1984). "Optical processing using outer-product concepts," *Proc. IEEE* **72, 931–941**.

Bakarat, R. (1987). "Optical matrix-matrix multiplier based on Kronecker product decomposition," *Appl. Optics* **26, 191**.

Bocker, R.P. (1974). "Matrix multiplication using incoherent optical technique," *Appl. Optics* **13, 1670–1676**.

Bocker, R.P. (1984). "Optical digital RUBIC cube processor," *Opt. Eng.* **23**, 26–33.

Bocker, R.P., Caulfield, H.J., and Bromley, K. (1983a). "Rapid unbiased bipolar incoherent calculator cube," *Appl. Optics* **22**, 804–807.

Bocker, R.P., Caulfield, H.J., and Bromley, K. (1983b). "Rapid unbiased bipolar incoherent calculator cube." *In:* "Advances in Optical Information Processing," (G.M. Morris, ed.), *Proc. SPIE* **388**, 205–211.

Bromley, K. (1974). "An optical incoherent correlator," *Opt. Acta* **21**, 35–41.

Casasent, D. (1984). "Acoustooptic linear algebra processors: Architectures, algorithms, and applications," *Proc. IEEE* **72**, 831–839.

Caulfield, H.J., and Abushagur, M.A.G. (1986). "Hybrid analog-digital algebra processors." *In:* "Optical and Hybrid Computing," Vol. II of the SPIE Institute Series (H.H. Szu, ed.). *Proc. SPIE* **634**,

Caulfield, H.J., Dvore, D., Goodman, J.W., and Rhodes, W. (1981). "Eigenvector determination by noncoherent optical methods," *App. Optics* **20**, 2263.

Caulfield, H.J., and Gruninger, J. (1981). "Algorithm improvements for optical eigenfunction computers," *Appl. Optics* **22**, 2075.

Caulfield, H.J., Gruninger, J., Ludman, J.E., Steiglitz, K., Rabitz, H., Gelfant, J., and Tsoni, E. (1986). "Bimodal optical computers," *Appl. Optics* **25**, 3128.

Caulfield, H.J., and Rhodes, W.T. (1981). "Acousto-optic matrix—Vector multiplication," *J. Opt. Soc. Am.* **71**, 1626.

Caulfield, H.J., Rhodes, W.T., Foster, M.J., and Horvitz, S. (1981). "Optical implementation of systolic array processing," *Opt. Commun.* **40**, 86–90.

Caulfield, H.J., Verber, C.M., and Stermer, R.L. (1984a). "Efficient matrix partitioning for optical computers," *Opt. Commun.* **51**, 213–216.

Caulfield, H.J., Horvitz, S., Tricotes, G.P., and Van Winkle, W.A. (1984b). Special Issue on Optical Computing, *Proc. IEEE* **72**.

Cheng, W.K., and Caulfield, H.J. (1982). "Full parallel relaxation algebraic operations for optical computers," *Opt. Commun.* **43**, 251.

Cutrona, L. (1965). *In:* "Optical and Electro-Optical Information Processing," (J. Tippet et al., eds.), MIT Press, Cambridge, Massachusetts.

Goodman, J.W. (1967). "Introduction to Fourier Optics," McGraw-Hill, New York.

Goodman, J.W., Dias, A.R., and Woody, L.M. (1978). "Fully parallel, high-speed incoherent optical method for performing discrete Fourier transforms," *Opt. Lett.* **2**, 1–3.

Goodman, J.W., and Woody, L.M. (1977). "Method for performing complex-valued linear operations on complex-valued data using incoherent light," *Appl. Optics* **16**, 2611.

Goutzoulis, A.P. (1984). "Systolic time-integrating acoustooptic binary processor," *Appl. Optics* **23**, 4095–4099.

Guilfoyle, P.S. (1983). *In:* "Bragg Signal Processing and Output Devices," (B.V. Markevitch and T. Kooij, eds.), *Proc. SPIE* **352**, 2.

Guilfoyle, P.S. (1984). "Systolic acousto-optic binary convolver," *Opt. Eng.* **23**, 20–25.

Heinz, R.A., Artman, J.O., and Lee, S.H. (1970). "Matrix multiplication by optical methods," *Appl. Optics* **9**, 2161–2168.

Jablonowski, D.P., Heinz, R.A., and Artman, J.O. (1972). "Matrix multiplication by optical methods: Experimental verification," *Appl. Optics* **11**, 174–178.

Johnson, R.L. (1982). "Numerical Methods," John Wiley, New York.

Krivenkow, B.E., Mikhlyaev, S.V., Tverdokhleb, P.E., and Chugui, Y.V. (1976). "Non-coherent optical system for processing of images and signals." *In:* "Optical Information Processing," (Y.E. Nesterikhin et al., eds.), Plenum Press, New York.

Monahan, M.A., Bocker, R.P., Bromley, K., Louie, A.C.H., Martin, R.D., and Shepard, R.G. (1975). "The use of charge coupled devices in electro-optical processing," *Proc. 1975 Intern. Conf. on the Appl. of Charge-Coupled Devices,* Naval Electronics Laboratory Center, San Diego, CA, Oct. 1975.

Psaltis, D., Casasent, D., and Carlotta, M. (1979). "Iterative color-multiplexed, electro-optical processor," *Opt. Lett.* **4**, 348.

Rhodes, W.T., and Guilfoyle, P.S. (1984). "Acoustooptic algebraic processing architectures," *Proc. IEEE* **72**, 820–830.

Schneider, W., and Fink, W. (1975). "Incoherent optical matrix multiplication," *Opt. Acta* **22**, 879–889.

Tamura, P.N., and Wyant, J.C. (1977). "Matrix multiplication using coherent optical techniques." *In:* "Optical Information Processing," (D. Casasent and A.A. Sawczuk, eds.), *Proc. SPIE* **83**, 97–104.

Westlake, J.R. (1975). "A Handbook of Numerical Matrix Inversion and Solution of Linear Equations," R.E. Krieger Publishing Company, Huntington, NY.

Wilkinson, J.H. (1965). "The Algebraic Eigenvalue Problem," Clarendon, Oxford.

Young, D.M., and Gregory, R.T. (1973). "A Survey of Numerical Mathematics," Addision-Wesley, Reading, Massachusetts.

8.

Optical Implementation of Neural Computers

Demetri Psaltis, David Brady, Xiang-guang Gu, and Ken Hsu

California Institute of Technology
Department of Electrical Engineering
Pasadena, California

Contents

1. Introduction. 251
2. The Basic Architecture 252
3. Three-Dimensional Storage of the Interconnection Weights 259
4. Adaptive Weights and Real-Time Holography 269
   Acknowledgements 274
   References 275

1.

Introduction

A neural computer is characterized by three properties: a) It consists of a large number of simple processing units (the "neurons"); b) each processing element is connected to many others, typically several hundred or several thousand; and c) the network is programmed to respond appropriately to inputs by adjusting the weights of the connections between neurons during a learning phase. Interest in this type of computer has emerged largely because the above characteristics are also part of the models that attempt to describe the operation of biological nervous systems. It is hoped that by building a computer that shares some of the characteristics of the biological systems, we will be able to address problems such as image understanding, which animals do exceedingly well but current machines do not. Unfortunately, due to the lack of a detailed knowledge of the operation of biological neural networks or an adequate theoretical understanding of how to use an adaptive, massively parallel, densely connected computer architecture, the practical use of neural networks for the solution of difficult computational problems remains mostly a goal. Nevertheless, there has been a great deal of progress on the theoretical side to justify optimism about future applications, and this has focused attention on the hardware realization of neural architectures. The computational power of neural computers arises from matching the computer architecture and the physical properties of the devices used in the implementation to the requirements of the problem. In other words, a neural computer is highly specialized, and it is therefore very difficult to derive its potential advantages on a general purpose computer. This provides strong impetus for advancing the technologies for the physical realization of neural computers in parallel and interactively with the theoretical development of neural network models.

Electronics (analog, digital, or hybrid) and optics are the two approaches under consideration for the hardware realization of neural networks. There are two basic components that need to be implemented: neurons and connections. The neurons are typically simple thresholding elements that can be implemented by a single switching device (i.e., transistor). The switching speed or the accuracy required for the neurons is not beyond the capabilities of current electronic technology. A practical neural computer may require millions of neurons operating in parallel. This requirement by itself is also achievable in electronics. However, each of the neurons must be connected to several thousand other neurons, and these connections must be modifiable so that learning can take place. While this massive connectivity is relatively difficult to achieve electronically, optics is particularly well suited for the realization of interconnections. In the remainder of this chapter we discuss how optical methods can be used to implement neural computers.

2.
The Basic Architecture

The basic architecture of an optical neural computer is shown in Fig. 8.1. The neurons are arranged as two-dimensional arrays in planes that are sep-

Fig. 8.1. _____

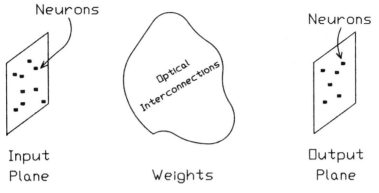

Optical neural computer architecture.

arated from each other by an optical system that specifies the interconnection between each neuron and other neurons in the same or adjacent neural planes. A variety of optical architectures for the realization of optical neural computers have been proposed (Psaltis and Farhat, 1985; Abu-Mostafa and Psaltis, 1987; Farhat, 1987; Owechko et al., 1987; Anderson, 1986; Yariv and Kwong, 1986; Fisher et al., 1986; Guest and Te Kolste, 1987; Athale et al., 1986), and most fit this basic architectural design. Spatial light modulators are used to simulate the two-dimensional array of neurons at the neural planes, whereas holograms, transparencies, and other passive optical elements comprise the optical interconnecting system. The feature of the architecture in Fig. 8.1 that gives it an advantage when compared with electronic implementations is the fact that it is constructed in three dimensions. This allows the active devices at the neural planes to be populated by processing elements only, since the interconnections are external to the plane of the neurons. The third dimension is used to store the information that is required to specify the connections between the neurons. It is important to keep in mind that in a large network (e.g., 10^6 neurons) that is densely connected (e.g., 10^3 connections per neuron), the weights represent a large database. We will see that the ability to store this information in three dimensions in the form of volume holographic interconnections provides the optical system with particularly high storage density. A second advantageous feature of the optical implementation is the relative ease with which learning can be accomplished as dynamic holography in photorefractive crystals. There may be other features of the optics that compare favorably with electronics in the context of neural net implementations, however, learning and three-dimensional storage of the weights are the most important. We will, therefore, focus on these two issues in this chapter. Of course there are important advantageous features for the electronic implementation as well. Electronics is a very mature technology, and the fabrication of analog VLSI chips for neural network applications requires only an adjustment rather than a major redevelopment of electronic technology. Moreover, or possibly as a consequence, there is much greater flexibility in designing electronic circuits so that they can implement a wide variety of functions. It is important therefore to clearly demonstrate that the unique properties of optics (three-dimensional and simple learning architectures) can indeed lead to major improvements in the capabilities of neural computers in order to justify the investment that is required to further develop this technology.

We begin by briefly describing a specific optical architecture that we experimentally demonstrated recently (Paek and Psaltis, 1987; Hsu et al., 1987) in order to provide a concrete example of the general architecture in Fig. 8.1. A schematic diagram of this architecture is shown in Fig. 8.2 and a

Fig. 8.2.

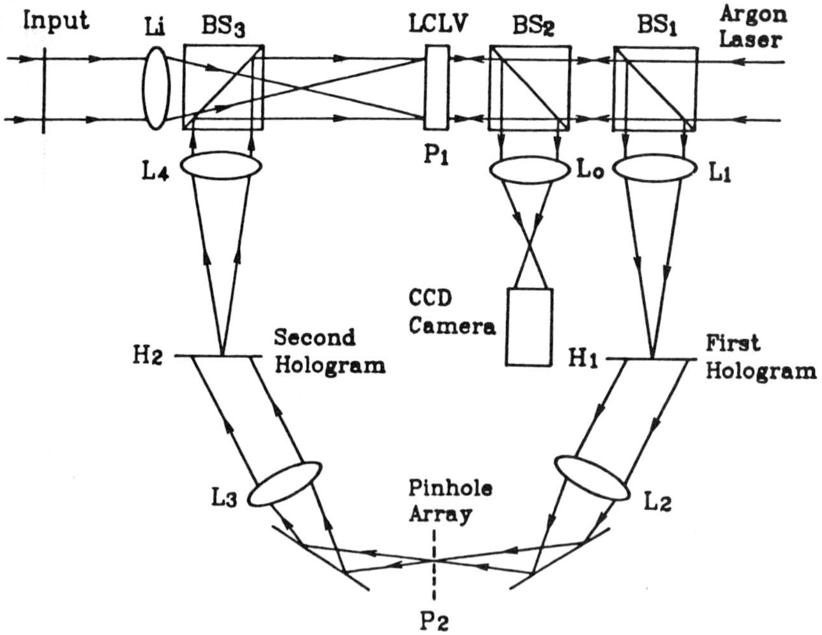

Optical auto-associative loop.

Fig. 8.3. _____

Experimental setup for the auto-associative loop.

photograph of the experimental apparatus is shown in Fig. 8.3. This processor is comprised of only one neural plane, which is the image thresholding device in Fig. 8.2. In the experiments, the neural plane was simulated by a Hughes liquid crystal light valve LCLV (Blecha et al., 1987). The LCLV consists of a photoconductive layer that is attached to a light-modulating liquid crystal layer. The reflectivity of the liquid crystal measured at each resolvable point is determined by the amount of light that is sensed on the photoconductor side at the same location. The input-output characteristic approximates a soft thresholding function if the device is exposed to sufficiently intense illumination. The input-output characteristic of the device used in the experiment is shown in Fig. 8.4. Each resolution element of the LCLV simulates a separate neuron, and, with the resolution of the device used being approximately 400 × 400 pixels, 160,000 neurons are simulated. Each of these neurons is connected to the rest by the two holograms and the rest of the optical components that surround the neural plane in Fig. 8.2. This architecture is organized as an auto-associative memory (Kochonen, 1984; Anderson, 1972; Amari, 1977; Hopfield, 1982) and it operates as follows. An input pattern is imaged onto the photosensitive side

Fig. 8.4.

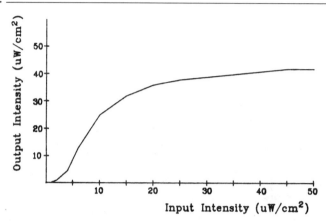

LCLV output versus input intensity with a 100-μW/cm^3 read beam.

of the LCLV by lens L_i and through beamsplitter BS_3. This then initializes the state of the neurons to this external image. Light from an argon laser illuminates the LCLV from the other side through beamsplitter BS_1, as shown in Fig. 8.2. A portion of the reflected light is diverted towards lens L_0 by beamsplitter BS_2, and lens L_0 forms an image of the neural plane onto a CCD television camera used to monitor the operation of the system. The portion of the light that propagates straight through BS_2 in Fig. 8.2 is Fourier transformed by lens L_1 and then it illuminates the hologram H_1. The light diffracted by H_1 is retransformed by lens L_2 and the result is displayed at the intermediate plane P_2. The optical system from the neural plane P_1 to the intermediate plane P_2 is a Vander Lugt correlator (Vander Lugt, 1964) that produces the correlation between the image at the neural plane and the image that results by Fourier transforming H_1. In this architecture the hologram contains several images that are arranged such that the individual correlations between the input and each of the stored images form spatially separated at P_2. The center of each of these correlation patterns is the inner product between the image at P_1 and each of the stored images. An array of pinholes is placed at P_2 that samples the light at the locations where these inner products form. The remainder of the optical system from P_2 back to the neural plane P_1 is essentially a replica of the first half, with the hologram H_2 storing the same set of images as H_1. Each of the light beams that emerges from one of the pinholes reconstructs in the aperture of the neural plane one of the images stored in H_2. The system is designed such that each image in H_2 is reconstructed by the beam formed by the inner product between the *same* image from H_1 and the current pattern at the output of the neural plane. Thus the light distribution that is incident on the photosensitive side of the LCLV is a linear combination of the images stored in the holograms with the "strength" of each image being proportional to the inner product between itself and the current state of the neural plane. Exposure of the LCLV to the reconstructions from H_2 will of course modify the reflectivity of the device, and it will tend to drive the state of the neurons towards the stored image with the highest inner product. Typically, the operation of the system is as follows. If the external image that is projected into the system is not similar to one of the images stored in memory, then the amount of light that makes it past the pinholes is very small, and essentially nothing happens in the loop; once the input is removed no information remains at the neural plane. If, however, the external input is sufficiently similar to one of the stored patterns, then this pattern builds up within the loop. When the input is removed, this stored image remains latched as a stable state of the system. This system can be thought of as a memory that associates each external input with one of the images that are stored in the holograms, provided that the input is sufficiently similar to one of the memories.

An example of experiments performed with this system is shown in Fig. 8.5. In this case four faces were stored in the holograms. An input image corresponding to half of one of the stored faces causes the system to latch onto that face (Fig. 8.5a). When a rotated version of another face (Fig. 8.5b) is used as the external input, the unrotated version of that face establishes itself as the stable state of the loop, and when the input is removed the unrotated image remains latched. Thus the system exhibits a degree of rotation (and also shift and scale) invariance. It is interesting to note that there is a pronounced trade-off between invariance and discrimination in this system that is mediated by the amount of gain in the loop. The gain is provided by the spatial light modulator at the neural plane. This is accomplished by illuminating it with read-out light that is brighter than the light incident on the photosensitive side. Gain is necessary to overcome the losses principally due to diffraction from the two holograms in the loop. If the gain is set high, then the loop generally recognizes highly distorted versions of the images in its memory, however, it also becomes susceptible to falsely recognizing unfamiliar objects. If the gain is lowered then its discrimination increases, but its tolerance to distortions also deteriorates. This limitation is not a consequence of the optical implementation but a consequence of the fact that a single-layer machine was simulated. It is well known that such a machine

Fig. 8.5. _____

(a)

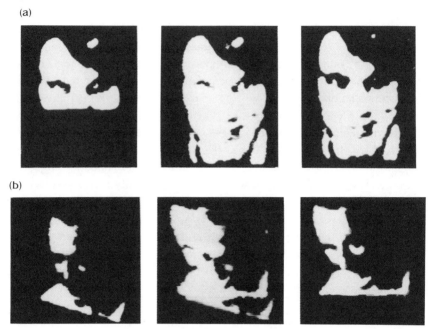

(b)

Experimental results from the associative loop. Shown in the figures are the
input (left), the response of the neural plane with the input present (middle),
and the latched output with the input removed (right) for the input being (a)
half a stored face (b) a rotated version of a stored face.

has limited capabilities (Minsky and Papert, 1988), particularly with regard
to the tradeoff between geometric distortions versus discrimination capability. This limitation can be overcome by the use of multilayered networks
whose optical implementation (Rumelhart and McClelland, 1986; Baum, 1987;
Wagner and Psaltis, 1987) is, at least in principle, straightforward as a cascade of single layers.

The experimental system described above demonstrates the type of optical
neural computer that can be implemented with currently available components, and it points clearly to the advantages of the optical approach, but
also to the areas where improvements are necessary. The number of neurons
that were simulated in this experiment was roughly equal to 160,000, and,
more importantly, each of these neurons was interconnected to all the rest,
simulating in excess of 10^{10} interconnections, with the weight of each connection being specified by the information recorded on the two holograms.
Notice that even though the weights of all these interconnections are fully

specified by the holograms, the connections are not fully loaded with information. It is in principle possible to store thousands of images in a network with this many connections (Venkatesh and Psaltis, 1985), and in our experiments we stored only four images. We will return to the issue of storage capacity shortly. Nevertheless, from an architectural point of view, the experiment clearly demonstrates the capability to optically simulate highly interconnected networks with a very large number of neurons. At the same time, this experiment also points to the deficiencies of the current optical implementation. The most obvious limitations of the system in Fig. 8.3 is its large size and the small number of images that were stored in the two holograms. Is it possible to drastically reduce the dimensions of the optical system while retaining the large number of neurons and connections that are being simulated? Is it possible to store a large number of images in an optical associative memory using practical training procedures? We address the first issue in the following section, and we discuss the second in Section 4.

3.
Three-Dimensional Storage of the Interconnection Weights

Let us contrast the basic neural computing architecture of Fig. 8.1 implemented using planar (Fig. 8.6a) versus volume (Fig. 8.6b) storage media (holograms) for recording the information necessary to specify the connections. We can obtain an estimate for the size of each system implementing a network of a given size without further knowledge of the details of the optical interconnection method. Let N_1 and N_2 be the number of neurons at the input and output planes, respectively. In order to independently connect each point at the input to each point at the output, $N_1 \times N_2$ connections need to be specified. If a planar hologram is used then at least one resolution element has to be devoted to represent each of the weights (Hong and Psaltis, 1986). A lower bound for the resolution element of a planar medium is λ^2, where λ is the wavelength of the read-out light. In practice the resolution may be several wavelengths in each dimension due to limitations of the recording medium or the optical system used to address the hologram. The area A of the hologram in Fig. 8.6a must satisfy the following inequality:

$$A > N_1 N_2 \lambda^2 . \tag{8.1}$$

The distance between either the input or output planes and the hologram

Fig. 8.6. _____

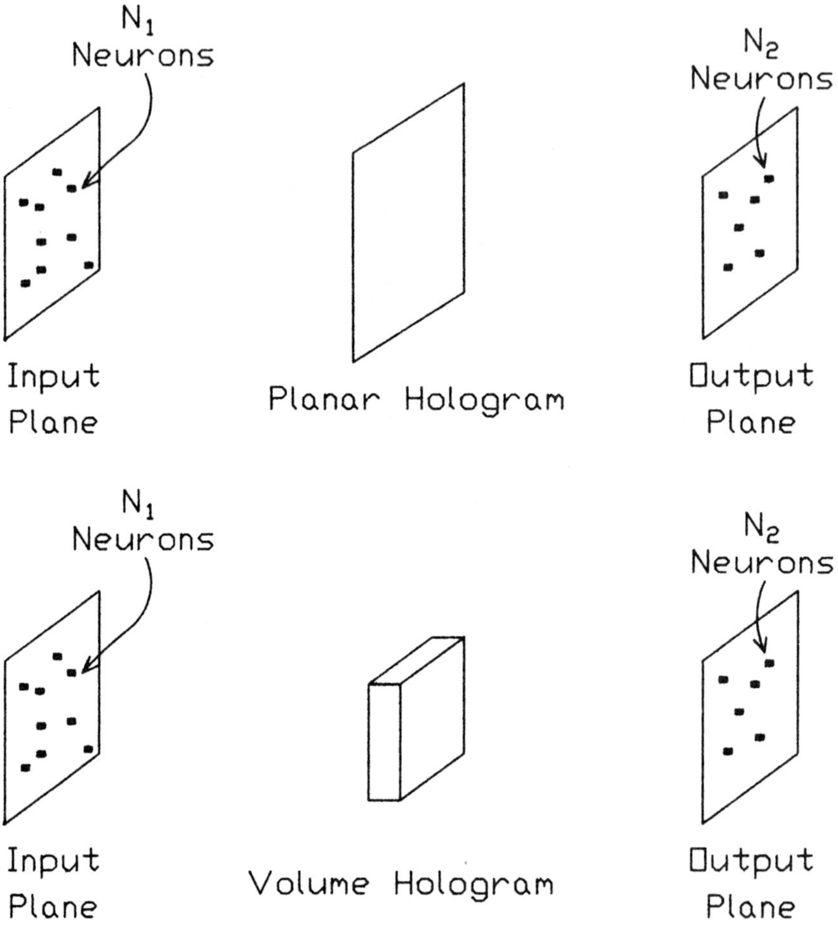

Optical neural architecture implemented with a planar hologram and a volume
hologram.

must be long enough to allow light from each of the neurons at the input
plane to expand and illuminate the hologram or vice versa. In a well-de-
signed optical system, at least one of these distances has to be comparable
to the transverse dimension of the hologram, assuming the numerical aperture of the optical system can be equal to 1 (Derstein, 1988). Thus the
volume V_p required to build the system of Fig. 8.6a must satisfy the following inequality:

$$V_p > A\sqrt{N_1 N_2}\,\lambda > (N_1 N_2)^{3/2}\lambda^{-3}. \qquad (8.2)$$

Using Eq. (8.2) we can estimate the density of connections per unit volume D_p achievable using a planar hologram:

$$D_p = \frac{(N_1 N_2)}{V_p} < (N_1 N_2)^{-1/2}\lambda^3 \text{ connections per unit volume.} \qquad (8.3)$$

If we go through a similar discussion for the case depicted in Fig. 8.6b, we find that the number of independent connections, $N_1 N_2$, and the volume of the storage medium V must satisfy the following inequality (Van Heerden, 1963; Psaltis et al., 1987; Psaltis et al., in press)

$$V > N_1 N_2 \lambda^3. \qquad (8.4)$$

The distance between either one of the neural planes and the volume hologram must be at least as long as the largest transverse dimension of the volume hologram. We assume that the volume hologram has a cubic shape, in which case each transverse dimension is equal to $V^{1/3}$ and we can derive an estimate for the volume V_v of the overall system of Fig. 8.6b

$$V_v > V + 2V^{1/3}\,V^{2/3} > N_1 N_2 \lambda^3. \qquad (8.5)$$

The corresponding density of connections D_v in this case is simply

$$D_v = \frac{(N_1 N_2)}{V_v} < \lambda^{-3} \text{ connections per unit volume.} \qquad (8.6)$$

Comparing Eqs. (8.3) and (8.6) we see that there is a potential for an improvement in storage density with the volume holographic system by a factor equal to $\sqrt{N_1 N_2}$. To appreciate the significance of this difference let us consider a specific example. Let the resolution of the planar recording medium be $(5\ \mu m)^2$ and let the resolution of the volume medium be $(5\ \mu m)^3$. Assuming that $\lambda = 1\ \mu m$, we calculate that in order to simulate $N_1 N_2 = 10^9$ interconnections with the three-dimensional storage medium we require a volume approximately equal to $.125\ cm^3 = (.5\ cm)^3$. The volume required to accomplish the same task using a planar medium is $\sqrt{10^9}$ times larger, or more than $(10\ cm)^3$.

The above discussion leads us to the conclusion that three-dimensional storage of the weights can lead to a very significant reduction of the overall size of the optical system. The question we address now is whether we can store information in volume holograms in the form of interconnections and approach the storage density predicted by Eq. (8.6). Consider again the system of Fig. 8.6b and let us set the number of resolvable points in any direction at the neural planes and at the volume hologram equal to N. Thus there is a total of N^2 pixels available at the input and output planes that are potentially available for the placement of neurons, and there is a total of N^3 "resolution volumes" or voxels in the three-dimensional hologram. If we attempt to interconnect every pixel at the input to all the pixels at the output then the total number of weights that need to be specified and recorded in the hologram would be N^4. Since we only have N^3 degrees of freedom available in the three-dimensional hologram, it is not possible to independently interconnect all the input pixels to all the points at the output. We need to select a subset of the available points at the input and output planes to be used for the placement of neurons such that the product of the number of input and output points does not exceed N^3. For instance, it is possible to independently interconnect $N^{3/2}$ input neurons to $N^{3/2}$ units at the output. We discuss next the procedures for determining *which* pixels are selected to be used at the input and output planes.

The architecture that we use for recording and implementing optical interconnections using a volume hologram is shown in Fig. 8.7. The volume hologram is a photorefractive crystal (Kuktarev et al., 1979; Hall et al., 1985) in all the experiments that will be discussed later on. A hologram that interconnects the input point A to the output point B is recorded as follows (Wagner and Psaltis, 1987). Light originating from A is collimated by lens L_1, it propagates through the crystal, and it is retroreflected back towards A by the phase-conjugating mirror in Fig. 8.7. Light from B propagates towards the left, it is collimated by lens L_2, and the two backpropagating

Fig. 8.7. _____

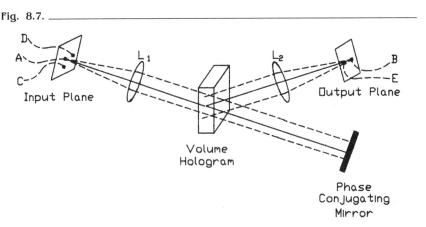

Recording geometry for implementing volume holographic interconnections.

beams interfere in the crystal and record a grating throughout its volume. This grating diffracts a portion of the forward (left-to-right) propagating wave from A into a plane wave that is focused by L_2 onto the point B at the output. In this manner point A is connected to point B, with the strength of the connection being determined by the modulation depth of the grating. Now suppose we introduce a new point C at the input plane that is vertically dispaced from A as shown in Fig. 8.7. Then light originating from C will produce a plane wave incident on the hologram at an angle that is vertically offset in the geometry of Fig. 8.7 from the angle of the plane wave resulting from the point A. This vertical angular offset of the incidence angle implies that the A $\mapsto$ B grating already recorded in the crystal will not diffract any of the light incident on the crystal due to phase mismatch (Kogelnik, 1969). Therefore, the point C, and also any other point that is vertically displaced from A, can be added as an input neuron location and independently connected to output points. However, if a point D is introduced at the input plane that is displaced horizontally from A, then the grating that is already recorded for connecting A to B is also perfectly matched for connecting D to a point E at the output that is horizontally displaced from B the output. In other words the specification of the A $\mapsto$ B connection automatically specifies the D $\mapsto$ E connection, and obviously these four points cannot be independently interconnected. This situation is schematically depicted in the momentum diagram of Fig. 8.8, showing the momentum mismatch due to the vertical separation of input points and the degeneracy that results when the input points are horizontally separated.

The positions of the neurons at the input and output planes are selected so that all degeneracies of the type described above are eliminated, thereby

Fig. 8.8. _____

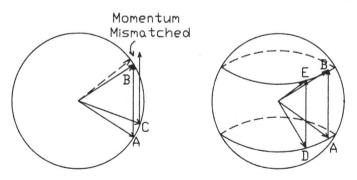

Momentum matching diagram showing mismatch and degeneracy.

Fig. 8.9.

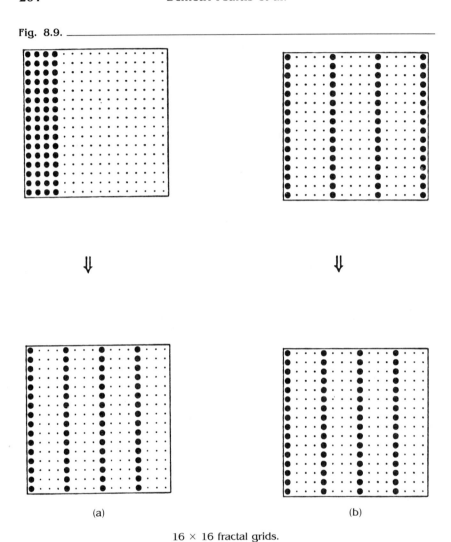

(a)   (b)

16 × 16 fractal grids.

ensuring that each grating in the hologram interconnects a separate pair of input-output points. The criterion for designing the sampling grids is as follows (Psaltis et al., 1987; Psaltis et al., in press)

No two points selected from the input sampling grid may form a rectangle with any pair of points selected from the output sampling grid.

Fig. 8.9 *continued.*

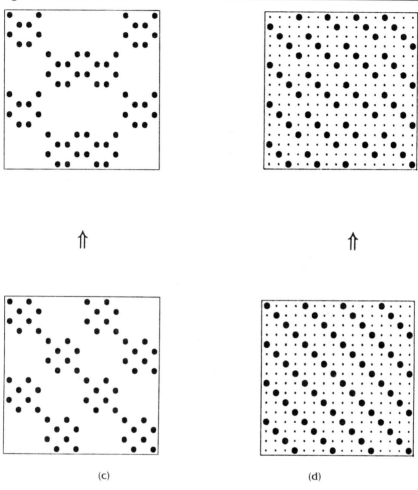

16 × 16 fractal grids.

We will describe how sampling grids can be designed based on the above criterion for the symmetric mapping $N^{3/2} \mapsto N^{3/2}$ case. Sampling grids for any mapping $N^d \mapsto N^{3-d}$ can be designed provided that $1 \leq d \leq 2$ (Psaltis et al., in press). The simplest way to design a $N^{3/2} \mapsto N^{3/2}$ mapping is as shown in Fig. 8.9a, which is drawn for the case $N = 16$. At the input plane, $\sqrt{N}$ columns of neurons are bunched together, and as a result the *maximum* horizontal separation between any two input neurons is $\sqrt{N} - 1$. The neurons at the output plane are arranged also in $\sqrt{N}$ columns, except that they are spaced $\sqrt{N}$ pixels apart. As a result the *minimum* horizontal separation between any two neurons at the output exceeds the maximum input separation and the requirement of the design criterion is satisfied. This sampling grid is not unique. Another way that neurons can be arranged is shown in Fig. 8.9b, where the input and output neurons are again arranged in $\sqrt{N}$ columns. However, the output rows are separated by $\sqrt{N}$ pixels as before, but the input neurons are now separated by $\sqrt{N} + 1$ pixels. It is easy to show that this arrangement also satisfies the design criterion. Shifting horizontally an entire row either at the input or output planes preserves the relative distances between neurons, and therefore different patterns can be created by shifting individual rows of the previous patterns. The sampling grid shown in Fig. 8.9c is created from shifted rows of the patterns in Fig. 8.9b, and it provides the most uniform sampling in terms of spreading equally the $\sqrt{N}$ neurons across the area of the plane. We refer to these patterns as *fractal sampling grids* since they can be thought of as patterns with fractal dimension $^3/_2$. The sampling grids shown in Fig. 8.9d were created by using the self-similar property of fractals. Starting with the same type of patterns as in Fig. 8.9c for $N = 4$, we obtain the larger patterns of Fig. 8.9d by replacing each of the neurons in the smaller patterns with the entire small pattern.

The importance of using the fractal sampling grids when volume holograms are used for the realization of interconnections can be demonstrated through a simple associative memory experiment. The objective is to record a hologram that produces the letter "B" when the letter "A" is presented at the input plane. This can be accomplished by connecting all the points in the input plane that comprise the letter "A" to all the output points that comprise the letter "B." All these connections can be simultaneously recorded using the same apparatus as before (Fig. 8.7), except the entire letters "A" and "B" are placed at the input and output planes, respectively. We might expect then that when the exposed hologram is illuminated with the "A," the "B" is obtained as the output (Gabor, 1948). We performed this experiment using a $LiNbO_3$ crystal and the result is shown in Fig. 8.10a. The reconstruction is highly distorted (ghost hologram) due to the accidental (degenerate) connections between input and output points. When the experiment is repeated with the same patterns sampled on the fractal grids of Fig. 8.9c, the distortion is completely eliminated, as shown in Fig. 8.10b. All the input neurons that comprise the input are connected only to the points on the desired output, thereby reconstructing an undistorted output pattern. Several weak diffracted points are also observable in the reconstruction of

Fig. 8.10.

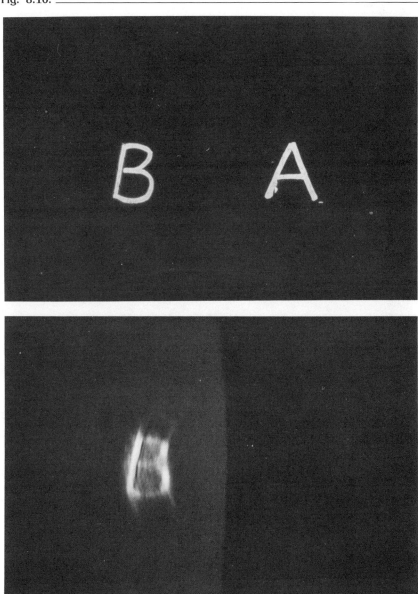

(a) Recording images and image reconstructed from a volume hologram formed without fractal grids.

Fig. 8.10 *continued.* _____

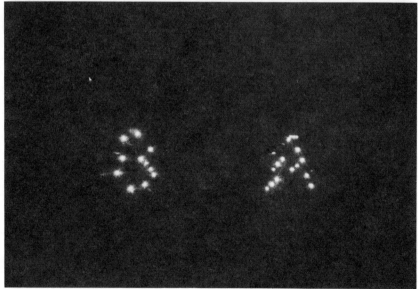

(b) Recording images and image reconstructed from a volume hologram formed using the fractal grids of Fig. 8.9c.

Fig. 8.10b, but these are all at output locations off the output sampling grid and hence do not interfere with the operation of the network.

4.
Adaptive Weights and Real-Time Holography

The use of the sampling grids described in the previous section guarantees that each grating stored in the hologram implements a separate interconnection. Since the number of distinguishable gratings that can be recorded in a crystal of volume V is approximately equal to the number of resolvable elementary volumes that can fit in the crystal, (V/λ^3), we have a way for storing information in the form of interconnections at very high density. The next issue we address is whether the physical mechanism used to record these gratings (the photorefractive effect) can indeed support such a large number of gratings superimposed in the same medium. Let η_0 be the maximum diffraction efficiency (in intensity) that may be obtained when a single grating is formed in the crystal using a single exposure. η_0 can easily be in excess of 50%. When $N_3 = N_1 N_2$ gratings are superimposed in the same crystal, the maximum diffraction efficiency of each grating is η_0/N_3 (Psaltis et al., 1988). This loss in diffraction efficiency is due to the fact that all the gratings must compete for the same finite resources available in the crystal. Specifically, when N_3 gratings are simultaneously recorded in a photorefractive crystal, the finite density of available traps (acceptors usually) limits the amplitude of each recorded holographic grating to $1/\sqrt{N_3}$ of the amplitude of a grating recorded alone. The intensity diffraction efficiency is proportional to the square of the amplitude of the recorded hologram, which leads to the $1/N_3$ loss in efficiency. In the architecture of Fig. 8.6b, each output neuron receives light from N_1 neurons at the input, and in a coherent implementation the light amplitude at each output neuron is the sum of the amplitudes of the light originating from all the neurons at the input layer. Hence the field incident on each output neuron is approximately N_1 times stronger than the field produced by the diffraction of a single grating. The detected intensity is the square of the field amplitude and hence the diffraction efficiency in intensity, including the coherent fan-in that is obtainable in a neural architecture, is $\eta_0 N_1^2/N_3 = \eta_0 N_1/N_2$.

The above discussion leads us to the conclusion that in architectures where $N_1 \approx N_2$, it is possible to superimpose an arbitrarily large number of gratings in the volume of a crystal without a significant loss in overall diffraction

efficiency. The next issue that must be addressed is how the strengths of all
these connections will be specified. We will see that the need to subject the
crystal to multiple exposures in order to load information in the weights of
the connections reduces the diffraction efficiency. We can gain an appre-
ciation for the loading problem by considering the holographic associative
memory example discussed earlier (Fig. 8.7). In an optical implementation,
the number of pixels in the images that can be associated to each other can
be quite large (easily is excess of 10^4 pixels on the fractal grids). From a
strictly information-theoretic point of view, without taking into consideration the limitations of the optical implementation, it is possible to store several thousand such associations by simply accumulating holograms on top
of each other through multiple exposures. However, the physics of the recording process introduces its own limitations. Let A_m be the amplitude of
the hologram that is recorded during the mth exposure in a sequence of M
exposures that record M associations. Then A_m is given by (Bløtekjaer, 1979;
Psaltis et al., 1988)

$$A_m = A_0(1 - \exp^{-t_m/\tau_w}) \exp\left(- \sum_{m'=m+1}^{M} \frac{t_{m'}}{\tau_e}\right), \qquad (8.7)$$

where A_0 is the saturation amplitude, t_m is the exposure time of the mth
hologram and τ_w and τ_e are the write and erase time constants, respectively.
The above equation shows that the recording created by the mth exposure is
partially erased by the $M - m$ subsequent exposures. The optimum exposure
schedule that will ensure that $A_m = A'_m$ for all m and m' is (Bløtekjaer, 1979)

$$t_m = \frac{\tau_e}{m}. \qquad (8.8)$$

Substituting the above equation in Eq. (8.7) and solving for M we obtain
an estimate for the number of exposures given a minimum acceptable amplitude A_m for each hologram.

$$M \approx \frac{\tau_e}{\tau_w} \frac{A_0}{A_m}. \qquad (8.9)$$

Eq. (8.9) reveals that the amplitude of each hologram A_m is inversely proportional to M. The diffraction efficiency is proportional to the square of
the amplitude of the recorded hologram, which leads us to the conclusion
that the diffraction efficiency of a holographic associative memory recorded
as M exposures in a photorefractive crystal is $\eta_0 N_1/N_2 M^2$ (Bløtekjaer, 1979).
The number of exposures that are required to fully load information in the

$N_1 N_2$ connections is $M = N_1$. The diffraction efficiency that we obtain when we use this optimum number of exposures is

$$\eta = \frac{\eta_0}{N_1 N_2} = \frac{\eta_0}{N_3}. \tag{8.10}$$

This simple result shows that if use the multiple-exposure method to fully load information in a set of N_3 connections that are superimposed in the same photorefractive crystal, we suffer a loss in diffraction efficiency by a factor N_3. This loss will have to be compensated by gain provided either at the neural planes or possibly through two-wave mixing amplification using an auxiliary photorefractive crystal.

The basic problem in loading neural interconnections into holographic media is that the dynamics of the holographic recording process must be made to match the dynamics of a useful neural model. In outer-product algorithms the interconnection weight w_{ij} taking the ith neuron into the jth neuron is a solution to the differential equation

$$\frac{d w_{ij}}{dt} = \alpha x_i x_j, \tag{8.11}$$

where x_i and x_j are the activities of the ith and j^{th} neurons. In the simulation of Eq. (8.11) using multiply exposed photorefractive holograms, the equation specifying the dynamics of the interconnections is

$$\frac{d w_{ij}}{dt} = \alpha x_i x_j - \beta w_{ij}. \tag{8.12}$$

As was described above, this discrepancy between the photorefractive response and the neural model limits the scale of the outer-product network that can be implemented using photorefractive crystals. There are two approaches to improving the performance of the multiple-exposure method described above. We can attempt to modify either the physical apparatus or the learning algorithm. We discuss below error-driven learning algorithms that may have superior performance over the simple multiple-exposure holographic associative memory.

The perceptron (Rosenblatt, 1961) is an example of a dynamic error-driven learning algorithm that can be implemented using photorefractive crystals. The perceptron consists of a set of input neurons with activities described by a vector $\mathbf{x}$ that drive a single-output neuron via a weight vector $\mathbf{w}$. The activity of the output vector is high if and only if $\mathbf{w} \cdot \mathbf{x} > \omega_0$ where ω_0 is a fixed threshold level. A perceptron is trained to separate a set of input vectors into two classes by updating the weight vector according to

$$\mathbf{w}(k + 1) = \mathbf{w}(k) + \alpha\mathbf{x}$$
$$\omega_0(k + 1) = \omega_0(k) + \alpha ,$$

(8.13)

where $\mathbf{w}(k)$ is the state of the weight vector at the discrete time k when $\mathbf{x}$ is presented for classification. α is zero if $\mathbf{x}$ is correctly classified and 1 (-1) if $\mathbf{x}$ is misclassified in the low (high) state. If training vectors from a set $\{\mathbf{x}\}$ are presented in sequence, Eq. (8.13) is known to converge on a weight vector implementing an arbitrary prescribed dichotomy if such a weight vector exists.

A particularly simple way to implement a perceptron in a photorefractive system is shown schematically in Fig. 8.11. The input to the system, $\mathbf{x}$, corresponds to a two-dimensional pattern recorded from a video monitor onto a LCLV. The LCLV transfers this pattern on a laser beam. This beam is split into two paths that cross in a photorefractive crystal. The light propagating along each path is focused such that an image of the input pattern is formed on the crystal. The images along both paths are of the same size and are superposed on the crystal. The intensity diffracted from one of the two paths onto the other by a hologram stored in the crystal is isolated by a polarizer and spatially integrated by a single output detector. The thresholded output of this detector corresponds to the output of a perceptron.

The ith component of the input to this system corresponds to the intensity

Fig. 8.11. _____

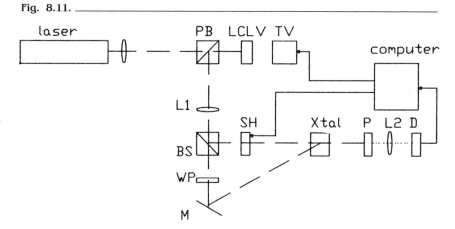

Optical implementation of the perceptron algorithm. PB is a polarizing beamsplitter. L1 and L2 are imaging lenses. WP is a quarter waveplate. M is a piezoelectric mirror. P is a polarizer. D is a detector.

in the ith pixel of the input pattern. The interconnection strength, w_i, between the ith input and the output neuron corresponds to the diffraction efficiency of the hologram taking one path into the other at the ith pixel of the image plane. In analogy with Eq. (8.13), w_i may be updated by exposing the crystal with the input along both paths. If the modulation depth between the light in the two paths is high, then if x_i is high w_i is increased. If the modulation depth is low, then if x_i is high w_i is reduced. The modulation depth between two optical beams can be adjusted by a variety of simple mechanisms. In Fig. 8.11 $m(t)$ is controlled using a mirror mounted on a piezoelectric crystal. By varying the frequency and the amplitude of oscillations in the piezoelectric crystal we can electronically set both $m(t)$ and $\phi(t)$ over a continuous range without changing the intensity in the optical beams or interrupting read-out of the system.

The architecture of Fig. 8.11 was implemented using a SBN60:Ce crystal. The 488-nm line of an argon-ion laser was used to record holograms in this crystal. Most of the patterns we considered were laid out on 10×10 grids of pixels, thus allowing 100 input channels. Ultimately, the number of channels that may be achieved using this architecture is limited by the number of pixels that may be imaged onto the crystal with a depth of focus sufficient to isolate each pixel along the length of the crystal.

Using this variation of the perceptron learning algorithm with fixed exposure times Δt_r and Δt_e for recording and erasing, we have been able to correctly classify various sets of input patterns. One particular set that we used is shown in Fig. 8.12. In one training sequence, patterns 1 and 2 were

Fig. 8.12. _____

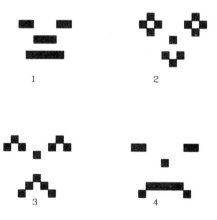

Training patterns.

Fig. 8.13.

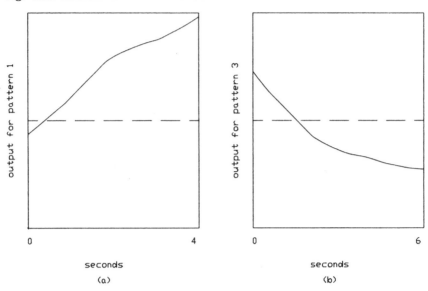

Detector output for patterns 1 and 3 during the second training cycle.

grouped together with a high output and patterns 3 and 4 together with a low output. After all four patterns were presented four times, the system gave the correct output for all patterns. The weights stored in the crystal were corrected seven times, four times by recording and three by erasing. Fig. 8.13a shows the output of the detector as pattern 1 is recorded in the second learning cycle. The dashed line in this figure corresponds to the threshold level. Fig. 8.13b shows the output of the detector as pattern 3 is erased in the second learning cycle.

The experiment described above was successfully carried out with up to 10 images, and it is very likely that the system can also be trained with more images. The challenge, however, still remains to develop practical procedures to go beyond these simple experiments and reach the full capabilities of optical neural computers that were derived in this chapter.

Acknowledgements

The authors gratefully acknowledge the numerous interactions they have had with Drs. Nabil Farhat, John Hong, Hyuk Lee, Eung Gi Paek, Kelvin Wagner, Jeff Yu, and Mr. Cheol-Hoon Park on the subject of optical neural computers. These interactions have contributed a great deal to the work discussed in this chapter.

We also thank Dr. R.R. Neurgaonkar from Rockwell Science Center for providing the SBN crystal used in one of our experiments.

This work is supported by the DARPA, the Air Force Office of Scientific Research, and the Army Research Office.

References

Abu-Mostafa, Y.S., and Psaltis, D. (1987). *Scientific American* **256**, 88.

Amari, S.I. (1977). *Biol. Cyber.* **23**, 175.

Anderson, D.Z. (1986). *Opt. Lett.* **11**, 45.

Anderson, J.A. (1972). *Mathem. Biosci.* **14**, 197.

Athale, R.A., Szu, H.H., and Friedland, C.B. (1986). *Opt. Lett.* **11**, 482–484.

Baum, E.B. (1987). "Proceedings of the IEEE Conf. on Neural Inf. Proc. Systems," Denver, November 1987.

Bleha, W.P., Lipton, L.I., Wiener-Arnear, E., Grinberg, J., Reif, P.G., Casasent, D., Brown, H.B., and Markevitch, B.V. (1978). *Opt. Eng.* **17**, 371.

Bløtekjaer, K. (1979). *Appl. Opt.* **18**, 57.

Derstein, M. (1988). Personal communication.

Farhat, N.H. (1987). *Appl. Opt.* **26**, 10.

Fisher, A.D., Fukuda, R.C., and Lee, J.N. (1986). "Implementations of adaptive associative optical computing elements," *Proc. SPIE* **625**, 196.

Gabor, D. (1948). *Nature* **161**, 777.

Guest, C., and Te Kolste, R. (1987). *Appl. Opt.* **26**, 5055.

Hall, T.J., Jaura, R., Connors, L.M., and Foote, P.D. (1985). *Prog. Quant. Electr.* **10**, 77.

Hong, J., and Psaltis, D. (1986). *Opt. Lett.* **11**, 812–814.

Hopfield, J.J. (1982). *Proc. Matl. Acad. Sci. USA* **79**, 2554.

Hsu, K., Brady, D., and Psaltis, D. (1987). "Proceedings of the IEEE Conf. on Neural Inf. Proc. Systems," Denver, November 1987.

Kogelnik, H. (1969). *Bell. Syst. Tech. J.* **48**, 2909.

Kohonen, T. (1984). "Self Organization and Associative Memory," Springer Verlag, Berlin.

Kuktarev, N.V., Markov, V.B., Odulov, S.G., Soskin, M.S., and Vinet-skii, V.L. (1979). *Ferroelectrics* **22,** 949.

Minsky, M.L., and Papert, S.A. (1988). "Perceptrons," MIT Press, Cambridge.

Owechko, Y., Dunning, G.J., Marom, E., and Soffer, B.H. (1987). *Appl. Opt.* **26,** 1900.

Paek, Z.E.G., and Psaltis, D. (1987). *Opt. Eng.* **26,** 428–433.

Psaltis, D., and Farhat, N.H. (1985). *Optics Lett.* **10,** 98–100.

Psaltis, D., Yu. J., Gu, X.G., and Lee, H. (1987). "Second Topic Meeting on Optical Computing," Incline Village, Nevada, March 16–18.

Psaltis, D., Brady, D., and Wagner, K. (1988). *Appl. Opt* **27,** 1752.

Psaltis, D., Gu, X.G., Lee, H., and Yu, J. (to be published). "Optical Interconnections Implemented with Volume Holograms."

Rosenblatt, F. (1961). "Principles of Neurodynamics: Perceptron and the Theory of Brain Mechanisms," Spartan Books, Washington.

Rumelhart, D.E., and McClelland, J.L. (eds.) (1986). "Parallel Distributed Processing, Volume 1," MIT Press, Cambridge.

Van Heerden, P.J. (1963). *Appl. Opt.* **2,** 393.

Vander Lugt, A.B. (1964). *IEEE Trans. Inform. Theory.* **IT-10,** 139.

Venkatesh, S.S., and Psaltis, D. (1985). "Conf. on Neural Network Models for Computing," Santa Barbara, California, April 1985.

Wagner, K., and Psaltis, D. (1987). *Appl. Opt.* **26,** 5061–5076.

Yariv, A., and Kwong, S.K. (1986). *Opt. Lett.* **11,** 186–188.

9.

Computer Synthesis of Diffraction Optical Elements

Voldemar P. Koronkevich

Institute of Automation and Electrometry
Siberian Branch of the USSR Academy of Science
Novosibirsk, USSR

Contents

1. Introduction. 278
2. Production of Diffraction Optical Elements 280
3. Practical Results: Elements of Diffraction Optical Systems 286
   3.1. Lenses 286
   3.2. Lenses with Uniform Energy Distribution in a Focal Spot 288
   3.3. Kinoform Axicons 290
   3.4. Lenses with a Ring Impulse Response 293
   3.5. Wavefront Correctors 294
   3.6. Circular Diffraction Gratings 295
   3.7. Diffraction Lenses with Mirrors 300
   3.8. Microlenses 301
4. Optical Systems with Diffraction Elements 301
   4.1. Hybrid Objectives 301
   4.2. Bifocus Microscope. 304
   4.3. Coding Systems 306
   4.4. Diffraction Interferometer 309
   4.5. Optical String 310
5. Conclusion 311
   References 312

Optical Processing and Computing
ISBN 0-12-064470-3

277

The late Invention of Telescopes has so exercised most of the Geometres, that they seem to have left nothing unattempted in Optics, no room for farther Improvement.

Isaac Newton. *Optical Lectures,* 1669

1.
Introduction

Progress in the technology of computer production of diffraction optical elements (DOEs) enlarges the base of conventional optical elements, which includes lenses, prisms, mirrors, and their combinations. Using diffraction effects, a wavefront can be transformed and the geometrical positions of point images can be varied. The diffraction structures synthesized by putting a microrelief onto surfaces or by local changes in the refractive index of materials make it possible to deviate, focus, split, or spatially modulate light beams.

For DOEs the optical path from the object to the image is not a continuous function of coordinates on the pupil. It can be given as $a + m\lambda$, where a is a small fraction of the wavelength λ, and m is an integer. Usual optical systems can be considered as a special cases ($m = 0$) of the diffraction elements. In this sense DOEs are sometimes called *generalized optical components* (Bryngdahl, 1975). Holograms and kinoforms are regarded as DOEs in the modern scientific literature. Below we shall use the term *diffraction optical elements* to indicate that the physical process is the basis of the wavefront transformation.

The new elements attract the attention of experts because of the following reasons:

(1) DOEs enable the performance of a wider class of transforms of wavefronts than do the conventional optical elements. They allow the construction of space-variant and spatially overlapping optical systems. In the first case the input image is subjected to space transforms, while in the second it is subjected to several different transforms at the same time. The optical information processing devices can be used to produce diffracting spatial filters, apodizing masks, etc.

(2) Because of their nature, DOEs can be made of thin substrates or films. Their weight and cost are practically independent of their aperture.

(3) The new elements can work in a wide spectral range, from the ultraviolet to the far infrared. They transmit powerful laser radiation without loss because of weak absorbtion in thin substrates, that is, they have a high radiation resistance.

(4) A number of elements whose production presents great difficulties for refraction optics and current technology can be implemented as diffraction elements. They are: Schmidt plates, axicons, phase filters, wavefront correctors, microlens matrices, etc.

(5) The number of optical components in a device can be reduced when DOEs are used, because the functional properties of several elements can be combined in a single element. For example, a mirror and a lens, an axicon and a lens, an interferometer and a lens, etc.

(6) The combination of classical optical elements with DOEs enables the improvement of optical image quality (resolution and contrast), of optical characteristics (field of vision and relative aperture), and reduction in the size and weight cost. In the old days, masters improved the quality of optical systems by *retouching*. By brilliant polishing up to fractions of a wavelength, they applied artificial defects (local and zonal) onto the objective surface, which decreased the wave aberration of the system as a whole. In fact, they intuitively used those fundamental principles that are the basis of operation of present-day optical systems containing refraction and diffraction elements.

(7) The dispersion properties of DOEs differ essentially from the dispersion properties of lenses made of usual glass, rare optical materials, or crystals. For most glasses, the relative partial dispersion is linearly dependent on the Abbe number. The dispersion of DOEs is essentially higher than that of known quartz, lithium fluoride, or fluorite glasses. Thus, when synthesizing the systems one can use DOEs together with the usual two kinds of glasses (crown and flint), instead of expensive materials, for the creation of high-quality apochromatic systems.

(8) The production technology of DOEs has nothing to do with the mechanical working of glass. It is based on the application of batch techniques similar to the production of integrated circuits, replicas of diffraction gratings, disks, compact disks, or books, when the techniques of photolithography or stamping from previously made matrices are used for duplication in large-scale production.

In practice, a number of characteristic features of DOEs should be taken into account:

- DOEs are characterized by many diffraction orders, and the optical power of each order is different and depends on the wavelength. The new elements are essentially chromatic, so the main field of their application is in laser systems that become more and more important from year to year.

- The DOEs diffraction efficiency depends on the shape of the structure profile. It approaches 100% only for phase gratings with a special *blazed* profile.

- Production of an arbitrary diffraction pattern with the *blazed* profile is a complicated technological task for which special equipment and technology are required for the production of the elements.

This chapter presents the results of mastering laser phototechnology for the production of new diffraction elements. For this we had to build a special-purpose laser photoplotter for the production of masks of the elements, to develop thermochemical technology for the recording of the diffraction structure, and also to master the techniques for the transfer of the DOE mask pattern to glass or other materials.

2.
Production of Diffraction Optical Elements

In order to gain an insight into the difficulties arising in DOE production, Fig. 9.1 shows the profiles of typical diffraction elements with a circular symmetry. The spherical refraction surface A is transformed to an ideal kinoform structure B by eliminating the areas of constant optical thickness $h = \lambda/(n - 1)$, because they introduce a phase delay that has no influence on the wavefront shape. The binary plate C with two phase quantization levels is the first approximation to the ideal kinoform lens B. The four-level element D whose calculated diffraction efficiency is $\sim 81\%$ is a quite good approximation to the theoretical profile B. The approximate notations for the real parameters of the element in visible light are shown in the figure. In fact, a DOE is a discrete phase structure. Each period of the grating profile is divided into regions of equal optical thickness. The phase in each region is $\phi_m(\lambda) = m\phi_1(\lambda)$ where $m = 0, 1, 2, \ldots, M - 1$. The discrete phase structure of a DOE is a sum of the microscopic Michelson echelons whose geometrical dimensions approach the wavelength of light. Creation

Fig. 9.1. _____

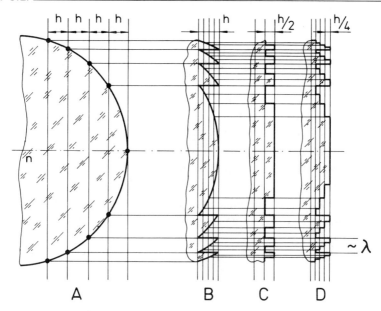

Synthesis of the phase profile of a diffraction optical element: A) refraction sphere, B) an ideal kinoform profile (Fresnel phase lens), C) a binary Fresnel plate (Rayleigh-Wood lens), and D) the kinoform lens produced by the photolithographic technique, where $h = \lambda/(n - 1) \sim \lambda/2 \sim 0.3$ μm ($n = 1.5$; $\lambda = 0.6$ μm).

of such a structure obviously presents difficulties. They cannot be overcome with the standard technique for synthesizing holograms by phototransformation of the enlarged DOE pattern (Collier et al., 1971).

It seems natural for the recording of diffraction structures to use a laser beam focused to the wavelength size as the main instrument of a precision computer-controlled photoplotter (Koronkevich et al., 1984). This manner of producing the element resembles the technique of pointillists in painting. The pattern structure is formed by overlapped points. The spatial frequency of the patterns can be as high as 1500 mm^{-1}. An acceptable recording speed can be achieved when working in a polar coordinate system. The developed photoplotter enables us to draw an amplitude pattern of the element mask, whose topology is then transferred to glass by photolithography (Sze, 1983).

The quality and accuracy of the masks determine if the finished elements conform to the preset characteristics. More stringent requirements are placed upon the accuracy of reproducing DOE topology than for photomasks of integrated circuits. This is conditioned by the fact that DOEs may have diameters as large as hundreds of millimeters. The dimensions of other features of the structure approach the wavelength of light. In addition, mutual positions of the features must sometimes be held to within several fractions of a wavelength. On the other hand, the DOE photomasks allow local defects that do not affect the operation of the element as a whole.

Figure 9.2 shows a scheme for a laser photoplotter (LPP) that enables one to produce photomasks with diameters up to 300 mm with elements of minimum dimensions of the order of 0.5 μm. The main LPP unit is a precision aerostatic spindle (1), at the end (2) of which a substrate with the material to be exposed is placed. The spindle is rotated by an electric motor (3) with an angle-code sensor (4) on its axis. The sensor stabilizes the rotational speed of the motor and determines the angle between the substrate and the recording laser beam. An argon laser (5) is used as a source of radiation.

Fig. 9.2. ──

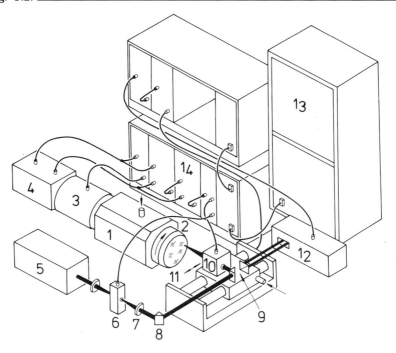

Laser photoplotter: 1, aerostatic spindle; 2, holder for DOE; 3, electric motor; 4, angular sensor; 5, laser; 6, acousto-optical modulator; 7, collimator; 8 and 9, prisms; 10, focusing system; 11, carriage of the X-Y table; 12, laser interferometer; 13, computer; 14, electronic control units.

Radiation from the laser passes through an acousto-optical modulator (6) with a power stabilizing system and a focusing objective (10) connected to the automatic focusing system. Both the objective and the microscope for recording control are mounted on a carriage (11) driven along the aerostatic guides by a linear motor and controlled by a laser interferometer (12). The corner cube (9) of the interferometer is connected to the traveling carriage (11). The laser interferometer, together with the linear driver control system, ensure discrete radial positioning of the recording spot, equal to 0.078 μm over the whole surface of the substrate. All units of the photoplotter are controlled by a computer (13).

In addition to a high spatial resolution in the radial direction, the photoplotter ensures a high precision control of the photomask angular position, which is important for high-quality recording of structures without circular symmetry. The problem of small discreteness along the angular coordinate has been solved by dynamical multiplication of the frequency of the signal from the angle-code sensor.

The mode of raster scanning (Chang et al., 1977) is taken as an operating mode for diffraction structure recording, where the photomask surface is exposed by two motions: spinning of the substrate and radial displacement of the recording spot. As soon as the coordinates of the beam coincide with coordinates of the pattern, it is exposed. The result is a dot or a track on the substrate surface. In the recording, the tracks are usually partially superimposed, so the step of radial displacement for each revolution of the substrate should be set to less than the size of the dot or the track.

The production technology of photomasks using LPP is based on the effect of thermochemical transformations in thin metal films (chromium, titanium, etc.) under intense laser radiation (Veiko et al., 1973; Koronkevich et al., 1985). Chromium films from 80- to 200-nm thick are used as the material. A chromium oxide layer is deposited on the film surface under thermal radiation of the laser. The rate of chromium oxide etching in selective etchants is many times less than the rate of chromium etching, which allows negative recording. Since thin chromium films adhere well to substrates, and have low heat conductivity and high durability, they can be used as the recording material.

According to the known models, thermochemical interaction between radiation of the laser and chromium films (Veiko et al., 1973) consists in depositing an oxide layer on the surface of exposed material, which then changes the physicochemical properties of the material.

For a high spatial resolution, the recording is performed by powerful nanosecond pulses, otherwise the resolution will decrease because of the effect of heat spreading over the film surface. Generally speaking, the required pulse recording presents some technical difficulties (for example, synchronization becomes more complicated, etc.) when the pattern topology is formed by raster scanning technique. Therefore, much attention in the investigation was given to increasing the spatial resolution with CW lasers.

The photograph in Fig. 9.3 shows a series of test paths recorded over a period of 10 μm with different laser beam intensities before the dark zone of the field and after etching with a selective etchant. When the recording

Fig. 9.3.

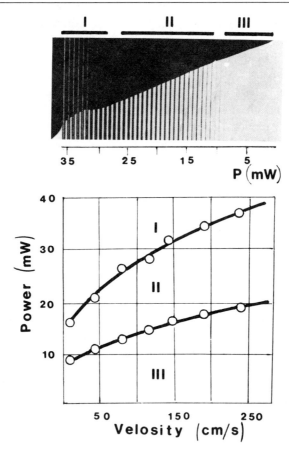

Test records in chromium film: I, region of chromium evaporation; II, region of thermochemical recording; III, region free from the influence of radiation.

spot intensity is high, the material of the film is partially evaporated (area I) and parapets are formed from chromium oxide. A decreased intensity results in a latent image (thermochemical recording in area II). As the intensity decreases the action of the laser radiation on the chromium films stops (area III). The dependence of the area of the latent image on the speed of translation of the light spot with a diameter of 0.8 μm is shown in Fig. 9.3 (bottom). For a speed of translation of the light spot of 2.5 m/s, the optimal intensity ranges from 10 to 30 mW, which corresponds to a flux density of $5-15 \times 10^5$ W/m^2. The spatial resolution of the thermochemical technique increases as the time of exposure decreases, due to the thermal mechanism of recording. At the speed of translation greater than 0.3 m/s (which corresponds to a characteristic exposure time of 5 μs), the limiting value of the optical system resolution of 1200 mm^{-1} is reached. The results of the investigation of spatial resolution are shown in Fig. 9.4. The tracks

Fig. 9.4.

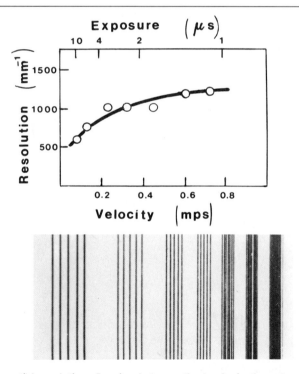

Test for spatial resolution. Spacing between the tracks in the sets are 4, 2.5, 2, 1.5, 0.7, and 0.5 μm, respectively. The curve shows the resolutions as a function of speed of the light spot and characteristic exposure times.

in the groups have a period from 2.5 to 0.5 μm at a relative beam traveling speed of 0.25 m/s with a chromium film thickness of 100 nm.

The development of the latent image by selective etching of the film is an important technological component. Experiments with a number of chromium etchants revealed that the highest selectivity coefficient, that is, the ratio between the average rates of etching of unexposed and exposed films, belongs to an etchant composed of $K_3Fe(CH)_6$ and NaOH aqueous solutions with a ratio of 1:9, although the highest rate of pure chromium etching can be achieved in the etchant with a ratio between the components of 1:2.7. For a highly selective etchant, perfect development of the latent image takes from 3 to 5 minutes.

The developed technology for DOE production comprises several steps:

- A substrate with an 80– to 200–nm thick chromium layer is exposed to a computer-controlled laser beam. The radiation flux density is set to 20–30% below the threshold for thermal chromium destruction (10^5 W/cm^2).

- The film is chemically treated in a selective etchant.

- The topology of the photomask pattern is transferred onto the glass by a photolithographic technique (Sze, 1983).

3.
Practical Results: Elements of Diffraction Optical Systems

3.1. Lenses

A diffraction lens is one of the simplest DOEs that is of prime importance in practice. Its complex transmittance is given by the relation (Clair, 1972)

$$T(\tau) = \sum_{k=-\infty}^{\infty} C_k e^{jk\tau^2/\lambda_0 f} \tag{9.1}$$

$$C_k = \begin{cases} 0 & k \neq mN + 1 \\ (-1)^m \dfrac{\sin[\pi(1/N + m)]}{\pi(1/N + m)} e^{-j\pi(1/N+m)} & \begin{matrix} k = mN + 1, \\ m = 0, \pm 1, \pm 2, \ldots \end{matrix} \end{cases}$$

where f is the focal length for the main wavelength λ_0, N is the number of steps of the phase relief, and τ is the radial coordinate in the plane of the lens.

As the light passes through the lens there occur the diffraction orders $k = mN + 1$, each in conformity with the terms of sum in Eq. (9.1), describing either converging or diverging light waves. A portion of the light energy in the kth order equals $(|C_k|)^2$ 100%.

Let us consider three special cases of particular importance:

(1) At $N \to \infty$ the diffraction efficiency in the first order approaches 100%. The lens phase profile corresponds to a blazed profile. Such a lens is usually called a *kinoform*.

(2) At $N = 2$ the DOE (Rayleigh-Wood lens) has real and virtual foci, and it functions as a combination of collecting and dispersing lenses with $f_k = f/k = f/(2m + 1)$. The energy of the light transmitted through the lens is distributed between the $+1$ and -1 orders. Each of them has a diffraction efficiency of approximately 40%.

(3) At $N = 4$ the energy is transferred to the $+1$ order. The diffraction efficiency is ~81%. In practice it is the most suitable case, because the light loss is not large and the technological difficulties in the synthesis of the profile can be overcome.

The radii of zones of the lens for the transformation of the parallel beam can be derived from the equation

$$\tau_m = \sqrt{m\lambda_0 f + m^2 \frac{\lambda_0^2}{4}} \qquad m = 1, 2, \ldots, M. \qquad (9.2)$$

The focal length of the lens for the first diffraction order is $f_1 = \tau_1^2/2\lambda_0$, and the value of chromatism of the position $\Delta f = -f \cdot \Delta\lambda/\lambda$ for the visible spectrum is equal to one third of the focal length. Chromatism of a lens made of common crown glass is known to be 20 times lower. For a lens with the number of zones over 10 the intensity distribution in the focal spot is practically the same as for a perfect glass lens (Slyusarev, 1975).

To illustrate what can be achieved with the laser photoplotter and thermochemical technology, some diffraction lenses with $(1 \div 3) \times 10^4$ concentric zones have been produced with a minimal period of the last zones equal to 0.7–1.2 μm with a ± 0.1 μm accuracy of the zone radii. The lenses were produced for a wavelength of 0.633 μm, with a practically limiting relative aperture for this type of elements of 1 and 1.3, and diameters of 23 mm and 47 mm. Figure 9.5 reproduces the focal spot ($f = 23$ mm) and the intensity distribution in the point image. The experimental results obtained are in good agreement with the calculation.

Fig. 9.5. _____

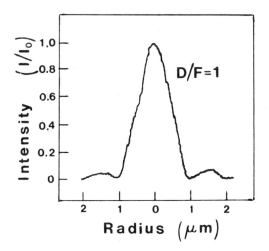

Point spread function.

3.2. Lenses with Uniform Energy Distribution in a Focal Spot

Effective recording of image and text information with laser printers depends on the intensity distribution over the light-beam cross section. With a Gaussian distribution, only one third of the energy is absorbed in view of the thresholding nature of the photoresponse of the material. The laser energy can be used to produce the best effect, and perfect recording is achieved by using a rectangular or a ring-shaped distribution of illumination in the plane of the photomaterial (Bryngdahl, 1978). This can be done with the only optical element operating simultaneously, both as a diffraction lens and an axially symmetrical phase grating.

The diffraction pattern in the far field of the circular phase grating shows a system of rings, and the intensity distribution in other orders depends on the profile of the grooves. In the limiting case when the radii of the rings are small (rough grating) the intensity distribution depends on the ratio between the grating period and the characteristic diameter of the incident beam. The transmission function of the DOE (lens + circular grating) can be represented as a product of the transmission functions of the diffraction lenses [see Eq. (9.1)] and the axially symmetrical phase mask.

The complex function for the phase mask transmittance has the form

$$T(\tau) = \begin{cases} 1 & R_1 < \tau < R \\ e^{j\pi} & \tau < R_1, \end{cases} \tag{9.3}$$

where R and R_1 are radii of the element zones.

The diffraction lens concentrates the laser beam to a circular focal spot with an intensity distribution on the cross section close to a Gaussian distribution. When the lens is supplemented with a phase grating, the energy distribution in the spot is described by the relation between the grating period and the entrance pupil diameter.

The field distribution in the DOE focus is described by a convolution of the impulse responses of the lens and the mask. As the element is illuminated with a plane wave, the intensity distribution in the focal plane can be found from the relation

$$I(\rho) = \frac{4\pi P}{(\lambda f)^2} \left[\frac{J_1(\zeta)}{\zeta} - \frac{J_1(\alpha\zeta)}{\alpha\zeta} \right]^2, \tag{9.4}$$

where $\zeta = 2\pi R\rho/\lambda f$, $\alpha = R_1/R$, P is the total radiation intensity, and ρ is a current coordinate of the focal plane. The energy distribution in the spot can be controlled through variation of the parameter α (i.e., varying the entrance pupil diameter).

The radius of the focal spot increases with α, and the distribution of the illumination becomes quasi-orthogonal. A further increase in α will lead to a ring-shaped distribution. Figure 9.6 shows the transmission functions of phase masks, the photographs of focal spots, experimental curves for the point spread functions, and the parameters of the elements. An important feature of the focal spot in laser printers is the power within a circle with a preset diameter. Figure 9.6 represents the results of the power measurements. The width of the track to be recorded, and the resolution and power of the laser, can be brought to optimal agreement with elements that combine the functions of a lens and a circular phase mask.

Fig. 9.6. _____

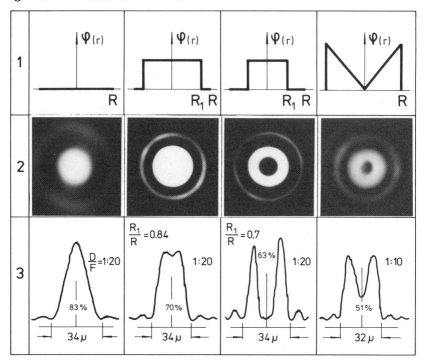

Axially symmetrical phase gratings. 1, phase functions of elements; 2, energy distribution in the focal spot; 3, point spread functions (%, energy in the first diffraction maximum).

3.3.   Kinoform Axicons

A glass cone or a lens with increased spherical aberration may achieve a refraction analogue to the axicon. When illuminated with a point source, an axicon forms a light line that coincides with the optical axis in the near field. This property is widely used in engineering industry to create a *reference direct line* to control the straightness of machine tools or the alignment of objects (Dyson, 1960). The measurement possibilities of telescopes, auto-collimators or interferometers can be widened by using axicons in their schemes (McLeod, 1960).

A kinoform axicon is a circular diffraction blazed grating. As mentioned above, the energy distribution in the far field behind the gratings has the form of a ring. In the near field the power density increases along a line normal to the axicon surface.

The intensity distribution across the cross section of a light line in the Fresnel approximation is described by the square of the Bessel function of zero order in the radial coordinate:

$$I(\rho) = \frac{4\pi\beta^2 L}{\lambda l(l + L)} \, J_0^2 \left(\frac{2\pi}{\lambda}\beta^2\right), \qquad (9.5)$$

where l and L are distances from the axicon to the source and the viewing plane, respectively; $\beta = \lambda/d(1 + L/l)$ is the angle between the rays and the optical axis in the viewing plane; and d is the period of the circular grating of the axicon.

To produce the kinoform axicon with a saw-toothed profile, successive photolithography (Mikhaltsova et al., 1984) with five masks produced on the laser photoplotter was used. Figure 9.7 shows the profile of the calculated axicon zones and a profilogram of the real obtained surface. The zone width is accurate to 1 μm, the maximal depth of the profile varies from the design value by $\pm(2 \div 6)\%$. As a result, besides the $+1, -5, +7, \ldots$ diffraction orders, where the light energy of an ideal element with six regular quantization steps has to be concentrated, there are some other orders in the axicon spectrum, even among them. The measurements have demonstrated that 6% of the total light flux reaching the axicon is lost by reflection and scattering, 1% and 1.6% go to the zero and the (-1)st orders, and 80% is concentrated to the useful $(+1)$st order.

Fig. 9.7. ⎯⎯⎯⎯⎯⎯⎯⎯⎯⎯⎯⎯⎯⎯⎯⎯⎯⎯⎯⎯⎯⎯⎯⎯⎯⎯⎯⎯⎯⎯⎯⎯⎯⎯⎯⎯⎯⎯⎯

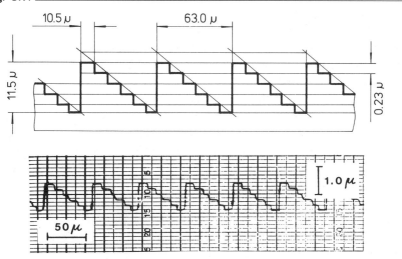

Calculation and real profiles of the axicon.

Fig. 9.8.

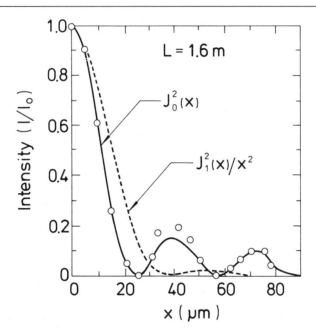

Intensity distribution in the interference field at $L = 1.6$ m behind the axicon. $J_0^2(x)$ is calculated and experimental values are shown for the axicon, and $J_1^2(x)/x^2$ is an Airy function.

The intensity distribution in the light line has been experimentally studied at various distances from the axicon illuminated with a plane wave. Figure 9.8 shows the intensity distribution in the diffraction pattern at $L = 1.6$ m. A good agreement between experimental and theoretical data is observed. It should be noted that the size of the central diffraction spot is narrower than the kernel of an Airy disk for the same aperture.

The axicon quality has been also checked in a Mach-Zehnder interferometer. Equidistance of the interferometer rings and a true circular form are fulfilled with $^1\!/_4$ of a fringe. The axicons in the interferometers enable one to have a conic reference wave (Bryngdahl, 1973). In this case the interference field is represented by circular fringes of equal thickness. Phase objects with circular symmetry can be easily checked using the interferometers. The results of checking phase are presented in (Mikhaltsova et al., 1984).

3.4.   Lenses with a Ring Impulse Response

Image-coding systems, devices for phase-object visualization, and setups for laser technology need optical elements that concentrate the light energy to a thin ring (Eu and Lohmann, 1973; Rioux et al., 1978; Bélanger and Rioux, 1978). An axicon and a lens can help to partially solve this problem. There is another technique—to use special diffraction elements, which have already been described (Koronkevich et al., 1985).

In the inverse problem the transmission function was found for an ideal element that forms a ring image in the focal plane:

$$T(\tau) = J_0\left(\frac{2\pi R_0}{\lambda f}\tau\right)\exp\left(-j\frac{\pi^2\tau^2}{\lambda f}\right), \tag{9.6}$$

where τ is the radial coordinate in the DOE plane and R_0 is the radius of the ring image. An ideal optical element with the transmission function $T(\tau)$ actually combines a lens and a transparency with an amplitude-phase transmission $J_0(2\pi R_0\tau/\lambda f)$. The possibility of producing an element with a different, purely phase version of the diffraction structure can be seen from the analysis of this function. Figure 9.9 represents the calculated formulae and the principal characteristic for DOEs of the three types that have been fabricated.

In the first element, the amplitude-phase filter transforms the incident plane wave to a conic wave front, and the lens then focuses it to a ring. The finest ring is formed for this case, although part of the energy is absorbed by the filter.

The transfer functions of the lenses forming the ring are axially symmetrical, so the corresponding DOEs have the form of circular phase gratings, with their centers on the optical axis. The calculated formulae for the radii of the element zones, corrected for spherical aberration, are given in the fifth column of Fig. 9.9. With the given radius of the ring R_0 and the distance f, the second element has the broadest zones, which is convenient from the point of view of production technology.

Photomasks of DOEs of the four types, with a light-beam diameter of 50 mm and a focal distance 150 mm, have been produced with the laser photoplotter. Amplitude masks for the elements are shown in Fig. 9.10. A ring of 8 μm width and 30 mm diameter was formed with the second element. The results of photomeasuring the ring cross section are in good agreement with the calculated results.

Fig. 9.9.

	$T(r)$	Analogue of DOE	Intensity distribution in a ring	r_m
1	$J_0(\frac{2\pi R_0}{\lambda f})\exp[-j\frac{\pi r^2}{\lambda f}]$		$\left|\frac{\sin y}{y}\right|^2$	$Y(\cos\frac{R_0}{f}mr)\cdot Y(\cos\frac{mr^2}{2f})=1$
2	$\exp[-j\frac{\pi}{\lambda f}(r-R_0)^2]$		$\left|\frac{3}{2}y^{-3/2}\int_0^y\exp(jt)t^{1/2}dt\right|^2$	$R_0\pm\sqrt{2m\lambda f+(m\lambda)^2}$
3	$\exp[-j\frac{\pi}{\lambda f}(r+R_0)^2]$		$\left|\frac{3}{2}y^{3/2}\int_0^y\exp(jt)t^{-2}dt\right|^2$	$R_0+\sqrt{R_0^2+2m\lambda(f^2+R_0^2)^{1/2}+(m\lambda)^2}$

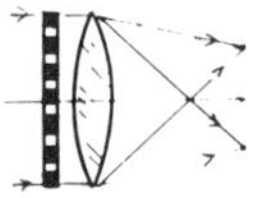

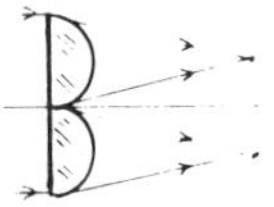

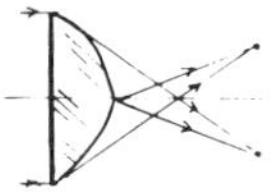

Elements with ring impulse response. The notations used:

$$y = \frac{2\pi R}{\lambda f}(R_0 - \rho);$$

R, the radius of linear aperture of the element; R_0, the ring radius; ρ, the polar coordinate in the focal plane; and $Y(\cdot)$, Heaviside step function.

3.5. Wavefront Correctors

Kinoform correctors are widely used in practice by designers of high-quality hybrid objectives and systems for certification of aspheric mirrors. The principal requirements imposed upon the correctors are high diffraction efficiency and precision production. The number of phase quantizations in a zone should therefore be no less than six to eight. There are no strict requirements on the efficiency of the correctors in the systems for certification of aspheric optics, because parasitic diffraction orders can be easily suppressed by spatial filtering.

For the production of a number of high-aperture hybrid objectives, and the certification of spherical mirrors, kinoform correctors have been created with the laser photoplotter. Figure 9.11 reproduces central zones for a set of photomasks of the kinoform corrector for the objective and its phase relief. The zones of the photomasks have a minimal size of 10 μm, with the boundary error no more than 1 μm.

Fig. 9.10. _____

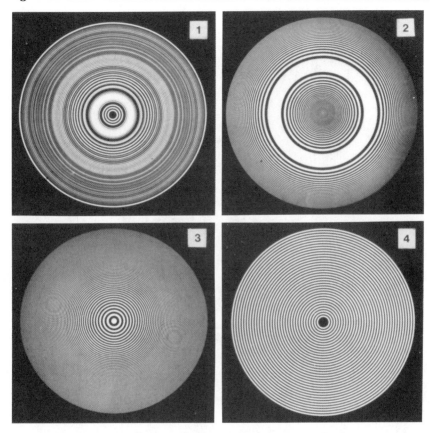

Structure of DOE zones with a ring impulse response. 1, 2, and 3 are masters
of the elements of Fig. 9.9; 4 is the axicon master.

A corrector with a binary phase profile 105 mm in diameter has been
produced for the creation of an aspherical wavefront in a system for the
certification of mirrors. An interferometer has been constructed on its basis
and the mirrors have been checked. Figure 9.12 shows the interferometer
field during the control of an aspherical mirror with a diameter of 1 m.

3.6. Circular Diffraction Gratings

The laser photoplotter can be used for the production of limbs, complex
code disks (Vedernikov et al., 1986), diffraction scales, and elements of the
Siemens star type (Bryngdahl, 1973), as well as for creating a helical ref-

Fig. 9.11.

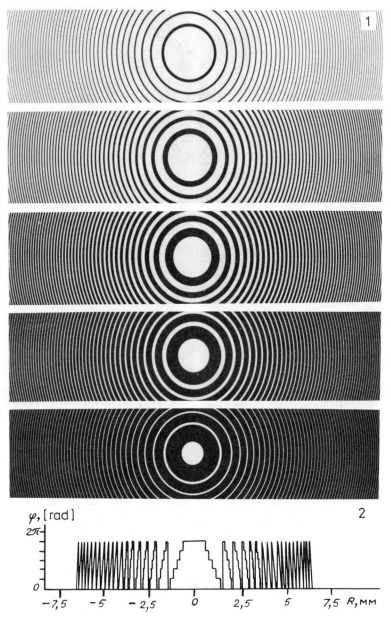

Structure of zones for masks and phase profile of the corrector: 1, topology of five masters; 2, phase profile shape.

Fig. 9.12.

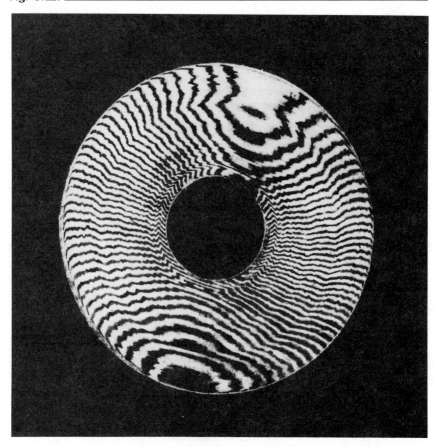

Field of view of the surface control interferometer.

erence wave in an interferometer. As opposed to standard amplitude divided scales, we now have an opportunity to synthesize gratings with marks that possess focusing ability and that allow the arrangement of cross optical communications in data coding.

Figure 9.13 represents a simplified picture of a fragment of the scale belonging to the diffraction code disk (Vedernikov et al., 1986). The scale is in the periphery of the disk and comprises four code tracks t_1, ..., t_4. Individual gradations in each track consist of elements of kinoform lenses. So, for example, sections t_1 and t_4 of the track belong to one lens, while those of the tracks t_2 and t_3 belong to another lens. The optical centers of these

Fig. 9.13.

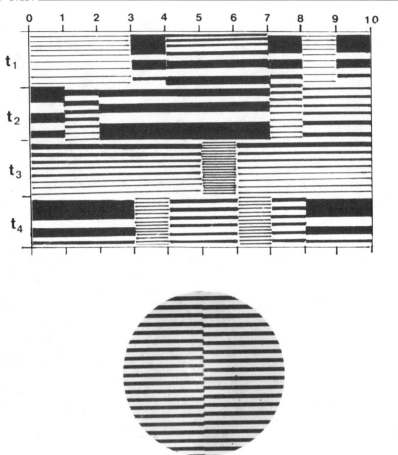

Code tracks of the diffraction scale. In the circle is a fragment of the boundary between two neighboring divisions.

lenses are shifted relative to each other, so the light is focused to points separated in space and is incident on different photocells. As the code scale is displaced in the direction of the arrow, the light is redistributed between the elements of the photocell array; a scale of this type works as a multifocus diffraction lens with one or several areas of light focusing, depending on the combination of codes.

Unlike well-known standard divided scales, the diffraction scales allow an improved reading accuracy for the limb position and increase the information capacity of the track and its noise stability owing to the control, among other factors, of the constancy of the sum of signals that are recorded from different sections of the track.

Fringes of equal thickness are used to determine the object shapes in two-beam interferometry. Decoding of the interferograms is usually difficult and computer processing is required. The problem becomes easier when a helical reference wave is used instead of the plane one (Bryngdahl, 1973). A reference wave with a helical surface enables the production of interferograms with fringes of equal thickness, directed radially from the center. A Siemens star can be used for this in the reference arm. It forms a linear phase gradient in the azimuth direction. When the errors on the shape of the controlled object have a circular symmetry, they can be easily interpreted and do not require computer processing. Figure 9.14 shows the pattern of central zones of the DOE for transformation of a plane wavefront to a converging helical front with an element focal length of 200 mm and a diameter of 40 mm. The intensity distribution in its focal plane is given in the same figure.

Fig. 9.14. ——————————————————————————————

1   2

Siemens star and the intensity distribution in its focal plane.

3.7. Diffraction Lenses with Mirrors

In the development of optical schemes for laser technology devices, it is advisable to combine the functions of two optical elements, one of them reflecting the light beam through a required angle (a mirror), while the other focuses it onto the material (a lens). The calculation of the topology of zones of the diffraction element that rotates the beam and simultaneously forms a nonaberration point image of a source is described by Lenkova (1985).

When γ is the angle between the element and the incident beam, the radius vector of the zone can be determined from the relation

$$\tau = \frac{\sqrt{2m\lambda(1 - \sin^2\gamma\cos^2\phi + m^2\lambda^2)} - m\lambda\sin\gamma\cos\phi}{1 - \sin^2\gamma\cos^2\phi} \ . \qquad (9.7)$$

Here ϕ is the polar angle in the element plane, and m is the number of the zone. The element zones represent a system of ellipses with their centers shifted along the long axis.

Let us note an interesting feature of the new element. When a mirror is added to the lens, the sign of the angular magnification changes. It becomes equal to $+1$. This means that negative principal planes that are twice the focal distance become positive. The positive principal planes of the lens are known to be harmless inclination points, i.e., a lens rotation about the positive principal point causes no changes in the direction of the beams going out from the focus. In the case considered, the harmless point will be shifted to twice the focal length. The latter advantage allows one to use the new element in optical measurement systems to compensate for the Abbe error (Bischoff, 1956).

Fig. 9.15. _____

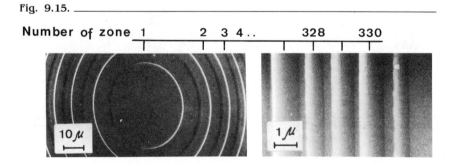

Microlens zone structure taken with an electron microscope.

3.8. Microlenses

A standard projection printing technique (Sze, 1983) can be used for the production of microlenses with a high numerical aperture ($\sim$0.45). The diffraction structure of the lens mask is recorded in an enlarged scale (5^x–10^x) with a laser photoplotter, and then it is projected with a reduction onto the glass plate covered with a resist. The projection system, i.e., a photopunch, allows the automatic operation and printing of lenses. Figure 9.15 demonstrates the quality of the produced lenses.

4.

Optical Systems with Diffraction Elements

4.1. Hybrid Objectives

In the calculation of objectives combining refraction lenses and diffraction elements, it is advisable to use available standard programs for the calculation of the beam path through the optical system and the programs for automatic correction of aberration and estimation of image quality. From a comparison between the imaging properties of a lens and a Fresnel zone plate, we can see that the DOE may be replaced by a thin equivalent refraction lens. In this case the calculation is as usual.

It is known that for the lens and the Fresnel plate (DOE) the following relations are valid:

$$(n - 1)x = \frac{y^2}{2f} \qquad \text{(Rayleigh formula)} \qquad (9.8)$$

$$m_p\lambda = \frac{y_p^2}{2f} . \qquad (9.9)$$

Correlating these formulae one can easily find the relation for a lens analogue of the diffraction element (Sweatt, 1979):

$$(n - 1)\frac{dx}{dy} = \frac{\lambda}{y_p - y_{p-1}} . \qquad (9.10)$$

In these formulae x is the lens thickness, n is the refractive index, m_p is the number of pth zone of the diffraction element, y is the height of the beam incident (aperture), and $y_p - y_{p-1}$ is the zone width.

Equation (9.10) makes it possible to carry out our calculation of refraction-diffraction optical systems using standard programs. For this the diffraction element is replaced by an infinitely thin lens with an artificially large refractive index $n > 10$. Then the equation for the lens surface meeting the requirements of this optical system is determined from aberration calculations and numerical optimization. The surface equation is usually given as a series

$$x = \frac{1}{2\tau}\, y^2 + A_2 y^4 + A_3 y^6 + \ldots, \tag{9.11}$$

where τ is the radius at the lens vertex, determined from the required focal length of the diffraction element, and A_2, A_3, ... are coefficients derived from the calculation. Equations (9.10) and (9.11) represent a system from which coordinates of the zones y_p of the kinoform can be derived.

The above technique of combining the diffraction and refraction elements was applied in the calculation of a hybrid objective designed for data output systems. The objective in Fig. 9.16 consists of a germanium lens and a kinoform element, with rather long back working distance and the input aperture removed for setting a scanning mirror in its plane. The principal calculated parameters for the objective are presented in Fig. 9.16.

Fig. 9.16. ———————————————————————————————

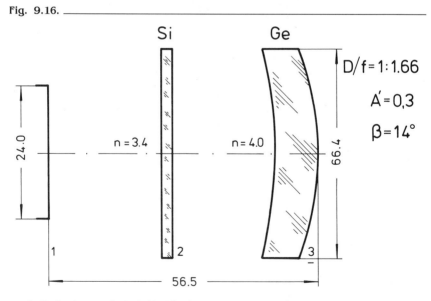

Optical scheme of a hybrid objective. 1, entrance pupil with a 24 mm diameter; 2, kinoform silicon corrector; 3, germanium lens. The field of view is 24 by 36 mm.

The germanium lens was produced by the conventional technique, and the kinoform corrector was made on a conventional silicon substrate by local removal of the material using photolithographic techniques. The production quality of the designed aspherical profile approximated by a step function (four steps per zone) was perfect, the deviation being no more that 0.01 fringe for $\lambda = 10.6$ μm. In Fig. 9.17 the dashed line shows the designed theoretical profile of the last corrector zone and the solid line indicates the steps of the real profile. An interferogram of three neighboring steps is shown in the bottom of the same figure. The height of the step can be easily controlled by displacement of the achromatic fringes, and it is in a good agree-

Fig. 9.17.

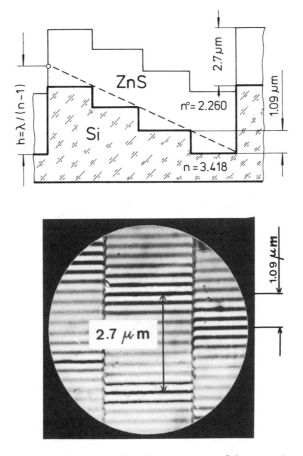

Interferogram and profile of the last zone of the corrector.

ment with the calculated value $h = \lambda/(n - 1) = 1.1$ μm. A diffraction efficiency of the kinoform of 79% was observed, which is near the theoretical value for the four-step profile. For better transmission the corrector was bleached by depositing a ZnS layer 6.1 μm thick. The second system of fringes from the upper surface of the bleached layer can be seen on the interferogram. The calculated data for the objective quality have been experimentally supported. A spatial resolution of 12 mm^{-1} was observed over the whole field at a contrast of 0.7. The characteristics and the degree of aberration correction of the objective correspond to those of a four-lens objective in conventional optics.

4.2. Bifocus Microscope

Matching microscopes with a higher depth of focus (Sze, 1983) are used for the observation of micro-objects arranged along the optical axis and for their alignment. The micro-objects (marks, crosswires, reticles) are usually spaced at 5- to 20-μm intervals for solving common tasks in contact printing, and at 10– to 100–μm intervals in x-ray lithography.

   We have investigated a microscope whose scheme comprises the diffraction elements: a Rayleigh-Wood lens or a kinoform plate with a special profile of zones in order to become bifocal. Refer now to Fig. 9.18, where an optical scheme with reversed beams is shown. The parallel beam incident onto lens 1 is split into two beams, because the Rayleigh-Wood lens works as a combination of scattering and collecting lenses. About 81% of the energy behind lens 2 is equally distributed between the foci of the $+1$ and -1 orders. The beams diffracted to the $+1$ order are focused ahead of the focal objective plane at point 3; the beams diffracted to the -1 order are focused at point 4. The distance between points 3 and 4 (for $f_1 \gg f_2$ and $f_1 \gg l$) can be found from a simple relation:

$$\delta = \frac{2f_2^2 f_1 \dfrac{\lambda}{\lambda_0}}{\left(\dfrac{\lambda_0}{\lambda}f_2\right)^2 - (l + f_2)} \approx \frac{2f_2^2 \lambda}{\lambda_0 f}. \tag{9.12}$$

Here λ_0 is the wavelength corresponding to the Rayleigh-Wood lens, and λ is an operating wavelength. The rest of the notation can be understood from Fig. 9.18. For $f_2 = 10$ mm, $f_1 = 1000$ mm, and $l = 0$, δ varies from 150 to 200 μm in the spectrum (656–486 nm). To eliminate chromatic aberrations, the spectral range of the light source should be limited to

Fig. 9.18.

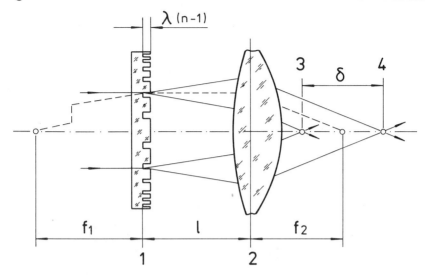

Optical scheme of a bifocus microscope. 1, Rayleigh-Wood lens; 2, microscope objective; 3 and 4, front and back foci, respectively.

$$\Delta\lambda \leq \left(\frac{\lambda}{D}\right)^{2} f_{1}. \qquad (9.13)$$

For $\lambda = 0.55 \times 10^{-3}$ mm, $D = 8$ mm, and $f_{1} = 1000$ mm, a spectral range of $\Delta\lambda \sim 5$ nm is allowed so that conventional light sources with interference light filters can be used. Scattered light resulting from diffraction orders higher that the first is an essential limitation of the considered bifocus system. This can be avoided using a special kinoform lens in the form of a circular zone plate. The phase relief inside even zones corresponds to the relief of a collecting lens, while that inside odd zones corresponds to a scatering lens. The lens profile is shown in Fig. 9.17 (top). To minimize wave aberrations, lenses with the longest possible focal length should be used, and the observed objects should be arranged in the focal planes of the bifocus systems.

Micro-objectives with 16x/0.2, ∞, and $f = 6.3/0.65$ were used in the experimental test of the microscope. The Rayleigh-Wood lens ($f_{1} = 1000$ mm, $\lambda_{0} = 0.55$ μm, $D = 8$ mm) was produced by reactive ion etching. The point spread function for the objective with a kinoform element is represented in Fig. 9.19. The light distribution near each of the foci is typical

Fig. 9.19.

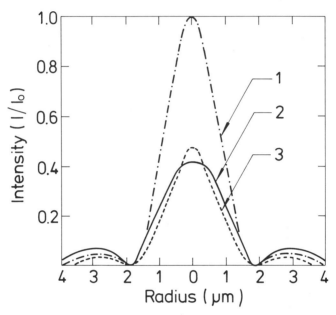

Point spread functions objectives. 1, without kinoform; 2 and 3, with the kinoform elements.

for a small primary spherical aberration. For a micro-objective without the kinoform element the first dark ring in diffraction spot 1 had a radius of 1.9 μm. For the bifocus system: the front focus radius was 1.85 μm and the back focus radius was 1.87 μm. The order of magnitude of spherical aberration in the bifocus system was found from the correlation of calculated and experimental curves; it was equal to 0.9 λ for each focus. The light-energy distribution between the front and back foci was 43.1% and 49.3%.

4.3. Coding System

Diffraction elements with a ring impulse response can be built into optical systems for direct and inverse geometrical image transformations. The latter is needed for coding and for reducing noise in the images of devices for data processing and communication.

Let us consider the scheme in Fig. 9.20. The transparency with an original image $\mathcal{U}_1(r, t)$ is set in front focal plane 1 of objective 2, DOE 3 being behind it. The transparency is illuminated with a monochromatic spatially incoherent light source (through a rotating ground glass, for example). The

Fig. 9.20.

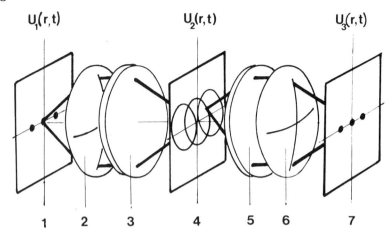

$$U_1(r,t) \qquad\qquad U_2(r,t) \qquad\qquad U_3(r,t)$$

1   2   3   4   5   6   7

Optical scheme of direct and inverse geometrical image transforms. 1, the input objective transparency; 2, the objective; 3, DOE; 4, the transformed object plane; 5, DOE; 6, the objective; 7, the output image plane.

transformed image $\mathcal{U}_2(r, t)$ is formed in plane 4 and represents a convolution of the original image $\mathcal{U}_1(r, t)$ with the square of the impulse response $|h_1(r, t)|^2$ of the DOE. The second unit of the optical scheme reconstructs the original image. In this case plane 4 is the input, element 5 acts similarly to 3, and in output plane 7 we have

$$\mathcal{U}_3(r, t) = \mathcal{U}_1(r, t) \otimes |h_1(r, t)|^2 \otimes |h_1(r, t)|^2 . \tag{9.14}$$

From Eq. (9.14), the reconstructed image is an exact copy of the original one, i.e., $\mathcal{U}_1(r, t) = \mathcal{U}_3(r, t)$, if the condition

$$|h_1(r, t)|^2 \otimes |h_1(r, t)|^2 = \delta(r, t) \tag{9.15}$$

is fulfilled, where $\delta(r, t)$ is a delta function.

Equation (9.15) describes the requirements on the impulse response of the DOE for the ideal reconstruction of the original image. In the simplest case condition (9.15) is met by ordinary lenses with their impulse response close to a δ function, and the optical system of Fig. 9.20 transfers the image from the input to the output plane. Optical elements 2 and 3 have their impulse responses in the shape of a ring δ function, which also satisfies Eq. (9.15). For real optical elements with a limited aperture, the impulse response represents a ring with a finite thickness. Therefore, the condition of reconstruction is fulfilled with a certain error leading to a lower resolution.

Figure 9.21 represents experimental results for the direct and inverse geometrical transformations of images consisting of three points, a line, and a
word. The optical scheme comprises objectives with a focal length of 50
mm and a synthesized element forming a ring with $R_0 = 10$ mm. The optical
system consisting of the objective and the DOE has been used twice—at the
steps of direct and inverse transformation. The transparency with an original
image is placed in plane 1 (top row of photographs). The picture of the
transformed image was taken in plane 4 (middle row). The developed film
was placed in plane 4 and the reconstructed image was observed in plane 7
(bottom row). The reconstructed image quality essentially depends on the
positioning accuracy of the transparencies and on the linear properties of the
photographic film.

Fig. 9.21. _____

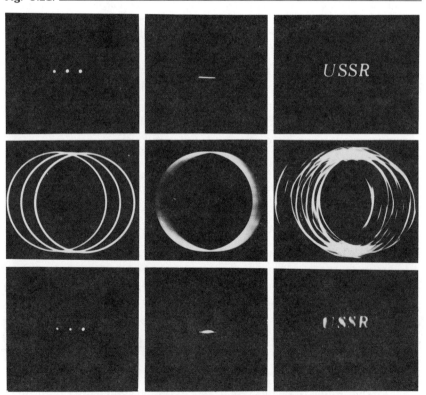

Examples of transforms. 1, points; 2, lines; 3, words.

4.4. Diffraction Interferometer

The high-quality Fresnel zone plates fabricated with the laser photoplotter enabled us to construct and investigate a diffraction interferometer based on two zone plates with different focal lengths (Koronkevich and Lenkova, 1984). Arranging the zone plates one after another and bringing their negative and positive focal planes into coincidence, one could observe fringes of equal thickness and rings of equal inclination. One of the interfering beams results from transmission through the first plate without deviation and diffraction on the second plate, while the second beam is the result of diffraction on the first plate and direct transmission through the second one.

The characteristic property of the interferometer is that the path difference approaches zero, and contrast fringes can be observed both with monochromatic and with white light (Fig. 9.22). Unlike other interferometers, this

Fig. 9.22.

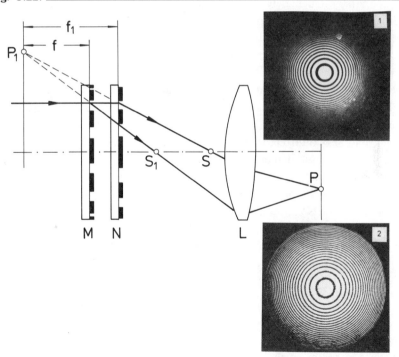

Diffraction interferometer for viewing the rings of equal inclination. M and N, phase lenses with their foci f and f_1; S and S_1, exit pupils; P and P_1, field of the interferometer and its image; 1, interferometric pattern in white light taken in plane P; 2, interferometric pattern in monochromatic light taken in plane P.

interference pattern is practically independent of the quality of the substrate. In addition, the interferometer is characterized by a high noise stability, because the interference beams are not separated.

A diffraction interfometer with two zone plates can be used for the alignment of objects and for matching the elements of microcircuits in photolithography. The thickness of the fringes or the amount of displacement of the center of the interference rings can serve as a measure of deviation from the preset direction. The diffraction interferometer is also suitable for visual demonstration of the interference effects arising from different positions of the pupils with respect to the plane of observation.

4.5. Optical String

To control the straightness of guides in heavy machine tools, and for the assembly of equipment, we have constructed a device where an axicon (circular grating) matched with a collimator objective served as the principal element. For practical purposes, we needed a light sightline with a 50 mm length and a cross section of no more that 500 μm behind a DOE. This can be fulfilled if the linear aperture of the diffraction element is equal to 100 mm.

Fig. 9.23 shows schematically the optical string. The radiation source S (a laser) illuminates the element KO. The field behind KO represents an interference pattern with the intensity distribution shown in Fig. 9.8. Views of the field at two different sections of the light line are shown in Fig. 9.23 (bottom). The multielement photoreceiver connected with the object is set at the point M (or some other point of the axis OM). The task is to find the displacement of the photoreceiver with respect to the sightline SOM.

The DOE zones can be calculated in the usual way if we equate the path differences of the peripheral (SKM) and of the central (SOM) beams. Hence the radius of the zones can be derived from the following formula:

$$
\tau_m = \sqrt{\frac{(f + m\lambda)^2 \sin\beta}{\cos^4\beta} + \frac{2fm\lambda + m^2\lambda^2}{\cos^2\beta} - \frac{(f + m\lambda)\sin\beta}{\cos^2\beta}}, \quad (9.16)
$$

where m is the zone number and β is angular aperture of the DOE on the image side.

From the results of the experimental test of the device, we were able to control a plate 36 m long with a mean-square error of 30 μm. It should be mentioned that the laser string is a very simple device that in fact consists of a single optical element.

Fig. 9.23.

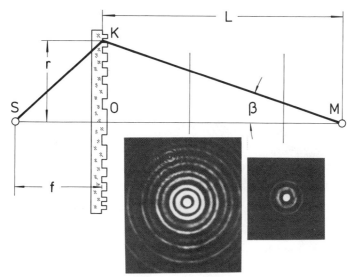

Optical string scheme.

5.

Conclusion

The results that have been described above illustrate attractive advantages and also some difficult problems in a new optical branch. The improvement of technology for computer synthesis of diffraction elements with an ideal kinoform profile is the main problem.

The development of classical optics technology began several hundred years ago. Its origin is related to the names of Galileo and Newton. Newton himself was an expert in optics; he produced a number of high-quality (for his time) optical elements. Present-day optical technology has brought to perfection the process of production of two types of precise optical surfaces: a sphere and a plane.

The application of laser computer phototechnology offers very new advantages in optics. The calculation and the production of an optical element are actually combined in the same technological process. We see a return to Newtonian times when the designer of a new element reproduced it by himself. The combination of the professions of optician-designer and fabricator will essentially change things and stimulate the appearance of new elements for which there are no analogues in classical optics yet. An optician will be able to master for the first time the art of fabrication of a precise optical surface of any arbitrary shape.

Diffraction optics is perfectly suitable for laser operation, and so the most efficient of its applications lie in the field of laser-beam transformations. Kinoform elements will give a new birth to laser systems for audio and image recording, data input/output, and information storage and processing. Another broad field of application of the new elements is for measurement devices in mechanical engineering: laser interferometers; optical systems for measuring information input; devices for the measurement of flatness and straightness, speed and acceleration, and angular rotations; and many other such devices.

References

Bélanger, P.A., and Rioux, M. (1978). *Appl. Opt.* **17,** 1080–1085.

Bischoff, W. (1956). *Feingeraetetechnik* **5,** (7).

Bryngdahl, O. (1973). *J. Opt. Soc. Am.* **63:** 1098–1104.

Bryngdahl, O. (1975). *Opt. Eng.* **14:** 426–435.

Bryngdahl, O. (1978). *J. Opt. Soc. Am.* **68:** 416–422.

Chang, T.H.P., Hatzakis, M., Wilson, A.D., and Broers, A.N. (1977). *Electronics* **10.**

Clair, J.J. (1972). "Synthèse Optique de Filtres d'Amplitude et de Phase Dits *Kinoform.*" Doctoral Thesis, Université de Paris VI, Paris.

Collier, R.J., Burckhardt, C.B., and Lin, L.H. (1971). "Optical Holography," Academic Press, New York.

Dyson, J. (1960). "Optics in Metrology," Pergamon Press, Oxford.

Eu, J., and Lohmann, A.W. (1973). *Opt. Commun.* **9:** 257–262.

Koronkevich, V.P., and Lenkova, G.A. (1984a). *Avtometriya* **3:** 61–67, (in Russian). English transl. in *Automatic Monitoring and Measuring.*

Koronkevich, V.P., Kiriyanov, V.P., Kokoulin, F.I., Palchikova, I.G., Poleshchuk, A.G., Sedukhin, A.G., Churin, E.G., Shcherbachenko, A.M., and Yurlov, Yu.I. (1984b). *Optik* **67:** 259–266.

Koronkevich, V.P., Poleshchuk, A.G., Churin, E.G., and Yurlov, Yu.I. (1985a). *Kvantovaya Elektronika* **12:** 755–761, (in Russian). English transl. in *Sov. J. Quantum Electron.*

Koronkevich, V.P., Palchikova, I.G., Poleshchuk, A.G., and Yurlov, Yu.I. (1985b). "Kinoform optical element with circular impulse response." Preprint No. 265. IAE SB USSR Ac. Sci., Novosibirsk (in Russian).

Lenkova, G.A. (1985). *Avtometriya* **6:** 7–12 (in Russian). English transl. in *Automatic Monitoring and Measuring.*

McLeod, J.H. (1960). *J. Opt. Soc. Am.* **50:** 166–169.

Mikhaltsova, I.A., Nalivaiko, V.I., and Soldatenkov, I.S. (1984). *Optik* **67:** 267–278.

Rioux, M., Tremblay, R., and Bélanger, P.A. (1978). *Appl. Opt.* **17:** 1532–1536.

Slyusarev, G.G. (1975). "Calculation of Optical Systems," Mashinostroyenye, Leningrad (in Russian).

Sweatt, W.C. (1979). *J. Opt. Soc. Am.* **69:** 486–487.

Sze, S.M., ed. (1983). "VLSI Technology," Bell Laboratories.

Vedernikov, V.M., Kiriyanov, V.P., Korolkov, V.P., Koronkevich, V.P., Poleshchuk, A.G., Sedukhin, A.G., Churin, E.G., Shcherbachenko, A.M., and Yurlov, Yu.I. (1986). "Laser technology of production of circular scales and code discs." Preprint No. 319. IAE SB USSR Ac. Sci., Novosibirsk (in Russian).

Veiko, V.I., Kotov, G.A., Libenson, M.N., and Nikitin, M.I. (1973). *Dokl. Akad. Nauk SSSR* **208:** 587–590 (in Russian). English transl. in *Sov. Phys.-Dokl.*

10.

Distortion-Invariant Pattern Recognition Using Circular Harmonic Matched Filters

Henri H. Arsenault

Laboratoire de Recherches en Optique et Laser
Département de Physique, Université Laval
Ste-Foy, P.Q., Canada

Contents

1. Introduction. 316
   1.1. Shift Invariance 317
   1.2. Rotation Invariance. 318
   1.3. Scale Invariance 318
   1.4. Intensity or Contrast Invariance 318
   1.5. Invariance to Distortion 318
   1.6. Invariance to Noise. 319
   1.7. Optics Versus Computers 319
2. Rotation-Invariant Matched Filters 320
   2.1 Centers of Expansion 323
   2.2 Rotation-Invariant Composite Filters 326
   2.3 Rotating Filter Method 327
   2.4 Real Filters 327
   2.5 CHC Phase Filters 328
   2.6 Scale-Invariant CHC Filters 328
3. Multiple CHC Methods 329
   3.1 Threshold Method 330

    3.2 Feature Space Methods 332
    3.3 Contrast-Invariant Methods 334
            3.3.1 Unit Vector Scalar Product Method 334
            3.3.2 Unit Vector Difference Methods 334
4. Sidelobe Reduction 336
5. Principal Component Filters 338
6. Conclusion 338
    References 339

1.

Introduction

In recent years, there has been a growing interest in the exploitation of image invariants in pattern recognition. Part of the reason for this interest stems from the need to deal with more complex images in various applications of automated image processing and from the need to process large images in real time. Patterns that may be shifted; rotated; scaled; distorted; different in texture, contrast, or shading; and degraded by signal-dependent noise must be recognized as identical or classified. Examples of such applications are robot vision and automatic processing of satellite or medical imagery. For some of the more critical applications, optical processing or hybrid opto digital techniques promise to allow faster processing of images.

Our own approach in this area has been to look for some part of the pattern that is invariant under the change of the target of interest, using methods that can be implemented optically.

Rotation-invariant pattern recognition or classification may be accomplished by using some invariant feature of the object as a matched filter. Such a useful feature is the circular harmonic component (CHC), which allows both rotation and shift invariance when used as a matched filter. CHC filters have been used either as computer-generated Vander-Lugt optical matched filters in optical correlators or as digital filters. The rotation invariance is obtained at the cost of a decrease in the signal-to-noise ratio and in the peak-to-sidelobe ratio. It was found that factors such as the proper expansion center, threshold shifting caused by varying noise levels, and high sidelobes can be critical enough to prevent the technique from functioning unless they are specifically addressed. Our recent research has been oriented towards improving the results by using multiple filters in parallel or sequentially, and by using linear combinations of filters (composite filters) as a single filter. We have also investigated real filters that do not require a reference beam to record the phase and techniques for using CHC filters on addressable modulators for real-time applications. Improved techniques for finding the best centers of expansion, for reducing sidelobes, and for minimizing the effects of noise on the threshold levels have also being developed.

We now briefly describe some types of invariants in images and how they may be dealt with.

1.1. Shift Invariance

Shift invariance is one of the two properties required for a system to be a linear filter (the other is that it satisfy the principle of superposition). Therefore if a recognition system uses a linear filter (for instance, a matched filter) it will automatically be shift invariant, that is, when the target is shifted, the output will shift by an equivalent amount with no other change.

The output of a linear filter with impulse response $h(x, y)$ is

$$R_{fh}(x, y) = \int \int_{-\infty}^{\infty} f(\sigma, \eta)h(x - \sigma, y - \eta)d\sigma \, d\eta, \qquad (10.1)$$

which can be represented symbolically by

$$R_{fh}(x, y) = f(x, y) \times h(x, y), \qquad (10.2)$$

where the symbol $\times$ means convolution. The correlation value of interest is

$$R_{fh}(0, 0) = \int \int_{-\infty}^{\infty} f(x, y)h(x, y)dx \, dy. \qquad (10.3)$$

If the target is the prototype for which the filter was made, $h(x, y) = f^*(-x, -y)$, and the output is

$$R_{ff}(0, 0) = \int \int_{-\infty}^{\infty} |f(x, y)|^2 dx \, dy. \qquad (10.4)$$

For techniques that do not use matched filters, such as moments or syntactic methods, shift invariance is not so direct, which is why such methods usually require some segmentation of the image. This means that a region of interest containing a potential object of interest must be isolated before the method can be applied, which is sometimes impossible in highly cluttered or noisy scenes such as aerial photographs, medical images, or images from imaging radars.

Since the circular harmonic component (CHC) filtering method described below uses a matched filter, shift invariance is automatically obtained. Thus multiple patterns in a scene may be detected or classified simultaneously.

1.2. Rotation Invariance

Rotation of a pattern is mathematically equivalent to a shift along the angular coordinate in polar coordinates. This suggests achieving rotation invariance by means of a coordinate transformation, a technique that is difficult to implement optically. Another way to achieve rotation invariance is to look for some part of the object that is invariant under rotation, an idea that naturally suggests a decomposition in polar coordinates. This idea leads to the circular harmonic decomposition, which is described below.

1.3. Scale Invariance

At first sight, one is tempted to say that a change of scale is equivalent to a radial translation in polar coordinates, like rotation is a translation along the angular coordinate. However, this is not the case: Rotation is a linear operation, that is, two successive rotations are equivalent to a single rotation by an angle equal to the sum of the angles of rotation. On the other hand, scaling is not a linear operation. Convincing experimental results have been published for achieving rotation invariance with linear filters, whereas the corresponding results for scale invariance are mostly preliminary. At this time, the best method for obtaining scale invariance involves the use of moments.

1.4. Intensity or Contrast Invariance

In many cases, the intensity or contrast of the patterns of interest in a scene are unknown or can change due to a change of illumination or other causes. Because matched filtering techniques usually detect the targets of interest by thresholding the output, a drop in the contrast of a target can cause its correlation peak to drop below threshold, causing it not to be recognized. In the absence of *a priori* information about the contrast, classical matched filters cannot correct for this effect without increasing the false alarm rate. A bonus of the multiple circular harmonic filter technique described below is that it can correct for such changes in contrast. Moment methods, which are briefly discussed in Section 2.6, have also been used to obtain contrast-invariant recognition or classification.

1.5. Invariance to Distortion

Rotation and scale changes discussed above are special kinds of distortions. Other distortions are small changes in shape such as are found in different font types for letters; other examples are small changes in shape caused by aberrations in optical systems or by differing perspectives in images. In the extreme, any object can be considered a distorted version of any other object. When it is necessary to classify different objects into arbitrary classes, the classifying system must consider all the objects of one class as identical. For example, if it was required to classify from photographs all American aircraft in one class and all Canadian aircraft in another, a Canadian F-18 and a Canadian B-747 would be considered indistinguishable, whereas a Canadian F-18 would be considered different from an American F-18 (the former is called a CF-18, to help avoid confusion, a fact of dubious value for automated pattern recognition). In a matched filter system, the output of the filter should be the same for all the objects belonging to one class, so from the point of view of the output, the objects are really indistinguishable. Composite filters discussed in Section 2.2 are able to accomplish this operation, discriminating between patterns having only slight differences, and this type of invariance can be combined with invariance with respect to position and orientation.

1.6. Invariance to Noise

Because invariant pattern recognition is still in the early stages of its development, there has been little study of the effects of noise on the methods. In addition, it has become apparent that methods based on the classical model of additive signal-independent noise, for which many powerful statistical techniques have been developed, is inadequate for many realistic cases, where the noise often depends on the signal, or where its statistics change over a complex image field. There are indications that those problems can be overcome, but much research will be necessary.

1.7. Optics Versus Computers

The advantage of optical systems over computers lies in the ability of optical systems to process data in a parallel manner. The classical optical correlator using a matched filter allows fully parallel matched filtering over an object field containing multiple target patterns. The output of such a filter is given by Eq. (10.1), where $f(x, y)$ is the input scene, $h(x, y)$ is the Fourier transform of the filter inserted into the Fourier plane of the correlator, and $R_{\mathrm{fh}}(x, y)$ is the output of the correlator. The inherent spatial invariance of this optical system, when combined with filters that are rotation invariant, allows pattern recognition that is invariant under both translation and rotation of the targets. Recent progress in optical modulators have injected new life into this correlator, because such modulators can be addressed optically and electronically, thus allowing rapidly changing the object or the filter for real-time applications.

Optical implementation of real-time pattern recognition is fast coming into its own and may be faster and cheaper than pure digital solutions, which require extremely fast computers. The possibility of implementing CHC filters as phase-only filters promises optical filters that can be electrically input on existing spatial light modulators in optical correlators at rates of more than 1000 frames per second. Rates of 20-frames-per-second pattern recognition have been demonstrated for the US military in trials with real aircraft (not rotation-invariant) using phase-only matched filters, and rates of 1000 frames per second have been attained in the laboratory. With this rate of 1000 filters per second, a CHC method using five filters could classify 200 input images per second. However, a single CHC composite phase filter using a single matched filter could classify 1000 input images per second! So the objective of a more complex classification of larger scenes (1000 × 1000 pixels) at frame rates of 30 frames per second does not seem an unreasonable objective for the next 5 years, considering the huge progress that has been made in both processing techniques and in spatial light modulators in the past few years, which is now picking up speed.

On the other hand, it is usually simpler to implement a given processing technique on a digital computer. The computer is usually more flexible but slower, at least in principle. It is usually advisable to simulate an optical method on a computer whenever this is possible; this makes it easier to evaluate performance, especially when the limitations are due to the algorithm. Most of the optical implementations described in this paper were previously carried out on a digital image processing system, and some of the methods have not yet been implemented in optical systems.

For real-time applications, the more promising approach is to use an optical system to do the time-consuming processing such as correlations and to do the post-processing operations such as thresholding and identification with a computer.

2.
Rotation-Invariant Matched Filters

During the last few years we have developed and studied some new methods for optical and digital pattern recognition based on the circular harmonic decomposition

$$f(r, \theta) = \sum_{m=-\infty}^{\infty} f_m(r) \exp(im\theta), \tag{10.5}$$

where

$$f_m(r) = \int_0^{2\pi} f(r, \theta) \exp(-im\theta) \, d\theta. \tag{10.6}$$

This decomposition has been used extensively in reconstruction from projections (Hansen and Goodman, 1978). The approach originally proposed and successfully implemented by us for simple objects was to use one of the circular harmonic components (CHC),

$$h_m(r, \theta) = f_m(r)e^{im\theta}, \tag{10.7}$$

as a matched filter to achieve rotation-invariant pattern recognition (Hsu et al., 1982; Hsu and Arsenault, 1982, 1983; Arsenault et al., 1984). Earlier, we had used a matched filter called the optimum circular filter (Yang et al., 1982; Yang et al., 1983) that turned out to be a zero-order CHC filter. Although this filter yields the maximum signal-to-noise ratio of a rotation-invariant matched filter, it is not very effective in discriminating between patterns. Later, using methods described in Section 3, more than one CHC component was used to achieve contrast-independent rotation invariance and to improve the discrimination ability of the filter.

Figure 10.1 shows how a pattern is built up from its CHC components. Most of the energy tends to be concentrated in the lower order components. Figure 10.2 shows how the energy in CHC components tends to decrease with the logarithm of the order m. This figure was calculated from the components of the letter of Fig. 10.3.

Figure 10.3 shows the $m = 1$ CHC of the letter E. When a matched filter made from this CHC was used on the scene of Fig. 10.4, all the patterns were detected with no false alarms.

When the object $f(x, y)$ is present in the scene with its center of expansion at coordinates (x_1, y_1), it is easily shown, using the orthogonality property of the CHCs, that the CHC filter of Eq. (10.7) yields the output

$$R_{ff}(x_1, y_1) = |f_m(0)|^2. \tag{10.8}$$

If a classical matched filter with $h(x, y) = f^*(-x, -y)$ had been used instead of the filter of Eq. (10.7), foregoing rotation invariance, the output peak value would be

Fig. 10.1.

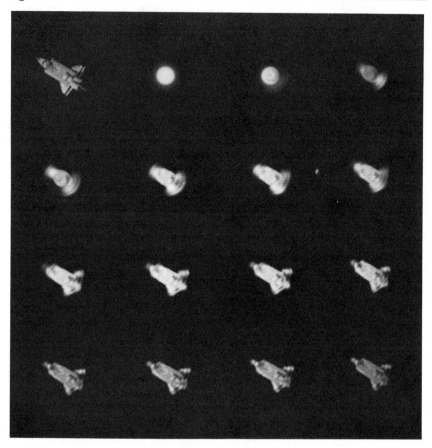

Circular harmonic components building up an object. On the top left is a photograph of the space shuttle, and the succeeding images show how the image
changes as circular harmonic components from 0 to ±15 are added to the image. (After Arsenault and Sheng, 1986.)

$$|f(0, 0)|^2 = \sum_{-\infty}^{\infty} |f_{\mathrm{m}}(0)|^2. \tag{10.9}$$

A comparison of the two expressions (10.8) and (10.9) shows that the price
paid to obtain rotation invariance with CHC filters is a drop in the signal-
to-noise ratio, since only one of the components of Eq. (10.5) is present in
the output. The same SNR as the classical matched filter can be obtained
by using multiple CHC filters and adding the correlation values; in this case

Fig. 10.2.

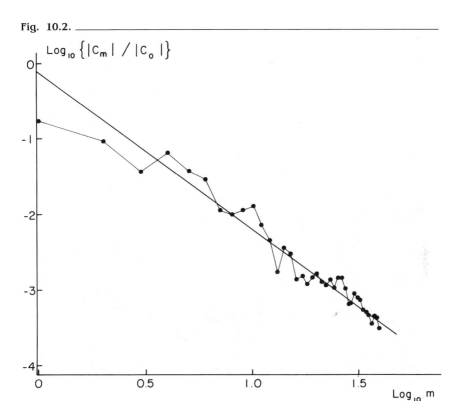

Output correlation peak $|C_m|$ of a rotation-invariant circular harmonic filter of the letter A decreases linearly with the log of the circular harmonic order m. (After Arsenault and Sheng, 1986.)

the price paid for rotation invariance is the time required for multiple filtering. The use of multiple CHC filters is discussed in Section 3.

2.1.   Centers of Expansion

The circular harmonic representation of a given function $f(x, y)$ changes with the center of expansion. The performance of CHC filters strongly depends on the choice of expansion center. If the center is chosen at random, the maximum correlation peak does not usually coincide with the center of expansion, which means that sidelobes are higher than the correlation peak (a phenomenon that is impossible in classical matched filters). This has been avoided in the past by searching for centers that yield the maximum correlation peak at the center of expansion. Such a center is called a proper

Fig. 10.3. _____

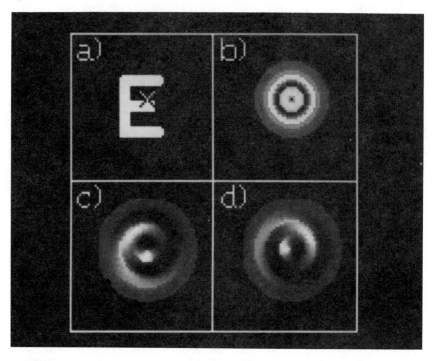

Rotation-invariant filter to recognize the letter E. a) The letter and the proper
center used shown by an x; b) the modulus squared of the first-order circular
harmonic component ($m = 1$); c) the real part of the CHC; d) the imaginary part
of the CHC. (After Hsu and Arsenault, 1982.)

center (Hsu and Arsenault, 1982; Sheng and Arsenault, 1987b). There is
usually more than one proper center for a given object and a CHC filter of
a given order. We have previously developed an iterative technique to find
a proper center, but there was no guarantee that the proper center found
would be the best.

It turns out that all the proper centers can be found by means of a relatively
simple and straightforward procedure that yields as a bonus a prediction of
the sidelobes of the correlation (Sheng and Arsenault, 1987b).

For a given CHC order m, the object of interest $f(x, y)$ is developed about
each point (x, y), yielding a family of CHC components

$$f_m(r; x, y)e^{-im\theta}. \tag{10.10}$$

The energy of each component of Eq. (10.10)

Fig. 10.4.

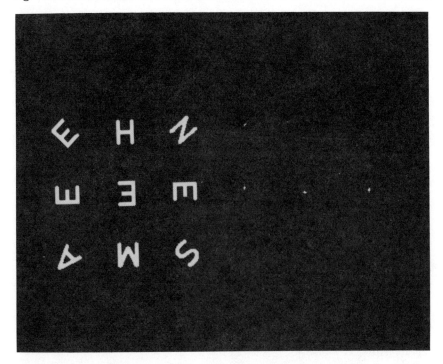

Recognition of the letter E with a circular harmonic filter. The left part of the photograph shows the scene containing three rotated letters E, and the right part shows the thresholded output with the correlation peaks corresponding to the three letters. (After Hsu and Arsenault, 1982.)

$$E_m(x, y) = \frac{1}{2\pi} \int_0^\infty |f_m(r; x, y)|^2 \, r \, dr \qquad (10.11)$$

is calculated for each point (x, y). The coordinates of the maxima of $E_m(x, y)$ are the proper centers, and the largest maximum is the proper center that will yield the largest correlation value. Furthermore, the secondary maxima have been shown to be good predictors of the positions and intensities of the sidelobes.

The amount of calculations necessary to find the best proper center is much reduced over previous methods, and the sidelobe prediction is added as a bonus. This technique solves the problem of the choice of a proper center for single CHC filters.

2.2. Rotation-Invariant Composite Filters

Composite matched filters, which are linear combinations of matched filters (Caulfield and Maloney, 1969; Caulfield and Haimes, 1980; Caulfield, 1980; Braunecker et al., 1979; Hester and Casasent, 1980; Casasent, 1984) can be used to improve the performance of CHC filters (Arsenault and Hsu, 1983; Schils and Sweeney, 1985, 1986, 1987; Arsenault, 1986). For two components, a composite CHC filter is

$$h_m(r) = af_m(r)e^{im\theta} + bg_m(r)e^{im\theta}, \tag{10.12}$$

where a and b are constants that are found by solving the matrix equation

$$\begin{bmatrix} F_mF_m & F_mG_m \\ F_mG_m & G_mG_m \end{bmatrix} \begin{bmatrix} a \\ b \end{bmatrix} = \begin{bmatrix} A \\ B \end{bmatrix}, \tag{10.13}$$

where A and B are the arbitrary outputs required when the inputs are, respectively, $f(x, y)$ and $g(x, y)$ (usually 1 and 0, respectively), and F_mF_m, G_mG_m, and F_mG_m are, respectively, the autocorrelations at $(0, 0)$ of $f_m(r)$, $g_m(r)$ and the cross correlation of $f_m(r)$ with $g_m(r)$. Each linear equation of Eq. (10.13) is found by correlating $h_m(r)$ with each input $f(x, y)$ and $g(x, y)$ and setting the output to the required respective values A or B. Equation (10.13) can be generalized to any number of inputs, but if the number of equations grows too large, the sidelobe problem, discussed later in this chapter, tends to get worse.

It may be shown that a composite filter is an optimum linear filter in the mean-square sense for detecting $f(x, y)$ when it is not known if the input is $f(x, y)$ or $g(x, y)$. We now consider what happens when the input object is rotated by an angle α. Using Eq. (10.12), it is a simple matter to show that Eq. (10.13) becomes

$$\begin{bmatrix} F_mF_m & F_mG_m \\ F_mG_m & G_mG_m \end{bmatrix} \begin{bmatrix} a \\ b \end{bmatrix} = \begin{bmatrix} A \\ B \end{bmatrix} \exp(im\alpha). \tag{10.14}$$

The solution (a, b) of the matrix equation (10.14) is the same as that of Eq. (10.13), multiplied by the phase factor $\exp(im\alpha)$. When we are interested only in the modulus of the output, the phase factor on the right side of Eq. (10.14) is irrelevant and Eq. (10.14) is equivalent to Eq. (10.13).

Consider now the possibility of using a composite filter using two CHC components of two different orders m and q

$$h_{mq}(r, \theta) = af_m(r) \exp(im\theta) + bg_q(r) \exp(iq\theta). \tag{10.15}$$

When the input is rotated by an angle α, the equations corresponding to Eq. (10.14) are

$$\begin{bmatrix} F_m F_m \exp(-im\alpha) & F_m G_q \exp(-iq\alpha) \\ F_m G_q \exp(-im\alpha) & G_q G_q \exp(-iq\alpha) \end{bmatrix} \begin{bmatrix} a \\ b \end{bmatrix} = \begin{bmatrix} A \\ B \end{bmatrix}. \quad (10.16)$$

It is easy to see that whereas the solution to Eqs. (10.14) does not depend on angle α except for a multiplicative constant, the solution to Eq. (10.16) does depend on angle. As a consequence, the modulus of the output of the filter is not constant when the input object is rotated (unless $m = q$). Another way to see this geometrically is that the modulus of the sum of two rotated vectors is constant only if the two vectors are rotated by the same angle. In Eq. (10.14), the angles are the same, whereas in Eq. (10.16) the angles are not the same.

We therefore reach the important conclusion that a circular harmonic filter using a finite number of CHC filters is rotation invariant only if all CHC components have the same order (or order zero). A CHC filter of the type of Eq. (10.16) does not yield an output with a constant modulus under rotation of the input.

CHC composite filters made from components having the same order can enhance the recognition capability of invariant recognition systems. A composite CHC filter was used in an optical processor for rotation-invariant recognition of letters F in the presence of letters E (Arsenault and Hsu, 1983). The use of composite CHC filters to reduce sidelobes is discussed in Section 4.

2.3. Rotating Filter Method

Schils and Sweeney (1985, 1986, 1987) introduced a filter also based on the CHC decomposition. They made a composite filter from CHC components of different orders for an object. The result was a filter that can yield a constant response when it is rotated only if the target of interest is present, and only at the center of expansion. This filter therefore requires each pixel of the output to be statistically analyzed to see if it remains constant when the filter rotates. It is therefore necessary, for optical implementations, to have a detector at each pixel of the output plane, in addition to using rotating filters. The method has been demonstrated using simple binary shapes on dark backgrounds.

2.4. Real Filters

Circular harmonic filters are complex filters. It would be very useful, not only for optical techniques but also for digital techniques, if a rotation invariant real filter could be found. For optical implementations, a complex filter needs to be stored as a hologram, which requires more space-bandwidth product on the recording medium. On the other hand, a real filter could be stored as a bipolar filter, which does not require recording a reference beam and which would require a much smaller storage capacity from the modulator. For real-time applications, the spatial light modulators available have a relatively low number of degrees of freedom; for instance, the electrically addressable Litton LIGHT-MOD magnetoptic modulator has a maximum of 128×128 pixels.

We have been doing research towards developing real rotation-invariant filters. So far, we have been successful only in making a real filter with partial rotation invariance (Arsenault et al., 1986), and the performance of this filter is inferior to that of normal CHC filters.

Shamir et al. (1987) and Rosen and Shamir (1987) have devised a real and binary filter that is invariant under rotation of the target. Like some of the filters described in this chapter, this recently developed filter has not yet been applied to complex scenes.

2.5. CHC Phase Filters

At the other end of the spectrum are filters using only phase information. Targets have been recognized using only the phase of the digital correlation with CHC filters, information that is usually thrown away in the CHC methods described above (Levesque and Arsenault, 1986). The targets used were those shown in Fig. (10.5), and multiple CHC filters were used. When four CHC components were used, the three space shuttles with bay doors closed were recognized with no false alarms. This scene is described in more detail in Section 4. The performance of CHC filters could be further improved by using both intensity and phase information from the correlation.

2.6. Scale-Invariant CHC Filters

Some attempts have been made to achieve scale invariance using matched filters (Szoplik and Arsenault, 1986). The best results so far for scale invariance have been obtained with invariant moments (Abu-Mostafa and Psaltis, 1984, 1985; Sheng and Arsenault, 1986, 1987a; Sheng and Duvernoy, 1985). Because these moment methods cannot at this time be implemented optically, they will not be described here.

acteristic vector will fall inside the sphere, with the result that the target will be missed.

Figure 10.7 shows the normalized images of two vehicles that were successfully classified by this method in the presence of noise. For this experiment, CHC filters of order 4, 6, and 8 were used. Table 10.1 shows the results for different levels of noise. For input images with a SNR better than 3, the target detection probability was better than 90%, with the false alarm rate smaller than 10%.

3.2. Feature Space Methods

Another method, proposed by Wu and Stark (1984), is to create a new vector **D** whose components are the difference between the two vectors **f** and **g**

$$\mathbf{D} = \mathbf{f} - \mathbf{g}. \qquad (10.20)$$

Fig. 10.7.

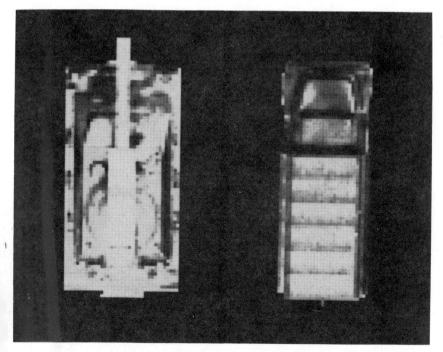

Normalized photograph of two vehicles used for recognition experiments using multiple CHC filters. (After Hsu and Arsenault, 1983.)

Fig. 10.5.

Aircraft patterns used for rotation-invariant recognition using only the phase of the correlation with the CHC filters. This scene was also used for the experiments corresponding to Fig. 10.9. (After Levesque and Arsenault, 1986.)

3.

Multiple CHC Methods

In the previous sections we have considered the use of CHC filters made from a single circular harmonic component or a linear combinations of CHCs. The use of multiple CHCs may improve the performance of invariant pattern recognition when single CHC filters do not yield satisfactory performance. Multiple filters may also be used to gain invariance over changes of contrast or intensity.

Hsu and Arsenault (1984) and Wu and Stark (1984) simultaneously introduced the idea of improving the CHC methods by using multiple CHC filters and combining the results. The former showed the possibility of discriminating between a tank and a truck by adding the correlation intensities from 3 CHC filters. Wu and Stark (1984) used a feature space containing the correlation values. A feature space was also later used by Arsenault and

Belisle (1985), who devised a method that was not sensitive to changes in target contrast, and in further work by Wu and Stark (1985).

We now briefly review the various multiple CHC methods. For each CHC filter, the correlation peak value is equal to

$$R_{ff}(0, 0) = |f_m(0)|^2, \qquad (10.17)$$

where m is the order of the filter. Let us denote the set of correlation values $|fm(0)|^2$ used as the components of a vector $\mathbf{f}$:

$$\mathbf{f} = [|f_0(0)|^2, |f_1(0)|^2, |f_2(0)|^2, \ldots, |f_N(0)|^2]. \qquad (10.18)$$

In practice, only a subset of the components are used to define the vector $\mathbf{f}$. A vector space whose coordinates axes are the values $\{f_i(0)|^2$ is then defined, and a given object is characterized by its coordinates in the feature space. Patterns may be classified by dividing the pattern space into decision areas, and an object is assigned to a given class when its vector is within the corresponding decision area. All the multiple CHC methods can be considered as special cases of decision functions in this feature space.

3.1. Threshold Method

To compare two objects $f(r, \theta)$ and $g(r, \theta)$, the vectors $\mathbf{f}$ and $\mathbf{g}$ must be compared to determine if an object is a target of interest. One way to do this is to use the criterion

$$\|\mathbf{g}\| < T, \qquad (10.19)$$

where T is a threshold satisfying $\|\mathbf{f}\| > T$. Note that when all the components are used, this method is equivalent to the classical matched filtering technique (except for the additional rotation invariance), since the total cross-correlation peak intensity is compared to the autocorrelation peak intensity of the prototype by means of thresholding.

Figure 10.6a shows the feature space for one method when only two components are used. The axes are the correlation intensities for each of two CHC components. The light gray areas correspond to the areas in decision space that correspond to the detection of the required target. The dark gray areas are the error sphere on the target. The light areas correspond to decision space that does not contain the target of interest. In this diagram, which corresponds to classical matched filtering for a target that has only two CHC components, the target is classified as a nontarget if it is inside the sphere of radius T, which represents the threshold. It is easy to see that if the contrast of the target falls below a certain value, the tip of the char-

Fig. 10.6.

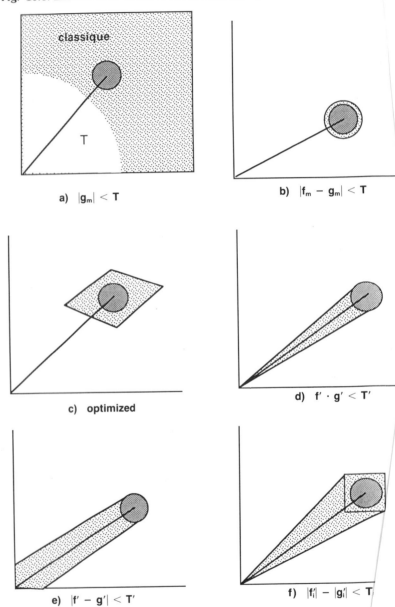

a) $|g_m| < T$

b) $|f_m - g_m| < T$

c) optimized

d) $f' \cdot g' < T'$

e) $|f' - g'| < T'$

f) $|f_i' - g_i'| < T$

Feature spaces corresponding to various multiple CHC methods. a) Th
b) vector difference; c) optimized vector difference; d) unit vector sca
uct; e) unit vector difference; f) individual unit vector difference.

TABLE 10.1

Statistical discrimination between a tank and a truck in the presence of noise. $P_{n.d.}$ = probability of nondetection; $P_{f.a.}$ = probability of false alarm[a].

Input SNR	1	1.3	1.6	2.0	2.5	3.0	3.5	4.0	4.5	5.0	6.0
$P_{n.d.}$	0.244	0.214	0.190	0.163	0.134	0.114	0.094	0.080	0.068	0.058	0.041
$P_{f.a.}$	0.243	0.213	0.190	0.161	0.135	0.111	0.095	0.080	0.067	0.057	0.039

[a] After Hsu and Arsenault, 1983.

The presence of a target is determined by the criterion

$$\|\mathbf{f} - \mathbf{g}\| < T, \qquad (10.21)$$

where T is a threshold. This method is illustrated in Fig. 10.6b. Only targets whose vectors fall within the light gray sphere will be classified as targets. From the figure it is seen that in this method also, if the contrast of the target drops too much, its vector will drop into the decision space for non-targets and the target will be missed.

Wu and Stark (1985) have also proposed a multiple-harmonic method using training samples and an optimizing technique to reduce the dimensionality. The feature space for this method is illustrated in Fig. 10.6c.

The previous methods are incapable of detecting low-contrast targets in the presence of high-contrast objects, because the moduli of the vectors are proportional to the contrast of the target. We now describe how a feature vector can be defined to be invariant to target contrast.

3.3.   Contrast-Invariant Methods

3.3.1.   Unit Vector Scalar Product Method

Let the unit vectors corresponding to $\mathbf{f}$ and $\mathbf{g}$ be $\mathbf{f}' = \mathbf{f}/f$ and $\mathbf{g}' = \mathbf{g}/g$. There are two ways to determine if two unit vectors $\mathbf{f}'$ and $\mathbf{g}'$ are parallel: one is to calculate the scalar product $\mathbf{f}' \cdot \mathbf{g}'$. If the two vectors are parallel the product is, of course, equal to unity, so an appropriate criterion to determine the presence of a target is

$$\mathbf{f}' \cdot \mathbf{g}' > T. \qquad (10.22)$$

Since the moduli of the vectors are normalized, in the absence of noise this method is insensitive to target contrast. The feature space corresponding to this method is shown in Fig. 10.6d. The decision space for the target is a cone with its apex at the origin.

3.3.2.   Unit Vector Difference Methods

The second way to determine if two unit vectors are parallel depends on the fact that if two unit vectors are parallel, their components are equal. A simple global criterion to determine the presence of a target is

$$\|\mathbf{f}' - \mathbf{g}'\| < T', \qquad (10.23)$$

which is similar but not equivalent to criterion (10.21), since in this case the moduli of the two vectors are equal, even when the objects are not the same. The decision space is shown in Fig. 10.6e. However, here we have gained insensitivity to differences of contrast. The application of this method to the recognition of pattern having different contrasts is shown in Fig. 10.8.

It is also possible to consider each of the components individually; then criterion (10.23) becomes

$$\left| \mathbf{f}_i' \right| - \left| \mathbf{g}_i' \right| < T_i \qquad (10.24)$$

for each component $\mathbf{g}_i'$ of the object. The feature space for this method is shown in Fig. 10.6f, where the decision spaces are not very different from those of Fig. 10.6d.

All of the multiple CHC methods described above are cases of minimum distance classifiers, a widely used technique in pattern recognition (Tou and Gonzales, 1974). These methods can be implemented optically by using the different CHC filters in succession and processing the output data digitally, a procedure that requires temporarily storing the output correlation values corresponding to each filter, but that can be done very rapidly because the number of digital operations is relatively small. Another method would be to process the data optically in parallel, an operation that would require one optical processor for each filter (three or five filters were typically used in the published experiments).

All the published results using the multiple CHC methods described above

Fig. 10.8.

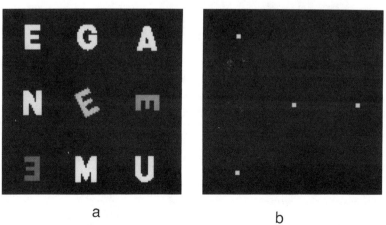

a

b

a) Scene containing four letters E having different contrasts. b) Output of the digitally processed correlation with multiple CHC filters showing the positions of the letters E detected. (After Arsenault and Belisle, 1985.)

used simple objects on black backgrounds. Research on the recognition and classification of complex gray-level objects on highly cluttered backgrounds is currently under way. Results obtained so far indicate that aircraft on air photographs can be recognized with very low error rates on backgrounds such as are found in air photographs, but the filters must be designed to reject the background.

4.

Sidelobe Reduction

Both composite filters and CHC filters tend to have high sidelobes, so when they are combined the sidelobe problem is compounded. High sidelobes tend to decrease the reliability of recognition by causing false alarms, and for applications such as the classification of aircraft, neither the simple CHC filter nor the composite filter of Eq. (10.5) yield a satisfactory performance.

One approach to sidelobe reduction is to use a composite filter with a radial dependence

$$h(r) = af_m(r) + b\zeta(r), \tag{10.25}$$

where $\zeta(r)$ is a rectangular matrix of one's (a uniform rectangle) the same size as the object (Arsenault et al., 1987). The filter is designed to recognize the object $f(x, y)$ and discriminate against a uniform background, so A and B are, respectively, equal to 1 and 0.

$$\begin{bmatrix} F_m F_m & F_m Z_m \\ F_m Z_m & Z_m Z_m \end{bmatrix} \begin{bmatrix} a \\ b \end{bmatrix} = \begin{bmatrix} 1 \\ 0 \end{bmatrix}, \tag{10.26}$$

where $F_m Z_m$ is the correlation between $f_m(r)$ and $\zeta_m(r)$ and $F_m F_m$, $Z_m Z_m$ are the autocorrelations of $f_m(r)$ and $\zeta_m(r)$. For the filter to recognize the object $f(x, y)$, to discriminate against the object $g(x, y)$, and to reduce the side-lobes, the constants (a, b) should simultaneously satisfy Eq. (10.25) and Eq. (10.13) [with $A = 1$, $B = 0$]), which is impossible. A compromise solution is possible by using the average between the two inconsistent solutions for (a, b) of Eq. (10.25) and Eq. (10.13). With this mean filter, the object $g(x, y)$ does not yield an output of zero, but there is no point in having a correlation of zero and high sidelobes.

This approach gives an overall filter performance that is much improved, as illustrated in Fig. 10.9 (Leclerc et al., 1988). The aim of this experiment was to recognize the three space shuttles in Fig. 10.5 against other aircraft, where the targets of interest are in positions 1, 4, and 6, counting clockwise from the upper left of the photograph. Note the space shuttle with the open bay doors at position 2, which is considered a nontarget for this experiment. In the following three-dimensional representations of the correlation peaks in Fig. 10.9, the space shuttle corresponding to position 1 is on the top. Figure 10.9a shows the intensity of the correlation peaks when only a second-order CHC of the space shuttle was used as a filter. It is not possible to recognize the three space shuttles using this method.

Fig. 10.9. _____

(a)   (b)

(c)

Sidelobe reduction with composite filters. The input scene is the same as that of Fig. 10.5. a) Output correlations when a single CHC filter was used; b) output when a composite filter was used; c) output when an antisidelobe component was added to the composite filter. (After Leclerc, Campos, and Arsenault, 1988.)

Figure 10.9b shows improved performance when a composite filter designed to detect the space shuttle and discriminate against the worst offender of the previous figure, target 8, was used. However, the three space shuttles still can not be recognized. Only when the composite filter is used with the antisidelobe filter can the shuttle can be correctly identified as shown in Fig. 10.9c. Other sidelobe reduction techniques are also under study.

5.
Principal Component Filters

We have been investigating other rotation-invariant filters than the filters based on the circular harmonic components. One possibility is to decompose an object into a sum of principal components (Jouan and Arsenault, 1987)

$$f(r, \theta) = \sum_k p_k(r)q_k(\theta), \qquad (10.27)$$

where $p_k(r)$ and $q_k(\theta)$ are principal components of the object. The $p_k(r)$ and $q_k(\theta)$ functions, being principal components, are completely determined by their eigenvectors λ_k, have less redundancy than the CHC components, and might allow a better performance in pattern recognition. The $q_k(\theta)$ are promising candidates for scale-invariant matched filters. Such filters are presently under investigation.

Another approach also under investigation is the decomposition of an object $f(r, \theta)$ into a sum of invariant functions

$$f(r, \theta) = \sum_j \sum_k a_{jk}s_k(r)t_k(\theta), \qquad (10.28)$$

where $s_k(r)$ and $t_k(\theta)$ are sets of orthogonal functions that do not depend on the object. In this approach, the object, $f(r, \theta)$ is completely determined by the set of coefficients a_{jk}. In addition to invariant pattern recognition, this decomposition could be used for image compression and for image mapping in applications such as content-addressable associative memories.

6.
Conclusion

The field of optical processing techniques for invariant pattern recognition is still in a state of rapid evolution. The use of multiple CHC filters and of composite CHC filters has led to considerable improvements in invariant pattern recognition. Considerable progress has been made in improved discrimination and in sidelobe reduction. Applications of CHC filters to low-light imagery is discussed elsewhere in this book. Some of the problems that are only partially solved include the effects of random noise and of highly cluttered backgrounds, and of aliasing caused by low resolution. The use of functions other than the circular harmonic components is also a promising area currently under investigation.

Because new and improved methods are being developed, often in response to new problems as research moves into more complex imagery, there have not been many systematic studies of the performance of the various methods. Most of the publications in this area are demonstrations of the feasibility of a new method using one or two examples. Studies such as those that are needed by systems designers would have been useless in the early stages of development of this field, because all the early methods are becoming obsolete as new more powerful techniques are being developed. As the field matures, such studies will begin to appear, and the performance of the various methods will be evaluated with respect to their advantages and shortcoming.

At this time, indications are that the composite CHC methods and the multiple CHC methods can recognize and classify complex objects, such as different aircraft, in the absence of a highly cluttered, high-contrast background. The problem of recognizing complex objects such as aircraft in the presence of a highly cluttered background is still the subject of active research.

The composite filter approach is more advantageous in principle than the multiple filter approach, because there is only one filter and the processing at the output plane consists only of determining whether each pixel is above or below a threshold. It is still too early to tell if multiple CHC filters can yield better results than composite CHC filters, because both methods are still being improved. However, new types of output plane processing may become feasible with the advent of associative memories. For example, a system using associative memories could yield directly corrected images of identified patterns on an output screen, thus giving the observer immediate information on both location and identity of recognized patterns.

References

Abu-Mostafa, Y.S. and Psaltis, D. (1984). "Recognition aspects of moment invariants," *Trans. IEEE Pattern Anal. Machine Intell.* **PAMI-6,** 698.

Abu-Mostafa, Y.S., and Psaltis D. (1985). "Image normalization by complex moments," *Trans. IEEE Pattern Anal. Machine Intell.* **PAMI-7,** 46.

Arsenault, H.H., and Hsu, Y.N. (1983). "Rotation-invariant discrimination between almost similar objects," *Appl. Opt.* **22**, 130–132.

Arsenault, H.H., Hsu, Y.N., and Chalasinska-Macukow, K. (1984). "Rotation-invariant pattern recognition," *Opt. Eng.* **23**, 705–709.

Arsenault, H.H., and Belisle, C. (1985). "Contrast-invariant pattern recognition using circular harmonics," *Appl. Opt.* **24**, 2072–2075.

Arsenault, H.H., and Sheng, Y. (1986). "Properties of the Circular harmonic expansion for rotation-invariant pattern recognition," *J. Opt. Soc. Am.* **25**, 3225–3229.

Arsenault, H.H. (1986). "Rotation invariant composite filters," *In:* "Nonlinear Optics and Applications," *Proc. SPIE* **613**, 239–244.

Arsenault, H.H., Ferreira, C., Levesque, M., and Szoplik, T. (1986). "Simple filter with limited rotation invariance," *J. Opt. Soc. Am.* **25**, 3230–3234.

Arsenault, H.H., Sheng, Y., and Bulabois, (1987). "Modified composite filter for pattern recognition in the presence of noise with a non-zero mean," *Opt. Comm.* **63**, 15–20.

Braunecker, J., Hauck, B.R., and Lohmann, A.W. (1979). "Optical character recognition based on nonredundant correlation measurements," *Appl. Opt.* **18**, 2746.

Casasent, D. (1984). "Unified synthetic discriminant function computational formulation," *Appl. Opt.* **23**, 1620.

Caulfield, H.J., and Maloney, W.T. (1969). "Improved discrimination in optical pattern recognition," *Appl. Opt.* **8**, 2354.

Caulfield, H.J., and Haimes, R. (1980). "Generalized matched filtering," *Appl. Opt.* **19**, 181.

Caulfield, H.J. (1980). "Linear combinations of filters for character recognition: A unified treatment," *Appl. Opt.* **19**, 3877.

Hansen, E.W., and Goodman, J.W. (1978). "Optical reconstruction from projections via circular harmonic expansion," *Opt. Comm.* **24**, 268.

Hester, C.F., and Casasent, D. (1980). "Multivariant technique for multiclass pattern recognition," *Appl. Opt.* **19**, 1758.

Hsu, Y.N., Arsenault, H.H., and April, G. (1982). "Rotation-invariant digital pattern recognition using the circular harmonic expansion," *Appl. Opt.* **21**, 4012–4015.

Hsu, Y.N., and Arsenault, H.H. (1982). "Optical pattern recognition using the circular harmonic expansion," *Appl. Opt.* **21**, 4016–4019.

Hsu, Y.N., and Arsenault, H.H. (1983). "Statistical performance of the circular harmonic filter for rotation-invariant pattern recognition," *Appl. Opt.* **22**, 2804–2809.

Hsu, Y.N., and Arsenault, H.H. (1984). "Pattern discrimination by multiple circular harmonic components," *Appl. Opt.* **23**, 841–844.

Jouan, A., and Arsenault, H.H. (1987). "Invariant principal components for pattern recognition," Paper MA1, OSA Annual Meeting, Rochester, NY, Oct. 18–23.

Leclerc, L., Campos, J., and Arsenault, H.H. (1988). "Sidelobe reduction techniques for invariant matched filters," *Appl. Opt.* (submitted).

Levesque, M., and Arsenault, H.H. (1986). "Rotation invariant pattern recognition using the phase of circular harmonic filter correlations," *Opt. Comm.* **58**, 161–166.

Rosen, J., and Shamir, J. (1987). "Distortion invariant pattern recognition with phase filters," *Appl. Opt.* **26**, 2315–2319.

Schils, G.F., and Sweeney, D.W. (1985). "Rotationally invariant correlation filtering," *J. Opt. Soc. Am.* **A2**, 1411.

Schils, G.F., and Sweeney, D.W. (1986). "Rotationally invariant correlation filtering for multiple images," *J. Opt. Soc. Am.* **A3**, 902–908.

Schils, G.F., and Sweeney, D.W. (1987). "Iterative technique for the synthesis of distortion-invariant optical correlation filters," *Opt. Lett.* **12**, 307–309.

Shamir, J., Caulfield, H.J., and Rosen, J. (1987). "Pattern recognition using reduced information content filters," *Appl. Opt.* **26**, 2311–2314.

Sheng, Y., and Arsenault, H.H. (1986). "Experiments on pattern recognition using invariant Fourier-Mellin descriptors," *J. Opt. Soc. Am.* **A3**, 771–776.

Sheng, Y., and Arsenault, H.H. (1987a). "Noisy-image normalization using low-order radial moments of circular-harmonic functions," *J. Opt. Soc. Am.* **A4**, 1176–1184.

Sheng, Y., and Arsenault, H.H. (1987b). "A method for determining expansion centers and predicting sidelobe levels for circular harmonic filters," *J. Opt. Soc. Am.* **A4**, 1793–1799.

Sheng, Y., and Duvernoy, J. (1986). "Circular Fourier-radial Mellin descriptors for pattern recognition," *J. Opt. Soc. Am.* **A3**, 885.

Szoplik, T., and Arsenault, H.H. (1985). "Shift and scale-invariant anamorphic Fourier correlator using multiple circular harmonic filters," *Appl. Opt.* **24**, 3179–3183.

Tou, J.T., and Gonzalez, R.C. (1974). "Pattern recognition principles," Addison-Wesley, Reading, MA.

Wu, R., and Stark, H. (1984). "Rotation invariant pattern recognition using a vector reference," *Appl. Opt.* **23**, 838.

Wu, R., and Stark, H. (1985). "Rotation invariant pattern recognition using optimum feature extraction," *Appl. Opt.* **24,** 179.

Yang, Y., Hsu, Y.N., and Arsenault, H.H. (1982). "Optimum circular symmetrical filters and their uses in pattern recognition," *Opt. Acta* **29,** 627.

Yang, Y., Chalasinska-Macukow, K., and Arsenault, H.H. (1983). "Digital and optical analysis of the optimum circular symmetrical filter in a character recognition system," *Opt. Acta* **30,** 189.

11.

Pattern Recognition Using Photon-Limited Images

G. Michael Morris

The Institute of Optics
University of Rochester
Rochester, New York

Contents

1. Introduction. 344
2. Photon Statistics and Detection Systems 346
   2.1. Inhomogeneous Poisson Processes 346
   2.2. Two-Dimensional, Photon-Counting Detectors 348
3. Correlation with a Deterministic Reference Function 350
   3.1. Statistics of the Correlation Signal 351
       3.1.1. Real-Valued Reference Functions 351
       3.1.2. Effects of Additive Noise. 357
       3.1.3. Effects of Detector Dead Time 359
   3.2. Scene Matching at Low Light Levels 360
   3.3. Distortion-Invariant Filters 372
       3.3.1. Rotation-Invariance Using Circular-Harmonic Filters 373
       3.3.2. Fourier-Mellin Descriptors 378
       3.3.3. Image Classification 379
4. Summary. 385
   Acknowledgments 386
   References 386

1.
Introduction

The spatial coordinates, the time of arrival, and the number of photoevents detected in a given area convey information about the classical irradiance of the input image. This underlying random process can be used to implement Monte Carlo schemes to estimate various features of the input image.

Low-light level (quantum-limited) images arise in many different areas, for example, astronomy, low-dose radiological imaging, and night vision applications. Rose (1977) has illustrated clearly that it does not take millions of detected photoevents for human observers to recognize an image. Theoretical work and computer simulations on low-light-level image restoration have been reported. Burke (1975) applied classical estimation theory to the image restoration problem. Goodman and Belsher (1976) investigated linear least-squares restoration of atmospherically degraded, photon-limited images. Barrett and Swindell (1981) discuss the effects of photon noise in radiological imaging systems; expressions for the SNR in various imaging systems, including the pinhole camera, coded-aperture imaging, and computed tomography are given.

Much of the two-dimensional, photon-counting detector development has been motivated by applications in low-light-level astronomy and spectroscopy (see Ford, 1979; Geary and Latham, 1981; Timothy, 1983).

In addition to these naturally quantum-limited situations, we have found that in many classical intensity situations it may actually be better to use photon-correlation methods to extract information about an input image. Even if there is an abundance of light, the use of photon-correlation methods, which at first may seem counterintuitive, can be justified by computational-efficiency arguments and by simplicity of implementation. Often only a sparse sampling (a small number of detected photoevents) of the input image is needed for accurate image recognition; hence, the time needed to detect, process, and make a recognition decision can be quite short. For example, consider a real-time, machine-vision application. Traditionally, one digitizes the input image using a two-dimensional detector, e.g., a CCD array, and a frame store. If the detector consists of, say, a 1000×1000 array of detector elements, one has to process a million data points. This is too much information for even very large computers to process in real time, so one generally transforms the input information into some sort of feature-space representation, e.g., through the use of edge-enhanced images, and makes the recognition decision based on this reduced data set.

An alternative approach to the machine-vision problem is to process low-light-level images. In this scheme photoevents are detected at the maximum rate that the detection/computer system can handle. One collects photoevents until there is enough information about the input scene to achieve an acceptable error rate for the given situation. In effect, one is letting nature sample (digitize) the input scene. Often it is found that a sparse sampling of an input scene is sufficient to make accurate recognition decisions. Because of the sparse sampling (compression) of the input image and the speed of available two-dimensional, photon-counting detectors, recognition decisions typically can be made in a few tens of milliseconds.

It is useful to divide photon-correlation systems into three categories:

(1)   Correlation with a fixed (deterministic) reference function

(2)   Double correlation

(3)   Triple correlation

In catetory (1), an input low-light-level (photon-limited) image is correlated with a deterministic reference function stored in computer memory. The principal application for these correlation systems is automatic pattern recognition. Basically, one is given a set of possible reference images and the goal is to decide automatically (without human intervention) which of the reference objects is most like the input object.

In double correlation systems, the input photon-limited image is correlated with itself (autocorrelation) or another photon-limited image (crosscorrelation). Double correlations yield information about object parameters such as object dimensions, velocity, and so on. Generally, with double correlations one obtains information about the magnitude of the amplitude correlation function, but the phase information is lost. The principal applications of double correlation systems have been in stellar speckle interferometry and studies of dynamic speckle (see Dainty, 1984; Newman et al., 1985; and Newman, 1986).

With the triple-correlation schemes, three photon-limited images are correlated. Triple correlations contain more information about the object than do double correlations. In particular, it is possible to obtain information about the phase structure of the image as well as information about the magnitude of the object's correlation function (Gamo, 1963; Bartelt et al., 1984; Lohmann and Wirnitzer, 1984). The experimental system to collect the required data is the same as that used for double correlation, only the subsequent processing is different. With the magnitude of the correlation function and phase information, one can reconstruct a diffraction-limited image even in the presence of atmospheric turbulence (Lohmann et al., 1983; Wirnitzer, 1985; Hofmann and Weigelt, 1987). The triple correlation is also insensitive to image position and rotation (Bartelt and Wirnitzer, 1985; Lohmann, 1986a, 1986b; Dainty and Northcott, 1986).

In this chapter we concentrate on pattern recognition systems in which a low-light-level input scene is correlated with a deterministic reference function stored in computer memory. In Section 2, the statistical properties of photon-limited images are reviewed. We also survey the salient features of the different types of two-dimensional photon-counting detectors that have been developed. Section 3 contains a discussion of the features of the correlation signal formed using a photon-limited input image and a real-valued (classical intensity) reference function stored in computer memory.

2.
Photon Statistics and Detection Systems

2.1. Inhomogeneous Poisson Processes

At low levels of illumination, an input scene $\hat{V}(r)$ can be represented as a two-dimensional collection of Dirac-delta functions, i.e.,

$$\hat{V}(\mathbf{r}) = \sum_{k=1}^{N} \delta(\mathbf{r} - \mathbf{r}_k), \qquad (11.1)$$

in which $\mathbf{r}_k$ denotes the spatial coordinates of the kth detected photoevent and N is the total number of detected photoevents. Of course, with an actual detector the photoelectric counts are not idealized points, but rather they occupy a finite area; this effect can be included by passing $\hat{V}(\mathbf{r})$ through a linear system in which the impulse response is equal to the point spread function of the detector (Barrett and Swindell, 1981). Although one does not want to ignore the finite spread of the detected photoevents, it does lead to helpful simplification in the notation.

In Eq. (11.1), the spatial coordinates $\mathbf{r}_k$ of the kth detected photoevent are random variables. The number of detected photoevents, N, may or may not be a random variable depending on how the experiment is performed. For example, N is not random for the case when a fixed number of photoevents is collected. On the other hand, if photoevents are collected for a fixed time interval τ, then from the theory of photodetection (see, e.g., Mandel, 1963; Mandel et al., 1964; Bertolotti, 1974; Saleh, 1978; Goodman, 1985) the conditional probability distribution for detecting N photoevents in the time interval $[t, t + \tau]$ from a detector of area A, given the classical image irradiance $V(\mathbf{r}, t)$, is an inhomogeneous Poisson process given by

$$P[N|V(\mathbf{r}, t)] = \frac{[\int_t^{t+\tau} dt' \int_A d^2r \lambda(\mathbf{r}, t')]^N}{N!} e^{-\int_t^{t+\tau} dt' \int_A d^2r \lambda(\mathbf{r}, t')}, \quad (11.2)$$

in which the rate function $\lambda(\mathbf{r}, t)$ is

$$\lambda(\mathbf{r}, t) = \frac{\eta V(\mathbf{r}, t)}{h \bar{v}}, \quad (11.3)$$

where η denotes the quantum efficiency of the detector, h is Planck's constant, and $\bar{v}$ denotes the mean frequency of the incident quasimonochromatic light.

Generally, $V(\mathbf{r}, t)$ is a random process and the conditional distribution given in Eq. (11.2) must be ensemble averaged to obtain the observable counting distribution. For example, if $V(\mathbf{r}, t)$ obeys negative exponential statistics, as in the case of polarized quasimonochromatic light emitted by a thermal source, then the observable counting distribution $P(N)$ obeys Bose-Einstein statistics when the integration time is small compared with the coherence time of the light (see, e.g., Goodman, 1985). However, if $V(\mathbf{r}, t)$ does not fluctuate significantly, i.e., $V(\mathbf{r}, t) = V(\mathbf{r})$, as in the case of illumination provided by a well-stabilized single-mode laser, the counting distribution is simply

$$P(N) = \frac{\bar{N}^N}{N!} e^{-\bar{N}}, \quad (11.4)$$

in which

$$\bar{N} = \frac{\eta \tau}{h \bar{v}} \int_A d^2r V(\mathbf{r}) \quad (11.5)$$

is the average number of detected photoevents. One notes that the distribution in Eq. (11.4) is applicable also for polarized thermal radiation when τ is much larger than the coherence time of the light (see, e.g., Bertolotti, 1974). In this case the fluctuations in the irradiance are smoothed out in the time integration and $V(\mathbf{r})$ represents the mean value of the irradiance.

In Eq. (11.1), the photoevent coordinates $\mathbf{r}_k$ are independent random variables. The probability density function for photoevent coordinates (see Goodman, 1985) is directly proportional to the classical intensity $V(\mathbf{r}_k)$, i.e.,

$$p[\mathbf{r}_k | V(\mathbf{r}_k)] = \frac{V(\mathbf{r}_k)}{\int_A d^2 r V(\mathbf{r})}. \qquad (11.6)$$

2.2. Two-Dimensional, Photon-Counting Detectors

Almost all of the two-dimensional photon-counting detectors that have been developed use a microchannel image intensifier (see, e.g., Lampton, 1981; Siegmund et al., 1985) in cascade with some type of anode assembly to record the position coordinates of the event. A number of anode assemblies have been used including silicon-intensified-target television cameras (Boksenberg, 1972; Boyce, 1977; Blazit et al., 1977), self-scanned (CCD) detector arrays (Loh, 1977; ITT, 1980; Johnson and Blank, 1981; Jorden et al., 1982; Tyson, 1986; Roberts et al., 1986), crossed-wire-grid anodes (Kellogg et al., 1979), multi-anode arrays (Timothy et al., 1979; Timothy et al., 1981; Timothy, 1985), resistive anodes (Lampton and Carlson, 1979; Firmani et al., 1982; Rees et al., 1980; Rees et al., 1981; McWhirter et al., 1982; Greenaway et al., 1982; Mertz et al., 1982; Tsuchiya et al., 1985), wedge-and-strip anodes (Anger, 1966; Martin et al., 1981; Siegmund et al., 1983; Siegmund et al., 1984; Schwarz and Lapington, 1985; Siegmund et al., 1986), and gray-coded masks used with a bank of photomultipliers (Papaliolios and Mertz, 1982; Papaliolios et al., 1985).

A schematic of a resistive-anode-type detector is shown in Fig. 11.1. An incident photon ejects an electron from a photocathode. The ejected photoelectron is directed into a stack of microchannel plates (typically arranged in a V- and/or Z-stack to prevent ion feedback) to achieve an electron gain of approximately 10^6 to 10^8. The resulting charge pulse is collected by the resistive-anode assembly. The resistive layer is terminated by electrodes at three or four locations around its perimeter, which provide the signals for the centroiding algorithm. When coupled to position-computing electronics, the detection system is generally capable of operating at count rates up to approximately 100,000/second with a spatial resolution of 400×400 elements (Firmani et al., 1982).

The choice of the anode assembly, of course, depends on the requirements imposed by the application. For example, detection systems that operate with only one detected photoevent in the device at a time can be used to

Fig. 11.1.

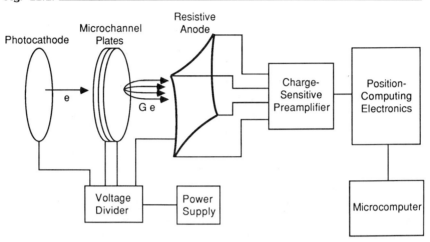

Schematic diagram of a resistive-anode, photon-counting detection system.

collect a specific number of photoevents; hence, N in Eq. (11.1) can be fixed, instead of random. These detectors can provide both the spatial coordinates and time-of-arrival informaiton for the detected photoevent. On the other hand, detection systems that utilize a detector array or a television tube to read out the position coordinates of detected photoevents are generally preferable in high-speed applications that involve moving objects or pulsed light sources. In these systems many events can be detected in a short time interval and then read out in a raster format. In these systems the time-of-arrival information of detected photoevents is not available and the number of detected photoevents for a fixed time interval τ is a random variable [see, e.g., Eqs. (11.2) and (11.4)].

The amount of additive noise due to dark counts depends primarily on the choice of the photocathode. With a blue-sensitive photocathode, e.g., a bialkali cathode (such as CS_3Sb), the dark-count contribution due to thermal emission of electrons from the cathode is typically less than 100 counts per second at room temperature. Whereas with a multialkali (e.g., $Na_2KSb:Cs$), one can expect to observe roughly 3000 dark counts per second at room temperature. Of course, it is always possible to reduce the effects of the dark count by cooling the photocathode. Other sources of dark count that are not so easily controlled include cosmic rays and fluorescence associated with the window material.

Dead-time effects in photon counters become increasingly important as the count rate increases. For the imaging photon-counting detectors, there exist two main sources of dead time. One is known as global dead time, which is the time it takes for the position-computing electronics to determine the position of a detected photoevent. For the resistive-anode device, such as that manufactured by Surface Science Laboratories, Mountain View, CA, the global dead time is on the order of 10 μsec for position sensing at a spatial resolution of 400 × 400 cells. Correction for global dead time effects has been discussed by Brown and Mackenzie (1985), Newman et al. (1985), and Newman (1986).

The other source of dead time in two-dimensional, photon-counting detectors is known as local dead time. Local dead-time effects are associated with individual channels in the microchannel plate. After detection of a photoevent, it is estimated that the recovery time of a given microchannel is on the order of 55 msec (Eberhardt, 1980). In the pulse-counting mode, the characteristics of local dead time resemble that of a paralyzable counter. Strictly speaking, the microchannel behaves as a paralyzable counter only if it discharges completely at every input event. Nicoli (1985) claims that the paralyzable dead-time model is applicable only up to a certain level of input count rates and that a more sophisticated model is needed to explain local dead-time effects in microchannel plates. When an imaging photon-counting detector is operated at high count rates and/or at high resolution (Timothy, 1985), local dead time can produce significant effects. One obvious effect is the reduction of image contrast. The effect of local dead time on the correlation signal used in pattern recognition studies is discussed below in Section 3.1.3.

3.
Correlation with a Deterministic Reference Function

Key features of a versatile vision system for robotics and target recognition include speed, reliability, and flexible illumination requirements. The primary objective for such a system is to develop a means for performing high-speed automatic identification of multiple objects, which may appear at unknown positions, orientations, or scales within a naturally illuminated input scene. As will be demonstrated in this section, the processing of photon-limited images can be used to achieve this goal. Our approach to this pattern-recognition problem is to store a reference function that describes the object of interest in computer memory, then to calculate the correlation between the input photon-limited image and the stored reference function. The recognition decision is based on the resulting value of the correlation. Section 3.1 contains a description of the statistical properties of the correlation signal. Examples of scene matching when the input image is correlated with an image of the reference object are given in Section 3.2. Reference functions that provide invariance to geometrical distortions, such as rotation, scale and position, and invariance to intrinsic object variations, e.g., changes in illumination, scene clutter, and so on, are discussed in Section 3.3.

3.1. Statistics of the Correlation Signal

Consider the correlation signal

$$C(\mathbf{r}) = \int d^2 r' \hat{V}(\mathbf{r}')R(\mathbf{r}' + \mathbf{r}) \tag{11.7}$$

obtained by cross correlating a photon-limited scene $\hat{V}(\mathbf{r})$, given in Eq. (11.1), with a deterministic reference function $R(\mathbf{r})$ stored in computer memory. Using Eqs. (11.1) and (11.7) gives

$$C(\mathbf{r}) = \sum_{k=1}^{N} R(\mathbf{r}_k + \mathbf{r}) . \tag{11.8}$$

Hence, the photon-limited correlation signal $C(\mathbf{r})$ is a random function since the event coordinates $\mathbf{r}_k$ are independent random variables with the probability density function specified in Eq. (11.6). As noted above, N, the number of detected photoevents, may or may not be random depending on how the input image is sampled.

To calculate $C(\mathbf{r})$, one uses the spatial coordinates of a given detected photoevent as an address. The offset coordinate $\mathbf{r}$ defines the location of reference-function window within the input scene, see Fig. 11.2. The procedure is to look up the value of the reference function stored at the address specified by $\mathbf{r} + \mathbf{r}_k$ and place that value in an accumulator; this operation is repeated for all N detected photoevents. The recognition decision is based on the resulting value of $C(\mathbf{r})$. In the treatment given here, $R(\mathbf{r})$ is taken to be a real-valued function. The results are readily extended to the case in which the reference function is complex (Isberg and Morris, 1986).

3.1.1. Real-Valued Reference Functions

3.1.1.1. Characteristic Function of $C(\mathbf{r})$

A convenient statistical quantity to calculate when using sums of independent random variables is the characteristic function of the process. The

Fig. 11.2.

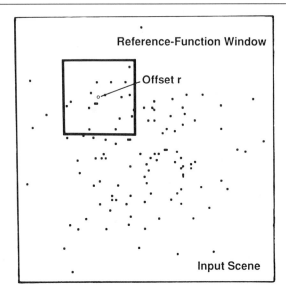

Input scene showing reference-function window at offset **r**.

characteristic function of a random variable **C** is defined by

$$\Phi(\omega) = \langle e^{i\omega C} \rangle = \int_{-\infty}^{\infty} dC\, P(C) e^{i\omega C}, \qquad (11.9)$$

where $\langle \ldots \rangle$ denotes an average over an ensemble of realizations and $P(C)$ represents the probability density function of the random variable **C**.

An expression for the characteristic function of $C(\mathbf{r})$ in Eq. (11.8) is derived in a manner similar to that for a shot-noise process (see Davenport and Root, 1958; Papoulis, 1965; Snyder, 1975).

First, we devide the reference function area into small patches $[\mathbf{r}_i', \mathbf{r}_i' + \Delta\mathbf{r}']$ of area $\Delta A_i = \Delta^2 r'$, and choose $\Delta\mathbf{r}'$ small enough that in the region $\mathbf{r}_i' < \mathbf{r}' < \mathbf{r}_i' + \Delta\mathbf{r}'$,

$$R(\mathbf{r}' + \mathbf{r}) \cong R(\mathbf{r}_i' + \mathbf{r}). \qquad (11.10)$$

The contribution to the correlation signal from area ΔA_i is then

$$\Delta C_i(\mathbf{r}) \cong R(\mathbf{r}_i' + \mathbf{r})n_i, \qquad (11.11)$$

where n_i denotes the number of detected photoevents that occur in area ΔA_i

in time interval τ. Note that $\Delta C_i(\mathbf{r})$ is the product of a constant $R(\mathbf{r}_i' + \mathbf{r})$ times the random variable n_i.

From Eqs. (11.9) and (11.11), we can write the characteristic function of $\Delta C_i(\mathbf{r})$:

$$\Delta\Phi_i(\omega) = \langle e^{i\omega R(\mathbf{r}_i' + \mathbf{r})n_i}\rangle. \tag{11.12}$$

Assuming that the random variables n_i are independent for nonoverlapping areas, the characteristic function of their sum from areas ΔA_i is equal to the product of the individual characteristic functions,

$$\Phi(\omega) = \langle e^{i\omega\Sigma_i R(\mathbf{r}_i' + \mathbf{r})n_i}\rangle. \tag{11.13}$$

If the photoevent counts in ΔA_i are Poisson-distributed [see Eqs. (11.4) and (11.5)], with the Poisson parameter

$$\bar{N}_i = \frac{\eta\tau}{h\bar{\nu}} V(\mathbf{r}_i')\Delta^2 r', \tag{11.14}$$

then

$$\Phi(\omega) = e^{[\eta\tau/h\bar{\nu}]\Sigma_i \Delta^2 r' V(\mathbf{r}_i')[e^{i\omega R(\mathbf{r}_i' + \mathbf{r})} - 1]}. \tag{11.15}$$

In the limit as $\Delta^2 r' \rightarrow 0$, the summation in Eq. (11.15) tends to an integral and $\Phi(\omega)$ becomes

$$\Phi(\omega) = e^{[\eta\tau/h\bar{\nu}]\int_A d^2 r' V(\mathbf{r}')[e^{i\omega R(\mathbf{r}' + \mathbf{r})} - 1]}, \tag{11.16}$$

where A is the area of the reference-function window.

It is useful to express $\Phi(\omega)$ in terms of the average number of photons in the input scene. This is accomplished by multiplying and dividing the argument of the exponential in Eq. (11.16) by $\int_A d^2 r' V(\mathbf{r}')$. This gives

$$\Phi(\omega) = e^{\bar{N}\int_A d^2 r' p[\mathbf{r}'|V(\mathbf{r}')][e^{i\omega R(\mathbf{r}' + \mathbf{r})} - 1]}, \tag{11.17}$$

where $\bar{N}$ [see Eq. (11.5)] is the average number of input-scene photoevents within the reference-window area A, and $p[\mathbf{r}'|V(\mathbf{r}')]$, given in Eq. (11.6), is the conditional probability density of event coordinates.

3.1.1.2. Moments of the Correlation Signal

Statistical moments of $C(\mathbf{r})$ are calculated easily using the characteristic function, i.e.,

$$\langle C^k(\mathbf{r})\rangle = (-i)^k \frac{d^k\Phi(0)}{d\omega^k}. \tag{11.18}$$

Using Eqs. (11.17) and (11.18), one obtains the following expressions for
the mean value and variance of $C(\mathbf{r})$:

$$\langle C(\mathbf{r}) \rangle = \bar{N} \int_A d^2r' \, p[\mathbf{r}'|V(\mathbf{r}')]R(\mathbf{r}' + \mathbf{r}), \qquad (11.19)$$

and

$$\sigma_p^2 = \langle C^2(\mathbf{r}) \rangle - \langle C(\mathbf{r}) \rangle^2 \qquad (11.20)$$

$$= \bar{N} \int_A d^2r' \, p[\mathbf{r}'|V(\mathbf{r}')]R^2(\mathbf{r}' + \mathbf{r}).$$

Equation (11.19) indicates that the expected value of $C(\mathbf{r})$ in Eq. (11.8) is
proportional to the cross-correlation function of the classical intensity input
scene $V(\mathbf{r})$ with the reference function $R(\mathbf{r})$. However, due to the inherent
statistical fluctuations of the photon-limited input scene, there is a variance
in the correlation signal as given by Eq. (11.20).

We can define the signal-to-noise ratio (SNR) of the correlation function
as the ratio of the mean value of the process to the rms deviation from the
mean, SNR $= \langle C(\mathbf{r}) \rangle / \sigma_p$. Using Eqs. (11.19) and (11.20) gives

$$\text{SNR} = \sqrt{\bar{N}} \, \frac{\int_A d^2r' \, p[\mathbf{r}'|V(\mathbf{r}')]R(\mathbf{r}' + \mathbf{r})}{[\int_A d^2r' \, p[\mathbf{r}'|V(\mathbf{r}')]R^2(\mathbf{r}' + \mathbf{r})]^{1/2}}. \qquad (11.21)$$

Notice that the statistical properties of the photon-limited correlation signal
are identical to that found if one were to evaluate the correlation signal using
a Monte Carlo scheme (see, e.g., Shreider, 1966; Rubinstein, 1981; Morris,
1985). We can therefore regard the correlation signal formed by a photon-
limited input scene and a deterministic reference function as an optical implementation of a Monte Carlo procedure to calculate definite integrals.

3.1.1.3. Probability Density Function for C(r)

A main quantity of interest for pattern-recognition studies is the probability
density function of the correlation signal, $P[C(\mathbf{r})]$, which is obtained by
taking the inverse Fourier transform of the characteristic function, i.e.,

$$P[C(\mathbf{r})] = \frac{1}{2\pi} \int_{-\infty}^{\infty} d\omega \Phi(\omega)e^{-i\omega C(\mathbf{r})}. \qquad (11.22)$$

Unfortunately, the Fourier inversion of the characteristic function in Eq.

(11.17), in general, cannot be evaluated in closed form. However, it is possible to obtain an estimate of $P[C(\mathbf{r})]$ numerically using fast-Fourier-transform (FFT) techniques.

Limit forms for $P[C(\mathbf{r})]$ can be found by expressing $P[C(\mathbf{r})]$ in terms of a power series and taking the inverse Fourier transform term by term (Morris, 1984a). One can represent the main exponential function in Eq. (11.17) as a Maclaurin series; this series representation is useful when $\bar{N}$ is small. In this case only the first few terms of the series are required.

For recognition of realistic scenes one would expect that the average number of detected photoevents $\bar{N}$, required to obtain reasonable error rates, is relatively large. Since both $\langle C(\mathbf{r})\rangle$ and σ_p^2 increase with $\bar{N}$, it is useful to consider the normalized process

$$\zeta(\mathbf{r}) = \frac{C(\mathbf{r}) - \langle C(\mathbf{r})\rangle}{\sigma_p}$$

in the limit as $\bar{N} \to \infty$. By expanding the exponential function in the exponent of Eq. (11.17) in a Maclaurin series, it is readily shown that the characteristic function, and hence the probability density function of $\zeta(\mathbf{r})$, tend to a Gaussian process as $\bar{N} \to \infty$, i.e.,

$$\lim_{\bar{N}\to\infty} \Phi_\zeta(\omega) = e^{-\omega^2/2}, \tag{11.23}$$

and

$$\lim_{\bar{N}\to\infty} P[C(\mathbf{r})] = \frac{1}{\sigma_p \sqrt{2\pi}} e^{-[C(\mathbf{r})-\langle C(\mathbf{r})\rangle]^2/(2\sigma_p^2)}. \tag{11.24}$$

3.1.1.4. Fixed Number of Detected Photoevents

In the previous sections it was assumed that the correlation signal is realized by detecting photoevents for a fixed time interval τ. Hence, provided that the assumptions concerning the image irradiance are valid, the number of detected photoevents in time interval τ is Poisson-distributed as given in Eq. (11.4). Mandel (1983) has suggested that an idealized light source, which emits a definite number of photons per message symbol, could provide the maximum information-carrying capacity for an optical communication channel. We achieve an analogous effect here by taking the number of detected photoevents N in the input image to be fixed, rather than Poisson distributed.

If the cross correlation of a photon-limited input scene with a reference function is performed by detecting a fixed number of photoevents N [see Eq. (11.8)], then by the central limit theorem (see, e.g., Gnedenko, 1963), the probability density function of the correlation signal will approach a Gaussian distribution, assuming that the number of detected photoevents is large, since the photoevent coordinates are statistically independent. In this case the mean value of $C(\mathbf{r})$ is given by

$$\langle C(\mathbf{r})\rangle = \left\langle \sum_{k=1}^{N} R(\mathbf{r}_k + r)\right\rangle, \qquad (11.25)$$

where $\langle \ldots \rangle$ denotes an average over an ensemble of photoevent coordinates. Using Eq. (11.6) and averaging term by term, one obtains

$$\langle C(\mathbf{r})\rangle = N \int_A d^2r'\, p[\mathbf{r}'|V(\mathbf{r}')]R(\mathbf{r}' + \mathbf{r}). \qquad (11.26)$$

Therefore, the mean value of the correlation signal has the same form as in the case when N is Poisson distributed, provided that $\bar{N}$ is replaced by N.

The variance, σ^2, is calculated in a similar manner. By definition,

$$\sigma^2 = \langle C^2(\mathbf{r})\rangle - \langle C(\mathbf{r})\rangle^2, \qquad (11.27)$$

Performing the calculation of $\langle C^2(\mathbf{r})\rangle$ directly using Eq. (11.8), one finds

$$\langle C^2(\mathbf{r})\rangle = N \int_A d^2r'\, p[\mathbf{r}'|V(\mathbf{r}')]R^2(\mathbf{r}' + \mathbf{r}) \qquad (11.28)$$

$$+(N^2 - N)\left[\int_A d^2r'\, p[\mathbf{r}'|V(\mathbf{r}')]R(\mathbf{r}' + \mathbf{r})\right]^2.$$

Using Eqs. (11.26)–(11.28), one finds the following expression for the variance of $C(\mathbf{r})$ with fixed N:

$$\sigma^2 = \sigma_p^2 - \frac{\langle C(\mathbf{r})\rangle^2}{N}, \qquad (11.29)$$

where σ_p^2 is the variance given in Eq. (11.20) with $\bar{N} = N$. Thus, when the number of detected photoevents is fixed, the mean value of the correlation signal is the same as when N is Poisson distributed. However, the variance of the correlation signal with fixed N, Eq. (11.29), is smaller than that obtained when N is Poisson distributed, Eq. (11.20).

3.1.1.5. Probability of Detection and False Alarm

The detection problem can be formulated by using the statistical theory of hypothesis testing (Helstrom, 1968). On the basis of the correlation signal $C(\mathbf{r})$, one must choose between two hypotheses: the null hypothesis, H_0— the reference function $R(\mathbf{r})$ is not present in the input scene $V(\mathbf{r})$; or the positive hypothesis, H_1—the reference function is contained in $V(\mathbf{r})$.

Under hypothesis H_0, the probability density function of the correlation signal is denoted by $P_0(C) = P[C(\mathbf{r})|V(\mathbf{r}') = N(\mathbf{r}')]$, where $N(\mathbf{r}')$ represents a noise (or false) image. Under hypothesis H_1, the probability density function of the correlation signal is denoted by $P_1(C) = P[C(\mathbf{r})|V(\mathbf{r}') = R(\mathbf{r}')]$ where $R(\mathbf{r}')$ is the reference image.

Usually the observer sets a threshold value C_T for the correlation signal. If $C(\mathbf{r}) > C_T$, hypothesis H_1 is chosen. Similarly if $C(\mathbf{r}) < C_T$, the observer chooses hypothesis H_0. However, because of the statistical nature of the signal, the observer occasionally makes an error, regardless of the value of C_T. The probability of choosing H_1 when H_0 is true is called the probability of false alarm and is given by

$$P_{\text{fa}} = \int_{C_T}^{\infty} dC P_0(C). \tag{11.30}$$

The probability of choosing H_1 when H_1 is true is called the probability of detection,

$$P_{\text{d}} = \int_{C_T}^{\infty} dC \, p_1(C). \tag{11.31}$$

The areas under the probability density curves that represent P_{fa} and P_{d} are illustrated in Fig. 11.3.

3.1.2. Effects of Additive Noise

With two-dimensional, photon-counting detectors, the dominant source of additive noise is associated dark counts due primarily to thermal emission of electrons from the photocathode. Let us consider the effects of additive noise on the correlation signal for the case when the number of detected photoevents is Poisson distributed. From Eq. (11.8), we have

$$C(\mathbf{r}) = \sum_{k=1}^{N_V} R(\mathbf{r}_k + \mathbf{r}) + \sum_{k=1}^{N_D} R(\mathbf{r}_k + \mathbf{r}), \tag{11.32}$$

Fig. 11.3.

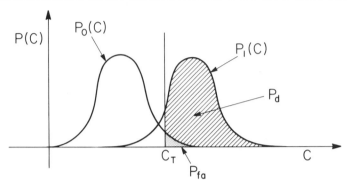

Probability density functions under hypotheses H_0 and H_1.

in which N_V is the number of detected photoevents due to the input scene $V(\mathbf{r})$ and N_D is the number of dark counts occurring in time interval τ. It readily follows that the mean value of the correlation signal is

$$
\langle C(\mathbf{r}) \rangle = \bar{N}_V \int_A d^2r'\, p[\mathbf{r}'|V(\mathbf{r}')]R(\mathbf{r}' + \mathbf{r})
$$

$$
+ \bar{N}_D \int_A d^2r'\, p[\mathbf{r}'|D(\mathbf{r}')]R(\mathbf{r}' + \mathbf{r}),
$$

(11.33)

and the variance is

$$
\sigma^2 = \bar{N}_V \int_A d^2r'\, p[\mathbf{r}'|V(\mathbf{r}')]R^2(\mathbf{r}' + \mathbf{r})
$$

$$
+ \bar{N}_D \int_A d^2r'\, p[\mathbf{r}'|D(\mathbf{r}')]R^2(\mathbf{r}' + \mathbf{r}),
$$

(11.34)

where $\bar{N}_V = \bar{N}$ in Eq. (11.5) and $p[\mathbf{r}'|V(\mathbf{r}')]$ is given in Eq. (11.6). $D(\mathbf{r}')$ represents the spatial distribution of dark counts, $\bar{N}_D = \int_A d^2r D(\mathbf{r})$ and $p[\mathbf{r}'|D(\mathbf{r}')] = D(\mathbf{r}')/\bar{N}_D$. Note that additive noise shifts the mean value of the correlation signal and increases the width of $P[C(\mathbf{r})]$ through σ^2. The effect of additive noise on the correlation signal is the same for all input images; hence, it is easy to take into account when setting the threshold value of the correlation signal to achieve a given probability of detection and false alarm.

3.1.3. Effects of Detector Dead Time

The photon-limited correlation signal in Eq. (11.8) can be written in the following form:

$$C(\mathbf{r}) = \sum_i n_i R(\mathbf{r}_i + r), \qquad (11.35)$$

where $\mathbf{r}_i$ represents the coordinates of the ith pixel of the reference image and n_i is the number of detected photoevents in the pixel [compare with Eq. (11.11)]. In most cases of practical importance for pattern recognition, the correlation signal in Eq. (11.35) will involve a large number of detected photoevents and one may invoke the central limit theorem to approximate the distribution of $C(\mathbf{r})$ to be Gaussian with the mean value given by

$$\langle C(\mathbf{r}) \rangle = \sum_i \langle n_i \rangle R(\mathbf{r}_i + \mathbf{r}) \qquad (11.36)$$

and the variance

$$\sigma_C^2(\mathbf{r}) = \sum_i \sigma_i^2 R^2(\mathbf{r}_i + \mathbf{r}), \qquad (11.37)$$

where $\langle n_i \rangle$ and σ_i^2 denote the mean and variance of the number of photoevents occurring in time interval τ for the ith pixel, respectively. Here, it is assumed that n_i and $n_j (i \neq j)$ are independent random variables.

To estimate the effects of local dead time on the correlation signal, suppose that there are m independent microchannels in a given pixel. In this case the mean value and variance of the ith pixel are given by

$$\langle n_i \rangle = m \langle n_{c,i} \rangle \qquad (11.38)$$

and

$$\sigma_i^2 = m \sigma_{c,i}^2, \qquad (11.39)$$

where $\langle n_{c,i} \rangle$ and $\sigma_{c,i}^2$ denote the mean and the variance of the number of detected photoevents in a single microchannel in the ith pixel, respectively.

The values of $\langle n_{c,i} \rangle$ and $\sigma_{c,i}^2$ are readily calculated from the counting statistics of a single, paralyzable counter (see, e.g., Feller, 1948; Libert, 1975). When the integration time τ is shorter than the local dead time τ_d, one finds

$$\langle n_{c,i} \rangle = \lambda_i \tau e^{-\lambda_i \tau_d} \qquad (11.40)$$

and

$$\sigma_{c,i}^2 = \langle n_{c,i} \rangle [1 - \langle n_{c,i} \rangle], \qquad (11.41)$$

where $\lambda_i = [\eta/(h\bar{v})]V(\mathbf{r}_i)A_c$ represents the count rate incident on the microchannel located at the ith pixel and A_c is the open area of the microchannel. Using Eqs. (11.36)–(11.41), one obtains

$$\langle C(\mathbf{r})\rangle = m \sum_i R(\mathbf{r}_i + \mathbf{r})\langle n_{c,i}\rangle \qquad (11.42)$$

and

$$\sigma_C^2(\mathbf{r}) \cong m \sum_i R^2(\mathbf{r}_i + \mathbf{r})\langle n_{c,i}\rangle, \qquad (11.43)$$

where we have assumed that $\tau \ll \tau_d$ so that $\langle n_{c,i}\rangle$ is much smaller than one and $\sigma_{c,i}^2 \approx \langle n_{c,i}\rangle$, that is, the process is approximately Poissonian with the rate parameter equal to $\langle n_{c,i}\rangle/\tau$. Therefore, the expression for the probability density function of event coordinates when local dead-time effects are present takes the following form:

$$p_d[\mathbf{r}_i|V(\mathbf{r}_i)] = \frac{V(\mathbf{r}_i)e^{-p[\mathbf{r}_i|V(\mathbf{r}_i)]R\tau_d/m}}{\sum_i V(\mathbf{r}_i)e^{-p[\mathbf{r}_i|V(\mathbf{r}_i)]R\tau_d/m}}, \qquad (11.44)$$

where $p[\mathbf{r}_i|V(\mathbf{r}_i)]$ is given in Eq. (11.6) and

$$R = \frac{m\eta A_c}{h\bar{v}} \sum_i V(\mathbf{r}_i)$$

is the total input rate of photoevents. Using Eq. (11.44) instead of Eq. (11.6), one can readily calculate the statistics of the correlation signal with dead time when the total number of detected photoevents is fixed [see Eqs. (11.20), (11.26), and (11.29)]. An illustration of the effects of dead time on the correlation signal is given in Section 3.2.

3.2. Scene Matching at Low Light Levels

The results in Section 3.1 are applicable for general reference functions and input scenes (Morris, 1984b; Morris et al., 1985). The capabilities of this low-light-level approach to pattern recognition can be predicted theoretically by studying the probability distributions of the correlation signal when the input scene (1) matches the reference function stored in computer memory, and (2) is a typical background image encountered in the given application. From these probability density functions, one can determine the number of detected photoevents that is required to achieve a given probability of detection and false alarm.

In this section we consider the correlation signal obtained when the input scene is correlated with a classical intensity image of the reference object. In this case the correlation output, $C(\mathbf{r})$ in Eq. (11.8), corresponds to that of a matched filter. When N, the number of detected photoevents, is Poisson distributed, the mean value and variance of the correlation signal are given in Eqs. (11.19) and (11.20), respectively. If N is fixed, the mean value and variance of $C(\mathbf{r})$ are given in Eqs. (11.26) and (11.29).

As a simple example, consider a reference image with a classical irradiance given by

$$R(\mathbf{r}) = R(x, y) = \begin{cases} 1 - |x/L| & ; -L \leq x \leq L, -L \leq y \leq L \\ 0 & ; \text{otherwise} \end{cases} \qquad (11.45)$$

and let the background (or false) image $B(x,y)$ be uniform; see Fig. 11.4.

Fig. 11.4. _____

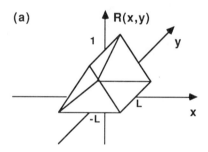

(a)

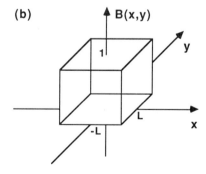

(b)

(a) Intensity distribution of reference image given in Eq. (11.45); (b) intensity distribution of background (or false) image.

When N is Poisson distributed, the characteristic functions $\Phi_0(\omega)$ and $\Phi_1(\omega)$ associated with the background and reference image, respectively, can be calculated using Eqs. (11.17) and (11.45) (Morris, 1984a). The probability density functions $P_0(C)$ and $P_1(C)$, see Section 3.1.1.5, are found numerically by taking the fast Fourier transform of $\Phi_0(\omega)$ and $\Phi_1(\omega)$. In these calculations it is assumed that the reference window offset $\mathbf{r} = 0$ and the ref-

Fig. 11.5. ──────────────────────────────────────

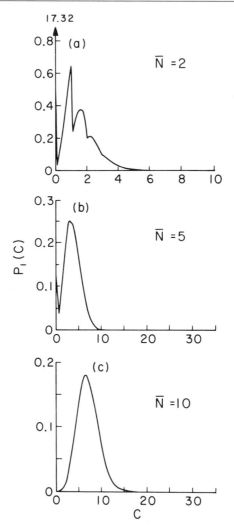

Probability density function $P_1(C)$ with (a) $\tilde{N} = 2$, (b) $\tilde{N} = 5$, and (c) $\tilde{N} = 10$.

erence image and the input scene have area $A = 4L^2$. In Fig. 11.5, the probability density function $P_1(C)$ is shown for several values of $\bar{N}$. Notice that as $\bar{N}$ gets large, $P_1(C)$ tends to a Gaussian form.

The probability density functions of the correlation signal under the null and positive hypotheses with different values of $\bar{N}$ are shown in Fig. 11.6.

Fig. 11.6. ───

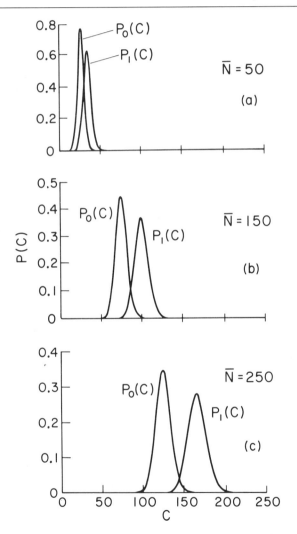

Probability density functions for null and positive hypotheses with (a) $\bar{N} = 50$, (b) $\bar{N} = 150$, and (c) $\bar{N} = 250$.

The mean value and variance of the correlation signal are calculated using Eqs. (11.19), (11.20), and (11.45). Under the null hypothesis [$V(x, y) = B(x, y)$], $\mu_0 = \langle C(0) \rangle = \bar{N}/2$ and $\sigma_0^2 = \bar{N}/3$. For the positive hypothesis [$V(x, y) = R(x, y)$], $\mu_1 = \langle C(0) \rangle = 2\bar{N}/3$ and $\sigma_1^2 = \bar{N}/2$. One sees that the theoretical values for the mean value and variance and the values obtained from the probability density functions in Figs. 11.5 and 11.6 are in good agreement.

The probability of detection and false alarm can be estimated easily by assuming $P_0(C)$ and $P_1(C)$ are Gaussian distributed with the mean values and variances given in the preceding paragraph. Figure 11.7 contains a plot of the probability of detection versus the probability of false alarm [receiver operating characteristic (ROC) curves] for different values of $\bar{N}$.

If greater accuracy is required in the tails of the probability density functions, one can use the variable-spacing technique reported by Richter and Smits (1974) or the saddlepoint approximation described by Helstrom (1978, 1979).

Let us now consider recognition of detailed images, such as the engraved portraits of George Washington, Abraham Lincoln, and Andrew Jackson

Fig. 11.7.

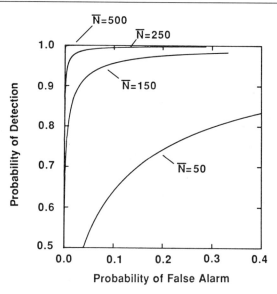

ROC curves for the reference and the background object shown in Fig. 11.4 for different values of $\bar{N}$.

Fig. 11.8.

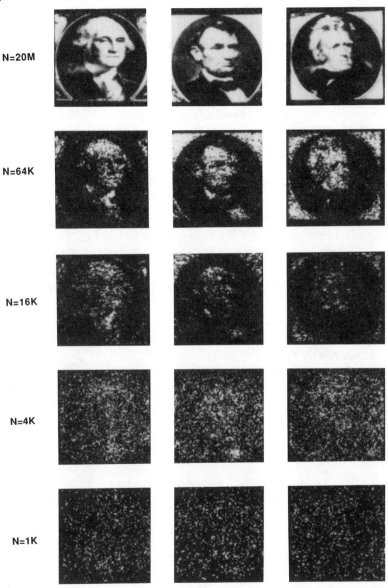

N=20M

N=64K

N=16K

N=4K

N=1K

Images of engraved portraits obtained using a two-dimensional, photon-counting detection system: first column, portrait of George Washington; second column, Abraham Lincoln; third column, Andrew Jackson. N is number of detected photoevents over the entire image. The spatial coordinates of each detected photoevent are digitized to 8-bit accuracy.

shown in Fig. 11.8. The photographs in Fig. 11.8 were obtained by imaging portraits from U.S. currency onto a two-dimensional, photon-counting detector (Electro-Optical Products Div., ITT Corporation, Model F4146M). The detector was connected to position-computing electronics (Surface Science Laboratories, Model 2401) to determine the spatial coordinates of detected photoevents. The spatial coordinates of the detected events were digitized to a spatial resolution of 256 × 256 pixels and then sent to a microcomputer for display. Illumination was provided by fluorescent room lights. Neutral-density filters were inserted between the imaging lens and the detector to reduce the count rate to approximately 50,000 counts/sec. In each image a fixed number of detected photoevents was collected. The number of detected events for the images in a given row is indicated at the left.

The probability density functions (PDFs) of the correlation signal in Eq. (11.8) are calculated using the images in the top row of Fig. 11.8. For fairly detailed imagery one expects that the number of detected photoevents will need to be relatively large for reliable recognition; hence, the approximation that the PDF of the correlation signal is Gaussian distributed should be fairly accurate.

Since the reference and input images have the same area A, we will again take the reference window offset $\mathbf{r} = 0$. For this case the correlation signal will be denoted by C,

$$C = C(0) = \sum_{k=1}^{N} R(\mathbf{r}_k) . \tag{11.46}$$

When N is fixed [see Eqs. (11.26) and (11.29)], the mean value and variance of C are

$$\langle C \rangle = \frac{N \int_A d^2 r V(\mathbf{r}) R(\mathbf{r})}{\int_A d^2 r V(\mathbf{r})} , \tag{11.47}$$

$$\sigma^{2c} = \frac{N \int_A d^2 r V(\mathbf{r}) R^2(\mathbf{r})}{\int_A d^2 r V(\mathbf{r})} - \frac{\langle C \rangle^2}{N} , \tag{11.48}$$

respectively.

The image of George Washington ($N = 20 \times 10^6$) (see Fig. 11.8) is used as the reference function $R(\mathbf{r})$. The number of pixels in the reference image is $N_{pix} = 128 \times 160 = 20,480$. Based on Eqs. (11.47) and (11.48), Gaussian PDFs of the correlation signal are calculated; these results are plotted in Fig. 11.9 for the case when the number of detected photoevents from the entire input image is (a) $N = 250$, (b) $N = 500$, and (c) $N = 1000$. Curve I is the PDF $P(C)$ of the correlation signal, C, in Eq. (11.46), when the input image is the portrait of George Washington. Curve II is the PDF when the input image is the portrait of Abraham Lincoln; and curve III is the PDF when Andrew Jackson's portrait is input.

Laboratory measurements of the correlation signal are shown in histogram form in Fig. 11.10. One thousand realizations of the correlation signal were made for each input image. In each realization the number of detected photoevents $N = 1000$. The solid curves are the theoretical predictions for the PDFs of the correlation signal assuming Gaussian statistics with the mean value and variance given by Eq. (11.47) and (11.48), respectively.

In operation, the recognition decision is based on a single realization of the correlation signal. N photoevents from the input image are detected, and the resulting correlation signal is compared with a threshold value C_T. If the value of the correlation signal exceeds C_T, the reference image is said to be present in the input; if not, the reference object is said to be absent. The probability of detection and the probability of false alarm are calculated in advance from the PDFs of the correlation signal when the input is the reference and a noise image, respectively. Figure 11.11 contains ROC curves for the portraits of Washington and Lincoln for different values of N. The portrait of George Washington was used as the reference function.

In Fig. 11.10, one sees excellent agreement between theoretical predictions (solid curves) and the laboratory measurements (histograms). It is important to note that in the theoretical predictions for the correlation signal, no corrections were made for additive noise or dead-time effects; these effects are simply not important when the count rate is 50,000 counts/sec and N is a few thousand counts. In the experiments, the dark-count rate was observed to be approximately 50 counts/sec. At a rate of 50,000 counts/sec, on average, there is only one detected photoevent out of a thousand that is associated with additive noise; hence, the contribution due to additive noise is negligible.

Similarly, for the count rate of 50,000 counts/sec, dead-time effects associated with the microchannel plates are not important. It is interesting, however, to ask at what count rate do dead-time effects become significant, and how does dead time affect the capability to distinguish between the

Fig. 11.9.

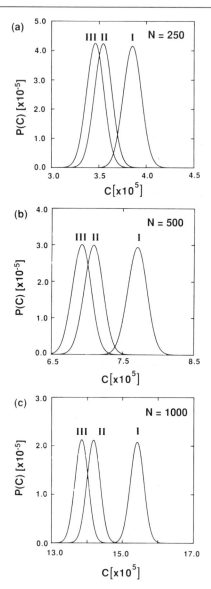

Probability density functions of the correlation signal when the input image $V(\mathbf{r})$ is the portrait of (I) George Washington, (II) Abraham Lincoln, (III) Andrew Jackson. The number of detected photoevents is (a) $N = 250$, (b) $N = 500$, and (c) $N = 1000$. The reference function $R(\mathbf{r})$ in all cases is the portrait of George Washington with $N = 20$ million (see Fig. 11.8). The reference image and input images contain 128×160 picture elements.

Fig. 11.10.

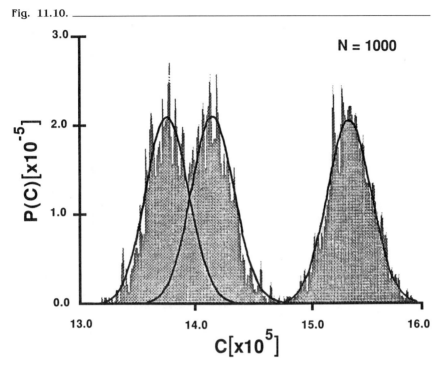

Histogram of correlation values obtained from laboratory measurements of the photon-limited correlation signal when the input object V(r) is the portrait of (I) Washington, (II) Lincoln, and (III) Jackson. In each realization the total number of detected photoevents N = 1000 (see bottom row of Fig. 11.8). The reference function was the portrait of Washington with N = 20 million.

various input images? The statistics of the correlation signal with dead time and fixed N can be obtained by using Eq. (11.44), instead of Eq. (11.6), to calculate the mean value and variance [see Eqs. (11.20), (11.26), and (11.29)]. Curves for the PDFs of the (auto)correlation signal predicted when the portrait of George Washington is both the input and the reference function are shown in Fig. 11.12a. Curve A is the PDF $P(C)$ of the correlation signal with no dead time. Curve B is the PDF of the correlation signal that would be found when the total input rate R = 500,000 counts/sec, and curve C is the PDF when R = 1,000,000 counts/sec. For curves B and C, it is assumed that N = 1000, m = 15 and τ_d = 50 msec. In Fig. 11.12b, PDFs for the correlation signal obtained when the input object: (I) Washington, (II) Lincoln, and (III) Jackson are shown. The image of Washington (N =

Fig. 11.11.

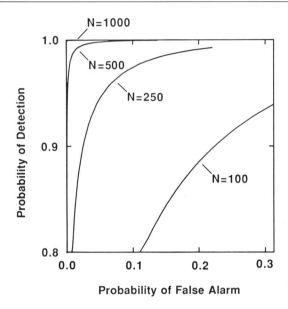

ROC curves for the portraits of Washington and Lincoln for different values of *N*.

20×10^6) is taken as the reference function; the number of detected photoevents $N = 1000$, $m = 15$, and $\tau_d = 50$ msec. The solid curves are the theoretical predictions for $P(C)$ assuming no local dead-time effects. The dotted curves are the theoretical predictions for $P(C)$ with local dead time assuming an input count rate of $R = 1,000,000$ counts/sec. In addition to the overall shift of the curves, notice that the separation between the PDFs for the various input images changes when local dead-time effects are included. In the calculation of $P(C)$ with local dead time, two basic assumptions are made: a given microchannel behaves as a paralyzable counter, and the channels in a given pixel operate as independent counters.

In summary, when the image of the reference object is used as the reference function and the input image is registered with respect to the reference image, we have found that often only a small number of detected photoevents from the input scene are needed to make an accurate recognition decision. While the requirement for image registration may be a limitation for some recognition problems, it may be well suited in other applications, such as recognition of spectral signatures. To identify spectral signatures, one can use a classical intensity image of a particular spectrum as the ref-

Fig. 11.12.

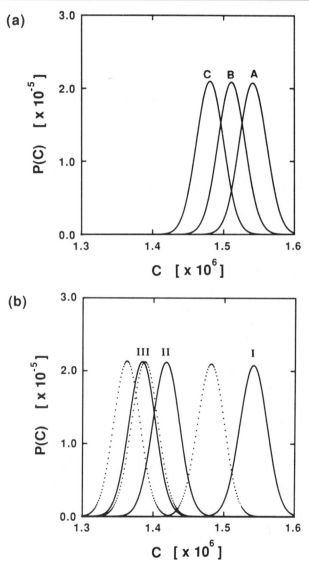

Effects of dead time on the correlation signal. (a) PDFs of the (auto)correlation signal found when the portrait of Washington is both the input image and reference function: (A) $P(C)$ with no dead-time effects, (B) $P(C)$ obtained when $R = 0.5$ million counts/sec, (C) $P(C)$ obtained when R is one million counts/sec. (b) PDFs of the correlation signal obtained when the input image is the portrait of (I) Washington, (II) Lincoln, (III) Jackson. In (I)–(III), the portrait of Washington [$N = 20$M] serves the reference function. Other parameters [see Eq. (11.44)] are: $m = 15$, $N = 1000$, and $\tau_d = 50$ msec.

erence function and correlate it with photon-limited input spectra detected in the output of a spectrometer.

However, when many objects are present in the input scene, or when the object(s) are in a cluttered, noisy environment, it becomes necessary to search the input scene for the presence of the object(s) to be identified. In this case the input scene is searched by scanning the reference-function window via the offset address **r** over the input scene [see Eq. (11.8) and Fig. 11.2] (Isberg and Morris, 1988). For example, if one considers the input scene to be composed of m independent cells and shifts the center of the reference window to each of the m locations in the input image, the probabilities of detection $P_{d,m}$ and false alarm $P_{fa,m}$ for detecting the reference object within input scene are readily calculated in terms of the probabilities of detection, $P_{d,1}$, and false alarm, $P_{fa,1}$, at a single cell (Goodenough, 1975; Barrett and Swindell, 1981). The number of detected photoevents needed to produce the required values of $P_{d,1}$ and $P_{fa,1}$ can be computed as discussed in Section 3.1.

To reduce the computation burden of the search, a two-stage search procedure can be used (see Vanderburg and Rosenfeld, 1977; Isberg and Morris, 1988). In the first stage of the search, each cell of the input scene is sampled using a small number of detected photons. The correlation threshold C_T is set so as to obtain the required probability of detection. The first stage of the search produces a small number of likely locations for the reference object—the probability of detection is high, but so is the probability of false alarm. In the second stage of the search, these likely locations are examined using an increased number of detected photoevents to obtain the required probability of false alarm.

3.3. Distortion-Invariant Filters

In most applications it is desirable to have an automatic recognition system that can tolerate certain variations in input images, which are not important as far as a recognition decision is concerned. These variations can be divided into two basic categories: geometrical distortions of the image (e.g., rotation, scale, and position) and intrinsic variations of the image (e.g., changes in illumination, image clutter, and object occlusions). One could approach this problem by using multiplexed filters in which a separate reference function (filter) is used for each scale and orientation of the input object, but this leads to a computationally intense system design that is difficult to implement.

A more elegant approach to the problem of image distortion is to choose a reference function $R(\mathbf{r})$ so that the correlation output is invariant to the distortion of the input image. Mellin transforms, which have scale- and position-invariant properties have been used (Casasent and Psaltis, 1976a, 1976b). Circular-harmonic filters, initially suggested by Hsu et al. (1982) and Hsu and Arsenault (1982), have proved useful for rotation-invariant pattern recognition (Hsu and Arsenault, 1984; Wu and Stark, 1984, 1985; Isberg and Morris, 1986; Arsenault, 1988). Fourier-Mellin descriptors for rotation, scale, and position invariance have also been reported (Sheng and Arsenault, 1986, 1987; Wu and Stark, 1986; Isberg and Morris, 1987). Other approaches to distortion-invariant filtering include synthetic discriminant filters (Casasent and Rozzi, 1984), and the "lock and tumbler" filter (Schils and Sweeney, 1986).

Intrinsic variations within images can be treated as a problem in image classification, i.e., the input image is to be identified as a member of some category or class of images. A broader interpretation of image classification reveals that image recognition in realistic environments is always, in fact, a sorting problem. Generally, input images are subject to clutter, variations in illumination, viewing angle, defects, occlusions, etc. By treating a set of images of a given object as an image class, one can formulate the problem of image recognition in realistic environments as an image classification problem. Among the most notable statistical classification algorithms are those proposed by Fukunaga and Koontz (1970), Foley and Sammon (1975), and the Hotelling trace algorithm (Fukunaga, 1972), all of which have been used in image-classification schemes (Leger and Lee, 1982a, 1982b; Gu and Lee, 1984; Casasent and Sharma, 1984; Wu and Stark, 1985; Wernick and Morris, 1986).

In this section we consider three examples of distortion-invariant filtering at low light levels. Experimental results for circular-harmonic filters, Fourier-Mellin descriptors, and maximum-likelihood image classification are given.

3.3.1. Rotation-Invariance Using Circular-Harmonic Filters

Any two-dimensional function $f(r, \theta)$ can be represented in terms of its circular-harmonic components as follows:

$$f(r, \theta) = \sum_{m=-\infty}^{\infty} F_m(r)e^{im\theta}, \qquad (11.49)$$

where

$$F_m(r) = \frac{1}{2\pi} \int_0^{2\pi} f(r, \theta)e^{-im\theta}d\theta .$$ (11.50)

In Eq. (11.49), $F_m(r, \theta) = F_m(r) \exp(im\theta)$ is said to be the mth circular-harmonic component of the function $f(r, \theta)$. Rotation-invariant filtering can be achieved by taking the reference function $R(\mathbf{r})$ in Eq. (11.8) to be the complex conjugate of a single (or multiple) circular-harmonic component(s) of the reference object, e.g.,

$$R(\mathbf{r}) = F_m^*(r, \theta) = F_m^*(r)e^{-im\theta} .$$ (11.51)

When the offset coordinate $\mathbf{r} = 0$, the correlation signal, $C(\mathbf{r}, \alpha)$, is an inner product of an input function $g(r, \theta + \alpha)$ rotated by an angle α with respect to the reference function $F_m^*(r, \theta)$:

$$C(0, \alpha) = \int_0^{2\pi} \int_0^{\infty} g(r, \theta + \alpha)F_m^*(r, \theta)r\,dr\,d\theta .$$ (11.52)

Using the expansion in Eq. (11.49) for $g(r, \theta + \alpha)$ and substituting into Eq. (11.52) yields

$$C(0, \alpha) = 2\pi e^{im\alpha} \int_0^{\infty} G_m(r)F_m^*(r)r\,dr ,$$ (11.53)

in which the modulus of $C(0,\alpha)$ attains its maximum value when $G_m(r) = F_m(r)$ as given by the Schwartz inequality. Notice that only the mth circular-harmonic component of the input contributes to $C(0, \alpha)$ in Eq. (11.52) owing to the orthogonality of the θ integration and that the rotation angle α appears only in the phase term $\exp(im\alpha)$. Hence, the modulus of $C(0, \alpha)$ is independent of the rotation angle of the input image. If the reference image is input, its orientation can be obtained from the ratio of the real and imaginary parts of the correlation signal. The rotation angle α is given by

$$\alpha = \frac{1}{m} \tan^{-1} \left[\frac{\text{Im}\{C(0, \alpha)\}}{\text{Re}\{C(0, \alpha)\}} \right] ,$$ (11.54)

which can be calculated easily when the correlation is implemented digitally. The rotation angle α is far more difficult to obtain in an optical implementation because most detection schemes are intensity based.

   The magnitude of the correlation peak obtained in Eq. (11.53) will depend on the particular harmonic that is chosen as the reference function. The magnitude of $C(\mathbf{r}, \alpha)$ also depends on the location of the point about which the reference object is expanded; this location is referred to as the expansion center. The magnitude of $C(\mathbf{r}, \alpha)$ will be an absolute maximum only when the "proper center" is chosen as the expansion center (Hsu et al., 1982). Several investigations using the centroid of the image (rather than the proper center) as an expansion center have been demonstrated to be effective for rotation-invariant image recognition (Hsu and Arsenault, 1984; Wu and Stark, 1984; Isberg and Morris, 1986).

Experiments to test the recognition capabilities of the photon-limited correlation scheme when a complex circular-harmonic filter is used as the reference function $R(\mathbf{r})$ were performed. In the experiments 35-mm-format input scenes, illuminated by an incoherent light source, were imaged onto a two-dimensional, photon-counting detector (ITT Corporation, Model F4146M). Neutral density filters were inserted to obtain a count rate of approximately 30,000 counts/sec. The (x, y) spatial coordinates of the detected photoevents were digitized to 8-bit accuracy and sent to a digital computer for processing. The number of detected photoevents, N, [see Eq. (11.8)] was fixed.

Figure 11.13 shows the input images and their associated circular-harmonic components used in the correlation experiments. The second ($m = 2$) circular-harmonic of the vise grips (computed about the centroid of the object) is taken as the reference function. The pliers and the movable-jaw wrench are used as false objects.

To test the performance of the circular-harmonic filter at low light levels, correlations between photon-limited tool images and the complex circular-harmonic reference function stored in computer memory were computed. Measurements were taken with the input reference object at various orientations (0, 90, 180, and 270 degrees with respect to the reference); the false objects were imaged onto the detector at the orientations shown in Fig. 11.13. Excellent agreement between theory and experiments was observed (Isberg and Morris, 1986). In accordance with theory, the magnitude of the correlation signal was found to be independent of the object-rotation angle α.

In Fig. 11.14, ROC curves are plotted for the vise grips (reference object) and the movable-jaw wrench (false object). Note that with $N = 3000$ detected photoevents, the probability of error is extremely small (approximately one error in 100,000 realizations). Based on theoretical predictions, one finds that if the image of the vise grips were used as the reference function (i.e., the matched-filter case), the same discrimination capability can be achieved with approximately 1000 detected photoevents. Hence, by increasing the number of detected events by only a factor of three, one can add rotational invariance into the recognition system.

Fig. 11.13.

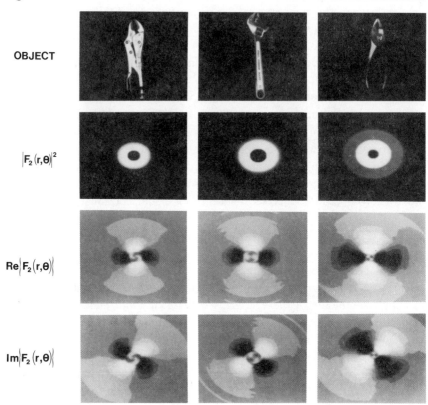

OBJECT

$\left|F_2(r,\theta)\right|^2$

$\mathrm{Re}\left|F_2(r,\theta)\right|$

$\mathrm{Im}\left|F_2(r,\theta)\right|$

Objects and associated second-order circular harmonics. First row, classical intensity images; second row, squared modulus of respective second circular-
harmonic components; third row, real parts of second circular-harmonic components; fourth row, imaginary parts of second circular-harmonic components.

Measurements of the accuracy to which the orientation angle α can be
predicted were also conducted. A histogram of the values of the orientation
angle α obtained using 1000 realizations of the complex correlation signal
is shown in Fig. 11.15. The number of detected photoevents in each realization was $N = 3000$. The rotation angle α is obtained by using Eq. (11.54).
The solid curve is the theoretical prediction for the probability density function $P(\alpha)$ for the rotation angle α. In this experiment the mean value and
variance of α were $89.6°$ and $0.705°$, respectively.

Fig. 11.14.

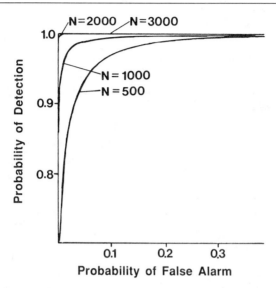

ROC curves for the vise grips (reference object) and the movable-jaw wrench
for different values of N.

Fig. 11.15.

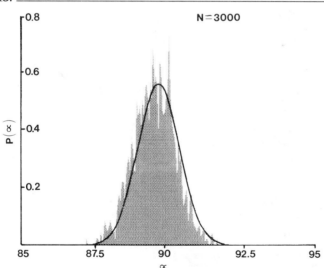

Histogram of laboratory measurements for the rotation angle α when the vise
grips are input at 90° with respect to the reference image. The number of detected photoevents in each realization is $N = 3000$.

3.3.2.   Fourier-Mellin Descriptors

Rotation-, scale- and position-invariant image recognition can be accomplished through the use of Fourier-Mellin descriptors (FMDs). In this method either the radial moments or the radial Mellin transform of dominant terms in the ciruclar-harmonic expansion of a reference object are computed about the centroid of the image. The modulus of these descriptors is used to define invariant features. The invariant features of an input scene are compared with the corresponding features of the reference object. A recognition decision is based on the sum of the squared differences of the features, D^2. If D^2 is less than some predetermined threshold value, the input is said to be the same as the reference. If D^2 exceeds the threshold, then the input is said to be different than the reference.

The invariant features $\Phi_{s,m}$ of the input image $V(\mathbf{r}) = V(r, \theta)$ are given by

$$\Phi_{s,m} = \frac{|M_{s,m}|}{|M_{s,0}|}, \tag{11.55}$$

where the Fourier-Mellin descriptors $M_{s,m}$ are

$$M_{s,m} = \int_0^{2\pi} \int_0^\infty V(r, \theta) r^{s-1} e^{-im\theta} dr d\theta. \tag{11.56}$$

The modulus of $M_{s,m}$ is invariant with respect to rotation and changes in position of the input image. If the Mellin transform variable s is pure imaginary, then the modulus of $M_{s,m}$ is also scale invariant. On the other hand, if the transform variable s is real (e.g., an integer), then the normalization by the 0th order descriptor [Eq. (11.55)] provides scale invariance.

Invariant features can be estimated using quantum-limited images in the following manner. If one chooses the reference function, which is stored in computer memory, to be

$$R(r, \theta) = r^{s-2} e^{-im\theta}, \tag{11.57}$$

where the coordinates (r, θ) are taken with respect to the centroid of the input image, the mean value of the subsequent photon-limited correlation signal is given by

$$\langle C_{s,m} \rangle = \frac{N \int_0^{2\pi} \int_0^\infty V(r, \theta) r^{s-1} e^{-im\theta} dr d\theta}{\int_0^{2\pi} \int_0^\infty V(r, \theta) r dr d\theta}, \tag{11.58}$$

where N is the number of detected photoevents. Notice that $\langle C_{s,m} \rangle$ is directly proportional to the classical intensity descriptor $M_{s,m}$ in Eq. (11.56). Also,

$$\frac{|\langle C_{s,m} \rangle|}{|\langle C_{0,m} \rangle|} = \frac{|M_{s,m}|}{|M_{s,0}|} = \Phi_{s,m} \qquad (11.59)$$

if different photoevents are used to compute $\langle C_{s,m} \rangle$ and $\langle C_{0,m} \rangle$.

The recognition capabilities of the photon-limited estimates of the FMDs were tested in laboratory experiments. A set of transparencies (35-mm format) were made using engraved portraits from U.S. currency, at relative magnifications of 1.0, 1.25, 1.5, and 1.75. These transparencies (input at various orientations) were imaged onto the two-dimensional, photon-counting detector. Five thousand detected photoevents were used to determine the location of the centroid of the input object in each case. The invarient features were computed using the reference function in Eq. (11.57) with $s = 2$ (after Sheng and Arsenault, 1986). The distance in feature space was computed between the quantum-limited input image and the reference image (George Washington with a relative magnification of unity). To test the theoretical predictions, one thousand measurements of the feature-space distance D^2,

$$D^2 = \sum_m [\Phi_{2,m}^{\text{input}} - \Phi_{2,m}^{\text{ref.}}]^2, \qquad (11.60)$$

were performed for each input image to provide accurate estimates for the mean values and standard deviations of D^2.

It was found that three circular harmonics ($m = 1$, 2, and 6) were sufficient to provide an error rate of 1×10^{-5} when 5000 detected photoevents were used to construct the estimates of the FMD for each value of m (Isberg and Morris, 1987). The probability density functions for D^2, based on experimental values for the mean values and variances of D^2 for the different input images, are shown in Fig. 11.16. In Fig. 11.16, a threshold value $D_T^2 = 0.08$ provides the error rate of 1×10^{-5} stated above.

3.3.3. Image Classification

In certain applications it may be desirable to ascertain the category or class of images to which an input image belongs. An image class may, for example, include images of a single scene in which variations in background content, illumination angle, and other attributes are included. Printed characters in various fonts may likewise compose a class of images. In this section photon-limited image correlation is applied to the problem of sorting two image classes. Advantages provided by this technique include the ability

Fig. 11.16.

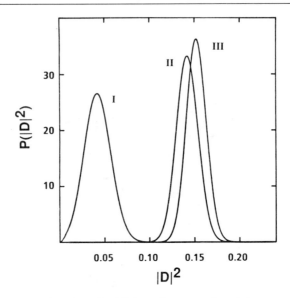

Probability density functions for D^2, based on experimental measurements of the mean value and variance of D^2 for the images of Washington, Lincoln, and Jackson. The invariant features $\Phi_{2,m}$ (m = 1, 2, and 6) of Washington were used as the reference.

of the system to operate in incoherent illumination and at low light levels. The system is also suitable for use in well-illuminated environments where it can be exploited for its rapid rate of operation. The high rate at which images can be identified arises from the efficiency of the photon-correlation calculation.

The photon-limited image consists of a histogram of the spatial coordinates of detected photoevents. Hence, a digitized photon-limited image takes the form of a two-dimensional array n. At zero offset, the cross correlation between of a photon-limited input image n and a reference function $R(\mathbf{r})$ is given by

$$C = \sum_i n_i R(\mathbf{r}_i), \qquad (11.61)$$

where $\mathbf{r}_i$ represents the coordinates of the ith pixel of the reference image and n_i is the number of detected photoevents in that pixel. In practice, most of the n_i's are zero; hence, the calculation consists simply of a summation of the values of the reference function $R(\mathbf{r})$ sampled at the spatial coordinates of the detected photoevents.

Our goal is to construct a reference function $R(\mathbf{r})$ that, when applied according to Eq. (11.61), yields useful information for class discrimination. The maximum-likelihood approach is found to be particularly well suited to the problem of sorting two classes of photon-limited images (Wernick and Morris, 1986).

The maximum-likelihood decision criterion (Melsa and Cohn, 1978) is to choose the hypothesis corresponding to the state that was most likely to have given rise to the observed data. The central quantity in the theory is the likelihood ratio ℓ, given by

$$\ell(\mathbf{n}) = \frac{p[\mathbf{n}|H^{(1)}]}{p[\mathbf{n}|H^{(2)}]},\tag{11.62}$$

where $\mathbf{n}$ represents the photon-limited input image and hypothesis $H^{(j)}$ ($j = 1, 2$) indicates that the input image is a member of class j. The procedure that we will use to classify an input image is as follows. When a photon-limited image $\mathbf{n}$ is input, the ratio $\ell(\mathbf{n})$ is calculated. To select the most probable source of the detected photoevents, class 1 is chosen when $\ell(\mathbf{n}) > 1$ and class 2 is chosen when $\ell(\mathbf{n}) < 1$.

To evaluate $\ell(\mathbf{n})$, training sets of prototype images must be used to provide information about the classes. The conditional probabilities appearing in Eq. (11.62) are then given by a weighted sum of the conditional probabilities associated with the prototype images for the class, i.e.,

$$p[\mathbf{n}|H^{(j)}] = \sum_{k=1}^{M_j} p[H_k^{(j)}]\,p[\mathbf{n}|H_k^{(j)}],\tag{11.63}$$

where $H_k^{(j)}$ indicates the hypothesis that the input image is the kth element of class j, $p[H_k^{(j)}]$ denotes the *a priori* probability for that image, and M_j represents the number of prototype images for class j.

The quantity $p[\mathbf{n}|H_k^{(j)}]$ can be specified by treating the photoevent counts in $\mathbf{n}$ as independent, Poisson-distributed random variables so that

$$p[\mathbf{n}|H_k^{(j)}] = \prod_i \frac{[s_{i,k}^{(j)}]^{n_i} e^{-s_{i,k}^{(j)}}}{n_i!},\tag{11.64}$$

where $s_{i,k}^{(j)}$ is the conditional mean for the number of detected photoevents in the ith pixel of image k of class j,

$$s_{i,k}^{(j)} = E[n_i|H_k^{(j)}].\tag{11.65}$$

For pictures of the same class, $s_{i,k}^{(j)}$ is approximately equal to the expected value of number of counts in the ith pixel of the average image $\mathbf{m}_j$ associated with class j, i.e.,

$$s_{i,k}^{(j)} \cong [\mathbf{m}_j]_i ,   \tag{11.66}$$

where

$$[\mathbf{m}_j]_i = \frac{1}{M_j} \sum_{k=1}^{M_j} s_{i,k}^{(j)} .   \tag{11.67}$$

Frequently, for convenience, the log-likelihood ratio $\ln\{\ell(\mathbf{n})\}$ replaces the likelihood ratio $\ell(\mathbf{n})$ as the decision parameter. Substituting from Eqs. (11.63), (11.64), and (11.66) into Eq. (11.62) and taking the natural logarithm, we obtain

$$\ln\{\ell(\mathbf{n})\} \cong \sum_i \ln\left\{\frac{[\mathbf{m}_1]_i^{n_i} e^{-[\mathbf{m}_1]_i}}{[\mathbf{m}_2]_i^{n_i} e^{-[\mathbf{m}_2]_i}}\right\}   \tag{11.68}$$

$$= \sum_i n_i \ln\left(\frac{[\mathbf{m}_1]_i}{[\mathbf{m}_2]_i}\right) + \sum_i \{[\mathbf{m}_2]_i - [\mathbf{m}_1]_i\} .$$

Comparing Eqs. (11.61) and (11.68), it is seen that the natural logarithm term serves as the reference function for maximum-likelihood image classification at low light levels; it is a component of a vector that can be calculated in advance and stored in computer memory. The term involving the difference of class means is a bias, which is independent of the input image; it simply changes the threshold value of $\ln\{\ell(\mathbf{n})\}$ that is used to decide between the two classes. Therefore, in operation, evaluation of the log-likelihood ratio reduces to the table lookup and addition procedure that we seek.

Experiments to compare the performance of various image-classification methods at low light levels have been performed (Wernick and Morris, 1986). In these experiments two object sets were used: characters (F's and R's) and tools (hammers and pliers), see Fig. 11.17.

Reference functions were constructed for maximum-likelihood classification, the Fukunaga-Koontz transform, and average filtering. The reference functions used in the character-recognition experiments are illustrated in Fig. 11.18. Notice that the prominent feature of each reference function suggests the distinction between an F and an R.

To evaluate the performance of the various algorithms we used as a figure of merit the number of detected photoevents required to reduce the probability of error (i.e., the fraction of decisions that are incorrect) to 10^{-4}. The results obtained for the various methods are summarized in Table 11.1. Note that, for both sets of object classes, the classification techniques have the

Fig. 11.17.

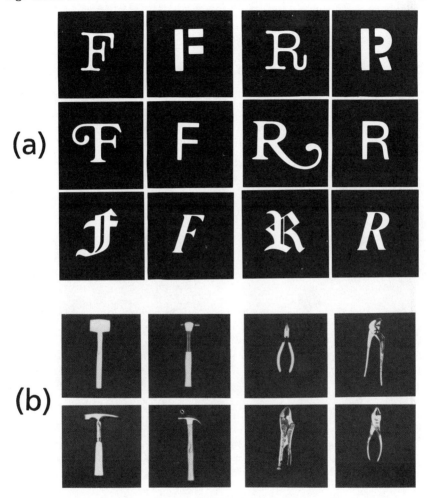

Image classes used in classification experiments. The character data set (a) consists of seven training (prototype) fonts and five test fonts; the tool data set (b) contains 10 training images and four test images for each class.

same performance ranking. In both cases the maximum-likelihood solution, Eq. (11.68), yields the best results.

The classification techniques illustrated above are designed for sorting of two image classes. The generalization to multiple classes is most readily obtained through application of a pairwise voting logic in which pairs of

Fig. 11.18.

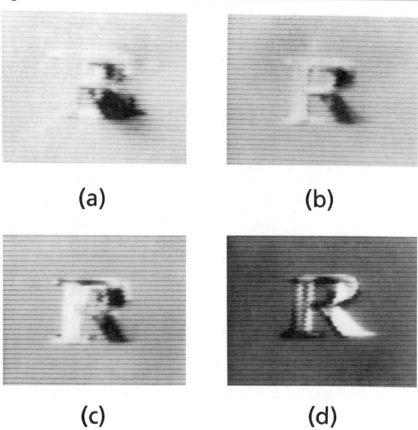

(a)   (b)

(c)   (d)

Reference functions for character discrimination: (a) maximum-likelihood detection; (b) difference of class means, (c), (d) Fukunaga-Koontz basis vectors. In each case, a bias is added for display purposes.

TABLE 11.1

Number of Detected Photoevents Required to Achieve a Probability of Error of 10^{-4}

Classification Technique*	Tools	Characters
Maximum likelihood	43	146
Difference of means	91	246
Fukunaga-Koontz	136	965

* Note that the performance of the various classification strategies has the same ranking for both sets of object classes.

image classes are successfully compared. On each pairwise decision, one class is eliminated. Thus, if K classes are to be considered, then $(K - 1)$ correlations must be performed. In a hard-wired system, many reference function may be applied in parallel to the incoming photoevent data. The resulting correlation values may be passed to a system that implements the voting logic.

4.
Summary

At low light levels, the mean value of the photon-limited correlation signal given in Eq. (11.8) is directly proportional to the classical-intensity correlation function [see Eqs. (11.19) and (11.26)]. Hence, it is clear that if a reference filter is to work well at low light levels it must also be a good filter at classical intensities. The rationale for the use of photon-limited images is twofold: a) the input scene may be naturally photon limited, b) given a classical-intensity input image, because of computational efficiency, in many cases it may be better to reduce the light level and use photon-correlation methods to process the images. Often only a sparse sampling (a small number of detected photoevents) of the input image is needed for accurate image recognition. The required processing [see Eq. (11.8)] is simply a table look-up and addition procedure. Hence, if the number of detected photoevents is not too large, the time needed to detect, process, and make a recognition decision can be quite short. For example, if 1000 photoevents are needed to distinguish between a set of objects and the detector/processing system can operate at a rate of one detected photoevent every 10 μsec, the total time needed to make a recognition decision is only 10 msec.

The statistical properties of the correlation signal are summarized in Section 3.1. The system to compute the correlation signal $C(\mathbf{r})$, formed by a photon-limited input scene and a deterministic reference function, is simply an optical implementation of a Monte Carlo scheme to calculate definite integrals.

Several reference functions for pattern recognition are examined. Examples of scene matching when the input image is correlated with an image of the reference object are given in Section 3.2 (see Figs. 11.4–11.12). In Section 3.3, distortion-invariant filters are considered. Experimental results that illustrate the use of circular-harmonic filters for rotation invariance (Figs. 11.13–11.15), rotation, scale, and position invariance (Fig. 11.16) and image classification (Figs. 11.17, 11.18 and Table 11.1) are given.

The hardware requirements to implement this photon-correlation scheme are minimal. The detection system (see Section 2.2) consists of a two-dimensional, photon-counting detector and position-computing electronics, which is connected to a microcomputer. The reference function is stored in computer memory. Furthermore, since the photon-correlation system is intensity based, it can operate with either spatially coherent or noncoherent radiation.

There are a number of potential applications for the methods discussed in this chapter. These include machine and robot vision, target recognition from video monitors, correlation tracking for vehicle guidance, active or passive night vision, automatic recognition of spectral signatures, and radiological and nuclear imaging.

Acknowledgements

The author wishes to thank T.A. Isberg, M.N. Wernick, and D.J. Cho for numerous and helpful discussions. Special thanks to D.J. Cho for his careful reading of the manuscript and editorial comments, and to T.A. Isberg for his assistance in the preparation of many of the figures. This work was supported in part by the U.S. Army Research Office and the New York State Center of Advanced Optical Technology.

References

Anger, H.O. (1966). *Instrum. Soc. Am. Trans* **5**, 311–334.

Arsenault, H.H. (1988). *In:* "Optical Computing and Processing," Academic Press, New York.

Barrett, H.H., and Swindell, W. (1981). "Radiological Imaging," Vol. II, Chap. 10, Academic Press, New York.

Bartelt, H., Lohmann, A.W., and Wirnitzer, B. (1984). *Appl. Opt.* **23**, 3121–3129.

Bartelt, H., and Wirnitzer, B. (1985). *Opt. Commun.* **53**, 13–16.

Bertolotti, M. (1974). *In:* "Photon Correlation and Light Beating Spectroscopy," (H.Z. Cummins and E.R. Pike, eds.), Plenum, New York, p. 41.

Blazit, A., Bonneau, D., Koechlin, L., and Labeyrie, A. (1977). *Astrophys. J.* **214**, L79–L84.

Boksenberg, A. (1972). *In:* "ESO/CERN Conference of Auxiliary Instruments for Large Telescopes," European Southern Observatory, Geneva, pp. 295–316.

Boyce, P.B. (1977). *Science* **198**, 145–148.

Brown, T.C., Mackenzie, K.K. (1985). *Aust. J. Phys.* **38**, 329–335.

Burke, J.J. (1975). *In:* "Proceedings of the 1975 International Optical Computing Conference," Institute of Electrical and Electronics Engineers, New York, p. 45.

Casasent, D., and Psaltis, D. (1976a). *Appl. Opt.* **15**, 1795–1799.

Casasent, D., and Psaltis, D. (1976b). *Opt. Eng.* **15**, 258–261.

Casasent, D., and Rozzi, W. (1984). *Opt. Eng.* **23**, 717–720.

Casasent, D., and Sharma, V. (1984). *Opt. Eng.* **23**, 492–498.

Dainty, J.C. ed. (1984). "Laser Speckle and Related Phenomena," 2nd ed., Springer-Verlag, Berlin. Chap. 7.

Dainty, J.C., and Northcott, M.J. (1986). *Opt. Commun.* **58**, 11–14.

Davenport, W.B., and Root, W.L. (1958). "An Introduction to the Theory of Random Signals and Noise," McGraw-Hill, New York, pp. 119–138.

Eberhardt, E.H. (1980). Technical Note #127, ITT Electro-Optical Products Div., Fort Wayne, IN.

Feller, W. (1948). *In:* "Studies and Essays," Courant Anniversary Volume, Interscience, New York, pp. 105–115.

Firmani, C., Ruiz, E., Carlson, C.W., Lampton, M. and Paresce, F. (1982). *Rev. Sci. Instrum.* **53**, 570–574.

Foley, D.H., and Sammon, Jr., J.W. (1975). *IEEE Trans Comput.* **C-24**, 281–289.

Ford, F.G. (1979). *Annu. Rev. Astron. Astrophys.* **17**, 189–212.

Fukunaga, K. (1972). "Introduction to Statistical Pattern Recognition," Academic Press, New York, p. 260.

Fukunaga, K., and Koontz, W.L.G. (1970). *IEEE Trans Comput.* **C-19**, 311–318.

Gamo, H. (1963). *In:* "Symposium on Electromagnetic Theory and Antennas," Pergamon, New York, pp. 801–810.

Geary, J.C., and Latham, D.W., eds., (1981). "Solid State Imagers for Astronomy." *SPIE Semin. Proc.* **290.**

Gnedenko, R.V. (1963). "Theory of Probability," Chelsea, New York, Chap. 8.

Goodenough, D.J. (1975). *SPIE Semin, Proc.* **47**, 199–204.

Goodman, J.W. (1985). "Statistical Optics," Wiley, New York.

Goodman, J.W. and Belsher, J.F. (1976). *SPIE Semin. Proc.* **75**, 141–154.

Greenaway, A.H., Lyons, A., McWhirter, I., Rees, D., and Cochran, A. (1982). *SPIE Semin, Proc.* **331**, 365–367.

Gu, Z.-H., and Lee, S.H. (1984). *Opt. Eng.* **23**, 727–731.

Helstrom, C.W. (1968). "Statistical Theory of Signal Detection," Pergamon, Oxford, Chap. 3.

Helstrom, C.W. (1978). *IEEE Trans. Aerosp. Electron. Syst.* **AES-14,** 630–640.

Helstrom, C.W. (1979). *IEEE Trans. Commun.* **COM-27,** 186–191.

Hofmann, K.-H. and Weigelt, G. (1987). *Appl. Opt.* **26,** 2011–2015.

Hsu, Y.-N. Arsenault, H.H., and April, G. (1982). *Appl. Opt.* **21,** 4012–4015.

Hsu, Y.-N. and Arsenault, H.H. (1982). *Appl. Opt.* **21,** 4016–4019.

Hsu, Y.-N. and Arsenault, H.H. (1984). *Appl. Opt.* **23,** 841–844.

Isberg, T.A., and Morris, G.M. (1986). *J. Opt. Soc. Am.* **A3,** 954–963.

Isberg, T.A., and Morris, G.M. (1987). *OSA Tech. Digest* **12,** 77–80.

Isberg, T.A., and Morris, G.M. (1988). *Proc SPIE* **976,** 160–167.

ITT Electro-Optical Products Div. (1980). Application Note #E22. Fort Wayne, IN.

Johnson, C.B., and Blank, R.E. (1981). *SPIE Semin. Proc.* **290,** 102–108.

Jorden, A.R., Read, P.D., and van Breda, I.G. (1982). *SPIE Semin, Proc.* **331,** 368–375.

Kellogg, E.M., Murray, S.S., and Bardas, D. (1979). *IEEE Trans. Nucl. Sci* **NS-26,** 403–410.

Lampton, M. (1981). *Sci. Am.* **245,** 62–71.

Lampton, M., and Carlson, C.W. (1979). *Rev. Sci. Instrum.* **50,** 1093–1097.

Leger, J.R., and Lee, S.H. (1982a). *J. Opt. Soc. Am.* **72,** 556–564.

Leger, J.R., and Lee, S.H. (1982b). *Appl. Opt.* **21,** 274–287.

Libert, J., (1975). *Nucl. Inst. Meth.* **126,** 589–590.

Loh, E.D. (1977). "A Search for a Halo Around NGC3877 with a Charge Coupled Detector," Ph.D. dissertation. Princeton University, Princteon, N.J.

Lohmann, A.W., Weigelt, G., and Wirnitzer, B. (1983). *Appl. Opt.* **22,** 4028–4037.

Lohmann, A.W., and Wirnitzer, B. (1984). *Proc. IEEE* **72,** 889–901.

Lohmann, A.W. (1986a). *Optik* **73,** 127–131.

Lohmann, A.W. (1986b). *Optik* **73,** 174–180.

Mandel, L. (1963). *In:* "Progress in Optics," (E. Wolf, ed.), Vol. 2, North-Holland, Amsterdam, p. 181.

Mandel, L. (1983). *Kinam Rev. Fis. Ser.* **C5,** 213–232.

Mandel, L. Sudarshan, E.C.G., and Wolf, E. (1964). *Proc. Phys. Soc.* **84,** 435–444.

Martin, C., Jelinsky, P., Lampton, M., Malina, R.F., and Anger, H.O. (1981). *Rev. Sci. Instrum.* **52,** 1067–1074.

McWhirter, I., Rees, D., and Greenaway, A.H. (1982). *J. Phys.* **E 15,** 145–150.

Melsa, J.L., and Cohn, D. (1978). "Decision and Estimation Theory," McGraw-Hill, New York.

Mertz, L., Tarbell, T.D., and Title, A. (1982). *Appl. Opt.* **21,** 628–634.

Morris, G.M. (1984a). *J. Opt. Soc. Am.* **A1,** 482–488.

Morris, G.M. (1984b). *Appl. Opt.* **23,** 3152–3159.

Morris, G.M. (1985). *Opt. Eng.* **24,** 86–90.

Morris, G.M., Wernick, M.N., and Isberg, T.A. (1985). *Opt. Lett.* **10,** 315–317.

Newman, J.D. (1986). "An Investigation of Dynamic Laser Speckle Phenomena using Photon-Limited Detection," Ph.D. dissertation. University of Rochester, New York.

Newman, J.D., Canas, A.A.D., and Dainty, J.C. (1985). *Appl. Opt.* **24,** 4210–4220.

Nicoli, A.M. (1985). "Dynamic Range of Microchannel Plate Photomultipliers," M.S. dissertation. MIT, Cambridge, MA.

Papaliolios, C., and Mertz, L. (1982). *SPIE Semin. Proc.* **331,** 360–364.

Papaliolios, C., Nisenson, P., and Ebstein, S. (1985). *Appl. Opt.* **24,** 287–292.

Papoulis, A. (1965). "Probability, Random Variables, and Stochastic Processes," McGraw-Hill, New York, Chap. 16.

Rees, D., McWhirter, I., Rounce, P.A., Barlow, F.E., and Kellock, S.J. (1980). *J. Phys.* **E 13,** 763–770.

Rees, D., McWhirter, I., Rounce, P.A., and Barlow, F.E. (1981). *J. Phys.* **E14,** 229–233.

Richter, W.J., Jr., and Smits, T.I. (1974). *J. Acoust. Soc. Am.* **56,** 481–496.

Roberts, E., Stapinski, T., and Rodgers, A. (1986). *J. Opt. Soc. Am,* **A3,** 2146–2150.

Rose, A. (1977). "VISION Human and Electronic." Plenum, New York.

Rubinstein, R.Y. (1981). "Simulation and the Monte Carlo Method," Wiley, New York.

Saleh, B. (1978). "Photoelectron Statistics," Springer-Verlag, Berlin.

Schils, G.F., and Sweeney, D.W. (1986). *J. Opt. Soc. Am* **A3,** 902–909.

Shreider, Y.A. ed. (1966). "The Monte Carlo Method," Pergamon, Oxford.

Schwarz, H.E. and Lapington, J.J. (1985). *IEEE Trans. Nucl. Sci.* **NS-32,** 433–437.

Sheng, Y., and Arsenault, H.H. (1986). *J. Opt. Soc. Am.* **A3,** 771–776.

Sheng, Y., and Arsenault, H.H. (1987). *J. Opt. Soc. Am.* **A4,** 1176–1184.

Siegmund, O.H.W., Clothier, S., Thorton, J., Lemem, J., Haper, R., Mason, I., and Culhane, J.L. (1983). *IEEE Trans. Nucl. Sci.* **NS-30,** 503–507.

Siegmund, O.H.W., Malina, R.F., Coburn, K., and Werthiemer, D. (1984). *IEEE Trans. Nucl. Sci.* **NS-31,** 776–779.

Siegmund, O.H.W., Coburn, K., and Malina, R.F. (1985). *IEEE Trans. Nucl. Sci.* **NS-32,** 443–447.

Siegmund, O.H.W., Lampton, M., Bixler, J., Chakrabarti, S., Vallerga, J., Bowyer, S., and Malina, R.F. (1986). *J. Opt. Soc. Am.* **A3,** 2139–2145.

Snyder, D.L. (1975). "Random Point Processes," Wiley, New York, Chap. 4.

Timothy, J.G. (1983). *Publ. Astron. Soc. Pacific* **95,** 810–834.

Timothy, J.G., Mount, G.H., and Bybee, R.L. (1979). *SPIE Semin. Proc.* **183,** 169–181.

Timothy, J.G., Mount, G.H., and Bybee, R.L., (1981). *IEEE Trans. Nucl. Sci.* **NS-28,** 689–697.

Timothy, J.G. (1985). *Opt. Eng.* **24,** 1066–1071.

Tsuchiya, Y., Inuzuka, E., Kurono, T., and Hosoda, M. (1985). *SPSE J. Imag. Tech.* **11,** 215–220.

Tyson, J.A., (1986). *J. Opt. Soc. Am.* **A3,** 2131–2138.

Vanderburg, G.J., and Rosenfeld, A. (1977). *IEEE Trans Comput.* **C-26,** 384–393.

Wernick, M.N., and Morris, G.M., (1986). *J. Opt. Soc. Am.* **A3,** 2179–2187.

Wirnitzer, B. (1985). *J. Opt. Soc. Am.* **A2,** 14–21.

Wu, R., and Stark, H., (1984). *Appl. Opt.* **23,** 838–840.

Wu, R., and Stark, H. (1985). *Appl. Opt.* **24,** 179–184.

Wu, R., and Stark, H. (1986). *J. Opt. Soc. Am.* **A3,** 954–963.

12.

Line Detection and Directional Analysis of Images

Tomasz Szoplik

Institute of Geophysics, University of Warsaw
Warsaw, Poland

Contents

1. Introduction. 391
2. Anamorphic Fourier Transform 392
   2.1 Definitions and Optical Implementations. 393
   2.2 Angular Relations in Anamorphic Spectra 396
   2.3 Applications. 399
3. Mesooptical Fourier Transform Microscope 402
   3.1 Structure of the Mesooptical Fourier Transform Microscope. 403
   3.2 Particle Track Analysis with the Mesooptical Fourier Transform
      Microscope 407
4. The Hough Transform 410
   4.1 Definition and Optical Implementations 410
   4.2 Some Applications 414
5. Conclusion 415
   References 416

1. Introduction

Visual information is stored in the form of images. Color or shades of gray, object outlines, and texture are the most important image variables that may be analyzed to understand an image. An elementary step in object shape determination is line detection. In the case of flat objects bounded with edges, a differentiation is necessary to get lines. Once the lines are available, they can be used to find an object shape and get into a recognition process. In this chapter, progress in line detection techniques is presented. Three approaches to the problem are discussed in connection with different applications.

The anamorphic Fourier transform (FT) is a straightforward generalization of a classical FT. It has a similar capability for image analysis, depending on the parameters of a transforming optical system. What makes the difference is spectrum anamorphosis resulting in nonlinear angular magnification of a spectrum. This allows very accurate directional analysis. The anamorphic FT was proposed for the purpose of seismogram analysis. Use of diffractive directional analysis has a long history in geophysical applications (Jackson, 1965; Dobrin, 1969; Bourrouilh, 1970; Arsenault et al., 1974; Duvernoy and Chałasińska-Macukow, 1981) and in the study of aerial photographs (Lendaris and Stanley, 1970; Harnett et al., 1978; Duvernoy, 1984).

The importance of high-energy physics has motivated vigorous research in the field of particle detection techniques. In some of those techniques final particle tracing is done in an optical way. One of examples is angular measurements in optical Fourier spectra of bubble-chamber photographs (Falconer, 1966). The mesooptical Fourier transform microscope is a new device for particle track detection in thick nuclear emulsions. It utilizes mesoopitcal elements, that is, a combination of spherical optics and axicons.

The third approach to the line detection problem is based on the Hough transform (HT). The significance of the HT is still growing, and its application area is becoming wider. The transform, originally proposed as a method for bubble-chamber photograph analysis (Hough, 1962), is now expanding its scope to several other fields of optical information processing. At present, the most important application of the HT is in robot vision systems. Because of the considerable popularity of the HT and of the existence of review papers (e.g., Maitre, 1985) the space devoted to this transform here is not proportional to its importance.

2.
Anamorphic Fourier Transform

G.G. Stokes first observed the equivalent imaging properties of a spherical lens with a focal length f and two adjacent and perpendicularly oriented cylindrical lenses with focal lengths f_x and f_y, both equal to f (Czapski and Culmann, 1920). This equivalence means that the two-dimensional optical image formation process can be considered as the sum of two independent one-dimensional operations. When an optical imaging system has different focal lengths in two perpendicular directions, the result is images with different lateral magnification. Anamorphic imaging systems composed of cylindrical lenses are more susceptible to aberrations than spherical systems (Montel, 1953; Wynne, 1954; Barakat and Houston, 1966). Nevertheless, imaging systems without rotational symmetry have found several important applications, and the most popular one is in panoramic cinema (Chrétien, 1927).

The work of Duffieux (1946) initiated the Fourier analysis approach to image formation theory. The transfer of concepts used in communication theory and electrical engineering appeared to be fruitful for understanding and describing optical systems. This gave rise to Fourier optics (Goodman, 1968; Gaskill, 1978; Stark, 1982). The crux of Fourier optics is the Fourier transforming property of a lens. Coherent, plane wave illumination of an object placed in the front focal plane of a spherical lens gives a two-dimensional Fourier spectrum in the back focal plane. Due to the circular symmetry of a spherical lens, such a Fourier transforming system is rotation invariant. In the following, we shall describe optical systems composed of crossed cylindrical lenses, which allow anamorphic Fourier transformations. Then the properties and applications of the anamorphic FT will be discussed.

2.1. Definition and Optical Implementations

The anamorphic FT can be accomplished in optical systems by means of several configurations (Szoplik et al., 1984). The simplest optical setup is shown in Fig. 12.1. Performance of a two-dimensional lens is achieved with two one-dimensional cylindrical lenses of unequal focal lengths f_x and f_y. The lenses are arranged in such a way that their back focal planes coincide. An object is placed in the x_1, y_1 plane or somewhere between the x_1, y_1 and x_2, y_2 planes. Illumination of an object with a coherent plane wave yields a spectrum with different scales in the x and y directions. This setup provides an object Fourier spectrum with two different phase factors in the x and y directions. This is acceptable when only the intensity distribution in the spectrum is of interest.

To get an exact anamorphic Fourier spectrum of an object the anamorphic transformer of Fig. 12.2 can be used. In the x direction acts the single cylinder L_x of focal length f_x placed in the central x_5, y_5 plane. In the y direction

Fig. 12.1.

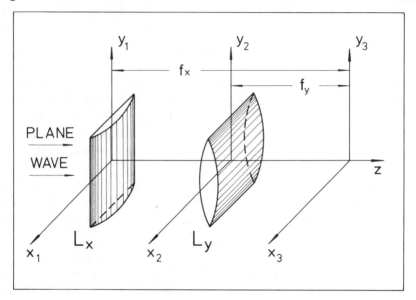

Illustrative anamorphic Fourier transformer composed of two crossed cylinders.

Fig. 12.2.

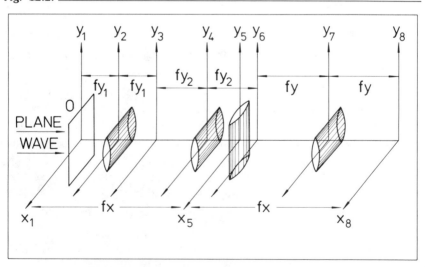

Anamorphic Fourier transformer accomplishing an exact Fourier spectrum.

there are three cylindrical lenses. Two of them, L_{y_1} and L_{y_2}, form a telescope giving an inverted image of the horizontal object structure in the x_6, y_6 plane. Then the image is transformed by the cylinder L_y. The focal lengths of the lenses used in the system must satisfy the condition

$$f_x = f_{y_1} + f_{y_2} + f_y \qquad (12.1)$$

to assure coincidence of the one-dimensional spectra in the output x_8, y_8 plane. The object transparency of complex amplitude transmittance $g(x_1, y_1)$, placed in the input x_1, y_1 plane, is illuminated with a coherent plane wave of amplitude A. Under the usual assumptions of paraxial propagation through thin lenses of sufficiently large apertures, the light field distribution $G(x_8, y_8)$ in the spectrum plane is given by

$$. \quad G(x_8, y_8) = \frac{A}{i\lambda} \sqrt{\frac{f_{y_2}}{f_{y_1} f_y f_x}} \exp\left(\frac{2\pi i}{\lambda} 2f_x\right) \times \int\int_{-\infty}^{\infty} g(x_1, y_1) \quad (12.2)$$

$$\cdot \exp\left[-2\pi i\left(\frac{x_1 x_8}{\lambda f_x} + \frac{y_1 y_8}{\lambda f_y f_{y_1}/f_{y_2}} \right) \right] dx_1 dy_1 ,$$

where λ is the wavelength. The spatial frequency scales in both directions are not equal due to the different focal lengths of the lenses. The ratio

$$\frac{f_x}{f_y f_{y_1}/f_{y_2}} = M \qquad (12.3)$$

is the coefficient of anamorphosis of the transformer. Substitution of M and

$$u = \frac{x_8}{\lambda f_x}, \qquad \text{and} \qquad v = \frac{y_8}{\lambda f_x}$$

into Eq. (12.2) leads to the definition of the anamorphic FT

$$\mathscr{F}_A\{g(x_1, y_1)\} = G_A(u, v) = G(u, Mv) \qquad (12.4)$$

$$= \int\int_{-\infty}^{\infty} g(x_1, y_1) \exp[-2\pi i(x_1 u + M y_1 v)] dx_1 dy_1 ,$$

where $\mathscr{F}$ denotes the FT operator, subscript A denotes anamorphic FT, and all proportionality factors are neglected. For the case of $M = 1$ the anamorphic FT reduces to the classical FT.

The anamorphic FT has the same properties as the classical FT (Gaskill,

1978; § 7–3 and 9–3). However, the scaling property of the anamorphic FT deserves an additional comment. Obviously, the bigger an object, the smaller is its anamorphic spectrum

$$\mathscr{F}_A\left\{g\left(\frac{x_1}{c}, \frac{y_1}{d}\right)\right\} = |cd|G_A(cu, dv), \qquad (12.5)$$

where c and d are real and nonzero constants. On the other hand, the larger the focal length of a transforming lens, the bigger is the spectrum. As a consequence, the anamorphic transform of a nonuniformly scaled object function (for example, the case of $c = 1$ and $d = 1/M$, where M is the coefficient of anamorphosis) leads to the classical Fourier spectrum

$$\mathscr{F}_A\{g(x_1, M y_1)\} = \left|\frac{1}{M}\right| \mathscr{F}\{g(x_1, y_1)\}. \qquad (12.6)$$

In turn, the classical transform of a stretched function gives the anamorphic spectrum

$$\mathscr{F}\left\{\left(x_1, \frac{y_1}{M}\right)\right\} = |M|G_A(u, v). \qquad (12.7)$$

Other optical implementations of an anamorphic transformer have been also proposed. They provide an exact spectrum (Andrés et al., 1985) or a spectrum with some additional phase factors (Szoplik et al., 1986). Surprisingly, the simplest arrangement of two crossed cylindrical lenses with nonparallel illumination (Andrés et al., 1985) gives additional control over the degree of anamorphosis of a spectrum. In this case, the coefficient of anamorphosis depends also on the position of a point source. With the same cylindrical lenses, one can get a larger coefficient of anamorphosis by using a spherical wave illumination. Additionally, the position of the object plane influences the size of the spectrum. This system is flexible and suitable for easy laboratory use.

2.2. Angular Relations in Anamorphic Spectra

A different scale of the one-dimensional transforms in an anamorphic Fourier spectrum results in the angular deformation of a spectrum. It is convenient to analyze angular relations in an anamorphic spectrum when Eq. (12.4) is represented in polar coordinates

$$G_A(\rho, \phi) = \int_0^\infty \int_0^{2\pi} g(r, \xi) \qquad (12.8)$$

$$\cdot \exp[-2\pi ir\rho(\cos \xi \cos \phi + M \sin \xi \sin \phi)]r\,dr\,d\xi,$$

where r, ξ are the object plane polar coordinates and ρ, ϕ are the radial and azimuthal spatial frequencies in the spectrum plane (Gaskill, 1978, p. 318).

Let us consider the spectrum of the sinusoidal diffraction grating

$$g(x_1, y_1) = 1 + \cos(2\pi\mu y_1), \tag{12.9}$$

where v is the spatial frequency. The grooves are oriented along the x axis, where the lens with the longer focal length is active. The grating rotated counterclockwise by an angle α

$$g(x_1, y_1) = 1 + \cos[2\pi\mu(-x_1 \sin \alpha + y_1 \cos \alpha)] \tag{12.10}$$

results in the following anamorphic spectrum

$$G_A(u, v) = \frac{1}{M} \delta(u)\delta(v) + \frac{1}{2M} \left[\delta(u + \mu \sin \alpha)\delta\left(v - \frac{\mu \cos \alpha}{M}\right) \right. \tag{12.11}$$

$$\left. + \delta(u - \mu \sin \alpha)\delta\left(v + \frac{\mu \cos \alpha}{M}\right) \right],$$

where the first term describes the zero-frequency part of the spectrum, which results from a constant bias. The second term describes two off-axis spectral points that appear at the azimuthal spatial frequency

$$\phi = \text{arc tg}(M \text{ tg } \alpha) + \frac{\pi}{2}, \tag{12.12}$$

where the constant $\pi/2$ shift is due to the fact that an edge diffracts perpendicularly to itself. In Fig. 12.3 plots of azimuthal frequencies $\phi - \pi/2$ versus angular orientation α are shown for $M = 2$ and 10. The diagonal shows the linear dependence of $\phi(\alpha)$ attained for the case of a FT made with a spherical lens. Despite their nonlinearity, anamorphic spectra are locked within subsequent quadrants. There is no spectrum overlap on adjacent quadrants, although the arc tangent function has a period π.

Angular magnification of azimuthal frequencies in an anamorphic spectrum with respect to rotation-invariant frequencies in a classical spectrum (equivalent to an object angular orientation) is well described with the coefficient $K(\alpha, M)$ defined as follows:

$$K(\alpha, M) = \frac{d\phi}{d\alpha}. \tag{12.13}$$

The coefficient of angular magnification K is a function of the coefficient of anamorphosis M and the rotation angle α in the object plane

Fig. 12.3.

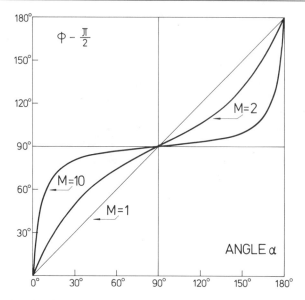

Plots of azimuthal frequencies $\phi - \pi/2$ versus angular orientations α of a diffraction structure calculated for three values of the coefficient of anamorphosis $M = 1$, 2, and 10.

$$K(\alpha, M) = \frac{M}{1 + (M^2 - 1) \sin^2 \alpha}. \tag{12.14}$$

Plots of $K(\alpha, M)$ for $M = 1$, 2, and 10 are shown in Fig. 12.4. The larger the coefficient of anamorphosis M is, the narrower is the range of angles of a spectrum with angular magnification greater than one. The angular magnification coefficient K exceeds unity for angles α given by

$$|\alpha| < \arcsin \sqrt{\frac{1}{M + 1}}. \tag{12.15}$$

The above relation defines the working range of the anamorphic transformer. However, the range of angles $\pm\alpha$ for which K is kept approximately constant is much smaller. When an accurate angular spectrum of an object is necessary, the anamorphic transformation must be repeated for object positions rotated every few degrees. Then, an unfolded angular spectrum having an angular extent of approximately $2\pi M$ may be obtained by a coherent superposition of spectra. The range of angles $\pm\alpha$ with maximum spectral angular magnification surrounds the direction where the lens with a larger focal length performs.

2.3. Applications

For seismological purposes, a large number of seismograms are routinely produced. One possible analytic tool is the optical directional analysis of

Fig. 12.4.

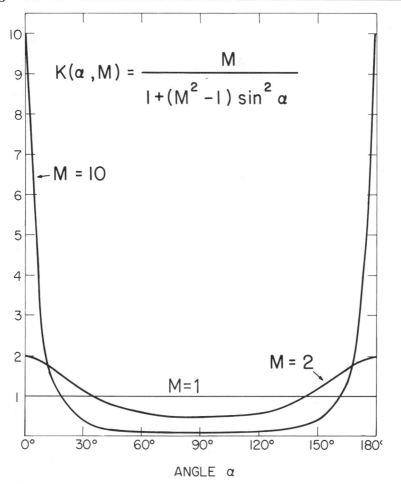

$$K(\alpha, M) = \frac{M}{1 + (M^2 - 1) \sin^2 \alpha}$$

← M = 10

M = 2

M = 1

0°   30°   60°   90°   120°   150°   180°

ANGLE α

Coefficient $K(\alpha, M)$ of angular magnification of spectra versus angular orientation α of a diffraction structure calculated for three values of the coefficient of anamorphosis $M = 1$, 2, and 10.

seismogram spectra. On the other hand, the angular analysis of anamorphic spectra can be used with respect to any object transparencies where directional order is important. An index of angular separability S of two diffracting structures in a transparency is defined by

$$S = \frac{I(\phi_1) + I(\phi_3) - 2I(\phi_2)}{I(\phi_1) + I(\phi_3)}, \qquad (12.16)$$

where $I(\ )$ are spectrum intensities measured through a narrow wedge at angles ϕ_1, ϕ_3, and ϕ_2, where two subsequent maxima and a minimum are located, respectively.

A comparison of the angular separabilities in rotationally symmetrical and anamorphic Fourier transformers has been made (Szoplik et al., 1986). In both cases, the angular contents of spectra were scanned through a wedge filter with the same limitation in the radial direction by the lower radius ρ_1 and the upper radius ρ_2. The wedge filter orientation was fixed in both systems. It was arbitrary in the spherical transformer. While in the anamorphic transformer, the filter was oriented along the y axis, where the largest angular magnification occurs. The angular extent β of the scanning filter was so small that the angular magnification coefficient K was constant and equal to M within the filter field. The experimental results are shown in Fig. 12.5. The spectral intensities $I(\rho_1, \rho_2, \beta)$ integrated over the wedge filter area

$$I(\rho_1, \rho_2, \beta) = \int_{\rho_1}^{\rho_2} \int_{(\pi-\beta)/2}^{(\pi+\beta)/2} |G_A(\rho, \phi)|^2 \rho\, d\rho\, d\phi \qquad (12.17)$$

are shown versus the object orientation. In an anamorphic case, rotation of an object by a small angle α causes rotation of a limited spectrum sector by an angle $\phi - \pi/2 = M\alpha$; see Eq. (12.12). This relatively longer spectrum sector is sampled with a fast detector through a fixed wedge and thus more samples are obtained. The method is equivalent to scanning with a wedge filter having an effective angular extent

$$\beta_{\text{eff}} = \frac{\beta}{K(\alpha, M)}. \qquad (12.18)$$

Another application of the anamorphic FT is connected with optical pseudocoloring techniques. This technique is used in optical image processing to encode in color the gray level or the spatial frequency content of an image (Bescós and Strand, 1978; Indebetouw, 1979; Mantock et al., 1980). Pseudocoloring has recently been used to improve the distinction between di-

Fig. 12.5.

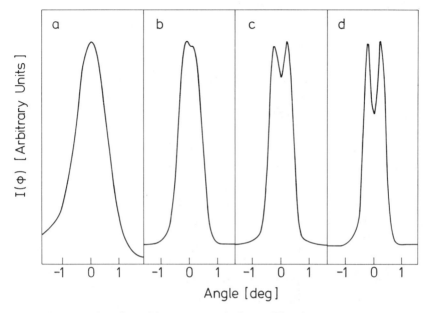

Angular spectrum of an object composed of two diffraction structures rotated with respect to each other by $\alpha = 0.5°$. Measurements made in: (a) a symmetrical transformer; (b) an anamorphic system with $M = 2.3$; (c) with $M = 2.6$; and (d) with $M = 3$ through the wedge filter of angular extent $\beta = 0.7°$.

rectional information (Nowak and Zając, 1983). A chromatic sector filter can be placed in the Fourier plane of a setup composed of spherical lenses with partially coherent illumination. A proper choice of filter colors allows direct observation of fine details that might be difficult to observe under other conditions (Pons et al., 1984). Insertion of chromatic sector filters into the anamorphic spectrum plane improves the distinction of angular details of an object. They act as sector filters of an effective angular extent that is smaller by a factor of $K(\alpha, M)$. An optical setup composed of anamorphic transformers can be arranged in such a way that undistorted pseudocolored images are obtained (Millán et al., 1988).

An optical correlator composed of anamorphic transformers may be used for pattern recognition purposes. An optional choice of coefficients M in both transformers allows arbitrary lateral magnifications of an output image (Szoplik and Arsenault, 1985a). Having an anamorphic correlator leads to the idea of an anamorphic matched filter. A holographic record of an anamorphic spectrum results in an anamorphic FT hologram (Szoplik and Arsenault, 1984). The use of such a hologram as a filter in an anamorphic correlator increases angular discrimination in character recognition (Bonet et al., 1986). On the other hand, the same hologram placed in a spherical 4-*f* correlator allows shift and scale-invariant pattern recognition. Obviously, the connection of a classical Fourier transform hologram with an anamorphic processor has a similar performance. To avoid the angular mismatch of the spectrum and the anamorphic Vander Lugt filter, the anamorphic filter based on one of the circular harmonics of an object function has been proposed (Szoplik and Arsenault, 1985b). With a computer-generated, anamorphic, circular harmonic filter, shift-, rotation-, and scale-invariant pattern recognition should be possible in principle.

3.
Mesooptical Fourier Transform Microscope

In recent years, some research in high-energy physics has been focused on elementary particles that contain a charm quark, such as charmed mesons and baryons. These particles have very short mean lives of $\tau = 10^{-12}$–10^{-15} sec. A particle of this kind is created in a primary nuclear event and decays after passing a path s, equal to some fraction of a micrometer up to a few hundred micrometers. For lifetime detection purposes, we need a device with a spatial resolution $\Delta x < s$. Several particle detectors have been elaborated up to now, such as bubble, streamer, proportional, and drift chambers; scintillator; emulsion; and silicon strips (Particle Data Group, 1986). In some of them, final track detection is made in an optical way. For example, photographs from a streamer chamber are optically analyzed. Also, holographic imaging techniques can be used for track analysis in a bubbler chamber (Falconer, 1966). Lately, this method has been improved and a spatial resolution of 2 μm in a 10 cm thick liquid volume was obtained (Royer, 1981). Undoubtedly, the best spatial resolution, close to 1 μm, is possible in a nuclear emulsion. The advantages of emulsions with respect to the other detectors mentioned above are low cost and archival storage of tracks. However, the long times required for analyses of recorded tracks is a serious drawback of nuclear emulsions. A developed emulsion has typical dimensions: $x = 20$ cm, $y = 10$ cm, and $z = 300$ μm. With an optical microscope each surface is scanned with a light beam of usually 50 μm diameter. The depth of field of an optical microscope in the object space is equal to

$$d = \frac{0.5\lambda n}{A^2} + \frac{340n}{A\Gamma} \ (\mu m), \qquad (12.19)$$

where the first term describes diffractional depth and the second the geometrical depth of field (Pluta, 1982). Numerical constants come from theoretical considerations and experimental measurements. λ is wavelength of the light, and n is the refraction index of the medium in front of the microscope objective. A is the object numerical aperture of an objective, and Γ is the magnification of the whole microscope. For $\Gamma = 100$, d changes from 20 μm to 80 μm for $A = 0.3-0.1$, respectively. That is, for $\Gamma = 100$, emulsion study requires several scans in depth. This is time consuming. In consequence, a majority of particle physicists have turned to electronic detectors.

In this section, we review an innovative technique of nuclear emulsion screening. A device called a mesooptical Fourier transform microscope (MFTM) allows a quick and simultaneous search of straight tracks of particles and determination of their positions, orientations, and vertices. In MFTM the diameter of the field of view analyzed at one shot is up to 500 μm, and the depth of field in the object space can be as large as 300 μm. These two important parameters of the MFTM are better by one order of magnitude each than those of an optical microscope. MFTM was developed in the Joint Institute for Nuclear Research (JINR) in Dubna near Moscow by a group of opticians headed by L.M. Soroko.

Let us comment on the device name. Mesooptics deals with optical elements that perform geometrical transformations with a change of dimensionality. For example, a point in the object space is transformed into a line in the image space. The first mesooptical device was an axicon (McLeod, 1954). Some problems connected with mesooptics have been considered in the past. Signal analysis in systems with dimensional transducers can be performed in sequence where signal dimensionality changes on subsequent stages (Bartelt and Lohmann, 1981). For the purpose of coherent optical processing of signals having a large time-bandwidth product, the old idea of a falling raster was developed and applied for signal correlation (Rhodes, 1981; Stoner et al., 1981). The proceedings of the SPIE conference, "Transformations in Optical Signal Processing" (Rhodes et al., 1981) deals with problems close to mesooptics. It is one of the most fascinating texts in optical processing of recent years.

3.1. The Structure of the Mesooptical Fourier Transform Microscope

Since 1982, when the first MFTM prototype was built (Soroko, 1982; Astakhov et al., 1983) a few improved versions have been constructed. Fig.

12.6 shows an arrangement of the MFTM with a mesooptical lens (Astakhov et al., 1984). A parallel beam of laser light passes through a lens L_1 of focal length f_1 to get a convergent beam illumination of a nuclear emulsion placed in the $x_1 y_1$ plane. The nuclear emulsion is thick, up to 300 μm after development, and $x_1 y_1$ is its median plane. There follows a mesooptical lens. Its concept is explained in Fig. 12.7 (Bencze and Soroko, 1985a). The performance of a mesooptical lens is similar to that of a negative axicon A, that is, a negative right circular cone, combined with a positive spherical lens L_2 in the same $x_2 y_2$ plane. Lens L_2 has focal length f_2 such, that

$$\frac{1}{f_2} = \frac{1}{d_{12}} + \frac{1}{d_{23}}, \qquad (12.20)$$

where d_{12} is the object-mesooptical lens distance and d_{23} is the distance be-

Fig. 12.6.

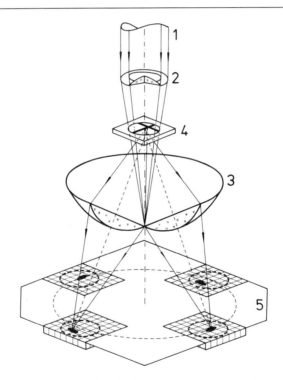

Diagram of the mesooptical Fourier transform microscope with a mesooptical lens. 1, HeNe laser illumination; 2, converging lens L_1; 3, mesooptical lens; 4, nuclear emulsion; and 5, output signal plane.

Fig. 12.7. _____

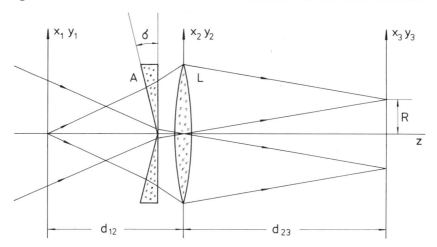

Explanatory representation of the mesooptical lens, where $x_1 y_1$ is the emulsion plane, $x_2 y_2$ is the mesooptical lens plane, and $x_3 y_3$ is the output signal plane. The negative axicon A with cone angle δ and the positive lens L_2 act together as a mesooptical lens. R is the radius of the mesooptical circular focus.

tween the mesooptical lens and output plane. Axicon A is characterized by a cone angle δ and its complex amplitude transmittance

$$p_a(x_2, y_2) = \exp[i\Delta\phi(x_2, y_2)] = \exp\left[\frac{2\pi i}{\lambda}(n-1)\,\mathrm{tg}\,\delta\,\sqrt{x_2^2 + y_2^2}\right]. \quad (12.21)$$

Due to its deflecting property, the mesooptical circular focus of radius R appears in the $x_3 y_3$ output plane

$$R = d_{23}(n-1)\,\mathrm{tg}\,\delta, \quad (12.22)$$

where n is the axicon index of refraction. The size of the focal spot is proportional to the area of illuminated nuclear emulsion. In spite of the axicon action, the MFTM optical system is shift invariant.

Fig. 12.8 shows another model of the MFTM that works with mesooptical mirrors (Astakhov et al., 1983). An analyzed emulsion is also illuminated with a convergent laser beam. The main part of light that is undisturbed by silver grains in the emulsion focuses in the center of the mesooptical lens or mirror and is stopped. Diffracted light is gathered by a mesooptical element. Mirrors are usually preferred because the preparation of mesooptical lenses is a difficult task.

In a recent MFTM prototype, a mesooptical mirror made of diamond-

Fig. 12.8. _____

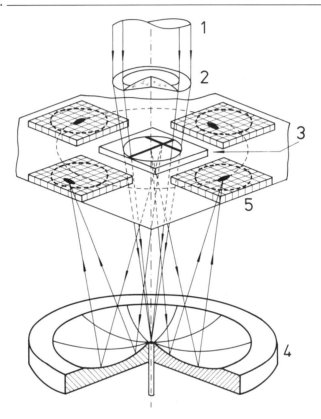

Diagram of the mesooptical Fourier transform microscope with a mesooptical
mirror. 1, coherent light illumination; 2, converging lens; 3, thick emulsion; 4,
mesooptical mirror; and 5, output signal plane.

machined metal alloy is used (Bencze et al., 1986b). The mirror is elliptically shaped and has circular symmetry around the device axis. The ellipse
is approximated with 600 straight segments, each having a width of 0.1 mm.
The mirror diameter is balanced to meet two opposite requirements. A large
mirror collects more diffracted light, but, on the other hand, the larger the
diameter, the shorter the depth of field in the object space. The mirror has
two foci in the output plane. One common focus is on the device axis. The
other forms a circle, shown in Fig. 12.8 with a broken line in the output
plane. The radial profile of the circular focus has a width of its intensity
distribution, measured at the half-height, equal to 1.5 μm. The angular aperture of half of the mirror is 25.7°, and the diameter of the point source

used in the measurement is 0.48 μm. This means that in the radial direction, a spatial resolution of the order of 1–2 μm is possible. The MFTM spatial resolution is influenced considerably by the shape of immersion base used with the nuclear emulsion.

Apart from the mesooptical lens and mirror, one more form of a mesooptical element has been considered for use in MFTM. It is a mesooptical kinoform with impulse response in the form of a circle (Bencze et al., 1986a). Its imaging properties were analyzed for different classes of input objects. The mesooptical kinoform performance was described in terms of Hilbert optics (Soroko, 1981), and the usefulness of mesooptical kinoforms in MFTM systems have been demonstrated. Research in the field of kinoforms carried out in the Institute of Automation and Electrometry in Novosibirsk is reviewed by V.P. Koronkevich in Chapter 9 of this book.

3.2. Particle Track Analysis with a Mesooptical Fourier Transform Microscope

The MFTM allows simultaneous search of particle tracks in the whole volume of a nuclear emulsion probed with the illuminating beam (Bencze and Soroko, 1985b). Each straight-line track gives rise to a pair of output signals. The output signal is not a track image, however. For each radial section of the MFTM, light diffracted on a track is imaged into two points. Output signal dots from all tracks that occur in the MFTM field of view appear on a circle having a width DM and an average radius R. D is the diameter of the field of view in the emulsion plane, and $M = d_{23}/d_{12}$ is a coefficient of linear magnification in the radial direction. The dot positions give information on angular orientation Φ of a track, its displacement r from the device axis, and its depth position in the object space. Angular orientation Φ is given by

$$\Phi = \begin{cases} \Sigma + \dfrac{\pi}{2} & \text{for} \quad \rho_1 < \rho_2 \\[2mm] \Sigma - \dfrac{\pi}{2} & \text{for} \quad \rho_1 > \rho_2 \end{cases}, \qquad (12.23)$$

where Σ is the angle of orientation of a line that connects output dots and goes through the output plane center. Distances from the left and right output signals to the system axis are ρ_1 and ρ_2, respectively. The distance r of a particle track from the system axis is

$$r = \frac{|\rho_2 - \rho_1|}{2 \cos \dfrac{\alpha}{2}}, \qquad (12.24)$$

where α is the angular aperture of the mesooptical element. Tracks occur in the object space on both sides of the $x_1 y_1$ median plane, because the emulsion thickness is much larger than the diameters of track grains. For tracks that are out of the median plane, the radial coordinates of both output signal dots are different. From this difference and its sign we get the depth position z of a track in the emulsion (Bencze and Soroko, 1985b). To find a track slope with respect to the median plane, two depth positions z are measured in two adjacent fields of view. Measurement of depth positions is possible due to the particular location of photodetectors in the output signal plane. They are distributed on a conical surface in such a way that diffracted light strikes them at normal incidence. In the MFTM, the spatial resolution in the z direction is four times less than in the horizontal directions. In order to improve the MFTM spatial resolution, the output signal is not observed in plane 5, as shown in Fig. 12.6 and 12.8. In practice, it is projected further and magnified, then detected with CCD arrays and fed into a computer. Cylindrical lenses used to shape both the beam that illuminates the emulsion and the output signal additionally improve the MFTM performance (Bencze et al., 1986b).

3.2.1. Measurement of Vertex Coordinates and of Track Orientation

Useful information is carried by light diffracted on silver grains of diameter 0.5–2 μm that form chains composed of 30 or more grains on 100 μm track lengths. The output signal contrast increases with the number of silver grains, but the internal structure of tracks is not reflected in the output signals. When a neutral particle is studied, this chain ends at a primary event vertex, and, after some micrometers, a secondary event occurs with two or more tracks. Tracks of particle decay products originate from the common vertex where a secondary event takes place. A track vertex can be detected even if it is outside an analyzed field of view. The radial and azimuthal coordinates of tracks originating in a vertex are represented on a Cartesian ρ, Ξ coordinate system. This representation will be discussed in the next section on the Hough transform. When all the tracks originate from the same vertex, their (ρ_i, Ξ_i) points lie on a sinusoid. In this way an easy classification of visible tracks is done. However, if an angular range of scattered particles is small, their respective (ρ_i, Ξ_i), points lie on a part of a sinusoid that can be approximated by a straight line.

The case when a track originates and ends within the field of view of the MFTM is of particular interest for particle physicists. The situation when a track ends within the field of view is shown in Fig. 12.9a. It is observed that output signals become shorter and, contrary to Eq. (12.23), have angular coordinates that differ by a value other than π. Therefore both dots must be measured to find out if the angular shift comes from the shorter track but not from two tracks of different angular orientation. When tracks become shorter, the output signals become fainter and the accuracy of measurements of the end positions decreases. This problem is still under study (Soroko, 1987a).

Figure 12.9b shows a track with a turning point. Such a track can be

Fig. 12.9. _____

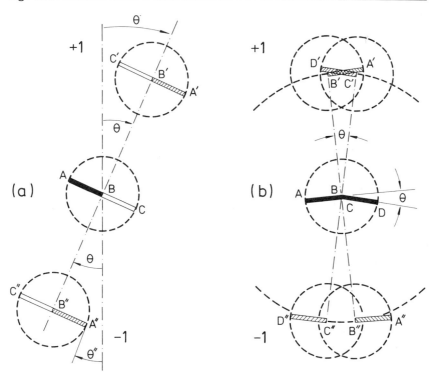

Particle tracks are shown in the central circles. Left and right output signals are shown in outer circles. (a) Particle track ends within the field of view. (b) Particle track vertex resulting from a nuclear event.

considered as a sum of shorter tracks AB and CD. Their mesooptical images
of orders $+1$ and -1 form different figures. In one case the output signals
overlap and in the other they are separated by a distance proportional to a
deflection angle. A simple measurement of separation length makes an excellent method for the determination of angular orientation of tracks. The
reported accuracy of analysis of angular scattering is about 0.02^0 (Soroko,
1987b). The measurement of separations between output signal dots and
their overlaps in both mesooptical images is a useful method to analyze short
tracts of particles between primary and secondary nuclear events that occur
within the field of view.

4.
The Hough Transform

The method and means for the recognition of complex patterns based on the
line-to-point transform was patented by Hough (1962). It was originally intended for the analysis of particle tracks on photographs taken in a bubble
chamber. In the beginning, the transform was not formulated in mathematical terms. Then, the method was developed and adapted for new uses, such
as the detection of curves in pictures (Duda and Hart, 1973), the tracking
of moving targets (Falconer, 1979), and other applications. It has been pointed
out that the HT is a special case of the Radon transform (Deans, 1981). For
a long time, the HT was used to digitally process images arriving at video
rates. Interest in robot vision systems has recently motivated research on
optical realizations of the HT. The extensive literature devoted to the HT
and to its applications in digital image processing was recently reviewed by
Maitre (1985).

4.1. Definition and Optical Implementations

An exact definition of HT can be derived as a particular two-dimensional
case of the Radon transform (Deans, 1981). Here, an Ockhamistic question
arises whether two names are needed for one transform. The Radon transform deals with projections in various multidimensional spaces. Along with
the central slice theorem, it forms the mathematical basis of computerized
tomography (Barrett, 1984). On the other hand, the HT is limited to two-
dimensional Euclidean image spaces and deals with coordinate transformations. Therefore, it is reasonable to keep both transforms apart, having
in mind the mathematical analogy.

For the case of a straight line $f(x, y)$ given in the normal form in the image x, y plane

$$f(x, y) = \begin{cases} 1, & (x, y) \in \rho_1 = x \cos \theta_1 + y \sin \theta_1 \\ 0, & \text{otherwise}, \end{cases} \qquad (12.25)$$

where θ_1 and ρ_1 are explained in Fig. 12.10; the HT is defined by

$$F(\theta, \rho) = \int\limits_{-\infty}^{\infty}\!\!\int f(x, y)\delta(\rho - x \cos \theta - y \sin \theta)dx\,dy \qquad (12.26)$$

$$= \begin{cases} 1, & \text{for } (\theta_1, \rho_1) \\ 0, & \text{otherwise}. \end{cases}$$

The transform of a straight line is a point (θ_1, ρ_1) in the parameter plane, see Fig. 12.10.

If an input object is the simplest possible, that is, a point

$$g(x, y) = \begin{cases} 1, & \text{for } (x_0, y_0) \\ 0, & \text{otherwise}, \end{cases} \qquad (12.27)$$

which can be written $g(x, y) = \delta(x - x_0)\,\delta(y - y_0)$, then

$$G(\theta, \rho) = \int\limits_{-\infty}^{\infty}\!\!\int \delta(x - x_0)\delta(y - y_0)\delta(\rho - x \cos \theta - y \sin \theta)dx\,dy \qquad (12.28)$$

$$= \delta(\rho - x_0 \cos \theta - y_0 \sin \theta).$$

Fig. 12.10. _____

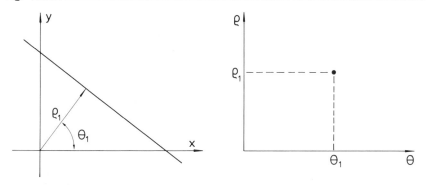

A straight line in the input image plane x, y is Hough transformed into the normal parameter plane θ, ρ.

An input point is Hough transformed into a sinusoidal curve $\rho = x_0 \cos \theta + y_0 \sin \theta$. This is shown in Fig. 12.11, where the point of intersection of a few straight lines is mapped onto a sinusoid. The sinusoid is composed of points that are the transforms of intersecting lines.

The generalized HT can be used for the detection of curves (Duda and Hart, 1973; Gorelik et al., 1975; Deans, 1981). To this end modification of Eq. (12.26) is necessary. To generalize a transform kernel, instead of a line equation that depends on two Cartesian coordinates in the input image plane, we take an equation of a family of curves

$$\rho = C(x, y; \xi), \tag{12.29}$$

where dependence on an additional parameter ξ appears. An arbitrary generalized function to be transformed may be written as

$$f(x, y) = a(x, y)\chi(c), \tag{12.30}$$

where $a(x, y)$ is the non-negative density of a curve and $\chi(c)$ is its characteristic function. Taking into account Eqs. (12.26), (12.29), and (12.30) the generalized HT can be defined by

$$F(\xi; \rho) = \int\int_{-\infty}^{\infty} a(x, y)\chi(c)\delta[\rho - C(x, y; \xi)]dxdy. \tag{12.31}$$

Fig. 12.11.

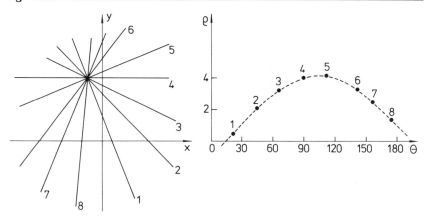

A bundle of straight lines that intersect at one point in the input image plane is Hough transformed into the parameter plane θ, ρ; respective angle-radius points form a sinusoidal curve.

Let us show how this definition works on an example of a family of concentric circles:

$$\rho = C(x_0, y_0; r_i). \tag{12.32}$$

The circles have a uniform density equal to one, $a(x, y) = 1$, and a characteristic function

$$\chi(c) = \begin{cases} 1, & (x, y) \in (x - x_0)^2 + (y - y_0)^2 = r_i^2 \\ 0, & \text{otherwise.} \end{cases}$$

Their transform is given by

$$F(\bar{\xi}, \rho) = \int\!\!\!\int_{-\infty}^{\infty} a(x, y)\chi(c)\delta[\rho^2 - (x - x_0)^2 - (y - y_0)^2]dxdy \tag{12.33}$$

$$= \begin{cases} 1, & \text{for } \rho = r_i \quad \text{and } \bar{\xi} = [x_0, y_0] \\ 0, & \text{otherwise.} \end{cases}$$

In this case the generalized HT parameter space is three dimensional.

There are a few optical systems accomplishing the HT (Eichmann and Dong, 1983; Gindi and Gmitro, 1984; Steier and Shori, 1986; Ambs et al., 1986 and Eichmann and Li, 1987), and some of them have evolved from incoherent optical Radon processors (Barrett, 1982). The HT kernel, that is, $\delta(\rho - x \cos \nabla - y \sin \theta)$ from Eq. (12.26), does not show a convolution-type dependence on the difference of coordinates. Therefore, the HT is space variant. Eichmann and Dong (1983) obtained a convolution-type kernel through a change to rotated coordinates. Thus an object to be transformed must rotate in the input plane of a 4-f type coherent processor. From the rotating spectrum of an input object, only one angular frequency is chosen with a fixed narrow vertical slit placed in the processor Fourier plane. In the output plane the signal is recorded on a translating photoemulsion through a narrow vertical slit. The angular dimension in the normally parametrized input is thus mapped onto one of the Cartesian parameter dimensions. The idea of performing a two-dimensional integration in two one-dimensional steps is important. However, the system is not useful because it contains two mechanically moving parts.

Figure 12.12 shows an optical system for producing an HT using coherent light (Steier and Shori, 1986). Instead of rotating an input object, a Dove prism is used (Gindi and Gmitro, 1984). The object beam rotation is twice that of the Dove prism. An anamorphic optical system images an input object and performs a one-dimensional FT in the vertical and horizontal directions, respectively. A vertically oriented CCD line detector records the zero-order component of the FT, which is proportional to one line of the HT at a fixed angular value θ. Angular scanning of the object is carried out by rotating the prism. The system allows the HT production at video rates. This coherent system is sensitive to phase variations of the input object. Therefore, a noncoherent setup with slightly modified optics has also been proposed (Gindi and Gmitro, 1984; Steier and Shori, 1986).

Space variance of the HT creates a serious problem for its optical implementations. Rotating an input object works well for straight-line mappings only. The generalized HT of Eq. (12.31) still awaits a practical optical implementation. In a recent and promising approach, a space-variant HT kernel is achieved by means of holograms with different impulse responses (Ambs et al., 1986; Eichmann and Li, 1987). The HT filter has the form of a matrix of Fourier subholograms. It is placed just behind a binary input image. Thus each subhologram interacts with an appropriate part of an input object, and hologram reconstructions form the parameter plane. Proper parameter coordinates are assigned to the output plane, and after threshold adjustment mapping of lines or curves onto points is possible. Thus the parameter $\bar{\xi} = [\xi_1, \xi_1]$ of the HT transform in Eq. (12.33) is found from the peak location, and a peak appears only when parameter ρ encoded in the hologram is matched to the input image content. This holographic implementation of the HT should lead to real-time processing of images with a large number of pixels.

4.2. Some Applications

The practical usefulness of the HT depends on the accuracy of input object mappings in the parameter space. The question is somewhat analogous to the resolution problem in both optical and digital systems. The HT performance is influenced by the kind of input object. It obviously deteriorates when the object signal is accompanied by noise and clutter. It depends on the existence of multiple signals. On the other hand, in optical and digital picture processors the HT accuracy depends on the number of detector pixels in the parameter space. A generally accepted rule of how to optimize a Hough transforming system does not exist yet. This research is still under development. A probabilistic assessment of the HT performance has been recently described (Maitre, 1986). Starting from a given probability density function within a photodetector retina in the image plane, the probability density function in the Hough parameter space was calculated. The two cases of rectangular and circular retinas were considered with a uniform and random distribution of feature points inside the retina.

Fig. 12.12.

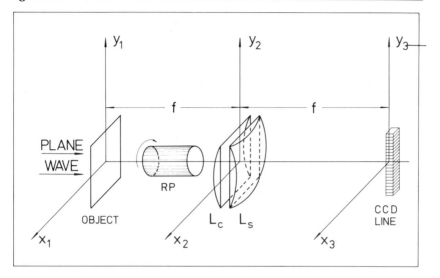

Optical implementation of HT. RP, rotating Dove prism, L_c and L_s, cylindrical and spherical lenses of focal length f form an anamorphic imaging-Fourier transforming system.

The most important applications of the HT are in the field of digital image processing. Up-to-date lists of publications can be found elsewhere (Maitre, 1985; Steier and Shori, 1986; Ambs et al., 1986). Many papers are connected with digital image processing systems for robots (e.g. Choraś, 1984). Recently, an associative network for detection of lines by means of a discrete version of the HT was developed for robot vision applications (Oyster et al., 1987). On the other hand, input images originating from various practical areas are digitally processed with the HT. These are chest radiographs, aerial photographs, seismograms, bubble chamber pictures, meteorological photos, and other applications. The HT is also used for the detection of missile trajectories (Falconer, 1979; Casasent and Krishnapuram, 1987). Recent progress in optical holographic implementations of the HT will increase the interest in real-time parallel processing based on this transform.

5.
Conclusion

Three new optical approaches to the problem of line detection and directional analysis of images have been presented.

The Hough transform has been a well-established tool in digital image processing for more than 20 years. Quite recently, when optical systems to achieve the transform were proposed, it also became useful in optical processing. The implementation of line-to-point and inverse mappings is easy and well developed. More complicated mappings of second or even higher order curves in the image space onto points in multidimensional parameter spaces have not been sufficiently explored yet.

The mesooptical Fourier transform microscope serves as an illustration that unconventional optics is necessary to solve certain difficult problems in line detection. The device is still under development. If all expectations are eventually fulfilled in practice, it probably will be the cheapest detection device in elementary particle physics. Preliminary results suggest that in some aspects the MFTM is better than a classical microscope for nuclear emulsion scanning.

The anamorphic FT is perhaps too simple a solution to the directional analysis problem to work well. There is no source of additional directional information in the system that can substantially increase the angular resolution. However, spectrum anamorphosis allows measurements with an effective aperture smaller than its physical extent and this improves practical results.

References

Ambs, P., Lee, S.H., Tian, Q., and Fainman, Y. (1986). *Appl. Opt.* **25**, 4039–4045.

Andrés, P., Ferreira, C., and Bonet, E. (1985). *Appl. Opt.* **24**, 1549–1552.

Arsenault, H.H., Seguin, M.K., and Brousseau, N. (1974). *Appl. Opt.* **13**, 1013–1017.

Astakhov, A.Ya., Komov, G.M., Sidorova, V.I., Skril, I.I., and Soroko, L.M. (1983). Commun. R13-83-119. JINR, Dubna (in Russian).

Astakhov, A.Ya., Bencze, G.L., Niedermayer, T.P., and Soroko, L.M. (1984). Commun. R13-84-277. JINR, Dubna (in Russian).

Astakhov, A.Ya., Bencze, G.L., Kisvàradi, A., Niedermayer, T.P., Nyitrai, G., and Soroko, L.M. (1985). Commun. R13-85-378. JINR, Dubna (in Russian).

Barakat, R., and Houston, A. (1966). *Opt. Acta* **13**, 1–30.

Barrett, H.H. (1982). *Opt. Lett.* **7**, 248–250.

Barrett, H.H. (1984). *In*: "Progress in Optics," (E. Wolf, ed.), Vol. XXI, Elsevier, Amsterdam, pp. 217–286.

Bartelt, H.O., and Lohmann, A.W. (1981). *Proc SPIE* **373**, 3–10.

Bencze, G.L., and Soroko, L.M. (1984). "ICO-13 Conf. Digest, Sapporo," pp. 146–147.

Bencze, G.L., and Soroko, L.M. (1985a). Commun. R13-85-136. JINR, Dubna (in Russian).

Bencze, G.L., and Soroko, L.M. (1985b). Commun. R13-85-137. JINR, Dubna (in Russian).

Bencze, G.L., and Soroko, L.M. (1985c). Commun R13-85-138. JINR, Dubna (in Russian).

Bencze, G.L., Palchikova, I.G., Poleshchuk, A.G., and Soroko, L.M. (1986a). Commun. R13-86-240. JINR, Dubna (in Russian).

Bencze, G.L., Kisvàradi, A., Nyitrai, G., and Soroko, L.M. (1986b). Commun, R13-86-630. JINR, Dubna (in Russian).

Bescós, J., and Strand, T.C (1978). *Appl. Opt.* **17**, 2525–2531.

Bonet, E., Ferreira, C., Andrés, P., and Pons, A. (1986). *Opt. Commun.* **58**, 155–160.

Bourrouilh, B. (1970). *Nouv. Rev. d'Opt. Appl.* **1**, 369–383.

Casasent, D., and Krishnapuram, R. (1987). *Appl. Opt.* **26**, 247–251.

Choraś, R.S. (1984). *Image Vision Comput.* **2**, 31–33.

Chrétien, H. (1927). *C.R. Acad. Sci. Paris* **184**, 1372–1374.

Czapski, S., and Culmann, P. (1920). *In*: "Geometrical Investigations of the Formation of Images in Optical Instruments," (M. von Rohr, ed.), H.M. Stationery Office, London, pp. 125–211.

Deans, S.R. (1981). *IEEE Trans. Pattern Anal. Machine Intell.* **PAMI-3**, 185–188.

Dobrin, M.B. (1969). *Appl. Opt.* **8**, 1551–1557.

Duda, R.O., and Hart, P.E. (1973). "Pattern Classification and Scene Analysis," Wiley, New York.

Duffieux, P.M. (1946). "L'Intégrale de Fourier et ses Applications à l'Optique," Rennes.

Duvernoy, J. (1984). *Appl. Opt.* **23**, 828–837.

Duvernoy, J., and Chałasińska-Macukow, K. (1981). *Appl. Opt.* **20**, 136–144.

Eichmann, G., and Dong, B.Z. (1983). *Appl. Opt.* **22**, 830–834.

Eichmann, G., and Li, Y. (1987). *Opt. Commun.* **63**, 230–232.

Falconer, D.G. (1979). SRI Internat., Techn. Note 202, Menlo Park.

Falconer, D.G. (1966). *Appl. Opt.* **5**, 1365–1369.

Gaskill, J.D. (1978). "Linear Systems, Fourier Transform, and Optics," Wiley, New York.

Gindi, G.R., and Gmitro, A.F. (1984). *Opt. Eng.* **23,** 499–506.

Goodman, J.W. (1968). "Introduction to Fourier Optics," McGraw-Hill, New York.

Gorelik, S.L., Pintsov, V.A., and Pintsov, L.A. (1975). *Avtometriya* **6,** 35–37 (in Russian). English transl. in *Automatic Monitoring and Measuring.*

Harnett, P.R., Mountain, G.D., and Barnett, M.E. (1978). *Opt. Acta* **25,** 801–809.

Hough, P.V.C. (1962). US Patent 3,069,654.

Indebetouw, G. (1979). *Appl. Opt.* **18,** 4206–4209.

Jackson, P.L. (1965). *Appl. Opt.* **4,** 419–427.

Lendaris, G.G., and Stanley, G.L. (1970). *Proc. IEEE* **58,** 198–216.

Maitre, H. (1985). *Traitement du Signal* **2,** 305–317.

Maitre, H. (1986). *IEEE Trans. Pattern Anal. Machine Intell.* **PAMI-8,** 669–674.

Mantock, J., Sawchuk, A.A., and Strand, T.C. (1980). *Opt. Eng.* **19,** 180–185.

McLeod, J.H. (1954). *J. Opt. Soc. Am.* **44,** 592–597.

Millán, M.S., Ferreira, C., Pons, A., and Andrés, P. (1988). *Opt. Eng.* **27,** 129–134.

Montel, M. (1953). *Rev. d'Optique* **32,** 585–600.

Nowak, R., and Zając, M. (1983). *Opt. Appl.* **13,** 39–46.

Oyster, J.M., Vicuna, F., and Broadwell, W. (1987). *Appl. Opt.* **26,** 1919–1926.

Particle Data Group (1986). *Phys. Lett.* **170B,** 1–350.

Pluta, M. (1982). "Optical Microscopy," PWN, Warsaw (in Polish).

Pons, A., Andrés, P., Ferreira, C., and Illueca, C. (1984). *J. Optics (Paris)* **15,** 65–67.

Rhodes, W.T. (1981). *Proc. SPIE* **373,** 11–19.

Rhodes, W.T., Fienup, J.R., and Saleh, B.E.A., eds. (1981). "Transformations in Optical Signal Processing," *Proc. SPIE* **373,** Bellingham.

Royer, H. (1981). *J. Optics (Paris)* **12,** 347–350.

Soroko, L.M. (1981). "Hilbert Optics," Nauka, Moscow (in Russian).

Soroko, L.M. (1982). Commun. D1-82-642. JINR, Dubna (in Russian).

Soroko, L.M. (1987a). Commun. R13-87-169. JINR, Dubna (in Russian).

Soroko, L.M. (1987b). Commun. R13-87-170. JINR, Dubna (in Russian).

Stark, H., ed. (1982). "Applications of Optical Fourier Transforms," Academic Press, New York.

Steier, W.H., and Shori, R.K. (1986). *Appl. Opt.* **25,** 2734–2738.

Stoner, W.W., Miceli, W.J., and Horrigan, F.A. (1981). *Proc. SPIE* **373,** 21–29.

Szoplik, T., Kosek, W., and Ferreira, C. (1984a). *Appl. Opt.* **23,** 905–909.

Szoplik, T., and Arsenault, H.H. (1984b). *J. Opt. Soc. Am.* **A1,** 1203–1205.

Szoplik, T., and Arsenault, H.H. (1985a). *Appl. Opt.* **24,** 168–172.

Szoplik, T., and Arsenault, H.H. (1985b). *Appl. Opt.* **24,** 3179–3183.

Szoplik, T., Chałasińska-Macukow, K., and Kosek, J. (1986). *Appl. Opt.* **25,** 188–192.

Vázquez, M.C., and Barcala, J. (1984). *Opt. Acta* **31,** 947–970.

Wynne, C.G. (1954). *Proc. Phys. Soc., London* **B-67,** 529–537.

13.

Incoherent Optical Processing and Holography

E.N. Leith

College of Engineering
University of Michigan
Ann Arbor, Michigan

Contents

1. Introduction 421
2. The Achromatization of Katyl 422
   2.1 Formation of a Fourier Transform Hologram 425
3. White Light Coherent Correlator 427
4. Further Development of White Light Filtering 428
   4.1 White Light Displays and Storage 431
   4.2 Monochromatic Extended Source Spatial Filtering 432
5. Construction of Diffractive Optical Elements 436
   References 438

1.

Introduction

During the past decade there has been extensive interest in carrying out holography and optical processing with light of reduced coherence, either spatial, temporal, or both. The objective is primarily to take advantage of the improved SNR offered by such coherence reduction.

Optical processing techniques carried out with incoherent light are by no means new; they are at least as old as the coherent techniques, and both can be traced back at least to the 1920s and 1930s. For example, correlation of two transparencies by moving one past the other and integrating the light emerging from the second transparency can be done either with coherent or incoherent light, and either way is indeed very old. Many of the older techniques are described in the 1977 book by Rogers[1].

The newer work has a recurring theme, namely, to accomplish with incoherent light operations that earlier had been restricted to the use of coherent light—operations such as the recording of Fresnel and Fraunhofer diffraction patterns, complete with phase as well as amplitude—thus permitting the construction of holograms, or arbitrary spatial filters, just as had earlier been done with coherent light. The techniques tend to be more complex, but the vastly improved SNRs may justify their use. Chavel and Lowenthal (1980) and Chavel (1980) have studied in considerable depth the SNR improvements due to partially coherent illumination, and their conclusions have been a strongly encouraging factor in the exploitation of incoherent systems. More recently, Yu et al. (1985) have studied the effect of noise in a partially coherent system. Although we limit our discussion to the new, post-1977 work, we nevertheless find the total amount and variety of the work to be overwhelming, so we by no means cover the whole area, but have aimed at a rather representative sampling.

Some of the techniques discussed are performed with broadband light but require spatial coherence. Others are performed with spatially incoherent, i.e., extended source light, but require monochromaticity. Seldom can both types of coherence requirements be simultaneously eliminated, although there are a few instances where this can be done. Finally, we note that the systems we describe as incoherent are in fact carried out in practice with partially coherent light; thus, we have used the terms *incoherent* and *partially coherent* interchangeably.

2.
The Achromatization of Katyl

One of the foundations of modern white light optical processing and holography is the work of Katyl, who in 1972 published three back-to-back papers:

one on the achromatization of the Fresnel hologram, one on the construction of Fresnel holograms in broadband light, and the third on the achromatization of the Fourier transform.

We describe in a basic physical way the method of Katyl for achromatizing the optically formed Fourier transform. Although the mathematical treatment can be rather complicated, the basic ideas can be understood in a rather simple and interesting way. The explanation we offer is not that of Katyl, which seems more suited to a lens design audience; ours is oriented to those in optical processing or basic physical optics.

We begin by noting that the Fourier transform of an object always occurs in the plane where the source is imaged (Fig. 13.1). The mask through which the source is imaged generates new waves, which, when projected back to the source plane, form a virtual image that has a size proportional to wavelength. This distribution, the Fourier transform of the object, is reimaged in the process of producing the Fourier transform as a real image. For example, let the object be a diffraction grating of spatial frequency f_0. Light impinging on the grating forms various orders that project back to the source plane as additional object points separated laterally from the actual source point. These source points have a lateral location proportional to wavelength. In the paraxial approximation the lateral position of these points is $x = F_c \lambda f_0$. Now, the two lenses, the collimator L_0 and the Fourier transform lens L_F, together reimage the source plane to the usual Fourier transform plane, typically the back focal plane of lens L_F. The magnification is $M_1 = F_F/F_c$, the ratio of the Fourier transform lens and the collimator lens focal lengths, since the source is at the front focal plane of L_c and the image forms at the back focal plane of L_F.

To achromatize the process, the magnification M should be inversely pro-

Fig. 13.1.

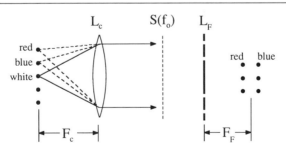

Optical system that compensates for the wavelength dependence of the scale of the Fourier transformation of a grating.

portional to wavelength to compensate for the wavelength dependence at
the source plane. We let L_f be a zone plate lens, or HOE, as described by
Katyl. The HOE has focal length inversely proportional to wavelength:
$F_F = F_{FO}(\lambda_0/\lambda)$, where F_{FO} is the focal length at the wavelength λ_o. The
magnification becomes $M_1 = (F_{FO}/F_C)(\lambda_0/\lambda)$, and the new, wavelength-in-
dependent lateral position of the imaged source points is $M_{1x} = F_{FO}\lambda_0 f_0$. The
result is a Fourier transform with scale independent of wavelength. Instead
there is now a longitudinal dispersion; for shorter wavelengths, the HOE has
a longer focal length, and the source image is then farther from the HOE
than it is for longer wavelengths (Fig. 13.1). Thus, it appears that we have
merely substituted one problem for another.

We require a second lens system that will appropriately shift the image
position as a function of wavelength while keeping the magnification wavelength independent. We now invoke the concept of the shift lens. We choose
(Fig. 13.2) two lenses, L_1 and L_2, separated by the sum of their focal lengths.
For all object positions, the magnification is just the ratio of the focal lengths,
F_2/F_1. Next, consider a third lens L_s placed at the common focal plane of
L_1 and L_2. This lens will cause the image to shift position, but the magnification is unaltered. This can be shown readily by simple algebra. Alternatively, we can argue from basic principles. The lens L_s is in fact a spatial
filter. The operation it performs is linear and spatially invariant. Therefore,
it cannot introduce magnification, since if it did it would not be invariant.
This argument should be quite compelling to those who are familiar with
spatial filtering. Those not convinced by this heuristic argument may prefer
just to calculate the magnification of this three-lens system, which is

$$M_2 = F_2/F_1 .$$

Fig. 13.2.

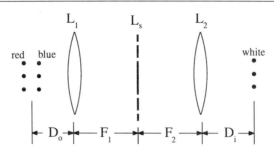

Spatial filtering system using the shift lens concept to compensate for longitudinal dispersion.

If we use a zone plate lens (HOE) for the shift lens, we can produce longitudinal dispersion, which calculations show will be proportional to wavelength. Thus, if we place the shift lens system downstream from the first portion of the optical system, and if we choose the available parameters properly, we can eliminate the longitudinal dispersion. Thus we form an achromatic Fourier transform. The compensation is only approximate and is useful only over a bandwidth of about 40 nm.

2.1. Formation of a Fourier Transform Hologram

Collins (1981) extended this work by integrating the achromatic Fourier transform system into an achromatic grating interferometer so as to form in broadband light a Fourier transform hologram that could be used as a spatial matched filter. The insertion must be made so that neither the achromatization of the Fourier transform system nor that of the interferometer will be compromised. Practically, this means that the lenses that form the achromatic Fourier transform system should encompass both branches of the interferometer, otherwise path differences will arise that cause the loss of fringes. The system, as given by Collins, is shown in Fig. 13.3. The grating G_2 is an off-axis Fresnel zone plate; thus it serves as both a grating element of the interferometer and as the lens L_F of the Fourier transforming system. The object-bearing plate extends through both beams of the interferometer, for path balancing purposes, but the object s is restricted to the portion of the plate that intercepts the upper beam.

Experimental results reported by Leon and Leith (1985) (Fig. 13.4) show the reconstruction of a Fourier transform hologram made in the presence of considerable noise. Figure 13.4a shows the reconstruction of a hologram made with monochromatic light. Figure 13.4b shows the reconstruction from

Fig. 13.3.

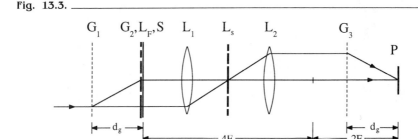

Final optical system combining Figs. 13.1 and 13.2 as described by Collins.

Fig. 13.4.

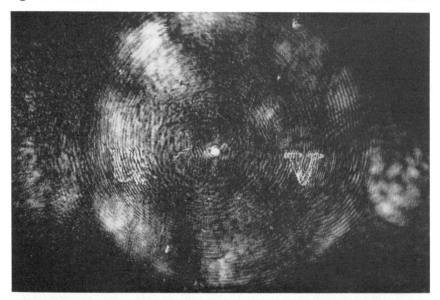

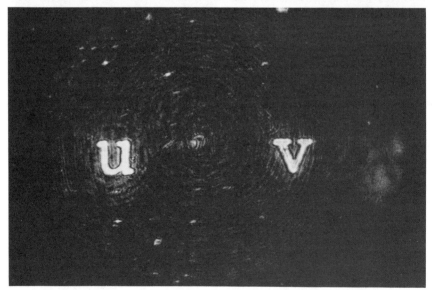

Image reconstruction from a Fourier transform hologram made in a noisy system. (a) Hologram made with monochromatic light; (b) hologram made in polychromatic light.

a hologram made in the same system, but with polychromatic light obtained by shifting a tunable dye laser over its 40-nm bandwidth during the exposure time, making the source effectively a spatially coherent polychromatic source of 40-nm bandwidth. The enormous noise reduction in the polychromatic case is apparent.

3.

White Light Coherent Correlator

A quite different approach to white light optical processing and holography was presented by Leith and Roth (1977) and Swanson (1981). The basic concept, as shown in Fig. 13.5, is that of a cross-correlation process that is inherently perfectly achromatic. A stationary mask $r(x, y)$ is imaged onto a moving mask $s(x - x', y)$, where the x' variable denotes the movement. The light emerging from the second mask represents the product rs. A lens of focal length F forms the Fourier transform of the product:

$$\int rs \exp\left(j \frac{xx''}{\lambda F} \right) dx, \tag{13.1}$$

where x'' is the coordinate of the Fourier transform plane. The cylindrical lens L_{cy} is introduced so as to form only a one-dimensional Fourier transform, i.e., a Fourier transform along the x'' dimension. The Fourier transform has the usual λ dependence. However, at the point $x'' = 0$, we have

$$\int r(x, y)s(x - x'', y) \, dx \tag{13.2}$$

The λ dependence has disappeared, thus rendering the process perfectly ach-

Fig. 13.5. _____

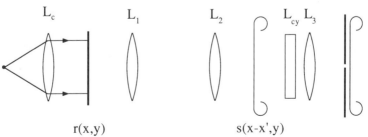

White light correlator.

romatic. Equation 13.1 can be described as a multichannel, one-dimensional cross correlation in which the operation is performed in the x direction only, for a continuous range of values of the variable y. By inserting this system into an achromatic interferometer, formed with diffraction gratings, the output can be placed on a carrier, thus preserving any phase distributions that may be generated. If r is an off-axis Fresnel zone plate and s is an arbitrary object transparency, then the output is the convolution of the object with a zone-plate point-spread function.

When the spatial carrier is introduced, the result is a conventional hologram, but dispersed in only one dimension. The hologram is of course generated only one line at a time, as the transparency s is moved through the system and a recording film moves past a slit at $x'' = 0$ on the output plane. In another arrangement, s is a one-dimensionally blurred image and r is the restoration function. The output is then the deblurred image. Experimental results were given for deblurring by Yang and Leith (1981).

A variant of this deblurring method was described by Leith (1980), in which the deblurring mask was a simple Ronchi ruling (a diffraction grating with rulings of square profile).

4.
Further Development of White Light Filtering

Morris and George (1980) have reported impressive results on achromatic spatial matched filtering using a system related to that of Katyl. Their system is described with respect to Fig. 13.6. The object is Fourier transformed by a lens combination consisting of a conventional lens L_1 and a pair of zone plate lenses L_2 and L_3, with L_2 being used as a negative lens and L_3 as a positive lens. They report that this compensation reduces the scale factor variation to only 15% of its value compared to a conventional nonachromatic system. The spatial matched filter, made with monochromatic illumination, embodies the usual holographic spatial carrier and therefore is grating-like; consequently, a compensating grating G is used to remove the dispersion produced by the filter. The spatially filtered result appears at the output.

Morris (1981a, 1981b) has described more sophisticated broad-spectrum Fourier transforming systems in which the achromatization is improved so that the usable wavelength band is significantly increased. This is accomplished by the use of holographic lenses in combination with glass doublets in which the wavelength dispersion is specially designed to correct the in-

Fig. 13.6.

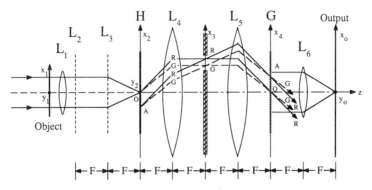

Spatial filtering system of Morris and George.

herent limitations of the conventional Katyl method, which uses holographic lenses in combination with conventional imaging lenses. They reported significant improvements in the broad-spectrum capability.

In related work, George and Shen-ge Wang (1984) have devised a system that creates a cosinusoidal transform that works with spatially incoherent broadband light and can therefore be used on an incoherently illuminated object scene. The system is essentially an optoelectronic hybrid system whose output is interfaced with a digital computer. A bias term is subtracted electronically. The optical system consists of an incoherent, broadband source that illuminates an object; the illumination then goes to a beam splitter and a pair of crossed roof prisms, and, finally through an achromatic Fourier transforming lens system to a detector array. The roof prisms produce, from an object $g(x, y)$, a pair of polarly symmetric images, $g(x, y)$ and $g(-x, -y)$. The lens system then produces an achromatic cosine transform from this image pair.

Yu (1983) has described a wide range of techniques for white light optical processing, some requiring spatial coherence, others not. The applications include: complex spatial filtering; pseudocolor displays; color image deblurring; color image subtraction; image subtraction with encoded, extended incoherent sources; the generation of multiple images; archival storage; and color restoration for faded color film. The techniques are quite varied, although there is one feature that underlies most of them: the use of diffraction gratings to place the input signal on a carrier and to disperse the light into a spectrum at the Fourier transform plane. We note that this use of gratings is quite different from that in our work, where the gratings have been used as elements of broad-source achromatic interferometers.

Many of the applications follow from the fundamental system shown in Fig. 13.7, which shows a standard coherent spatial filtering system in which a diffraction grating is overlain on the input plane. At the Fourier transform plane P_2 the light is spread into three diffracted orders (assuming the grating produces no higher orders). Of interest is one of the diffracted orders. In the first order, the light is spread into a spectrum of colors. The object spatial frequency spectrum is repeated for each wavelength component of the source; each spectrum is displaced in proportion to the wavelength. If the spatial frequency on the grating is sufficiently high, the light at any location α in the frequency plane can be considered monochromatic. We can place an array of spatial filters H_1, H_n in this plane; each filter will see the object spatial frequency at a different wavelength, and each will perform the appropriate spatial filtering operation. Since the object spatial frequency spectrum has a scale proportional to wavelength, each filter will have to have a different scale factor so as to be correct for the wavelength it encounters. The second lens L_2 forms a spatially filtered image of the object for each wavelength. These many images combine incoherently, after having traversed different paths in the optical system. This incoherent addition will average out noise from defects in the optical system, such as scatterers, etc. The result is an image that is free from the noise that plagues the typical coherent optical system. Yet, the system is essentially a coherent one, for which the laws of coherent spatial filtering apply. In reality, the system is a multichannel coherent system, with as many separate channels as there are discernibly different wavelength components, each channel having noise that is essentially uncorrelated with that of the other channels.

The filter (or filter band) H can perform many tasks. For example, it can

Fig. 13.7.

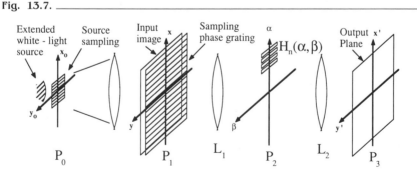

Typical system used by Yu for achromatic optical processing.

be a deblurring filter to correct a linear, or motion, blur of a photograph. It could be a filter for subtraction of two different input signals.

If the object is a color photographic transparency, the possibilities become quite interesting. Since the illuminating source contains all wavelengths, it appears that there is the possibility of the optical processing of a color object. Yu has shown experimental results of deblurring of a color photograph and of color image subtraction, i.e., taking the difference between two color images.

4.1. White Light Displays and Storage

White light techniques have produced some interesting devices in the areas of display and archival storage. Jiang (1982) has described a very convenient pseudocolor encoder and reader. In one mode of operation, two similar images are superimposed in such a way that portions of the image that are identical appear white, whereas portions that are different appear in color. The key element of the device is a diffraction lens (HOE) that, between images and object plane, disperses the illuminating white light into its spectrum, allowing color selection.

The same system also permits the mapping of photographic density into color. The image is modulated with a grating pattern, either before or at the time of insertion into the system. The basic principle is that the image formed in the zeroth order of the overlaying grating is a negative, whereas the image formed in the first order is a positive. The object film is illuminated by a white light source in which the red is removed, resulting in a greenish image. Also, the object is illuminated by a red source (HeNe laser) so that the two images superimpose. Ordinarily, the result would simply be a black-and-white image. However, if the first image is formed in the zeroth order of the object grating and the second in the first order, the result is the superposition of a negative image in green and a positive image in red. Consequently, light areas of the object form a predominantly green image, whereas dark areas form a predominantly red image; hence, the image is coded so that density is mapped into color variations.

Several methods of color storage of color transparencies have been demonstrated, all related to a color photographic process discovered originally by Ives, in which color is encoded onto black-and-white film by spatial frequency (Ives, 1906), that is, the red component is modulated onto a spatial frequency carrier, the green onto a second spatial frequency carrier, and the blue onto a third, all carriers differing either in magnitude or direction.

The readout is accomplished with a white light source with appropriate spatial filtering, and the image can be in true color, or with the colors rearranged, depending on the output spatial filtering arrangement.

Ih reported such a method in 1975, using coherent, Fourier transform methods. Yu et al. (1980) recorded three separate images of a color transparency, each coded with a Ronchi ruling in different orientations, in a manner similar to Ives, so that the three primary colors were modulated onto three different spatial carriers. In another technique, by Chen and Cheng (1983), a Mach Zehnder interferometer, adjusted for broad-source fringes, is illuminated with a laser source, with the spatial coherence reduced by the usual means of a rotating ground-glass diffuser. The object transparency is placed in one branch of the interferometer and is imaged to the fringe localization plane. An image plane hologram is thus formed with partially coherent light. The hologram is read out with a white light source, and spatial filtering is done to select the desired wavelength band in which to form the image. Because of the coherence reduction in both the making and readout process, the image will be very free from noise. To extend the process to color pictures, the process is repeated three times, using a HeNe laser to provide red, and an argon to provide green and blue; each color component resides on a differently oriented fringe pattern, permitting the different images to be separated by spatial filtering.

4.2. Monochromatic Extended Source Spatial Filtering

Perhaps the most significant accomplishment in spatially incoherent optical processing has been the two-pupil method of modulation transfer function synthesis by which incoherent illumination acquires the full range of spatial filtering capability that is achieved by coherent methods. The basic papers are by Gorlitz and Lanzl (1977), Lohmann (1977), and Rhodes (1977), all arriving independently at their particular form of the two-pupil method. A few months later, an independent experimental paper by Stoner (1977) gave convincing evidence of the power of the two-pupil method. A powerful analysis method for the technique was given by Stoner (1978) and Cartwright (1984).

This work was continued by Angell (1988), who, among other contributions, achromatized the interferometric process by the use of grating elements for the interferometer and thereby demonstrated bandpass spatial filtering using arbitrary, diffusely reflecting objects and perfectly incoherent, while light from an extended source.

The two-pupil method takes on various forms. We limit our discussion to only one, which we now describe in a rather physical way. First we consider a conventional coherent spatial filtering system (Fig. 13.8), wherein an object with amplitude transmittance s is imaged through a spatial filter H to give an output field $u = s \circledast h$, where h and H are a Fourier transform pair, and $*$ means convolution. If the illumination is spatially incoherent, the system becomes linear in intensity and the output intensity is $1 = |u|^2 \circledast |h|^2$ or, alternatively, $F\{1\} = S\,[H \circledast H]$, which states that the image has a Fourier transform that is the product of the object Fourier transform multiplied by the autocorrelation function of the mask amplitude transmittance H ($\circledast$ means correlation). This is a rather depressing result, stating that if spatial filtering is done in an incoherently illuminated system, the transfer function realized is only the autocorrelation function of the filter mask H. Autocorrelation functions tend to be rather uninteresting transfer functions; they are inherently low pass and the synthesis possibilities are very meager.

However, as shown in Fig. 13.9, when two conventional spatial filtering systems are placed in a two-beam interferometer adjusted for broad-source fringes and the output fringe pattern is recorded as an image-plane hologram, a most interesting result ensues. When the recorded pattern is read out in the first order, the image has the form (to within a constant)

$$u = |s|^2 * h_1 h_2{}^* \tag{13.3}$$

or

$$F\{u\} = \zeta[H_1 \circledast H_2], \tag{13.4}$$

where ζ is the Fourier transform of $|s|^2$. The image has been modified by a transfer function that is not merely an autocorrelation function, but rather a cross correlation; and unlike the autocorrelation function, the cross corre-

Fig. 13.8. ────────────────────────────

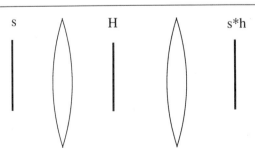

Coventional coherent spatial filtering system.

Fig. 13.9. _____

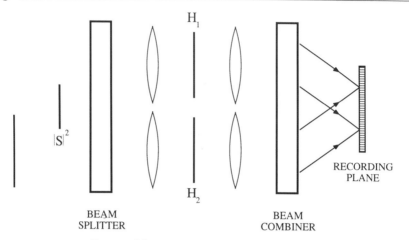

Two-pupil incoherent spatial filtering system.

lation function is most interesting indeed. First, the cross correlation $H = H_1 \circledast H_2$ of two functions takes on the same range of values that either H_1 or H_2 can by itself, which is to say that the incoherent modulation transfer function H has the full range of filter synthesis capabilities that can be manifested by a coherent system. Further, there is an infinite number of synthesis possibilities; essentially, we can choose H_1 in an infinite number of ways, and for each H_1 there exists a corresponding H_2 such that $H_1 \circledast H_2$ yields the desired result.

A recent form, embodying the basic principals of the early authors plus subsequent improvements, is shown in Fig. 13.10. This system, taken from Angell, works with arbitrary light. The light from a microscope illuminator is passed through a diffuser and thus is both white and spatially incoherent.

Fig. 13.10. _____

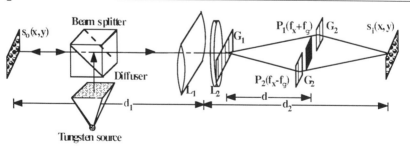

White light spatial filtering system with two-pupil system (after Angell).

Fig. 13.11. _____

Spatially incoherent high pass filtering of a 3-D object in white light.

A prism beam splitter directs the light onto an arbitrary, diffusely reflecting, three-dimensional object at normal incidence, and the reflected light then passes through the beam splitter onto the two-pupil spatial filtering system. The interferometer is formed from diffraction gratings and is therefore achromatic. The lens that images the object to the output plane is upstream from the interfereometer, so that it does not have to image the fringe structure; hence its entire spatial frequency passband can be used for imaging the object. The filters H_1 and H_2 consist of an on-axis stop and a pair of symmetrically-placed off-axis slits; thus the cross correlation is bandpass. The filter thus performs edge enhancement. The cylindrical lens is required to compensate the astigmatism that the gratings introduce. Although the interferometer is achromatic, the spatial filtering system is not, and therefore the passband is λ dependent. However, the edge sharpening operation, the λ dependence is inconsequential; all that is required is that the system be bandpass for all wavelengths, and this condition is met. For more sophisticated filters, such as the matched filter or stop-band filter, the filtering system would have to be achromatized, most likely in the manner of Katyl. Fig. 3.11 shows an example of edge sharpening on a real-world object (a gear).

The two-pupil system has many variants; its flexibility is enormous. Many other directions of implementation are described by Lohmann and Rhodes (1978). Here we have stressed the so-called pupil interaction mode, in which the transfer function is produced by the multiplicative interaction of the two-pupil masks H_1 and H_2. Alternatively, there are the non-pupil interaction modes, in which the transfer function is formed by the linear combination of the two pupil masks, with arbitrary phase between the two.

5.
Construction of Diffractive Optical Elements

A number of methods for the construction of diffractive (or holographic) optical elements have been described. Swanson (1983) has described the construction of diffraction lenses in monochromatic, extended source illumination. The basis for the system is the grating interferometer, which forms high-contrast fringes, unlimiting by the source size (Fig. 13.12). The upper branch contains a lens, which images plane A to the output. In the process, the planar wavefront is converted into a spherical wave. The lower branch contains a pair of lenses, arranged in the afocal mode, that is, separated by the sum of their focal lengths. This arrangement results in an incident plane wave being converted into an emerging plane wave. If rays that split from the same source point at the initial grating are brought together at the output,

Fig. 13.12.

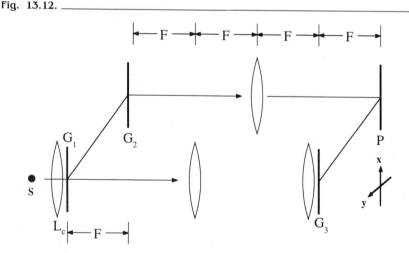

System for recording diffractive optical elements in spatially incoherent light.

interference occurs with broad source illumination and the recorded fringes thus form a zone plate, i.e., a diffraction lens. The two lenses in the lower branch might appear unnecessary, since if they were absent the result would still be a plane wave impinging on the output plane. These lenses are, however, needed for two reasons. First, the lens in the upper branch inverts the wavefront, and so the wavefront in the lower branch must also be inverted. A second reason is more subtle. The Fresnel-diffraction propagation distances must be the same in both beams. For the upper beam, this distance is from the source to plane A. The lower branch must then also image plane A to the input. We note that, for broad source incoherent illumination, as opposed to polychromatic illumination, the optical paths do not have to be equal; however, the Fresnel diffraction distances do have to be equal. The improvement in image quality between fringe paterns formed in the system with coherent light and with incoherent light is considerable (Fig. 13.13).

Leon (1987) has further investigated the construction of HOEs with incoherent light and has devised a new interferometer, formed with mirrors and prisms, to obtain high-quality broad source fringes.

Leith and Hershey (1985) have described two methods for producing fringes of arbitrary profile with incoherent light using the grating interferometer. In these methods, multiple beams from various diffraction orders of the gratings are combined after appropriate spatial filtering, which adjusts the attenuation and phase of the combining beams. The first method uses monochromatic, spatially incoherent light, but the synthesis is coherent in that the system is linear in field. The second method uses polychromatic, extended source light, and here the synthesis is incoherent in that the system is linear in irradiance. Iemmi et al. (1987) as well as Chen et al. (1985), have used these techniques to produce sawtooth fringes, which can be recorded to form blazed gratings.

Leith and Shentu (1986) have described a method of diffraction tomography using monochromatic, spatially incoherent light and the grating interferometer, in which the grating interferometer performs, under incoherent illumination, a Fourier decomposition of the object in the longitudinal and in one lateral dimension; the Fourier components are displayed in the output as fringe patterns located in different planes. The object can be reconstructed by recording the contrast and phase of the fringe patterns, reading them into a digital computer, and doing a matrix inversion to put the Fourier components back together.

The incoherent work has added immeasurably to the field of optical processing and holography, and produced many quite surprising results. The

Fig. 13.13.

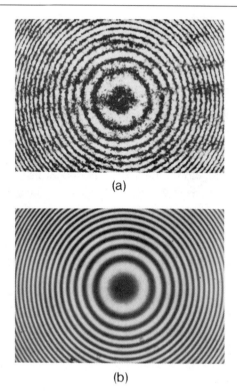

(a)

(b)

Zone plate pattern produced with (a) coherent light and (b) incoherent light in the same optical system.

usefulness of the incoherent techniques will eventually be determined; the decision is not in yet. It seems likely that some of these methods will prove durable.

References

Angell, D. (1988). "Incoherent spatial filtering with the grating interferometer," PhD thesis, University Microfilms.

Cartwright, S. (1984). "Incoherent optical processing: A coherence theory approach," *Appl. Opt.* **23,** 318.

Chavel, P. (1980). "Optical noise and temporal coherence," *J. Opt. Soc. Am.* **70,** 935.

Chavel, P., and Lowenthal, S. (1980). "Noise and coherence in optical image processing. II. Noise fluctuations," *J. Opt. Soc. Am.* **68,** 721.

Chen, H., and Cheng, Y. (1983). "Low-noise multicolor archival storage with broad source interferometric imaging," *Appl. Opt.* **22,** 2790.

Chen, H., Hershey, R., and Leith, E. (1988). "Sawtooth profile fringes with a two-grating interferometer," *Appl. Opt.* **27,** 1193.

Collins, G. (1981). "Achromatic Fourier transform holography," *Appl. Opt.* **20,** 3109.

George, N., and Wang, Shen-ge. (1984). "Cosinusoidal transforms in white light," *Appl. Opt.* **23,** 787.

Gorlitz, D., and Lenzl, F. (1977). "Methods of zero-order non-coherent spatial filtering," *Opt. Comm.* **20,** 68.

Iemmi, C.C., Simon, J.M., and Ratto, J.O. (1987). "Synthesis of asymmetrical profiles from a double grating interferometer," *Appl. Opt.* **25,** 1822.

Ih, C.S. (1975). "Multicolor imagery from holograms by spatial filtering," *Appl. Opt.* **14,** 438.

Ives, H.E. (1906). "Improvements in the diffraction process of color photography," *Br. J. Photog.* **609.**

Jiang, Y.G. (1982). "Simplified color image-processing system using a dichronated gelatin holographic element," *Appl. Opt.* **21,** 3138.

Katyl, R.H. (1979). "Compensating optical systems. Part 1: Broadband holographic reconstruction; Part 2: Generation of a hologram with broadband light; Part 3: Achromatic Fourier transforms, *Appl. Opt.* **18,** 4025.

Leith, E. (1980). "Image deblurring using diffraction gratings," *Opt. Lett* **5,** 70.

Leith, E., and Hershey, R. (1985). "Transfer functions and spatial filtering in grating interferometers," *Appl. Opt.* **24,** 237.

Leith, E., and Roth, J. (1977). "White light optical processing and holography," *Appl. Opt.* **16,** 2565.

Leith, E., and Shentu, L. (1986). "Tomographic reconstruction of objects by grating interferometer," *Appl. Opt.* **25,** 907.

Leon, S. (1987). "Broad source fringe formation with a Fresnel biprism and a Mach-Zehnder interferometer, *Appl. Opt.* **26,** 5259.

Leon, S., and Leith, E. (1985). "Optical processing and holography with polychromatic point source illumination," *Appl. Opt.* **24,** 3638.

Lohmann, A. (1977). "Incoherent optical data processing of complex data," *Appl. Opt.* **16,** 261.

Lohmann, A., and Rhodes, W. (1978). "Two-pupil synthesis of optical transfer functions," *Appl. Opt.* **17,** 1141.

Morris, G.M ., and George, N. (1980). "Frequency plane filtering with an achromatic optical transform, *Opt. Lett.* **5,** 446.

Morris, G.M. (1981a). "Diffraction theory for an achromatic Fourier transform," *Appl. Opt.* **20,** 2017.

Morris, G.M. (1981b). "An ideal achromatic Fourier transform processor," *Opt. Comm.* **39,** 143.

Rhodes, W. (1977). "Bipolar pointspread function by phase switching," *Appl. Opt.* **16,** 265.

Rogers, G.L. (1977). "Noncoherent Optical Processing," John Wiley and Sons, New York.

Stoner, W. (1977). "Edge enhancement with incoherent optics," *Appl. Opt.* **16,** 1451.

Stoner, W. (1978). "Incoherent optical processing via spatially offset pupil masks," *Appl. Opt.* **17,** 2454.

Swanson, G. (1981). "Recording of one-dimensional holograms in white light," *Appl. Opt.* **20,** 4267.

Swanson, G. (1983). "Interferometric recording of high quality zone plates in spatially incoherent illumination," *Opt. Lett.* **8,** 45.

Yang, G., and Leith, E. (1981). "White light image deblurring." *Appl. Opt.* **20,** 3995.

Yu, F.T.S. (1980). "White light processing technqiue for archival storage of color films," *Appl. Opt.* **19,** 2457.

Yu, F.T.S. (1983). "Optical Information Processing," John Wiley and Sons, New York.

Yu, F.T.S., Shaik, S., and Zhuang, S.L. (1985). "Noise performance of a white-light optical processor. II. Spatially partially coherent illumination," *Appl. Phys.* **B36,** 11.

14.

Generalized Matched Spatial Filters with Optimum Light Efficiency

Katarzyna Chałasińska-Macukow

Institute of Geophysics
Warsaw University
Warsaw, Poland

Contents

1. Introduction. 442
2. Light Utilization Problems in Optical Correlators 443
3. Phase-Only Matched Filtering 446
   3.1. Enhanced Discrimination Capability of the Phase-Only Filter 446
      3.1.1. High-Pass Matched Filtering 447
      3.1.2. Results of Discrimination by Using MSF_h and POF 448
   3.2. Scale and Rotation Sensitivity of the Phase-Only Filter 451
   3.3. Various Realizations of the Phase-Only Filter 452
      3.3.1. Continuous Phase-Only Filters 452
      3.3.2. Binary Phase-Only Filters 453
      3.3.3. Composite Phase-Only Filters. 454
4. Matched Filtering Using Tandem Component Filters 455
   4.1. Tandem Component Filters 457
   4.2. Character Recognition Using Tandem Component Filters 458
   4.3. Binary-Phase Version of Tandem Component Filters 462
5. Conclusion 463
   References 464

1.

Introduction

Matched filtering was a widely used method of pattern recognition (Turin, 1960), even before Vander Lugt's introduction of matched filtering into coherent optics (Vander Lugt, 1964). Correlation methods have played a very important role in optical information processing. Matched filtering is a powerful technique because it can search an input scene for the desired pattern without scanning. The matched spatial filter realization is very simple, especially now that such filters can be made digitally (see, e.g., Lee, 1978; Dallas, 1980) and incorporated into optical processors (hybrid systems) (Leger and Lee, 1982). Using digital methods one can easily modify the filter, depending on the application, by making it more sensitive to between-class variations for better enhancement of small differences between classified objects or by making it less sensitive to within-class variations such as rotation, translation, magnification, etc. (Almeida and Indebetouw, 1982; Hsu and Arsenault, 1982; Leger and Lee, 1982; Merkle and Lorch, 1984; Wu and Stark, 1984).

For several applications, however, the light efficiency of the optical correlator is not satisfactory (Caulfield, 1982; Horner, 1982). The basic problems are the light losses due to the holographic spatial filters used. Light losses may be produced by absorption or by diffraction into orders not used in the processing step. In ordinary holography, there are well-known methods of increasing the light efficiency of the filter, but it is always much smaller than unity even if phase recorders are used (Cathey, 1974).

Recent works have shown that the problem of low light efficiency of optical correlators can be avoided with the help of several types of pure phase filters used as generalized matched spatial filters. One type of phase-only filter (POF) was proposed by Horner and Gianino (1984); another, the tandem component filter (TCF), was proposed by Bartelt (1984). Both kinds of filters assure a theoretical light efficiency of 100% independently of the object function. This performance is important for optical pattern recognition, especially in the case of compact optical processors or in applications using spatial light modulators (Casasent et al., 1987; Davis et al., 1987; Flannery et al., 1986; Gregory, 1986; Gregory and Huckabee, 1985). The first results obtained with the use of phase-only filtering (Bartelt, 1984; Horner and Gianino, 1984) initiated a series of studies analyzing the possibilities of more complicated phase-only filters, continuous as well as binary.

This chapter demonstrates different realizations of generalized matched spatial filtering with optimum light efficiency and discusses the performance of such optical processors. The filters discussed are called *generalized matched spatial filters* because information about the reference target registered on the filter is reduced or modified, and the optical processor does not give an exact correlation-type operation similar to the one obtained with a conventional matched spatial filter.

2.
Light Utilization Problems in Optical Correlators

The low light efficiency of optical matched spatial filters is due to the fact that for most object functions light power in the Fourier spectrum is very unevenly distributed. Usually it is maximum at zero spatial frequency and rapidly decreases towards higher spatial frequencies. Light efficiency of an optical processor depends on what fraction of the input light power is converted into the output peak. Horner introduced a very useful measure for light efficiency of optical pattern recognition systems, called by Caulfield (1982) the *Horner efficiency*. The definition of the light efficiency η_H is

$$\eta_H = \frac{\text{power measured at the correlation peak}}{\text{power in the object beam}}, \tag{14.1}$$

For an optical correlator one obtains

$$\eta_H = \eta_D \frac{\displaystyle\iint\limits_{S_c} |f(x, y) ** h(x, y)|^2 \, dx_0 d y_0}{\displaystyle\iint |f(x, y)|^2 dx dy}, \tag{14.2}$$

where η_D is the diffraction efficiency of the recording medium, $f(x, y)$ is the input function, $h(x, y)$ is the reference function of the searched target, and the operator ** indicates two-dimensional correlation. x, y and x_0, y_0 are Cartesian coordinates in the input plane and in the output plane, respectively, and S_c is the correlation peak spot.

In the Fourier transform plane the analogous formula takes the form (Gianino and Horner, 1984)

$$\eta_H = \eta_D \frac{\displaystyle\int\limits_{-\infty}^{\infty}\!\!\int |F(u, v)|^2 |H(u, v)|^2 \, du dv}{\displaystyle\int\limits_{-\infty}^{\infty}\!\!\int |F(u, v)|^2 du dv}, \tag{14.3}$$

where $F(u, v)$ and $H(u, v)$ are the Fourier transforms of the input function and of the reference function, respectively, and u, v are spatial frequencies in the Fourier transform plane.

For the matched spatial filter

$$H(u, v) = F^*(u, v), \qquad (14.4)$$

where * indicates the complex conjugate of the Fourier transform and

$$\eta_H = \eta_D \frac{\int\int\limits_{-\infty}^{\infty} |F(u, v)|^4 \, du \, dv}{\int\int\limits_{-\infty}^{\infty} |F(u, v)|^2 \, du \, dv}. \qquad (14.5)$$

If $f(x, y) = h(x, y) = \text{rect}(x/a) \, \text{rect}(y/a)$ one obtains $\eta_H = 44.4\%$ if $\eta_D = 1$ (Horner, 1982). Thus even with a simple object function and with a perfect medium the best light efficiency that can be obtained is equal to 44.4%. For the inverse filter

$$H(u, v) = \frac{1}{F(u, v)}, \qquad (14.6)$$

and the efficiency is equal to $\eta_H \sim 0.01\%$.

The value of the light efficiency η_H thus depends on the kind of recognition problem that must be solved. Light efficiency as well as discrimination capabilities depend strongly on the spatial frequency characteristic of the filter. The low-frequency information with the highest light power is of very little value for discrimination. Usually, for a pattern recognition filter, the greatest discrimination capability yields extremely low light efficiency (Caulfield, 1982; Szu, 1985).

The problem of compromise between discrimination capability and light efficiency almost always arises in optical pattern recognition methods using as a reference target only partial information about the object.

Any reference target $f(x, y)$ may be decomposed into orthogonal functions $h_i(x, y)$

$$f(x, y) = \sum_i h_i(x, y), \qquad (14.7)$$

and any single orthogonal component $h_j(x, y)$ can be used as a reference.

In this case the light efficiency η_H^j of the optical processor with one component $h_j(x, y)$ takes the form

$$\eta_H^j = \eta_D \frac{\displaystyle\int\int_{-\infty}^{\infty} \left| \sum_i H_i(u, v) \right|^2 |H_j(u, v)|^2 \, du \, dv}{\displaystyle\int\int_{-\infty}^{\infty} |F(u, v)|^2 \, du \, dv}, \qquad (14.8)$$

and because of the orthogonality of the expansion, Eq. (14.8) reduces to

$$\eta_H^j = \eta_D \frac{\displaystyle\int\int_{-\infty}^{\infty} |H_j(u, v)|^4 \, du \, dv}{\displaystyle\int\int_{-\infty}^{\infty} |F(u, v)|^2 \, du \, dv}. \qquad (14.9)$$

Light efficiency for a filter using one component as a reference target is always smaller than that for a conventional matched spatial filter [see Eq. (14.5)].

One useful application of orthogonal decompositions for optical pattern recognition is the rotation-invariant optical pattern recognition method using the circular harmonic expansion (Arsenault et al., 1984; Hsu, 1982; Hsu et al., 1982). To accomplish rotation-invariant pattern recognition, any single harmonic component can be used as a reference. It has been proven that if the target pattern is real and positive, the zero-order circular harmonic component is the strongest one among all the components. The general tendency for high-order circular harmonic components of the pattern is to be weaker, similar to the Fourier spectrum decrease at high spatial frequencies (Hsu, 1982). Thus, the zero-order component assures maximum light efficiency (Yang et al., 1982), but is not able to discriminate between similar objects. To improve discrimination capability, higher circular harmonic components are used and the price to be paid is a loss in light efficiency (Hsu, 1982; Arsenault et al., 1984). In some cases the degree of discrimination varies almost inversely with the Horner efficiency (Caulfield, 1982; Caulfield and Weinberg, 1982).

3.

Phase-Only Matched Filtering

In general the Fourier transform of the object is complex

$$\mathcal{F}\{f(x, y)\} = A(u, v) \exp[i\varphi(u, v)], \qquad (14.10)$$

where $\mathcal{F}$ is the Fourier transform operator, and $A(u, v)$ and $\varphi(u, v)$ are the amplitude and the phase, respectively.

The relative roles played by phase and amplitude information in the Fourier domain to preserve the accuracy of the restored image has been discussed in many recent papers (Oppenheim, 1981). The general result of this discussion in the image processing field is that the phase information is more important than the amplitude information. "Is the same true in the case of a matched filter?" is a question posed by Horner and Gianino (1984). They presented the results of a computer simulation and compared the phase only filter with the classical matched spatial filter.

The phase-only filter $F_\varphi(u, v)$ is defined as (Caulfield, 1982; Horner and Gianino, 1984)

$$F_\varphi(u, v) = \exp[-i\varphi(u, v)] \qquad (14.11)$$

by setting the modulus $A(u, v)$ in Eq. (14.10) equal to unity. It is very simple to prove, by substituting the transmittance of the phase-only filter $F_\varphi(u, v)$ into Eq. (14.3), that the light efficiency for this filter is maximum and is equal to one if the diffraction efficiency is equal to one. This is a major advantage of this filter and the reason why much recent work has been initiated to analyze the performance and the various realizations of such filters.

3.1. Enhanced Discrimination Capability of the Phase-Only Filter

The computer simulation made by Horner and Gianino (1984) proved that the phase-only filter yields superior discrimination between similar objects (capital O and G). Table 14.1 shows a comparison between the results ob-

TABLE 14.1

Correlation Results for Noise-Free Inputs*

Object	Peak Intensity		(%)	
	MSF	POF	MSF	POF
G	1.	57.6	27.2	100
O	0.92	35.3	27.7	100

* After Horner and Gianino (1984).

tained by using a matched spatial filter (MSF) and a phase-only filter (POF) for noise-free inputs (Horner and Gianino, 1984). The results of Table 14.1 are interesting because they show that the phase-only filter not only assures 100% light efficiency, but also enhances the discrimination capability. This situation is far from that described in the previous part of this chapter, where improved discrimination capability was paid for with lower light efficiency.

3.1.1. High-Pass Matched Filtering

The phase-only filter performmance can be easily explained using a simple model of this filter consisting of a conventional matched filter $A(u, v)$ $\exp[-i\varphi(u, v)]$ preceded by an amplitude-only filter $A(u, v)^{-1}$ (Horner and Leger, 1985). The amplitude-only filter preceding the conventional matched filter has a reciprocal response that acts as a high-pass filter. The better ability of discrimination between similar objects is the result of the domination of high spatial frequencies in the impulse response of the phase-only filter.

The high-pass characteristic of the phase-only filter suggests comparing the discrimination capability of this filter with that of the high-pass matched spatial filter, which has enhanced discrimination capability (Chałasińska-Macukow and Nitka, 1987b).

There are several practical methods of increasing the discrimination capability of matched spatial filters (Binns et al., 1968; Vasilenko and Cybulkin, 1985; Wintzer, 1974). The most popular method consists of removing low spatial frequencies by using opaque stops or slits centered on the optical axis as an additional filter in the Fourier transform plane. The other method, leaving only the edge information, is to differentiate the reference target. For two-dimensional functions an additional filter with circular symmetry with a transmittance proportional to the distance from the optical axis gives a good approximation to the first derivative (Binns et al., 1968; Vasilenko and Cybulkin, 1985).

A particularly simple and effective optical method for increasing the discrimination by partial differentiation that does not require any additional filter is to overexpose the spectrum information of the target from which the filter is made (Binns et al., 1968; Chałasińska-Macukow and Nitka, 1987a).

All the filters mentioned above can be described by the formula

$$\text{MSF}_h = S(u, v)\, A(u, v)\, \exp[-i\,\varphi(u, v)]. \qquad (14.12)$$

The index h means high-pass matched spatial filtering and $S(u, v)$ is an additional filter with a high-pass characteristic (prefiltering). The prefiltering

$S(u, v)$ can take various forms. The most popular methods of prefiltering are as follows:

In the case of using the opaque stop with a radius equal to a

$$S(u, v) = 1 - \text{circ}\left(\frac{r}{a}\right),\qquad(14.13)$$

where

$$\text{circ}\left(\frac{r}{a}\right) = \begin{cases} 0 & \text{if } r > a \\ \dfrac{1}{2} & \text{if } r = a \\ 1 & \text{if } r < a \end{cases}$$

and r is the distance from the optical axis;

in the case of using the first derivative approximation as a reference target

$$S(u, v) = u^2 + v^2.\qquad(14.14)$$

The phase-only filter in this approach is also the high-pass matched spatial filter with the prefiltering

$$S(u, v) = A(u, v)^{-1}.\qquad(14.15)$$

3.1.2. Results of Discrimination by using MSF_h and POF

The digital analysis presented by Chałasińska-Macukow and Nitka (1987b) contains a comparison of the discrimination capability between the different characters by means of the phase-only filter with analogous results obtained by using a high-pass matched spatial filter. The high-pass matched spatial filter was made by using an opaque stop simulation on the optical axis [(Eq. 14.13)] with radius a equal to the average radius of the central maximum of the Fourier transform of the reference target. In the case considered, the reference target for all the filters was the character A, and the problem was to recognize the reference character A from among a set of tested characters A, X, D, O, U, and Y, by using the phase-only filter and a high-pass matched spatial filter. The digital results are presented in Figs. 14-1 to 14-3 and Table 14.2. Figures 14.1 to 14.3 show the normalized output peaks for the various filters. The results obtained for the matched spatial filter were considered as the reference case to which the other results were compared. For both, modified filters output peak is much sharper than the matched spatial filter peak. The signal-to-noise ratio in the output plane is the worst for the high-pass matched spatial filter because of the sidelobes generated by diffraction from the opaque stop.

Fig. 14.1. —————————————————————————————————

Output signal for the phase-only filter. (After Chałasińska-Macukow and Nitka, 1987b.)

Fig. 14.2. —————————————————————————————————

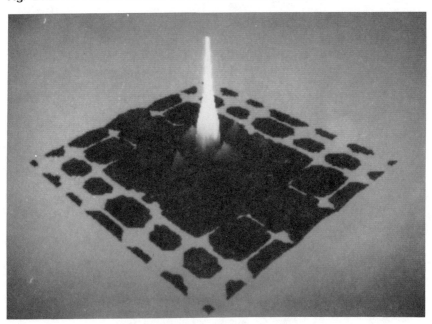

Output signal for the high-pass matched spatial filter. (After Chałasińska-Macukow and Nitka, 1987b.)

Fig. 14.3. _____

Output signal for the matched spatial filter. (After Chałasińska-Macukow and Nitka, 1987b.)

Table 14.2 shows the normalized output peak values for the three filters: phase-only filter (POF), high-pass matched spatial filter (MSF_h), and matched spatial filter (MSF). The two first filters have similar enhanced discrimination capability as compared with the matched spatial filter. This compar-

TABLE 14.2

Discrimination of Characters with the Use
of Various Types of Filters*

Object	Peak Intensity		
	POF	MSF_h	MSF
A	1.	1.	1.
D	0.18	0.3	0.5
O	0.21	0.34	0.57
Y	0.21	0.34	0.34
U	0.18	0.27	0.41
X	0.34	0.32	0.64

* After Chałasińska -Macukow and Nitka (1987b).

ison proves that the phase-only filter belongs to the class of matched spatial filters with enhanced discrimination capability.

Optical results of discrimination (Chałasińska-Macukow and Nitka, 1987b) obtained by means of an overexposed matched spatial filter and an optically made phase-only filter also confirm this conclusion.

3.2. Scale and Rotation Sensitivity of the Phase-Only Filter

The results of comparing the scale and rotation sensitivity of the phase-only filter with that of the conventional matched spatial filter, made by Gianino and Horner (1984), are presented in Figs. 14.4 and 14.5. The incident signal for the computer simulation was the capital letter G, and both filters were also matched to the same letter. Figure 14.4 shows the peak value of power in the correlation spot plotted against the angle of rotation in either direction for both filters. At the 70% response point, the response of the phase-only filter is approximately seven times more sensitive to rotation than the matched spatial filter. The effect of scale changes in the incident letter G on the

Fig. 14.4.

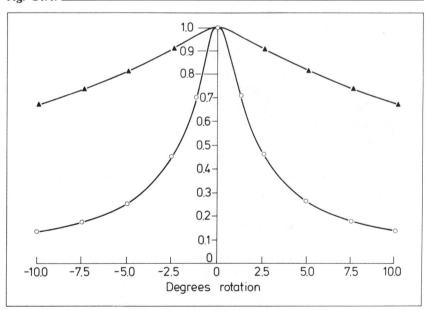

Correlation versus angle of rotation of the incoming signal relative to the filter. Data for the POF is indicated by circles; data for the MSF is indicated by triangles. (After Gianino and Horner, 1984.)

Fig. 14.5. _____

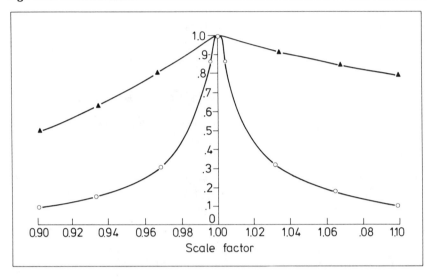

Correlation versus the scale factor of the incoming signal relative to the filter.
Data for the POF is indicated by circles; data for the MSF is indicated by triangles. (After Gianino and Horner, 1984.)

variations in the peak value of correlation power is shown in Fig. 14.5 for
both filters mentioned above. A scale change by a factor of k (where k can
be smaller than unity or larger than unity) is defined as $g'(x, y) = g(kx, ky)$. The curves show that at the 90% response point the phase-only filter
is approximately nine times more sensitive to scale change than the matched
spatial filter.

The greater sensitivity to scale changes and to rotation of the incident
signal is the result of the high spatial frequency domination in the impulse
response of the phase-only filter. Anderson and Anderson (1987) have demonstrated that the phase-only filter is just as sensitive to scale changes as
the high-pass matched spatial filter.

3.3. Various Realizations of the Phase-Only Filter

3.3.1. Continuous Phase-Only Filters

Optical realization of the phase-only filter assures that the phase function of
the filter is continuous and can be accurately reproduced in the correlation
step. The phase-only filter can be made optically by holographic methods

(Chałasińska-Macukow and Nitka, 1987a, 1987b). The phase-only Fourier hologram, having recorded only phase information about the Fourier transform of the reference target, plays the role of the phase-only filter. Such a phase-only Fourier hologram can be recorded optically using the setup shown in Fig. 14.6 (Zetsche, 1982; Chałasińska-Macukow and Nitka, 1987b). This is a typical setup for the optical realization of the phase component of the Stroke inverse filter (Stroke and Hallova, 1972). An additional filter (optical prefiltering) with the amplitude component $A(u, v)^{-1}$ inserted in the first Fourier transform plane levels the Fourier amplitude of the object function to a constant. This element can be obtained by recording the intensity of the Fourier transform function on a photographic plate that is processed with $\gamma = 1$. The object wave from the object transmitted through the additional filter (Fig. 14.6) and in the back focal plane leaves only the phase term of the Fourier transform of the object i.e., $\exp(i\varphi(u, v))$. In this plane the phase-only Fourier hologram can be recorded by adding a plane reference wave. Such a filter is used as a standard off-axis holographic filter and requires a high-resolution recording medium.

This kind of phase-only filter was used by Chałasińska-Macukow and Nitka (1987b) for the optical analysis of discrimination capability.

3.3.2. Binary Phase-Only Filters

The continuous filter accurately reproduces the reference phase-only function. However, in some applications there are several advantages of restricting the filter function to binary values only (Horner and Leger, 1985). This approach is especially useful for real-time applications with spatial light

Fig. 14.6. _____

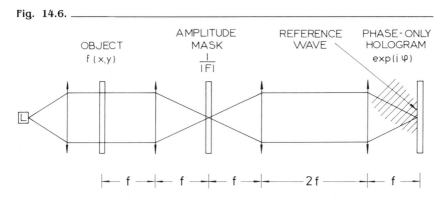

Optical setup for POF recording. (After Chałasińska-Macukow and Nitka, 1987b.)

modulators (Cottrell et al., 1987; Davis et al., 1987; Flannery et al., 1986; Psaltis et al., 1984) that cannot handle a large amount of information because the resolution of the spatial light modulators is limited. The spatial light modulators work well in a binary phase-only mode and can be used to generate spatial filters of this type (Cottrell et al., 1987; Davis et al., 1987; Flannery et al., 1986). A binary process is easier to control and two-phase levels can be set accurately.

One of the major advantages of a binary phase-only filter is that it can be recorded without a carrier frequency directly on the phase medium (nonholographic spatial filters), assuring operation in an in-line optical recognition architecture. Light losses by diffraction into orders not used in the processing step can be avoided by this method. Such phase-only filters are known as *kinoforms* (Lesem et al., 1969).

There are many methods of generating binary phase-only filters (Akahori, 1973; Akahori, 1986; Gallagher and Liu, 1973). One method is to approximate the continuous phase function with two discrete levels (Horner and Leger, 1985). This approach produces quantization errors (Goodman and Silvestri, 1970; Horner and Bartelt, 1985), but the correlation result from such a binary phase-only filter is comparable with the correlation from a continuous phase-only filter with a somewhat higher noise level (Horner and Leger, 1985). Table 14.3 shows a comparison between the performances of a matched spatial filter (MSF), a phase-only filter (POF), and a binary phase-only filter (Bi-POF) in terms of optical efficiency, signal-to-noise ratio (SNR) and peak correlation intensity (Bartelt and Horner, 1985).

3.3.3. Composite Phase-Only Filters

The high sensitivity of a phase-only filter to scale changes and to rotation of the input signal can severely limit the filters for practical applications.

TABLE 14.3

Light Efficiency, SNR, and Peak Intensity for
Various Types of Correlation Filters*

Filter	η_H (%)	SNR	Peak Intensity
MSF	0.8	6:1	1.
POF	13.8	51:1	256.
Bi-POF	4.7	29:1	87.

* After Bartelt and Horner (1985).

To avoid this problem, as in the case of matched spatial filters, various versions of composite phase-only filters, also known as *synthetic discriminant function filters* were developed (Casasent and Rozzi, 1986; Horner and Gianino, 1985; Kallman, 1986; Rosen and Shamir, 1987.)

The comparison between phase-only synthetic discriminant function filters (SDF/POF) and standard synthetic discriminant functions filters made by Horner and Gianino (1985) demonstrated that:

(1)   With the same optical input energy, the correlation intensity using the SDF/POF will be approximately 49 times greater than with the standard SDF filter.

(2)   The decrease by a factor of 10 in the area of the correlation spot makes it possible to detect another target in the field of view.

(3)   The signal-to-noise ratio increases on the average by a factor of 3.7.

The simplified version of the SDF/POF using biphase quantization works almost as well.

Rosen and Shamir (1987) have proposed another version of a composite filter for distortion-invariant pattern recognition. They have introduced a new kind of phase-only filter, the modified phase-only filter (MPOF) with partial rotation invariance, and incorporated this filter into a composite phase-only filter (CPF). The main objective of this work is the development of a pattern recognition approach taking into consideration the resolution limitations of the presently available spatial-light modulators. The performance of this filter has been demonstrated by computer simulation. The qualitative comparison of the rotation sensitivity of the new phase-only filter (MPOF), and of the composite phase-only filter (CPF) with the phase-only filter (POF) and the matched spatial filter (MSF) made by Rosen and Shamir (1987), is presented in Fig. 14.7.

4.
Matched Filtering Using Tandem Component Filters

Another type of pure phase filter was proposed by Bartelt (1984, 1985). He proposed an optical subsystem consisting of two separate elements (tandem component) to modify a general wavefront with a pure phase structure. Such a tandem component allows a general wavefront modification with a theoretical light efficiency of 100%, independently of the object function.

Fig. 14.7. _____

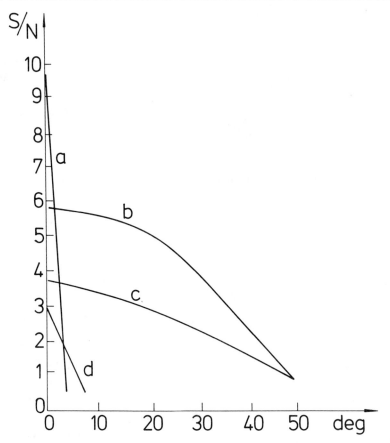

Qualitative comparison of the rotation sensitivity for four filters: a) POF, b) CPF, c) MPOF, d) MSF. (After Rosen and Shamir, 1987.)

One of the applications of the tandem component is a correlation-type measurement. With this component it is possible to transform an object function into an almost perfect peak in the output plane of the recognition system with 100% light efficiency (Bartelt, 1985). The tandem component filter (TCF) does not give an exact correlation similar to the one obtained with a conventional matched filter. As in conventional matched filtering, all the information from the Fourier transform of an object is used in this recognition operation, but, as opposed to a conventional correlator, this system is space variant.

4.1. Tandem Component Filters

The tandem component filter is composed of two computer-generated phase-only elements. A single synthetic phase-only element is known as a *kinoform* (Lesem et al., 1969). There are many configurations of tandem component systems depending on the applications (Bartelt, 1984). The basic optical correlator using a tandem component filter (Bartelt, 1985) is shown in Fig. 14.8. It is a 4-f optical processing system with two phase-only elements P_1 and P_2 located, respectively, in the object plane and in the Fourier transform plane. The first phase element $P_1(x, y)$ placed in the object plane in contact with the object $O(x, y)$ levels the Fourier amplitude of the object to a constant. The second phase element $P_2(u, v)$ is placed in the Fourier transform plane and sets the phase of the Fourier transform to a constant. Therefore, immediately after the second element, both the amplitude and the phase of the Fourier transform of the object are constant and the wavefront is uniform. The Fourier transform of such a function will yield a perfect diffraction-limited peak in the output plane of the optical system shown in Fig. 14.8.

The main problem in the application of the tandem component to matched spatial filtering is the computer generation of the two phase-only elements $P_1(x, y)$ and $P_2(u, v)$ satisfying the given constraints. The tandem component filter has to be matched to the object $O(x, y)$. To level the amplitude in the Fourier transform plane, the object function $O(x, y)$ can be multiplied by a phase function $P_1(x, y)$, which is a solution of the equation

$$\mathscr{F}\{O(x, y)P_1(x, y)\} = A(u, v) \exp[i\phi(u, v)], \qquad (14.16)$$

where $\mathscr{F}$ is the Fourier transform operator, and $A(u, v)$ and $\phi(u, v)$ are the

Fig. 14.8. _____

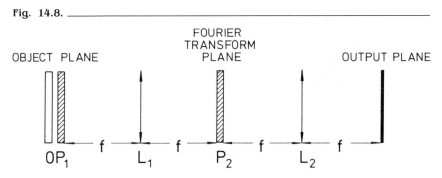

Optical correlator employing a tandem component filter composed of two pure phase filters P_1 and P_2.

amplitude and the phase of the Fourier transform of the product of the object function $O(x, y)$ and of the phase-only function $P_1(x, y)$. In solving Eq. (14.8), the following condition must be satisfied

$$A(u, v) = A = \text{const}(u, v). \tag{14.17}$$

The solution must be of the form

$$P_1(x, y) = \exp[i\varphi(x, y)], \tag{14.18}$$

where $\varphi(x, y)$ is the phase distribution of the first phase-only element.

The second phase-only element $P_2(u\ v)$, whose purpose is to set the Fourier phase to a constant, takes the form

$$P_2(u, v) = \exp[-i\phi(u, v)]. \tag{14.19}$$

The output function of the optical system with such a tandem component filter is

$$R(x_0, y_0) = \mathscr{F}^{-1}[\mathscr{F}\{O(x, y)P_1(x, y)\}P_2(u, v)], \tag{14.20}$$

which is equal to

$$R(x_0, y_0) = [O(x, y)P(x, y)] * \tilde{P}_2(x, y), \tag{14.21}$$

where x_0, y_0 are Cartesian coordinates in the output plane, $\tilde{P}_2(x, y)$ is the Fourier transform of the second phase-only element $P_2(u, v)$ of the tandem component filter, and the symbol * indicates a convolution.

A tandem component filter composed of such phase-only elements matched to the object function $O(x, y)$ yields a uniform wavefront after the second phase element and a perfect peak in the output plane of the system, but only is the input plane of the system contains the object $O(x, y)$. For any other input function, the peak is degraded.

4.2. Character Recognition Using Tandem Component Filters

Chałasińska-Macukow and Arsenault (1987, 1988) presented a digital character recognition using a tandem component filter.

A tandem component filter generated digitally was matched to the character A, composed of 64×64 pixels. Each phase-only element was generated separately. The generation of the element $P_1(x, y)$ is equivalent to solving a discrete version of Eq. (14.16) with the constraints $A(u, v) = \text{const}(u, v)$. A closed form solution cannot usually be found, except for certain special cases (Bartelt, 1984). This suggests the use of an iterative algorithm. The object-dependent phase element can be calculated by means of several algorithms (Akahori, 1986; Fienup, 1982; Gallagher and Liu, 1973;

Hirsch et al., 1971). For this purpose a method that attempts to approach the optimum results by alternating between the object plane and the Fourier plane during each iteration and modifying the result after each iteration was chosen (Bartelt and Horner, 1985; Fienup, 1982).

The iterative scheme used is represented in Fig. 14.9. To begin the iteration, a uniform phase function is selected. Constraints are introduced in the Fourier plane and in the object plane. In the Fourier plane the amplitude $A_i'(u, v)$ after each iteration is replaced by $A(u, v)$, where

$$A(u, v) = 1 \qquad \text{if } A_i'(u, v) < 1 \qquad (14.22)$$

$$A(u, v) = 1 - \epsilon \qquad \text{if } A_i'(u, v) > 1.$$

The value $\epsilon = 0.9$ was used to accelerate the convergence, and the index i indicates the iteration number. In the object plane, the amplitude $a(x, y)$ of the true object replaces the amplitude $c(x, y)$ after each iteration.

The convergence obtained by this method is shown in Fig. 14.10. The error E_i is calculated after each iteration in the Fourier transform plane by the formula

$$E_i = \frac{\left\{ \sum_{u,v} [A - A_i'(u, v)]^2 \right\}^{1/2}}{N^2}, \qquad (14.23)$$

Fig. 14.9. ───────────────────────────────

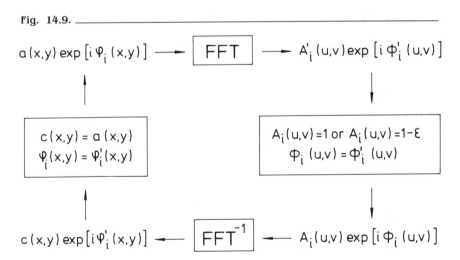

Diagram of the iteration scheme used to compute the first phase element P_1 of the TCF. (After Chałasińska-Macukow and Arsenault, 1987.)

Fig. 14.10.

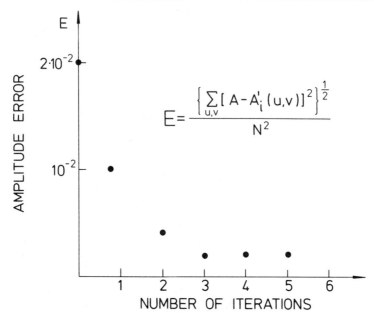

$$E = \frac{\left\{ \sum_{u,v} [A - A'_i(u,v)]^2 \right\}^{\frac{1}{2}}}{N^2}$$

Amplitude error calculated after each iteration in the Fourier plane. (After Chałasińska-Macukow and Arsenault, 1987.)

where A is the required constant level of the amplitude and N^2 is the number of pixels.

The tandem component filter matched to the letter A calculated by this method was obtained after five iterations.

The tandem component filter matched to the letter A was used to recognize the reference character A among the set of tested characters A, X, D, O, U, and Y. The results were compared with those obtained for the same set of characters using a conventional matched spatial filter and a phase-only filter. The results from this digital calculation are presented in Figs. 14.11a–14.11c and in Table 14.4. Figures 14.11a–14.11c show the normalized output peaks for different filters. All the filters were matched to the same character A. In the case of the tandem component filter of Fig. 14.11c, the output function is almost a delta function. The sharpness of the output peak is the major advantage of the tandem component method.

Table 14.4 gives the normalized output peak values for all tested characters using the three filters mentioned above. The phase-only filter has the best discrimination ability. The performance of the tandem component filter

Fig. 14.11.

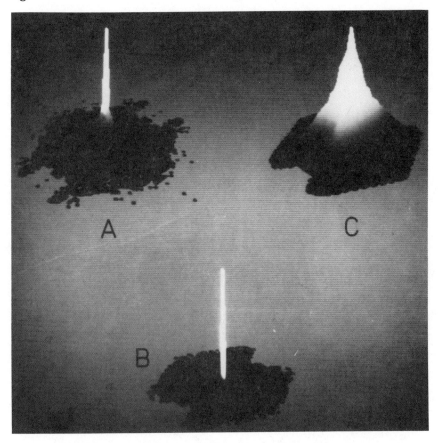

Output signal for: A) POF, B) TCF, and C) MSF. (After Chałasińska-Macukow and Arsenault, 1987.)

is almost identical to that of the conventional matched spatial filter. This result is easy to understand when one remembers that the phase-only filter can be considered as a high-pass filter with enhanced discrimination capability. On the other hand, the tandem component filter's spatial frequency characteristic is more similar to that of a conventional matched filter.

This kind of filter can be useful for some recognition problems where complete information about the object is necessary, for example, for recognition among any set of objects whose spectra have identical phase distributions, which would be ambiguous to a phase-only filter. Also in the

TABLE 14.4

Recognition of the Character A by Using
MSF, POF, and TCF*

| | Peak Intensity | | |
Object	MSF	POF	TCF
A	1.	1.	1.
D	0.5	0.18	0.44
O	0.57	0.21	0.51
Y	0.5	0.21	0.45
U	0.41	0.18	0.42
X	0.64	0.34	0.63

* After Chałasińska-Macukow and Arsenault (1987).

between-class discrimination problem, filters with enhanced discrimination capabilities might be too sensitive to small variations. In such cases, it might be convenient to use a tandem component filter with its high light efficiency and sharp output signal instead of a conventional matched filter. The disadvantage of tandem component filters associated with the space-variant properties of the operation can be reduced using a periodic filter $P_1(x, y)$ (Bartelt, 1985).

4.3. Binary-Phase Version of Tandem-Component Filters

Bartelt and Horner (1985) proposed a binary-phase version of a tandem-component filter (Bi-TCF). Simultaneously they proposed the use of the

TABLE 14.5

Light Efficiency, SNR, and Peak Intensity for
Various Types of Tandem-Component Filters*

Filter	η_H (%)	SNR	Peak Intensity
MSF	0.8	6:1	1
TCF	91.1	409:1	1853
Bi-TCF	31.8	87:1	590
Bi-TCF-Opt.	58.8	153:1	1090

* After Bartelt and Horner (1985).

overcompensation algorithm to improve the design and performance of the binary tandem component filter. Table 14.5 (Bartelt and Horner, 1985) compares the three versions of tandem component filters: the continuous tandem component (TCF), the binary tandem-component filter (Bi-TCF), and the optimized binary tandem-component filter (Bi-TCF-Opt) using the overcompensation algorithm, with a conventional matched spatial filter (MSF) in terms of optical efficiency, signal-to-noise ratio, and peak correlation intensity. All these filters are much better than the classical matched filter, not only in terms of light efficiency, but also in terms of SNR and peak intensity. The comparison of the effect of phase binarization on the tandem component filter with the effect of phase binarization on the phase-only filter (see Table 14.3) shows that the first effect is less critical than the second.

5.
Conclusion

Various types of phase-only filters discussed in this chapter have many advantages as compared with conventional matched spatial filters. They assure a theoretical light efficiency of 100% independent of the object function. This is very important for optical pattern recognition, especially in the case of compact optical processors designed to work in industrial or space environments where size and power are important parameters or for real-time applications with spatial light modulators.

Initial experiments suggest that the binary versions of phase filters can be effectively implemented in real-time optical processors, because spatial light modulators work well in the binary phase-only mode. This binary process is easier to control, and two-phase levels can be set accurately. The binary-phase approach has several additional advantages. There is no reason to write the binary-phase filters as holograms, and they do not require high resolution of the recording medium. They can be written without a carrier frequency directly onto a spatial light modulator, avoiding the light losses by diffraction into orders not used in the processing step and function in an in-line configuration in optical recognition systems.

Recent pattern recognition results obtained by means of various kinds of phase-only filters discussed in this chapter are very promising. Other versions of such phase-only methods, coherent as well as using a broad spectral band (Javidi and Yu, 1986), are under investigation.

References

Akahori, H. (1973). "Comparison of deterministic phase coding with random phase coding in terms of dynamic range," *Appl. Opt.* **12**, 2336–2343.

Akahori, H. (1986). "Spectrum leveling by an iterative algorithm with a dummy area for synthesizing the kinoform," *Appl. Opt.* **25**, 802–811.

Almeida, S.P., and Indebetouw, G. (1982). "Pattern recognition via complex spatial filtering," *In:* "Applications of Optical Fourier Transforms," (H. Stark, ed.), Academic Press, New York, pp. 41–88.

Anderson, C.S., and Anderson, R.C. (1987). "Comparison of phase-only and classical matched filter scale sensitivity,", *Opt. Eng.* **26**, 276–279.

Arsenault, H.H., Hsu, Y.N., and Chałasińska-Macukow, K. (1984). "Rotation-invariant pattern recognition," *Opt. Eng.* **23**, 705–709.

Bartelt, H.O. (1984). "Computer-generated holographic component with optimum light efficiency," *Appl. Opt.* **23**, 1499–1502.

Bartelt, H.O. (1985). "Applications of tandem component filter: An element with optimum light efficiency," *Appl Opt.* **24**, 3811–3816.

Bartelt, H.O., and Horner, J. (1985). "Improving binary phase correlation filters using iterative techniques," *Appl. Opt.* **24**, 2894–2897.

Binns, R.A., Dickinson, A., and Watrasiewicz, B.M. (1968). "Methods of increasing discrimination in optical filtering," *Appl. Opt.* **7**, 1047–1051.

Casasent, D., and Rozzi, W.A. (1986). "Computer-generated and phase-only synthetic discriminant function filters," *Appl. Opt.* **25**, 3767–3772.

Casasent, D., Xia, S.F., Lee, A.J., and Song, J.Z. (1987). "Real-time deformation invariant optical pattern recognition using coordinate transformations," *Appl. Opt.* **26**, 938–942.

Cathey, W.T. (1974). "Optical Information Processing and Holography," John Wiley & Sons, New York, pp. 162.

Caulfield, H.J. (1982). "Role of Horner efficiency in the optimization of spatial filters for optical pattern recognition," *Appl. Opt.* **21**, 4391–4392.

Caulfield, H.J., and Weinberg, M.H. (1982). "Computer recognition of 2-D pattern using generalized matched filters," *Appl. Opt.* **21**, 1699-1704.

Chałasińska-Macukow, K., and Arsenault, H.H. (1987). "Pattern recognition using tandem component filter," *Proc. of SPIE* **813**, 289–290.

Chałasińska-Macukow, K., and Arsenault, H.H. (1988). "Performance of the tandem component filter for pattern recognition," *Optics Commun.* **65**, 334–338.

Chałasińska-Macukow, K., and Nitka, T. (1987a). "Phase-only Fourier hologram as an optical matched spatial filter." *Proc. of SPIE* **673**, 188–191.

Chałasińska-Macukow, K., and Nitka, T. (1987b). "Phase-only filter as matched spatial filter with enhanced discrimination capability," *Optics Commun.* **64**, 224–228.

Cottrell, D.M., Davis, J.A., Schamschula, M.P., and Lilly, R.A. (1987). "Multiplexing capabilities of the binary phase-only filter," *Appl. Opt.* **26**, 934–937.

Dallas, W.J. (1980). "Computer-generated holograms." *In:* "The Computer in Optical Research," (B.R. Frieden, ed.), Springer Verlag, Berlin, Heidelberg, pp. 291–365.

Davis, J.A., Heissenberger, G.M., Lilly, R.A., Cottrell, D.M., and Brownnell, M.F. (1987). "High efficiency optical reconstruction of binary phase-only filters using the Hughes liquid crystal light valve." *Appl. Opt.* **26**, 929–933.

Fienup, J.R. (1982). "Phase retrieval algorithms: A comparison," *Appl. Opt.* **21**, 2758–2769.

Flannery, D.L., Biernacki, J.S., Loomis, J.S., and Cartwright, S.L. (1986). "Real-time coherent correlator using binary magnetooptic spatial light modulators at input and Fourier planes," *Appl. Opt.* **25**, 466–468.

Gallagher, N.C., and Liu, B. (1973). "Method for computing kinoforms that reduces image reconstruction error," *Appl. Opt.* **12**, 2328–2335.

Gianino, P.D., and Horner, J.L. (1984). "Additional properties of the phase-only correlation filter," *Opt. Eng.* **23**, 695–697.

Goodman, J.W., Silvestri, A.M. (1970). "Some effects of Fourier domain phase quantization," *IBM J. Res. Dev.* **14**, 478–484.

Gregory, D.A. (1986). "Real-time pattern recognition using a modified liquid crystal television in a coherent optical correlator," *Appl. Opt.* **25**, 467–469.

Gregory, D.A., and Huckabee, L.L. (1985). "Acoustooptically addressed Fourier transform matched filtering," *Appl. Opt.* **24**, 859–862.

Hirsh, P.M., Jordan, J.A., and Lesem, L.B. (1971). "Method of making an object-dependent diffuser," *U.S. Patent* 3,619,022.

Horner, J.L. (1982). "Light utilization in optical correlators," *Appl. Opt.* **21**, 4511–4514.

Horner, J.L., and Bartelt, H. O. (1985). "Two-bit correlation," *Appl. Opt.* **24**, 2889–2893.

Horner, J.L., and Gianino, P.D. (1984). "Phase-only matched filtering," *Appl. Opt.* **23**, 812–816.

Horner, J.L., and Gianino, P.D. (1985). "Applying the phase-only filter concept to the synthetic discriminant function correlation filter," *Appl. Opt.* **24**, 851–855.

Horner, J.L., and Leger, J.R. (1985). "Pattern recognition with binary phase-only filters," *Appl. Opt.* **24**, 609–611.

Hsu, Y.N. (1982). "Shift-and-Rotation Invariant Pattern Recognition," *Ph.D. thesis,* Laval University, Quebec.

Hsu, Y.N., and Arsenault, H.H. (1982). "Optical pattern recognition using circular harmonic expansion," *Appl. Opt.* **21**, 4016–4019.

Hsu, Y.N., Arsenault, H.H., and April, G. (1982). "Rotation-invariant digital pattern recognition using circular harmonic expansion," *Appl. Opt.* **21**, 4012–4015.

Javidi, B., and Yu, F.T.S. (1986). "Performance of a noisy phase-only matched filter in a broad spectral band optical correlator," *Appl. Opt.* **25**, 1354–1358.

Kallman, R.R. (1986). "Optimal low noise phase-only and binary phase-only optical correlation filters for threshold detectors," *Appl. Opt.* **25**, 4216–4217.

Leger, J.R., and Lee, S.H. (1982). "Hybrid optical processor for pattern recognition and classification using a generalized set of pattern function," *Appl. Opt.* **21**, 271–287.

Leger, J.R., and Lee, S.H. (1982). "Signal processing using hybrid systems." *In:* "Applications of Optical Fourier Transforms," (H. Stark, ed.), Academic Press, New York, pp. 131–207.

Lee, W.H. (1978). "Computer-generated holograms: Techniques and applications." *In:* "Progress in Optics," (E. Wolf, ed.), vol. XVI, North-Holland, Amsterdam, pp. 121–232.

Lesem, L.B., Hirsch, P.M., and Jordan, J.A. (1969). "The kinoform: A new wavefront reconstruction device," *IBM J. Res. Dev.* **13**, 150–161.

Merkle, F., and Lorch, T. (1984). "Hybrid optical-digital pattern recognition," *App. Opt.* **23**, 1509–1516.

Oppenheim, A.V., and Lim, J.S. (1981). "The importance of phase in signals," *Proc. of the IEEE* **69**, 529–541.

Psaltis, D., Pack, E., and Venkatesh, S. (1984). "Optical image correlation with a binary spatial light modulator," *Opt. Eng.* **23**, 698–703.

Rosen, J., and Shamir, J. (1987). "Distortion invariant pattern recognition with phase-filters," *Appl. Opt.* **26**, 2315–2319.

Stroke, G.W., and Hallova, M. (1972). "Attainment of diffraction-limited imaging in high resolution electron-microscopy by *a posteriori* holographic image sharpening I," *Optik* **35**, 50–65.

Szu, H.H. (1985). "Matched filter spectrum shaping for light efficiency," *Appl. Opt.* **24**, 1426–1431.

Turin, G.L. (1960). "An introduction to matched filters," *IRE Trans. Inform. Theory* **IT-6,** 311–329.

Vander Lugt, A. (1964). "Signal detection by complex filtering," *IEEE Trans. Inform. Theory* **IT-10,** 139–145.

Vasilenko, G.I., and Cybulkin, L.M. (1985). "Golograficzeskije rozpoznajuszczije ustrojstwa," *Radio i Swiaz.* Moskwa (in Russian).

Wintzer, G. (1974). "An examination of the suitability of holographic low-pass, high-pass and band-pass filters for the recognition of characters featuring a semantically simple structure," *Optica Acta* **21,** 697–707.

Wu, R. and Stark, H. (1984). "Rotation-invariant pattern recognition using a vector reference," *Appl. Opt.* **23,** 838–840.

Yang, Y., Chałasińska-Macukow, K., and Arsenault, H.H. (1982). "Digital and optical analysis of the optimum circular symmetrical filter in a character recognition system," *Optica Acta* **30,** 189–197.

Zetzche, Ch. (1982). "Simplified realization of the holographic inverse filter: A new method," *Appl. Opt.* **21,** 1077–1079.

15.

Optoelectronic Analog Processors

Evgeny S. Nezhevenko

Institute of Automation and Electrometry
Siberian Branch of the USSR Academy of Sciences
Novosibirsk, USSR

Contents

1. Introduction. 469
   1.1. Review of the Research on Optoelectronic Analog Computing in the Institute of Automation and Electrometry in Novosibirsk 471
2. Optoelectronic Analog Feedback Processors 472
3. Optoelectronic Pipeline Processors 477
   3.1. The Principle of Optoelectronic Pipeline Processors 478
   3.2. Graphical Presentation of Optoelectronic Pipeline Processors 479
      3.2.1. Multichannel Convolution 479
      3.2.2. Multichannel Signal Processors 480
      3.2.3. Two-Dimensional Correlation 481
      3.2.4. Matrix Multiplication 483
4. Optoelectronic Pipeline Correlator 484
5. Conclusion 486
   Acknowledgments 487
   References 487

1.

Introduction

Optical analog computing (OAC) has passed a number of stages during its development. The paper published by Vander Lugt et al. (1965) can be taken as the origin of OAC, if we do not take into account the preholographic period when incoherent correlators were the only type of optical computing systems. The multiple advantages provided by multiplication of the image spectrum by complex or real functions have given an appreciable impetus to OAC. There was a burst of publications in this field after the paper mentioned above. In the course of time, however, some significant limitations of coherent holographic processors were revealed. The main difficulties were:

(1) Difficulties arising with real-time input of images (high speed is required) or with filters (real-time writing of holograms is required).

(2) The high positioning accuracy required of the elements in coherent processors and the resulting sensitivity to environmental mechanical effects.

(3) The high sensitivity to phase distortions of optical elements, increasing the cost of coherent processors.

The above limitations were gradually overcome. A great variety of controlled transparencies have been developed, based on several different principles (electro-optical, magneto-optical, liquid crystal, etc.), including transparencies for the realization of dynamic holographic filters. The last two limitations were removed by the advent of holographic intensity correlators (Lohmann, 1968). This was achieved at the expense of bipolarity lost during filtering and, thus, the lost possibility of preprocessing images simultaneously with their correlation. The latter, however, was compensated by the possibility to realize the preprocessing immediately on the controlled transparency. Holographic correlators are not widely used, in spite of the advances in the development of holographic elements and in system architectures. This is probably associated with the particular properties of holographic elements.

At the same time, another trend towards overcoming the principal functional limitations of optical processors was developed. The range of problems solved with OAC using correlation processing only was really too narrow. Hence there was an attempt to enlarge it through the construction of optical feedback computers able to solve a great variety of problems such as image reconstruction, adapting, the solution of differential equations, etc. This idea was directed first to the development of passive, and then of active, systems (Jablonowski and Lee, 1973; Ferrano and Hausler, 1980).

Important steps in overcoming the functional limitations of optical analog processors were the work on their application to operations in two-dimensional matrices. At first, holographic systems were used for this purpose (Heinz et al., 1970). Then they were followed by incoherent parallel processors and, in the last few years, by pipeline (systolic) processors (Casasent, 1984).

At present, the development of pipeline processors has become one of the principal trends in OAC (Psaltis, 1984; Monahan et al., 1975; Athale and Lee, 1984). Practically all the problems that can be solved by parallel processors can be pipelined. In addition, most of the information to be processed is obtained either from natural time variations of signals or by the scanning of parallel arrays (e.g., TV scanning). Parallel processing is therefore often unadvisable. Parallel-serial real-time information processing is more suitable. Serially arriving vectors are appropriate subjects for pipeline processing.

The principal steps of OAC development are summarized above. This chapter only presents work in the field carried out at the Institute of Automation and Electrometry of the Siberian Branch of the USSR Academy of Sciences in Novosibirsk. Primary emphasis is given to two directions that seem to be the most promising. They are optoelectronic feedback systems and optoelectronic pipeline processors.

1.1. Review of the Research on OAC at the Institute of Automation and Electrometry in Novosibirsk

The first holographic coherent correlators were intended for recognition of one-dimensional signals (Nezhevenko, 1971). At that time, methods were developed that allowed the calculation of arbitrary measures of similarity between appropriate signals (in the form of contour and silhouette images) and the reference to be recognized. Further development of holographic correlators was connected with the recognition of two-dimensional signals (Kozlov et al., 1976). In this paper holographic filters with a bipolar impulse response were proposed and studied. The filters allowed simultaneous image recognition and preprocessing such as differentiation with finite differences. The same idea was used for the dimensional inspection of objects having complex shapes, where the filter impulse response represented a field of limits (Boldyreva et al., 1976).

Later, the theoretical foundations were developed and the practical realization of holographic intensity correlators was proposed (Potaturkin, 1979; Potaturkin et al., 1980) on the basis of an idea put forward by Lohmann (1968). Intensity correlators differ from coherent correlators by being less sensitive to inaccurate adjustment of their elements and by their greater in-

dependence to phase distortions of optical elements. Systems for image recognition based on a holographic intensity correlator with a controlled transparency, used for the input and the preprocessing of recognized images,
have been described (Nezhevenko et al., 1981).

In our first work on matrix multiplication (Nezhevenko and Tverdokhleb,
1972), coherent light and addressing of light beams with mirrors were used.
After that (Krivenkov et al., 1976) incoherent matrix multipliers with a matrix multiplication accuracy better than 0.5% were proposed and studied.

To develop the equipment for OAC systems a series of projects on controlled transparencies of the PROM type were carried out (Grekhov et al.,
1976; Kotlyer et al., 1977). As a result, high-resolution (up to 30 lines/
mm) and sensitive (10^{-6} J/cm^2) transparencies were produced.

Below, we consider in detail our research on optical analog feedback systems and pipeline optoelectronic processors.

2.
Optoelectronic Analog Feedback Processors

In spite of rapid progress in digital computing, analog computers retain their
value. They are indispensable for the real-time computing of differential
equations and for some other cases where high-speed computing is required
without a high accuracy. It seems attractive to create optical analog computers that would enable one to solve (by analogy with electronic computers
solving common differential equations), for example, partial differential
equations. To achieve this goal a complete set of functional units comparable
to the units of an electronic analog computer are needed. They are summing
and integrating (space and time) units, nonlinear converters, etc. A version
of OAC based on electro-optical controlled transparencies has been described (Nezhevenko, 1979; Nezhevenko and Gofman, 1984).

The main principles of OAC are as follows:

(1)   Neither intensity nor amplitude changes, but a phase shift between
      ordinary and extraordinary beams, produced by the electro-optical
      effect, is used as a physical carrier of information, that is, as an
      algebraic computer variable. This allows the realization of bipolar
      operations, a problem that creates a bottleneck for both incoherent
      and, to a higher degree, for coherent processors. The phase shift is
      also advantageous from another point of view, namely, it is more
      noise resistant than intensity, and especially amplitude, variations.

(2) The application of time scanning is a universal principle of functional transformations and image transfer between OAC units. This
operation is practically unrealizable in systems where amplitude or
light intensity are used as a computer variable. In systems where the
phase shift serves as an information carrier, the time-scanning operation can be easily performed. The spatial distribution of the phase
shift $\phi(x, y)$ is transmitted through an element that compensates for
the phase shift sequentially in time according to the function $V(t)$.
The $V(t)$ function is introduced by an element referred to as a *time
phase modulator*. Thus, one can easily determine the instant when

$$\phi(x_o, y_o) - kV(t) = 0,$$

because the light is linearly polarized at the point (x_o, y_o).

(3) The OAC systems are constructed from individual functionally com-
pleted modules, which can be grouped and matched without the use
of special elements. This can be achieved by the standardization of
input/output signals. In particular, when a time scan is used, data
communication between units is possible with the help of binary
signals.

The basic elements of optoelectronic analog computers are:

(1) A controlled light-light transparency (CT) shown in Fig. 15.1. Any
space-time modulator based on the linear electro-optical effect may
be used as a CT. The CT output phase shift $\phi_3(x, y, t)$ is the computer variable resulting from the input phase distribution $\phi_1(x, y, t)$
and the controlled intensity signal $f_2(x, y, \tau)$

$$\phi_3(x, y, t) = \phi_1(x, y, t) \pm k \int_0^T f_2(x, y, \tau) \, d\tau, \qquad (15.1)$$

where k is a constant and the sign depends on the applied voltage
$V(t)$ polarity.

(2) A time phase modulator is shown in Fig. 15.2. The output phase
shift $\phi_3(x, y, t)$ results from the input phase shift $\phi_1(x, y)$ and the
controlled voltage $V(t)$

$$\phi_3(x, y, t) = \phi_1(x, y) + kV(t). \qquad (15.2)$$

(3) A spatial threshold element is shown in Fig. 15.3. It is an inertial-
less element that converts a gray-level light distribution to the binary
form

Fig. 15.1.

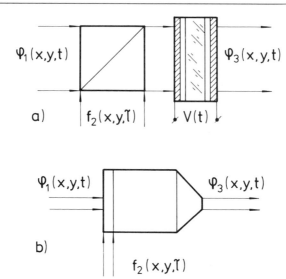

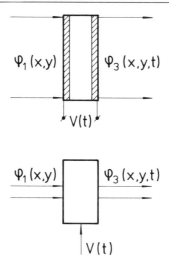

Optical (a) and block (b) schemes of a controlled light-light transparency (CT). $\phi_1(x, y, t)$ and $\phi_3(x, y, t)$ are input and output phase shift distributions, respectively; $f_2(x, y, \tau)$ is a controlled intensity signal; $V(t)$ is the CT voltage.

Fig. 15.2.

$\varphi_1(x,y)$ $\varphi_3(x,y,t)$

$V(t)$

$\varphi_1(x,y)$ $\varphi_3(x,y,t)$

$V(t)$

Optical (a) and block (b) schemes of a time phase modulator. $\phi_1(x, y)$ and $\phi_3(x, y, t)$ are input and output phase shifts, respectively; $V(t)$ is a controlled voltage.

Fig. 15.3. ───

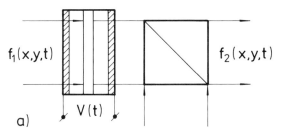

a)

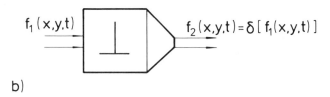

b)

Optical (a) and block (b) diagrams of a threshold element. $f_1(x, y, t)$ is a distribution of an input light intensity with gray levels. $f_2(x, y, t)$ is an output binary distribution of light intensity.

$$f_2(x, y, t) = \begin{cases} 1, & \text{if } f_1(x, y, t) \le \epsilon, \quad \text{where } \epsilon \ll (f_1)_{max} \\ 0, & \text{otherwise.} \end{cases} \quad (15.3)$$

With the above devices and some common elements of optical information processing systems, such as filters, transparencies, and photodetectors, the following units can be assembled: algebraic summers and multipliers, integrators and differentiators, functional converters, logic modules, etc. The above units are described in detail elsewhere (Nezhevenko and Gofman, 1984). The present chapter only illustrates their use in an optoelectronic analog processor intended for the solution of a partial differential equation by an iteration method.

Let us solve the Dirichlet problem for the Poisson equation in a rectangle.

$$\frac{\delta^2 U(x, y)}{\delta x^2} + \frac{\delta^2 U(x, y)}{\delta y^2} = f(x, y), \quad U(x, y)|_\Gamma = \Phi(\theta), \quad \theta \in \Gamma, \quad (15.4)$$

where Γ denotes rectangle boundaries and the equation on the right represents boundary conditions.

It is well known that a simple iteration method used for a two-layer iteration circuit results in a differential equation

$$\beta \frac{U_{n+1}(x, y) - U_n(x, y)}{\tau} + \Delta U_n(x, y) = f(x, y), \qquad (15.5)$$

where Δ is the Laplacian.

If we take the stabilizing operator β as unitary, the solution of the problem is then reduced to the iteration procedure:

$$U_{n+1}(x, y) = U_n(x, y) + \tau[f(x, y) - \Delta U_n(x, y)], \qquad (15.6)$$

$$U_n(x, y)|_\Gamma = U(x, y)|_\Gamma.$$

The sign-variable Laplacian can be represented as a difference of two functions

$$\Delta U(x, y) = U(x, y) - \tilde{U}(x, y),$$

where $\tilde{U}(x, y)$ can be derived by a usual image defocusing.

The block diagram of the optoelectronic analog processor for the above iteration procedure is given in Fig. 15.4, and the optical implementation is shown in Fig. 15.5. The nth approximation of the calculated function $U_n(x, y)$ is formed on CT2. In the path we have: the time modulator TM2; a polarizer

Fig. 15.4. —————————————————————————————————————

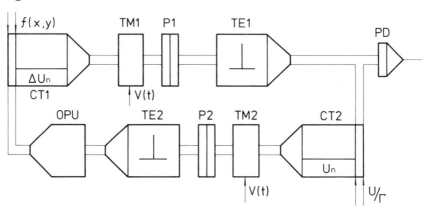

Block diagram of the optoelectronic analog processor for the iteration procedure. $f(x, y)$ is a controlled intensity signal arriving at the controlled light-light transparency CT1. The nth approximation of $U_n(x, y)$ is formed on CT2. TM1 and TM2 are time phase modulators with $V(t)$ controlled voltages; P1 and P2 are polarizers; TE1 and TE2 are threshold elements; PD is a photodetector; OPU is an optical processing unit.

Fig. 15.5. _____

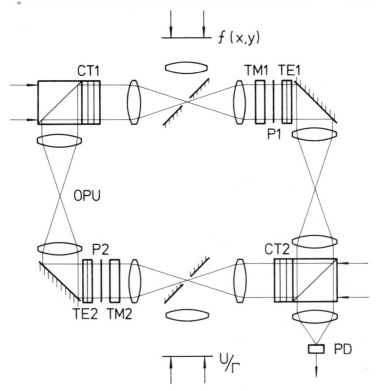

Optical scheme of the optoelectronic analog processor with conditions similar to that of Fig. 15.4.

P2; a threshold element TE2; an optical processing unit OPU, where the Laplacian of the function $U_n(x, y)$ is computed. The function $f(x, y)$ is subtracted from $U_n(x, y)$ on CT1. The difference formed on CT1 is summed up with $U_n(x, y)$ on CT2, $U(x, y)\,|_\Gamma$ being printed into the function $U_n(x, y)$ at each iteration. As a result, after some iterations the solution $U(x, y)$ will be obtained on CT2. Repeatability is controlled by a difference signal detected from the photodetector PD.

3. _____
Optoelectronic Pipeline Processors

Optoelectronic pipeline processors (OPPs) are closer to practical application despite the fact that their development began recently. This is because the parallel-sequential information processing in such processors makes the input of data much easier than in massively parallel processing systems. The construction of OPPs is simpler due to the well-developed production technology of basic optoelectronic devices such as light-emitting diodes, diode lasers, acousto-optical cells, CCD arrays, and so on that are used in those processors.

Before dwelling on this subject, we present a remark concerning the terminology. The term *pipeline processor* is used here. We believe that the systolization of optical computing essentially limits the functional possibilities of processors, because it assumes only local interconnections. On the other hand, the possibility of realizing complex global interconnections in optics is one of the most important advantages that makes it competitive with electronics.

3.1. The Principle of Optoelectronic Pipeline Processors

The main distinctive feature of OPPs is parallel-sequential data input at a certain rate and data output at the same rate (Gofman et al., 1986a). Figure 15.6 shows the general structure of a pipeline processor. It consists of an input unit for electric-to-light signal conversion; a unit for the optical readdressing of input signals; a modulator, where the transformation kernel is given; a unit for the optical readdressing of the modulated signal; and an output unit providing summation and shifts of signals.

The processor performance consists of the following steps. The input data enter the OPP sequentially in time, in the form of vectors representing either the lines of an image or instantaneous sections of signals that arrive via multiple channels. The input unit converts each vector pixel to a light signal. The optical system, consisting of two readdressing units and a modulator, presets an algorithm of input vector processing. The resulting two-dimensional light distribution is projected upon the light-sensitive surface of the

Fig. 15.6. _____

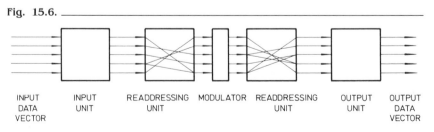

INPUT   INPUT   READDRESSING   MODULATOR   READDRESSING   OUTPUT   OUTPUT
DATA   UNIT   UNIT   UNIT   UNIT   DATA
VECTOR   VECTOR

General structure of the optoelectronic pipeline processor.

output unit. The next line is then fed to the OPP input unit in the time T that the pipeline simultaneously shifts by a single step, and the next vector is processed. The result is added to the previous one, and so on. The result in the output unit is also output sequentially at the rate T. The output vectors are delayed with respect to the input vectors by the pipeline delay time mT. Of course, a limited class of signal- and image-processing algorithms can be realized in the above implementation. However, it includes algorithms of correlation, convolution, spectral analysis, matrix multiplication, etc.

3.2. Graphical Presentation of Optoelectronic Pipeline Processors

An analytical description of the OPP structure is rather tedious and does not vividly represent its operation. We believe that a graphical description in terms of a signal-flow graph (SFG) is more suitable (Kung, 1984). Let us consider the structures of the processors and the corresponding SFGs for four signal- and image-processing algorithms.

3.2.1. Multichannel Convolution

Multichannel convolution algorithms, such as FPR filtering or transversal filtering, can be described by the expression

$$y_n(k) = \sum_{l=1}^{L} x_n g_n(l - k), \qquad n = 1, 2, \ldots, N. \tag{15.7}$$

Figure 15.7 shows the SFG for the realization of the above algorithms. All signal processing operations in the processor can be easily followed. The SFG inputs correspond to light emitters in the input unit. The edges marked with lower-case letters $g_{11}, \ldots, g_{pq}$ represent multiplication with the modulator. The edges without marks and the vertices correspond to various readdressings with multiplication and summation of the light energy. The edges with the index D match with signal delays in the output unit. The input unit represents an array of light sources oriented along the line. The first readdressing unit provides transfer of the energy of each source onto the column. The kernel $g_n(l)$ is written in the nth column of the modulator. The second readdressing unit is a projecting unit. The output unit is a two-dimensional structure that provides accumulation and shifts of light distributions between the columns.

Fig. 15.7.

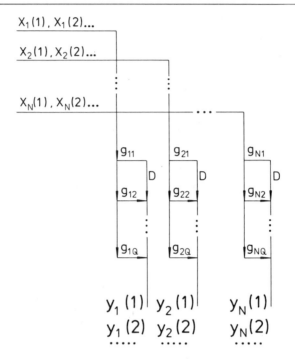

Signal-flow graph for the multichannel convolution algorithm. X, input matrix;
g, kernel of an algorithm; D, signal delay; Y, output matrix.

3.2.2. Multichannel Signal Processors

Multichannel seismic signal processing systems often use the procedure of summation of signals from multiple sensors with different delays:

$$y_m(k) = \sum_{n=1}^{N} x_n(k - \tau_{mn}), \qquad m = 1, \ldots, M. \tag{15.8}$$

Figure 15.8 represents a SFG for the realization of this procedure in OPP. Unlike in Section 3.2.1, here the light fluxes from all sources are summed on each column. The first readdressing unit transmits the energy of the light sources to nonoverlapping areas of the modulator. The second unit (de-multiplier) matches the light distributions behind the modulator on the light-sensitive surface of the output unit, and a set of delays τ_{mn} in the form of binary masks is written in each area of the modulator.

Fig. 15.8.

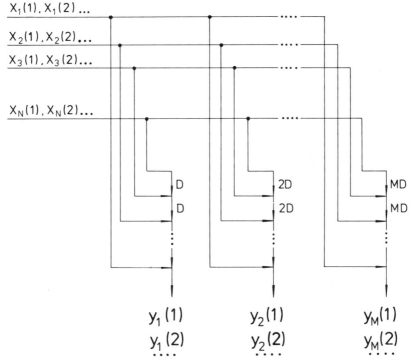

Signal-flow graph for the multichannel seismic signal processor. X, input matrix; mD, signal delays; Y, output matrix.

3.2.3. Two-Dimensional Correlation

A two-dimensional correlation of the image $x(m, n)$ with the reference $g(m, n)$ is described by the expression:

$$y(p, q) = \sum_{m=1}^{M} \sum_{n=1}^{N} x(m, n)\, g(m-p, n-q). \qquad (15.9)$$

The corresponding SFG is shown in Fig. 15.9. The first readdressing unit transmits the energy of each light source to the entire modulator where the reference $g(m, n)$ is written (there are dozens of them in a real processor). The second readdressing unit projects the plane of the modulator onto the photosensitive surface of the output unit. Images of the reference from different light sources are shifted by one resolution cell of the photosensitive

Fig. 15.9.

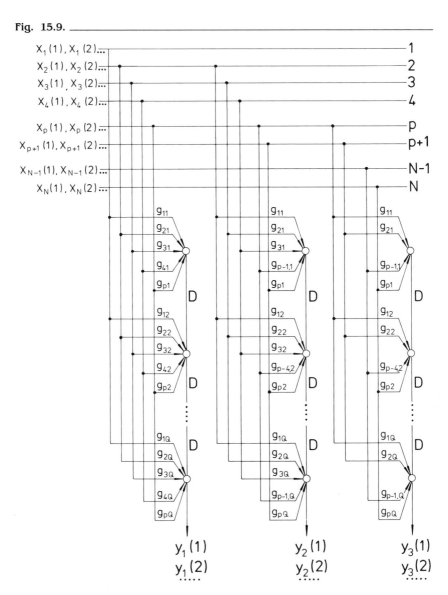

Signal-flow graph for the two-dimensional correlator. *X*, input image matrix; *g*, reference matrices; *D*, signal delay; and *Y*, output matrix.

medium for the nth light source with respect to the $(n-1)^{th}$. The latter can be achieved by special light addressing behind the modulator.

3.2.4. Matrix Multiplication

Figure 15.10 shows a SFG for the matrix multiplication operation. The input unit represents an array of light sources that are oriented along the column. The first readdressing unit transmits the energy of each light source to a line. The second readdressing unit projects this transposed matrix onto the modulator. Elements of the multiplicand matrix are fed to the input unit, as shown in the figure. The product matrix is formed in a pipeline delay time proportional to the number of elements in one column of the multiplicand matrix.

The distinguishing feature of the above processors is the identity of the input unit, the modulator, and the output unit. Reprogramming is performed by the replacement of readdressing units and of the information written on the modulator. In this respect OPPs are analogous to digital signal processors (DSP), which can be programmed as special-purpose processors to solve one problem or another in a rather wide class. It is therefore reasonable to refer to the devices of the above class as optoelectronic signal processors (OSP). It is probable that, similarly to DSPs whose development is directed towards the creation of single crystal processors, future OSPs will take the

Fig. 15.10. _____

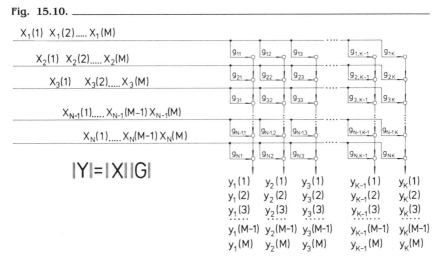

Signal-flow graph for the matrix multiplier. X, multiplier matrix; G, multiplicand matrix; Y, product matrix.

form of a monoblock sandwich programmable in an optical way for solving all kinds of problems.

We now give a brief description of typical features of individual units. The input unit is an array of light sources, whose number is equal to the dimension of the input unit. Light-emitting diodes or diode lasers are used as light sources. Direct operation can be provided directly by sensors that transform a physical value to a light flux (e.g., fiber optic sensors). The readdressing units may be based either on conventional optical elements (lenses, prisms, and wedges), on fiber optical elements, or on holograms. Phototransparencies and other kinds of controlled transparencies can be used as modulators. A CCD array working in the temporal storage delay mode is an optimal version of the output unit.

Accuracy is one of the main problems of analog systems in general and especially for optical systems. For the OPP under consideration the problem is not so acute as for other analog optical processors. The point is that almost all of the OPP units, i.e., the input unit, the readdressing units, the modulator, and the CCD array, are either initially discretized in space or they can be discretized by rastering. Therefore, digital-to-analog coding can be used here, with K columns of the CCD array for each channel instead of one. As a result, the OPP accuracy is improved by a factor of A^k, where A is the dynamic range of the CCD array.

4.
Optoelectronic Pipeline Correlator

Let us consider an OPP that performs a two-dimensional correlation of a fragment of a TV image with several references (Gofman et al., 1986b). The correlator is built according to the scheme described in Section 3.2.3. The input unit is an array of 16 LEDs. The modulator is a photographic or controlled transparency. The first readdressing unit is a common collecting lens, while the second one is a special addressing mirror combined with projection optics. Figure 15.11 shows the signal processing steps. A 16 × 312 fragment (Fig. 15.11a) is cut out from the input TV frame and is pre-processed (contoured) in the electronic path (Fig. 15.11b). Then 16 line elements are input to the processor from LEDs, each of them illuminating the whole transparency (Fig. 15.11c). The mutual correlation function obtained from the second readdressing unit is stored as a charge relief on the CCD array. The next line then follows, the charge relief is shifted by one

Fig. 15.11.

a   b   c   d   e

Steps of signal processing in the optoelectronic pipeline correlator. (a) the initial image fragment; (b) the contoured image fragment; (c) the etalon transparency; (d) the output correlation function; (e) the sections of the correlation
function.

line, and so on until all the last line. As a result, the correlation functions
of the chosen fragment and the arrays of references are computed (Fig. 15.11d).
Figure 15.11e shows a section through the maxima of the correlation functions.

An external view of the correlator is shown in Fig. 15.12. With a rather
simple construction, it provides a computing performance of 1.5×10^9 operations per second, where one multiplication and addition are counted as
one operation.

Fig. 15.12.

External view of the optoelectronic pipeline correlator.

This correlator has the following features:

(1) All electronic units of the correlator work with frequencies that are not higher than TV frequencies. Global synchronization is performed by TV signals from the CCD array. Both factors together assure extremely simple and reliable electronics in the correlator.

(2) References are input to the correlator in the form of images but not holograms. This allows easy real-time input.

(3) The correlator has no units that require precise adjustment and is stable to vibrations. With an integrated input unit the correlator can be rather small.

5.
Conclusion

Optoelectronic analog processors have not justified their expectations yet because they are not widely used. There are several reasons for this. Some fundamental limitations have been revealed in coherent holographic processing systems and they are especially evident in view of the intensive development of digital signal processors that offer a wide range of functional possibilities. Electro-optical analog computing systems with feedback seem to be rather promising. They are well suited for computational problems involving two-dimensional functions, that is, problems where accuracy is more important than the speed of operation. However, for this kind of system there is not an adequate element basis yet.

Optoelectronic pipeline processors with parallel-sequential data inputs are close to practical application. A complete element basis is already available for them now. Providing both high computing performance and extremely simple construction, they are quite competitive with digital processors in some applications. We believe that OPP characteristics such as computing performance, accuracy, size, and energy consumption will be improved considerably soon. To this end there is a need for further development of special purpose elements: integrated one-dimensional and two-dimensional arrays of light sources, controlled code-light transparencies (at present, light-light transparencies are primarily used), and CCD arrays.

Acknowledgements

The author is grateful to M.A. Gofman and V.I. Feldbush for fruitful discussions and to L.A. Gibina for assistance in the experiments.

References

Athale, R.A., and Lee, J.N. (1984). *Proc. IEEE* **72**, 931–941.

Boldyreva, I.S., Butorin, V.A., Bychkov, R.M., Volkov, V.I., Koronkevich, V.P., and Nezhevenko, E.S. (1976). *Avtometriya* **3**, 67–72 (in Russian). *English transl. in Automatic Monitoring and Measuring.*

Casasent, D. (1984). *Proc. IEEE* **72**, 831–849.

Ferrano, G., and Hausler, G. (1980). *Opt. Eng.* **19**, 442–451.

Gofman, M.A., Nezhevenko, E.S., and Feldbush, V.I. (1986a). *Report Intern. Seminar Optical Computing—'86, Novosibirsk 1986,* pp. 1–12.

Gofman, M.A., Nezhevenko, E.S., Korzhov, E.N., and Polezhaev, V.P. (1986b). "*Proc. 6th All-Union Workshop Opt. Inf. Proc., Frunze 1986,*" pp. 81–82 (in Russian).

Grekhov, Yu.N., Kotlyar, P.E., Nezhevenko, E.S., Feldbush, V.I., and Shadeev, N.I. (1976). *Pisma v Zh. Tekh. Fiz.* **2**, 457–462 (in Russian). *English transl. in Sov. Tech. Phys. Lett.*

Heinz, R.A., Artman, J.O., and Lee, S.H. (1970). *Appl. Opt.* **9**, 2161–2168.

Jablonowski, D.P., and Lee, S.H. (1973). *J. Opt. Soc. Am.* **63**, 1306.

Kotlyar, P.E., Nezhevenko, E.S., and Feldbush, V.I. (1977). *Izv. Akad. Nauk, SSSR, Ser Fiz.* **41**, 792–797 (in Russian). *English transl. in Bull. Acad. Sci. USSR, Phys. Ser.* **41**(4), 119–123.

Kozlov, O.A., Nezhevenko, E.S., and Potaturkin, O.I. (1976). *Avtometriya* **6**, 36–44 (in Russian). *English transl. in Automatic Monitoring and Measuring.*

Krivenkov, B.E., Mikhlyaev, S.V., Tverdokhleb, P.E., and Chugui, Yu.V. (1976). *In*: "Optical Information Processing," (Yu.E. Nesterikhin, G.W. Stroke, and W.E. Kock, eds.), Plenum Press, New York, pp. 203–217.

Kung, S.-Y. (1984). *Proc. IEEE* **72**, 867–884.

Lohmann, A.W. (1968). *Appl. Opt.* **7**, 561–563.

Monahan, M.A., Bocker, R.P., Bromley, K., and Lonie, A. (1975). "*Digest Internat. Opt. Comp. Conf. IEEE, Washington, D.C. 1975,*" pp. 25–33.

Nezhevenko, E.S. (1971). *Avtometriya* **6,** 43–46 (in Russian). *English transl. in Automatic Monitoring and Measuring.*

Nezhevenko, E.S., and Tverdokhleb, P.E. (1972). *Avtometriya* **6,** 21–26 (in Russian). *English transl. in Automatic Monitoring and Measuring.*

Nezhevenko, E.S. (1979). *In* "Optical Information Processing," Nauka, Leningrad, pp. 35–60 (in Russian).

Nezhevenko, E.S., Khotskin, V.I., and Potaturkin, O.I. (1981). *Opt. Appl.* **11,** 143–150.

Nezhevenko, E.S., and Gofman, M.A. (1984). *Optik* **67,** 199–210.

Potaturkin, O.I. (1979). *Appl. Opt.* **18,** 4203–4205.

Potaturkin, O.I., Nezhevenko, E.S., and Khotskin, V.I. (1980). *J. Opt. (Paris)* **11,** 305–309.

Psaltis, (1984). *Proc. IEEE* **72,** 962–974.

Vander Lugt, A., Rotz, F.B., and Klooster, A., Jr. (1965). *In* "Optical and Electro-optical Information Processing," (J.T. Tippett, D.A. Berkovitz, C.L. Clapp, C.J. Koester, and A. Vanderburgh, Jr., eds.), MIT Press, Cambridge, Mass, pp. 125–141.

Index

achromatic Fourier transform, *see* Fourier transform
achromatization, 428, 434
anamorphic Fourier transform, 398–402, 402–405
  angular relations in, 402–405
  definition, 401
  hologram, 407
  scaling property, 402
anamorphic optical correlator, 407,
approximate solutions, 229, *see also* matrix
associative memory, 255–257
axicon, 410–411
  complex amplitude transmittance, 411
bacteriorhodopsin, 118–140
  photocycle of, 119
  recording materials, 119–140
bimodal optical computer, 234, 240, 242, 246
  see also logic data processing; optical analog computing
binary Fresnel plate, *see* Rayleigh–Wood lens
biochrom film, 121–132
  nonlinear polarization effects in, 131
  photoinduced anisotropy in, 122–126
  polarization four-wave mixing in, 126–130
  see also purple membrane
biopolymers for optical processing, 103–140
bonding pads, 21
bosons, 3

Bragg selectivity, 9
broadcast capability, 7
  see also interconnects
capacitive loading, 4, 20, 24
characteristic impedance, 15, 23
character recognition, 454, 464
  see also circular harmonic filter
charge-transport
  model, 62, 63
  process, 65
  see also efficiency
circular diffraction grating, 290, 295–299
  blazed, 290
Circular harmonic (CHC)
  components 316, 318, 320
  filter, 320–324
    autocorrelation peak intensity, 330
    center of expansion, 321, 323, 324
    cluttered backgrounds, 319, 336, 339
    invariance to contrast, 318–334
    invariance to distortion, 318
    invariance to noise, 319
    principal component, 338
    rotating filter method, 327
    see also filter; optical pattern recognition
  multiple CHC methods, 328, 330, 334, 338
  phase filters, 328
  single CHC methods, 319–325
clock
  distribution, 23
  generator, 28

489

clock, *cont'd*
  skew, 25, 28
coax, 22
coefficient
  of anamorphosis M, 401
  of angular magnification, 403–405
  electro-optic, 67
  fiber amplification 48
  see also stimulated Mandelstam–Brillouin
      scattering; stimulated Raman
      scattering
coherence, spatial, 428
complex filters, *see* filter
composite matched filter, *see* filter
computational complexity, 227
constant brightness theorem, 16, 17
controlled light transparency, 479–483
control unit, 191
correlator, *see* optical correlator
coupling loss, 11
cross correlation, 439
  peak 330
  see also optical correlator
data array, 213
data search techniques, 213–220
  greater (less than) search, 218
  between limits search, 218
  match (mismatch) search, 217
data structures, re-arrangement of, 203–210
  cyclic single coordinate shift, 209
  page transfer, 204
  row masking, 204
  row multiplexing, 206
  row transfer, 205
  single-coordinate shift, 207
deblurring, 437
  of color photographs, 437
  with white light, 438
decision space 334
degeneracy of volume gratings, 263
detection probability 332
dichromated gelatin, 9, 11, 105–110
diffraction efficiency, 67, 96–97
diffraction lens, 286–289, 293, 300–301
  complex transmittance of, 286
  focal length of, 287
  microlens, 301
  with mirror, 300
  radii of zones, 287
  with ring impulse response, 293, 306

  with uniform energy in focus, 288–289
  see also hologram
diffraction optical element (DOE), 278–311
  circular diffraction grating, 295–299
  kinoform axicon, 290–292
  lens, 286–289, 293, 300
  lens with mirror, 300
  microlens, 301
  production of, 280–286
  properties of, 278–280
  wavefront corrector, 294–296
  see also holographic optical element
digital image processing 320
diode laser, 146
  bistable double-section (D^2), 175–179
  buried heterostructure, 146
  Fourier holography with, 154–161
  GaAlAs/GaAs, 147–149
  generation formulae, 175
  hysteresis, 177
  injection current 150
  mode locking, 152
  multi-quantum-well (MQW), 11, 147,
    183
  optical logic gates on 174, 179
  pulse frequency, 150
  short pulses by, 150, 154
  threshold current, 146
discrimination ability, *see* filter
drive power, 12, 15, 18
efficiency, 9, 10, 11
  charge-transport, 75, 88–89, 97
  diffraction, 80, 95
  grating recording, 68, 86, 97–98
  see also filter; quantum efficiency;
    photorefractive
eigenvalue problem, *see* matrix
electro-optic
  coefficient, 67
  effect, 66
electrorefractive effect, 66
exposure schedule, 270
false alarms 332, 336
fan-in, 15, 16
fan-out, 7, 10, 15
feature space 329–334
fermions, 3
fiber amplification coefficient, 48
fibers, 5
filter

discrimination ability, 321, 450
  enhanced, 452
Horner efficiency, 449
inverse 450, 459
light efficiency, 448
matched, 316, 321, 431, 441
  bipolar, 328
  CHC, *see* Circular harmonic
    complex, 328
  composite 326, 327, 336, 338
  conventional, 449
  generalized, 448
  high-pass, 453
  over-exposed, 453
  real and binary, 328
  rotation-invariant 320, 321
phase-only, 320, 448, 452
  binary, 448, 459
  composite, 460
  continuous, 458
  modified, 461
sensitivity
  rotation, 457, 460
  scale, 457, 460
spatial frequency characteristic, 450
synthetic discriminant function
  phase-only, 461
  standard, 461
tandem component, 461
  binary, 468
  digitally generated, 464
white-light *see* white light
see also CHC, optical pattern
    recognition, optoelectronic
format conversion, 228
Fourier transform, achromatic, 431
fractal sampling grids, 266
Fresnel phase lens, 281
gates, 1
gate-to-gate interconnect, *see* interconnects
gelatin planar waveguide, 112–118
  with bis azido compounds, 111
  bistability in, 113
  phase and polarization effects in, 117
  self-propagation in, 115
generalized optical element, 278
geometrical image transformation, 306–308
grating,
  space-charge, 66
  see also efficiency; photorefractive

ground plane, 4, 14
halophilic bacteria, 118
Hamming distance, 262
hologram
  Fresnel, 429
  planar, 259–262
  storage capacity of
    volume, 259–268
    waveguide, 169–174
holographic interconnect, *see* interconnects
holographic optical element, 431, 434, 442
  see also kinoform, optical system with
      diffracting elements
holography, real-time, 106–110, 133–137
  in dichromated gelatin, 106–110
  in purple membrane suspension, 133–137
Hough transform, 416–421
  definition, 416–419
  imaging, 8
  optical implementation of, 419–420
H-tree, 25, 26
impulse response, 317
incoherent optical processing, 427
index of angular separability S, 406
information
  amplitude, 452
  phase, 452
injection laser (IL), *see* diode laser
integrated optics, 6
interaction length, 43
interconnects
  chip-to-chip, 20
  dynamic, 4
  free space, 7, 8
  gate-to-gate 2, 18, 19
  holographic, 8, 9, 16, 37
inverter, 24
kinoform, 280, 287, 290–292, 294, 302–
      306, 460, 463
  axicon, 290–292
  corrector, 294–296, 302–303
  see also holographic optical element
laser photoplotter, 282
  technology of photomasks, 283–286
laser, *see* diode laser
leakage currents, 30
Light emitting diode (LED), 10
liquid-crystal light valve, 255
logic data processing, 213–218
  addition, 214

logic data processing, *cont'd*
  multiplication, 216
  multiplication of vectors, 202
  vector-matrix multiplication, 214
  see also matrix
matched filter, *see* Circular harmonic filter
matrix
  complex, 233
  condition number, 230, 237, 239
  eigenvalue problem, 226, 229, 243
  ill-conditioned, 239, 245
  inversion, 226, 243
  multiplication, 489
  norm, 229
  optical, 233
  preconditioning, 230
  see also optical computations, singular
    value decomposition
matrix–matrix multiplier, 224, 234
Maxwell equation, 65
mesooptical Fourier transform microscope
    (MFTM), 408–416
  performance, 413–416
  structure, 409–413
mesooptics, 409
  lens, 410–413
  mirror, 411–413
minimum distance classifiers, 335
model
  charge compensation, 70
  charge-transport, 68–69, 72–73, 75, 98
  photogeneration, 74–75
  photorefractive recording, 72, 79, 83
  realistic, 73, 83
  transport analysis, 84
moments, invariant, 328
multichannel convolution, 485–486
multichannel signal processor, 486–487
multiple target patterns, 317, 319
  see also Circular harmonic; filter
mutual
  coherence function, 164
  propagation law, 164
  spectral density, 164
neural network, 252
  adaptive, 269–274
neuron, 251
noise, 319
nonlinear fiber optical element, 40
  characteristic curves, 42
optical analog computing, 475–479

see also filter
optical associative loop, 255–259
optical computations, 231, 234, 237
  accuracy, 232, 236, 239
  speed, 235
optical computer, *see* associative memory;
    bimodal optical computer; optical
    correlator; filter; logic data
    processing; optical analog computing;
    diode laser; optoelectronic, computer;
    neural network
optical correlator, 166, 319
  correlation peak intensity, 449, 452
  light efficiency, 449
  normalized correlation peak, 454
  white-light, 433
  see also filter
optical fiber switching element, 53
optical interconnections, 259–269
  see also interconnects
optical pattern recognition
  distortion invariant, 461
  rotation invariant, 451
  space variant, 461
  see also Circular harmonic; filter
optical pre-processor, 191, 193–201
  resolution of, 198
optical system with diffracting elements,
    301–310
  bifocus microscope, 304–306
  coding system, 306–308
  diffraction interferometer, 309–310
  lens with refracting and diffracting
    elements, 301–304
  optical string, 310
  see also holographic optical element
optics versus computers 319
optimum circular filter, 321
  see also Circular harmonic; filter
optoelectronic
  analog feedback processor, 478–483
  computer, 191
  pipeline correlator, 490–492
  pipeline processor, 483–492
parallel optical memory, 191
paraphrase code, 202
pattern recognition, *see* Circular harmonic;
    filter; optical pattern recognition
Pauli exclusion principle, 3
perceptron, 271–272
phase matching, 36, 263

phase-locked loop, 30
phase-only filter, *see* filter
photoelectronic parallel processor, 191–193, 210–213
photogeneration process, 73–75
photorefractive perceptron, 269–274
photorefractrive
  charge-transport, 61, 65, 96
  effect, 64
  efficiency, *see* quantum efficiency
  grating, 67–68
  recording, 69, 93
    enhanced recording techniques, 92
    grating, 62–63, 76, 78–83
    running grating technique, 93–94
    stationary illumination technique, 92
    see also model
  sensitivity, 59–67
prefiltering, 453, 459
principal component filters, *see* filter
proper expansion center, *see* Circular harmonic
purple membrane, 118–140
  electro-optical effect in, 138
  recording materials, 119–140
  suspension, 133–139
quantum efficiency, 10
  absolute, 62, 97
  ideal, 96
  photogeneration, 60, 63–64, 83
  see also efficiency
quantum limits, absolute, 98
  see also quantum efficiency
Rayleigh–Wood lens, 281, 287, 304–305
real and binary filter, *see* filter
recording sensitivity
  initial, 83
  maximum, 86
  see also efficiency; photorefractive
reflection grating, 9
responsivity, 10
rotating filter method, *see* Circular harmonic
rotation invariance *see* Circular harmonic
routing, 4, 23
sampling grids, *see* fractal sampling grids
scale invariance, *see* Circular harmonic; filter

sensitivity, *see* photorefractive; grating; efficiency
sidelobes, 316, 323–326
  reduction of, 336, 338
  see also filter
signal-flow graph, 485–489
signal to noise ratio 322
singular value decomposition, 227
skin effect, 12
spatial filtering
  with extended source, 438
  systems, 435, 441
    see also correlation
    two-pupil method, 439
spatial threshold element, 479–483
stimulated Mandelstam–Brillouin scattering, 34–36
  gain coefficient, 40
  inverter, 42
stimulated Raman scattering, 34–36
  amplifier, 41
  differential amplification coefficient, 47
  gain coefficient, 38
  generator, 46
  inverter, 46
Stokes waves, 36–55
  frequency shift of, 38
  threshold power for, 39
stray capacitance, 14
terminated line, 12, 22, 23
threshold current, 20
threshold voltage, 9
time phase modulator, 479–483
transimpedence amplifier, 28
transmission grating, 9
two-dimensional correlation, 487–488
two-pupil method, *see* spatial filtering
Vander Lugt correlator, 256
vector–matrix multiplier, 224, 232
velocity of propagation, 22
waveguide, 6, 17
white light
  correlator, *see* optical correlator
  filtering, 434
  techniques, 437
zone plate lens, 431
  see also kinoform